Library of
Davidson College

Cuban Foreign Policy

Caribbean Tempest

Pamela S. Falk

Lexington Books
D.C. Heath and Company/Lexington, Massachusetts/Toronto

To E.C.W.

Library of Congress Cataloging in Publication Data

Falk, Pamela S.
  Cuban foreign policy.

  Bibliography: p.
  Includes index.
  1. Cuba—Foreign relations. I. Title.
F1776.2.F34   1985   327.7291   81-47890
ISBN 0-669-05127-6

Copyright © 1986 by D.C. Heath and Company

All rights reserved. No part of this publication may be reproduced or transmitted in any form or by any means, electronic or mechanical, including photocopy, recording, or any information storage or retrieval system, without permission in writing from the publisher.

Published simultaneously in Canada
Printed in the United States of America on acid-free paper
International Standard Book Number: 0-669-05127-6
Library of Congress Catalog Card Number: 81-47890

Contents

Preface vii

Acknowledgments ix

Introduction xiii

Part I History of Cuban Foreign Policy 1

1. Foreign Policy in the New Republic 3

Early Foreign Policy Objectives 4
Cuba's Constitution 7
Cuban Leadership and International Relations 7
U.S. Occupation—1906 to 1909 9
The Foreign Policy of World War I 10
Foreign Affairs and the Student Movements of the 1920s 10
The Pan-American Conference in Havana 12
International Mediation in the 1930s 13
Rise of Cuban Communism 15
Cuba in World War II 16
Postwar Cuba 17
1953: The Beginning of the Revolution 18

2. Cuba's Relations in the Western Hemisphere 21

Stage One: Fidel Castro's Experience 22
The 1960s 24
Early Military Approaches 24
Other Revolutionary Examples 26
Cuba and Latin American Communism 27
Reaction in Latin America 28
Latin America's Ideological Direction: Hegel Plus Marx Plus Einstein Equals Haya de la Torre 28

Che Guevara 30
Insurgency in Venezuela 30
Other Roads to Revolution in Latin America 32
Cuba in Argentina 33
Revolutionary Strategies: The Guerrilla Foco 34

Part II Diplomacy and Insurrection in the Western Hemisphere 39

3. Diplomacy and Foreign Policy 1960–1980 41

Break with the United States 41
The White Paper on Cuba 43
Isolation and Internationalism 43
Foreign Policy Activism in 1979: Revolution in Grenada 46
1980s Shifts 47
Cuba and Nicaragua 48

4. Cuban Assistance to El Salvador and Insurgency through the 1980s 57

U.S. and Cuban Involvement 58
The 1970s and the Roots of Present Conflict 59
El Salvador's Opposition and Outside Forces 60
The White Paper on El Salvador 62
Latin America and Its Reaction 65
Cuba and Colombia's M-19 Movement 66
Cuba and Puerto Rico in the 1980s 70
Cuba's Role in the South Atlantic Crisis 71
U.S. Reaction to Cuba and the Falklands/Malvinas 73
Cuba in the 1980s 73
Cuba's Latin American Regionalism 74

Part III Cuba's New Frontier: African Assistance Programs 81

5. Cuba's African Assistance Programs 83

Angola, 1974 to 1976: Operation Carlota 83

6. Ethiopia and the Costs of Cuba's African Assistance 95

Ethiopia: 1977 to 1979 95
Other Medical and Technical Assistance in Africa 101
Costs of Cuba's African Policies 102

Part IV International Economic Policy and International Decision Making 111

7. Cuba's International Presence 113

Sino-Cuban Relations 113
Cuba's International Diplomacy 114
Cuba's Relations with Western Europe and Southeast Asia 115
Cuba's Relations in the Middle East 116
How Foreign Policy Is Made 117

8. The Dollars and Cents of Cuba's Foreign Economic Policies: The Cost of Soviet Aid 127

Cuba's International Trade: An Overview 128
Cuba's Trade with Socialist Countries, 1970 to 1985 131
Cuba's Trade with Nonsocialist Countries, 1970 to 1985 136
Future of Cuba's International Trade Agreements 138

9. Conclusions 151

Modern Cuban Foreign Policy: The Break with Spain 152
Break with the United States: Alliance with the Soviet Union 155
Cuba's Foreign Policy of Internationalism: "Bonapartismo" and Sovietization 157
Dominance and Divergence 159
Contemporary U.S. Policy 163
U.S. Policy Interests 166
Strategies for U.S. Policymakers 167

Factsheet 173

Appendix A: Cuban Heads of State 177

Appendix B: Cuban Ambassadors to the United Nations and Representatives to Washington, 1959–Present 179

Appendix C: Treaty of Paris between Spain and the United States, 1898 181

Appendix D: The *Platt Amendment* 185

Appendix E: Guantánamo Bay Lease Agreements 193

Appendix F: Report of the Secretary of War 1906: *Cuban Pacification* 197

Appendix G: Letters Relating to the Cuban Missile Crisis 209

Appendix H: Excerpts from the Speech Given by Fidel Castro Analyzing the Events in Czechoslovakia, 23 August 1968 229

Appendix I: The Constitution of the Republic of Cuba, 1976 237

Appendix J: Cuban Leadership and Government Structure before January 1980 Reorganization 251

Appendix K: Government and Communist Party of Cuba 259

Appendix L: Note on Statistics 263

Appendix M: Cuban Central Budget 267

Appendix N: Cuban Military Capability: 269

Appendix O: Economic and Trade Date 273

Appendix P: Joint Ventures in Cuba 289

Appendix Q: Interviews by the Author 301

Bibliography 305

Index 328

About the Author 337

Preface

Since its earliest days as an independent republic, Cuba has tried to exert its influence in all parts of the world. This book focuses on Cuba's effect on its neighbors in Central and South America and in Africa.

My interest in this book began in 1971, when I came across a text on the Spanish-American War that made no reference to Havana, even though that war was fought by Cuba for its independence from Spain. When I visited Cuba, I was frequently reminded by my Cuban hosts of the sinking of the U.S.S. *Maine*. Either Spain, Cuba, or the United States itself, the story goes, sank the ship, thus initiating the conflict that determined Cuba's future.

The rusting hulk was raised from the deep on 2 February 1912, and towed out to sea, ceremoniously removing all vestiges of the colonial memento. An obelisk was built in downtown Havana, near the Malecón, Havana's seawall, as a monument to the historic ship. The eagle, which rested on the top of the monument, had been knocked off during a demonstration against the United States. Pablo Picasso had agreed to design a dove in its stead, but the plan was never completed.

The research for this book was based on interviews with U.S. and Cuban government officials, policy analysts, and business executives, as well as representatives of governments in South America and the Caribbean. The representatives from almost every nation in the region, including several heads of state and former heads of state, were remarkably candid and generous with their time. Cuba's 1959 Revolution, as well as its subsequent foreign policy choices, present profound philosophical questions to many of these government officials. Understanding Cuba has been particularly troublesome to them because their own countries have had parallel experiences with colonialism.

Unlike the majority of studies of postrevolutionary Cuba, which have focused on specific aspects of Cuba's political and economic systems, this book limits itself to a policy-oriented analysis of Cuba's foreign economic and political affairs. The objective of this book was not to reexamine U.S.-Cuban relations and U.S. policy in the region, but, rather, to examine Cuba's foreign programs, particularly in Latin America and Africa, and to analyze the example that Cuba sets for developing nations. Many studies of post-1959 Cuba balance social achievements of the postrevolutionary government against policies that restrict domestic personal liberties.

The premise of this book is that a balance sheet appraisal is not possible between social reform and personal injustice in the history and politics of the Cuban government before and after the 1959 Revolution. I have tried to let the facts speak for themselves.

This book relies principally on primary sources such as interviews with government leaders, national legislation, party resolutions that concern policy, bilateral and multilateral treaties, actions in international organizations, and statements by government leaders to leaders of other states. A nation's foreign policy, unlike its domestic policy, is not articulated in a body of laws. As a result, motives for foreign involvement must be gleaned from government documents and actions over several years.

The policies of the Cuban government change. The conclusions in this book reflect the evolution of international policies and Cuba's foreign relations. The book, therefore, invites further analysis as new events demand it.

Acknowledgments

The nature of Cuban politics and the ominous relationship between the U.S. and Cuba, particularly since 1959, have had a discernible affect on the state of political analysis itself; few analysts of Cuban affairs agree on which issues and which approach are appropriate. As a result, I am indebted to dozens of scholars, government officials (U.S. and Cuban), Cuban-Americans, and Latin Americans, who have offered both first-hand data and critical advice during the eleven years I have written on Cuban affairs. I am most grateful to the editorial and production staffs at Lexington Books, who graciously accepted revisions to the manuscript as events and political changes and my own insights warranted them; I would especially thank Marilyn Weinstein Ehrlich, Jamie Welch-Donahue, and Kevin Ahern for their commitment to perfection and hard work during the past three years, and to Pamela Walch Constantine, Mary Ann Greene, Karen Storz, Nancy Herndon, and Richard Tonachel. I am indebted to Grace Darling Griffith for putting me on track with this dedicated publishing group. My colleagues at the Americas Society and the Center for Inter-American Relations, particularly Russell E. Marks, Jr., the former President, have earned my gratitude for affording me an opportunity to work in the field of inter-American relations. To Russell Marks I am indebted for immense professional and intellectual support and hours upon hours of discussion and debate about political and economic issues within Latin America and Cuba. For administrative assistance at the Americas Society, and for keeping track of programs with calm and skill, I thank Lauretta Cohen, and for early research assistance, Beatrice Hernández.

My academic colleagues have been a source of constant encouragement, especially the Hunter College's faculty of the Department of Political Science during my seven years on the faculty, particularly by giving me the opportunity to teach Cuban government and history. With sadness, I remember the help of a Hunter College colleague, the late Professor Manuel Urrutia-Lleó, Cuba's first President after 1959, who agreed to speak with me about a subject which profoundly troubled him. New York University's Department of Politics provided the intellectual training during my graduate education, which led first to my doctoral dissertation and finally to this book. Much of the research was made possible by the financial assistance of the politics department, including the Penfield Fellowship for Studies in Diplomacy, International Affairs, and Belles Lettres. I thank Christopher Mitchell who unfailingly kept me on the track and Professors Louis Koenig and Gisbert Flanz. For early discussions of my manuscript on domestic political process in Cuba, during the graduate seminar on Latin America at Columbia University, I am grateful to Douglas Chalmers. I especially appreciated comments on several drafts of an early manuscript by Professor Jorge I. Domínguez of Harvard University and I thank Robert Bond for his critical examination of the manuscript. My special thanks go to experts and analysts who read the book and commented on Cuban affairs to me: Ambassador Ambler H. Moss; Antonio Navarro; Lord Hugh Thomas, of the London-based Center for Policy Studies, whose landmark work on Cuba provides immeasurable historical information; *New York Times* correspondent Alan Riding; Karl E. Meyer, for a lengthy first-hand account of a then-reporter's view of the Sierra Maestra and Castro in 1958; and to numerous colleagues and panelists at Conferences on Cuban-U.S. relations who helped me to understand aspects of Cuba's foreign policy: William LeoGrande, Susan Kaufman Purcell, and the Council of Foreign Relations Cuba group.

Because the method of the book was to rely to the greatest extent possible on primary sources and interviews, I am deeply indebted to many Cuban and U.S. government officials for answering countless questions and for arranging both formal and informal interviews with visiting dignitaries. Knowing full well that neither government would, by definition, agree with all my analysis and certainly not with many conclusions, both the U.S. government and Cuban government were remarkably forthright and helpful. I must thank many present and former U.S. State Department officials who have read drafts of the book and generously made vital critiques and suggestions. For their extensive comments I thank Senator Daniel P. Moynihan, Congressman Ted Weiss, Kenneth W. Skoug, Jr., desk officer at the State Department Cuba desk, and his predecessor Myles Frechette, who offered hours of analysis, and Ernesto Betancourt of Radio Martí, who provided a first-hand description of the revolutionary Twenty-sixth of July Movement, and Cuban government officials in New York, Washington, and Havana. Several officials discussed issues regularly in addition to the formal interviews listed in the appendix of this book. I thank Ambassador Ramón Sánchez-Parodi, head of the Cuban Interest Section in the Czech Embassy in Washington, former Ambassador Raúl Roa Kourí, and Ambassador Oscar Oramas Oliva, ambassadors of Cuba to the United Nations, as well as many members of the U.N. Mission and the Ministry of Foreign Relations in Cuba: Carlos Ciaño, Ramón Prado, Mary Gentile, and Ricardo Alarcón. I thank them for the invaluable opportunities and interviews that they arranged, particularly with Cuban Vice-President Carlos Rafael Rodríguez and for an official government invitation (at my expense) to conduct interviews in Cuba.

No book could be completed on such an extensive period of Cuban history without the cooperation of several research libraries, library staffs, and resources of research institutes. Without the Center for Cuban Studies and its executive director, Sandra Levinson, much less information would be known about Cuba in the United States. I have also been greatly assisted by the library staffs of the John F. Kennedy Library in Boston; the New York University Library; and the Hunter College and Columbia University libraries. I have also been aided by the Cuban-American Committee and the Cuban American National Foundation.

This book would not have been completed without the tireless research efforts and endless information digging by Gabrielle Brussel, my research assistant at the Center for Inter-American Relations. In her tenure as teaching assistant, research intern, and research assistant, she spent countless hours researching and writing and traveling to every library in the New York, Washington, and Boston corridor, making herself somewhat of an expert in her own right in both investigative methods as well as on the subject of Cuba. I owe a great debt to my friends who have been supportive during the process of writing this book, and to a friend, *New York Times* editor Tom Wallace, for editing the first draft of the final manuscript. With deep affection, I acknowledge the contribution of the late Professor Kalman Silvert to the study of Cuban affairs, and for his examination of the first study I completed under his supervision of Cuban political institutions in 1974. I wish to share all the credit with my colleagues; any blame for the conclusions, I bear myself.

Finally, I wish to thank Edward C. Wallace, my husband, the scope of whose contribution is impossible to describe, for rigorous editing, intellectual guidance, and unending emotional support. And, my deep respect and affection I owe to my parents, Richard R. Falk and Corinne Falk, for their early and continuing inspiration.

Fidel Castro in Miami, Florida, addressing a meeting before going to Mexico in 1953.

Introduction

Since the 1890s, Cuba has been making headlines in foreign newspapers. Relative to its size, its resources, and its location, Cuba has received a disproportionate amount of world attention. Why Cuba, a small, one-crop island in a sea dotted with islands, has figured so prominently in international relations for three-quarters of a century is not easy to fathom. Much of the answer lies in its foreign policy.

Cuban foreign policy has sought not only to develop formal diplomatic relations and trade ties with other nations but also to serve as a strategic tool in Cuba's quest for influence. Over the years, Cuba has experimented with different foreign programs, each of which has reflected a common theme: to secure international recognition of Cuba as an autonomous nation. The goal has been to draw international attention to Cuba's plight and thus to enlist political and economic support.

Whether one remembers the U.S.S. *Maine* or the missile crisis or the State Department's 1961 White Paper on Cuba, it is clear that Cuba has been noticed. This notice has brought Cuba economic aid and support for its "internationalist" movements. It has not, however, brought either the international perception or the reality that Cuba has been in the twentieth century the master of its destiny.

The first step to understanding Cuban foreign policy is to understand Cuba's relationship with the three major powers that have played such a large part in its history: Spain, the United States, and the Soviet Union. Cuba's fight for independence from Spain was based on its long-held desire for democratic government and self-rule. It was a battle fought in Cuba after most nations of Latin America had won their independence. Cuba's independence movement writers, such as José Martí and Ignacio Agramonte, were inspired by the liberatión struggles of Simón Bolívar and by those fought in other parts of the hemisphere, including the American Revolution, about which Martí wrote while self-exiled in New York City.

Cuba had great importance to Spain: it was the largest and most prosperous of the Antillean nations. Through the 1860s, Cuba fought for independence. After an unsuccessful independence battle, and twenty years of skirmishes, fighting broke out again in 1895. At the end of the century, revolutionary leaders sought U.S. help. Although this call for international assistance was a key strategy of the early independence leaders, it soon became clear that Theodore Roosevelt's

Rough Riders were not true liberators—although their importance in ousting Spain should not be overlooked.

The Spanish-American War was a war between two superpowers for control of a territory. Consequently, in the first half of the twentieth century, the United States made many of the decisions about the direction of Cuban affairs. During this period, Cuba attempted to forge an aggressive and visible foreign policy—which would become a cornerstone of foreign affairs.

Cuban politics during the first half of the twentieth century became increasingly corrupt, and the message of Cuba's early independence philosophers sparked a new generation of leaders of rebellion, culminating in the revolution that brought Fidel Castro to power. In the years immediately following the 1959 Revolution, Cuban leaders were forced to break economic and political ties with the United States and set up a radically different government. In the midst of this chaotic transition, Cuba turned to the Soviet Union to relieve it of U.S. influence, and again, rapidly, the tables turned.

From 1961 through the following two decades, Cuba's relationship with the Soviet Union became central to its foreign policies, and it became the common perception that Cuba was, to some degree, fighting proxy wars for Moscow in Africa and Central America. As Cuban leaders continued military training and aid to guerrillas in at least a dozen nations of Central and South America in the 1970s and 1980s, Cuban programs appeared to be in Moscow's interest. Similarly, in Africa, Cuba's massive military program—in which it sent tens of thousands of combat soldiers—was on a par with that of the Soviet Union. Simultaneously, Cuba's international economic agreements began to shape Cuba's options. Its commitment to the eastern European Council for Mutual Economic Assistance (CMEA) limited Cuba's ability to trade in the future with the West.

But, Cuba's interest in thrusting itself onto the world stage through its foreign policy was established long before 1959 and continued after the revolution. While Cuban foreign programs reached out during the 1980s to every nation in Central and South America as well as to Africa and the Middle East, Cuba's close ties with the Soviet Union brought it prominence as a world power in the midst of a conflict between the East and the West. In the 1980s—with as much fervor as it has argued the point in the 1890s—Washington argued that the Caribbean Basin was the strategic underbelly of the United States and the Achilles heel of NATO.

Cuban foreign policy in the mid-1980s appears to be based on four objectives: to hold power and leverage in the international system; to react and respond to the actions of the United States and to remain visibly independent of Washington; to aid insurgencies with military might in Latin America and Africa, regardless of the common perception that its compass is the same as Moscow's; to broaden its diplomatic relations; and finally, to develop its economy.

From the Andes to the Ogaden, Cuba's leadership has sought to portray it as a small developing nation that has dared to challenge its neighbor to the North. Ultimately, Cuba's foreign policy successes and failures must be evaluated on the basis of both Cuba's definition of its foreign policy objectives and international perceptions, particularly Third World judgment of these foreign programs.

Part I
History of Cuban Foreign Policy

Colonel Theodore Roosevelt and his Rough Riders, 1898.

1
Foreign Policy in the New Republic

The struggle for Cuban independence from Spain during the last half of the nineteenth century left a stamp on Cuban foreign policy that endures today. A principal objective of Cuban independence movement leaders, such as José Martí, Antonio Maceo, Carlos Manuel de Céspedes, and Ignacio Agramonte, was to establish not only national autonomy but international recognition as well. Their strategy was to draw international attention to Cuba's struggle against Spain and to use that attention as a lever. To internationalize their struggle, they spent time—sometimes on diplomatic missions and sometimes in exile—traveling to Mexico, Guatemala, and the United States. This pattern has been repeated often; by 1980 Cuba had provided military assistance to insurgent groups in every Central and Latin American country at one point in their history.

When Cuba gained independence in 1898, the military assistance provided by the United States gave Washington considerable influence over Cuban politics. Although Cuba would continue to set an independent tone in its foreign policy pronouncements, the extensive involvement of the United States in Cuban affairs was undeniable. The United States alleged that military and financial assistance were merely being supplied to assist in Cuba's transition and to protect U.S. interests. It was clear, however, that in the earliest years of independence Havana's foreign policy reflected the demands made on it by a neocolonial administration.

In 1910 Cuba demonstrated its international leadership by assisting revolutionaries in Mexico, and in the Chaco War in 1935. These international involvements were consistent with U.S. interests and were supported by the United States. Similarly, World War I provided a platform for Cuba to demonstrate its leadership capabilities and to reveal its longing for autonomy. By the 1930s, however, Cuba's opposition parties and student groups were establishing relations with the heads of other nations and with opposition leaders in Latin America, Africa, and Europe, and were laying the groundwork for support of new leadership and a new direction.

In the first half of the twentieth century, particularly before the Platt Amendment was abrogated in 1934, the United States exerted a heavy hand in Cuban internal politics. In a very real way the United States was calling the shots and preventing Havana from shaping Cuba's future. This juxtaposition of domestic frustration with a new political system which did not satisfy Cuba's need to rule itself on the one hand, and an aggressive and internationally visible foreign policy on the other, was to become the hallmark of Cuba's diplomatic relations. Tragically, these foreign policy positions would also serve as a distraction from domestic corruption and ultimately as evidence of the misplaced priorities of Fulgencio Batista in the 1930s and 1940s.

Despite the obvious contradictions of such an approach, it is not unusual for a developing nation, newly independent, to establish a bold and assertive foreign policy to compensate for domestic frustrations and internal failures. In the case of Cuba, after many years of fighting Spain, the independence leaders discovered that pressure from the North had in many respects simply supplanted colonial rule. Cuba began to understand its strategic significance to the United States as it had somewhat painfully learned its value to Spain during the 1860s and 1870s. Cuba began to develop a foreign policy that utilized this strategic and political value as a lever with other world powers. In 1959 Cuba's programs and ideology changed dramatically, but themes remained in its international relations that dated back to its entry into the world arena with its internationalized struggle against Spanish colonial rule and its birth as an independent republic.

Early Foreign Policy Objectives

Cuban leaders emerged from the war of independence (1895-1898) fatigued. Few nations in the hemisphere have fought such long and arduous wars. Even the name which history has given the conflict seemed to reflect the dashed hopes of the Cuban freedom fighters: the Spanish-American War, a war that had been fought on Cuban soil and was the culmination of almost a half of a century of turmoil.

The details of the battle for independence have been described by many others. The fighting began in 1895; the U.S. battleship *Maine* was sent by the United States and was blown up outside Havana harbor in February 1898. The United States, blaming the loss of the U.S.S. *Maine* on Spain, allied with Cuba and declared war against Spain. In December 1898 after Spain's defeat, Spain and the United States signed the Treaty of Paris, which granted independence to Cuba and awarded other Spanish territories, such as Puerto Rico, to the United States as war booty.

Cuba, however, learned for the first time a lesson that it would be reminded of several times in the next century: its geopolitical blessings could also be its downfall. The battle had been taken from the Cubans—as had the glories of victory—by its North American neighbor. Cuba's importance to the United States—as its importance had been to Spain—stemmed from its proximity to the sea lanes of the Caribbean that carried trade with Latin America. The building of the Panama Canal heightened Cuba's strategic value. In military terms, Cuba would be the *watchdog* of the Caribbean because of its location and its size, and its sugar would supply the United States and western Europe.

In the struggle for independence from Spain, Cuban revolutionaries had enlisted the aid of a world power—a neighbor—only to discover that the ally expected much more from Cuba than friendship; the United States expected allegiance. Half a century later in a struggle to establish independence from the United States, Cuba enlisted the aid of another world power, the Soviet Union, which in turn also demanded allegiance. In both instances an aggressive and ambitious foreign policy was created to internationalize the struggle.

Cuba's philosophical leaders had preached revolution during the thirty years of struggle against Spain. Carlos Manuel de Céspedes was a principal fighter in the first war against Spain in 1868, which began with the famous Grito de Yara rebellion against Spanish colonialism. Ignacio Agramonte drafted a manifesto of Cuban rights, the Constitution of Guainaro, for a rebel convention in April 1869. This constitution called for the abolition of slavery (with some exceptions) and the annexation of Cuba to the United States. It was in this early period that Cuba sought to bring the United States in as an ally to help it break ties to Spain. Insurrections occurred throughout the island. The rebels sought international recognition of the state of war in Cuba. Some Latin American presidents, including Mexico's President Benito Juárez who had himself been at war in the mid-nineteenth century with the United States, recognized the rebel cause.

From Cuba's day as a colony fighting for independence, Cuban rebels learned their foreign affairs rule: international recognition would be the key to international leverage. No one implemented this strategy more astutely than did José Martí, a writer who founded the Cuban Revolutionary party while in exile. (A curious aspect of Martí's immortality is the acknowledgment which his contributions received from both the government of Fidel Castro in Cuba after the 1959 Revolution and from Castro's opponents. Posters of Martí prominently display his writings in Havana in the 1980s, but, ironically, the Reagan administration named its broadcast program "Radio Martí.")

Unlike Agramonte, Martí predicted the possible dilemmas that Cuba would face in transferring alliances to the United States. Martí's Manifesto of Monte Cristi cautioned against U.S. interference in Cuban affairs. Although U.S. involvement in Cuba during most of Martí's life (he was born in 1853) was minimal, by the time he died in 1895—just as the war for independence was beginning—he was warning against strong U.S. relations for Cuba. He had lived in New York during his years in exile and perhaps it was there that he grew to know the importance that the United States placed on a strong alliance with Cuba. In his final letter before he died, he cautioned,

> I have lived inside the monster [the United States] and I know its entrails; my sling is David's.[1]

Cuba's earliest foreign policy of broadening diplomatic contacts was established during the independence struggle. Cuban independence leaders were successful in bringing their plea to Latin America, and many Latin American leaders established close contact with Cuba during this period. The famous Venezuelan liberator of

Latin America, Simón Bolívar—along with Mexican and Colombian independence leaders—stated his support of independence for Cuba as well as for Puerto Rico in the late 1800s.

Puerto Rico also aided the Cuban independence fight. Independence leaders in Puerto Rico supported Cuba's goal of autonomy, and Puerto Rican generals fought in Cuba's war with Spain in the 1890s. There was a strong sense of commitment by Puerto Rican leaders to Cuba's independence. This early alliance continues to link Cuba's leaders to staunch support for Puerto Rican independence. In the 1980s, Rubén Berríos Martínez, the head of the Puerto Rican Independence party (PIP), stated:

> One has to understand Puerto Rican and Cuban history. After all, José Martí's revolutionary party was established to fight for Cuban independence and promote independence for Puerto Rico. Our soldiers and generals went to fight in the Cuban revolution for independence in the last century and thus Cuba has an historical debt and obligation . . . there was no such thing as a Puerto Rican independence movement or a Cuban independence movement; it was a Puerto Rican-Cuban movement.[2]

Indeed, when Puerto Rico's independence leader Don Pedro Albizu Campos was in jail, Cuba's President Carlos Prío Socarrás cabled the Puerto Rican government for his release.

These early relationships were the foundation for Cuba's internationalism of the 1980s. Support for Cuba's independence from Spain came from all parts of the region and dated back to 1849 when Venezuelan General Narciso López supported Cuba.

As for the United States, it entered Cuba's war of independence for several reasons. Among them was the inflammatory reporting of William Randolph Hearst and Joseph Pulitzer, which aroused support for what was seen as a fight for Cuba's right to self-rule. U.S. intervention was supported by almost all parties in the United States Congress.

Before war was declared, Spain made concessions and offered an armistice to Cuban insurgents, but the United States ignored them. By the time Congress declared a state of war on 25 April 1898, congressional support for war was overwhelming.[3] European nations tried to mediate. Cuba had successfully internationalized its battle and its call for independence. Just before the United States intervened in the war that was being fought between Cuba and Spain, Great Britain, France, Germany, Austria, Russia, and Italy signed a letter asking that they be allowed to participate in the conciliation effort. Doubtless Europe had its interest in assisting Cuba and preventing U.S. intervention in Cuban affairs. Balance-of-power politics played no small part. Nonetheless, a portentous feature of Cuba's independence struggle was that it had launched and successfully carried out an international struggle for autonomy.

The war was over in 1898, yet for the next four years the United States occupied Cuba militarily and appointed military governors. Appointed by the United States, Leonard Wood (promoted to Major-General in 1903) was military commander of Santiago from 1898 to 1899 and military governor from 1899 until 1902 when Cuba's constitution was written and the Cuban Republic was formed. He had organized the Rough Riders with Theodore Roosevelt and commanded the attack on Santiago de Cuba. Although the United States had argued that Cuba was entitled to self-rule, William Jennings Bryan, then a U.S. army colonel, stated the U.S. view at the time: "Washington is in greater danger just now than Cuba. Our people defended Cuba against foreign arms; now they must defend themselves and their country against a foreign idea—the colonial idea of European nations."[4] President William McKinley began to argue that Cuba was not stable enough to protect itself from European colonialism. McKinley's message to Congress, Bryan argued, was to take possession of Cuba, to establish a stable government, and then to "turn that government over to the Cuban people."[5] The concept of U.S. national security, thus stated, became the underlying—and perilous—basis of U.S. reaction to Cuba for decades to follow.

Cuba's Constitution

Ironically, Cuba's first constitution was written in 1901 during the U.S. occupation. Appended to Cuba's own constitution was a U.S. army appropriations bill that had been passed by Congress and signed by President McKinley. The bill contained an amendment, proposed by Senator Orville H. Platt, which established the right of the United States to intervene militarily in Cuban affairs. Two years later in 1903, the United States and Cuba endorsed the amendment in the form of a treaty.

The Platt Amendment became a powerful symbol of Cuba's frustrated independence struggle. Similar frustrations were being experienced in nations throughout the Western hemisphere. The United States was building a canal in Panama through the Central American isthmus, and in 1902 Venezuela experienced a crisis resulting from European intervention, which made Venezuela particularly sympathetic to Cuba's dilemma.

In 1903 Cuba consented to lease the military bases in the port cities of Guantánamo and Bahía Honda to the United States for an indefinite period of time for an annual rent of two thousand dollars (later increased to five thousand dollars) which gave the United States possession of the Isle of Pines (today the Isle of Youth). The United States claimed that in order to fulfill the requirements of the Platt Amendment it would be necessary to establish bases not only at Bahía Honda and Guantánamo but also at Cienfuegos and Nipé. The Platt Amendment, as well as the bases that were established as a result of this legislation, were anachronisms in their own time. Colonialism as an international trend, did not, however, fade until after World War II.

Cuban Leadership and International Relations

Cuba's first president, Tomás Estrada-Palma, viewed foreign policy as a key to international prestige. Like the majority of presidents who followed him, Estrada-

Palma made foreign policy one of his first items of business after he was sworn in as president on 20 May 1902. In the three years before Estrada-Palma came to office, the U.S. occupation under the military administration of General Leonard Wood, military governor of Cuba, had created a substantial presence of U.S. troops in Cuba. Estrada-Palma, eager to create the fact and appearance of a new independent republic, encouraged the Cuban Congress to increase expenditures in the national budget to assume the cost of domestic defense. He quickly enlarged Cuba's armed forces.[6]

Estrada-Palma had special reasons for developing a distinctive foreign policy. His election had been suspect, and he thus lacked credibility. Several congressional representatives involved in his administration were sent to jail for corruption and fraud. The United States was continuing to exercise a strong hand in Cuba's politics, and in May 1904 Theodore Roosevelt argued that the United States should be able to intervene to protect Cuba. Roosevelt's Corollary to the Monroe Doctrine (the address of President James Monroe to Congress on 2 December 1823 in which Monroe argued that the United States would regard European colonialism in the Western hemisphere "as dangerous to our peace and safety") was the modern justification for the repeated U.S. military interventions that followed.[7]

Estrada-Palma's increase in Cuba's military forces, however, also served U.S. interests since the United States hoped that Cuban soldiers would be able to defend U.S. interests throughout the Caribbean. As a result, he was able to secure the concession from the United States that not all of the bases that had been agreed to in 1903 were necessary, and the U.S. settled for continuing leases on the bases at Guantánamo and Bahía Honda.

Although Cuba's economy was flourishing and becoming increasingly tied to U.S. investment, the fraud that began to increase in domestic politics undermined the administration of Estrada-Palma. Cuban opposition parties were beginning to learn that if domestic politics seemed too unstable, the United States would intervene. This fact of life became part and parcel of Cuban politics.

Cuba's earliest foreign policy became one of leverage with outside intervention. The most obvious rule was that the party that could manipulate and persuade the United States to assist it would be able to wedge some space in the Cuban political system.

Despite the danger that the United States perceived to be posed by western Europe, and particularly Germany, to Cuba, Cuba's new independent government began to establish relations with western Europe. Nonetheless, Cuba's principal foreign relations remained aligned with the United States. As Estrada-Palma's Republican party supported him and Liberal party opposition grew, the United States sent William H. Taft, secretary of war, and Robert Bacon, assistant secretary of state, to Havana to attempt to mediate the crisis.

Estrada-Palma's attempt to reinforce his own domestic military force to combat the possible rebellion failed, and he requested military assistance from the

United States. Taft and Bacon ignored his request. They issued a report arguing that the only effective response would be to establish another provisional U.S. administration in Cuba.[8] The United States, directed by Secretary of State Elihu Root, responded to the ineffectiveness of the Cuban Army by offering to replace the government of Estrada-Palma.[9] In August of 1906, between fifteen thousand and twenty-four thousand soldiers revolted. The public perception that Estrada-Palma was corrupt in the reelection campaign of 1905 brought widespread support for the rebellion. In September Estrada-Palma resigned. The next day, the United States sent two thousand marines to Havana and established a provisional government. The liberals had been successful in using the United States to influence Cuban domestic difficulties. The first Cuban presidency had ended in failure, the United States was back in charge, and the Cuban government was far from its goal of an independent government. U.S. government-appointed Provisional Governor William Howard Taft was succeeded in October 1906 by Charles E. Magoon, who served until 1909.

U.S. Occupation—1906 to 1909

During the three years of U.S. occupation, Cuba had virtually no independence in foreign policy decision making. The occupation for the two years after Estrada-Palma resigned was substantially different, however, from the first occupation. Magoon had been sent by Roosevelt to govern within the context of an independent Cuban republic. No doubt because he had been governor of the Panama Canal Zone, Magoon emphasized the strategic importance of Cuba and Latin America to the United States. Access to sea lanes had an important strategic value to the United States as well as to Europe. From the days of President Monroe, the United States had felt it was necessary to guard against intervention by Europe. In Monroe's 1823 address to Congress, he announced the principle of U.S. protection of the Western hemisphere. Although Magoon's experience was not in the military, he stressed the theme of Cuba's strategic value to Cuban politicians from the day he arrived.

Magoon's administration politicized government positions. However, he did encourage the Cuban Congress to pass legislation to replace Spanish statutes. As Theodore Roosevelt was completing his term, he declared that U.S. intervention in Cuba would cease at the end of his term. According to the plan, Cuba would be ruled by its own leaders and U.S. troops would depart. The influence of Theodore Roosevelt, known for his distrust of Latin America as a whole and in particular for his description of Cubans as "that cheating mañana lot," came to an end. U.S. influence and manipulation, however, did not cease.

In 1908 Cuba again held elections, and José Miguel Gómez was sworn in as president in 1909. For the four years that followed Gómez reestablished Cuban priorities. He won the return of one additional U.S. base at Bahía Honda, leaving the United States only Guantánamo. Within a few months of Gómez's installation, Cuba's economy improved and sugar prices increased. Gómez stayed in office, corrupt as he was, until the elections of 1912, when conservative candidate Mario García Menocal was elected.

The Foreign Policy of World War I

When the United States entered World War I in April 1917, Cuba was under great pressure to follow suit. The liberals were immediately criticized; domestic squabbles in Cuba served to divide the country at a time when it needed to be unified. Economic links to the United States were important, and in fact essential, both to the United States and to France and the Allied nations. Sugar was to be principally supplied by Cuba.

On 7 April 1917, Menocal declared to the Cuban Congress that Cuba would support the United States in World War I. Latin America was divided over the war. Nations that remained neutral included Argentina, Chile, Colombia, Mexico, Paraguay, El Salvador, and Venezuela; those that broke diplomatic relations with Germany and the Central Powers but did not declare war were Bolivia, the Dominican Republic, Ecuador, Peru, and Uruguay.[10] Cuba favored a declaration of war for two reasons: first, Cuba was able to exert its leadership role, and, second, Cuba's economy clearly benefitted from the sale of sugar to the United States.

To guarantee the suppression of the liberals' revolt, Menocal asked the United States to send troops. Within months three thousand U.S. soldiers were again in Cuba. They stayed for five years. While sugar was being sold to Allied forces, Cuba experienced the most prosperous period in its history. During 1914, Cuba's entire sugar harvest was sold to supply the war effort.

Cuba declared war on the Germans but did not send soldiers. An interesting aspect of Cuba's assistance, however, was the technical and medical assistance it sent to France, including approximately 100 doctors and medical personnel.[11] However small, this was Cuba's first technical assistance mission in a war effort. As a foreign policy program it would become the rule rather than the exception.

In 1920 elections were held for the Cuban presidency. Fearing a repeat of the events of 1905 and 1916, the United States sent special envoy General Enoch Crowder to watch the elections. The presidency was won by Alfredo Zayas, who took office in 1921, guided by Crowder, who exerted significant influence but held no formal political title.

Foreign Affairs and the Student Movements of the 1920s

The election of Alfredo Zayas was in part the result of pressure by the administration of President Woodrow Wilson to protect U.S. sugar interests in Cuba. Between

1921 and 1925, however, during the Zayas administration, new international contacts were made, not by the Cuban government, but by the Cuban student movement, which was increasing its membership and activism.

The precedent for a schism in Cuba's foreign relations was set during the first two decades of the century. During the 1920s, international relations expanded on two levels: first, formal policymaking was carried out by a corrupt and firmly implanted group of politicians (supported by the United States), and, second, informally, a network of opposition (including the student movement, the Anarchist-Syndicalist movement, and the Cuban Communist party) was making international contacts. These opposition groups established international connections that provided a network of refuge and assistance through the 1950s and during Castro's revolution of 1957 to 1958.

One of the principal student radicals of the 1920s, whose call to arms spurred the rebellions of the next decade, was Julio Antonio Mella. Just as Agramonte did in the early nineteenth century, Mella gave life to a seminal opposition movement of the twentieth century. Through it Mella was establishing international prominence and support for a national rebellion. It was a mutual response to a domestic administration that was becoming increasingly more corrupt and repressive.

Cuba's university movement was encouraged, in part, by parallel university movements in other nations of Latin America. Only five years before Cuba's major university demonstrations began, Argentina had a major student revolt, and the rector of the University of Buenos Aires, José Arce, had traveled to Cuba and conferred with the University of Havana's rector, Carlos de la Torre, who had himself become an advocate of reform.[12]

University reforms were enacted after student demonstrations organized by Mella and the Students' Federation (FEU), but the students had successfully proven their power as a social force within Cuba—a force that foreshadowed deep-seated unrest within the middle class of the next generation.

Mella inspired other revolutionary groups within the country. Mella's generation of students preceded Fidel Castro at the university, but it was this model of student-led rebellion that Castro would adopt. Mella organized the Revolutionary Students' Congress which founded an institute named after Cuba's independence leader—the Universidad Popular José Martí.[13]

Mella had dreams (as Castro would) of Latin American unity. He proposed a Latin American League of Students. In 1924 elections again were called, and the Liberal party supported General Gerardo Machado, who would ultimately extend his term of presidency and establish a repressive rule in Cuba until he was overthrown in 1933.

In 1925 a series of strikes opened the way for Machado's repressive policies. In ensuing months, Machado began to destroy the labor movement as well as the Communist and Socialist parties. Mella was arrested. Within a few months, Machado effectively wiped out all political opposition in Cuba. He consolidated his power by controlling armed forces and purging the army of officers who were other than loyal allies.

The parties that Machado successfully repressed were not, however, to disappear from Cuban society. The 1917 Russian Revolution had made an impact on the development of Communist parties in Cuba as well as in the rest of Latin America, and it was in part through these Communist parties that early international connections were made. Although the United States had established relations with Cuba as a major trading partner from the beginning of World War I, it had done nothing to integrate itself into the intellectual development of Cuba. Unlike the United States, the Soviet Union had had links with Cuba and Latin America since the 1917 Revolution, and it strengthened those links during the 1920s. In August 1925 the Cuban Communist party was founded, and Julio Antonio Mella joined the Communist party, which in 1925 joined several splintered groups to form the Cuban National Workers Confederation (CNOC).[14]

Machado traveled to the United States to assure U.S. business executives that domestic politics would not interfere with their business practices. The strong arm that Machado exerted on the Cuban people was to have an ominous effect within a few years. In 1927 the United States began to notice the power that Machado was accumulating, and Stokely Morgan, the head of the State Department's Latin American Affairs Division, cautioned Machado that U.S. policymakers would not approve of changes in the Cuban constitution that Machado sought.[15] This pressure, however, was to no avail. In April 1927 the Cuban Congress, at Machado's request, extended the term of the Cuban presidency from four to six years, thus relieving Machado of the need to seek reelection.[16]

The Pan-American Conference in Havana

In 1927 when Machado went to Washington to invite President Calvin Coolidge to attend the sixth Pan-American Conference in Havana, he was greeted by U.S. business leaders, including J.P. Morgan and representatives of the Chase National Bank and the National City Bank.[17] In international circles this gathering signified U.S. support of Machado's repressive tactics.

In 1928 Coolidge went to Havana for the Pan-American Conference at a time when support for Machado was waning domestically. In effect, Coolidge's trip underscored the strong approval of the United States and gave Machado a mandate to continue to oppress his domestic opponents. As Machado's relations with the United States improved, his crackdown on domestic opposition increased. The crackdown on opposition parties became more severe, and Julio Antonio Mella went into exile in Mexico, where he was assassinated in January 1929.

The repression became so fierce that in September 1929 the U.S. Senate Foreign Relations Committee suggested that the United States might again have to intervene in Cuban politics.[18] U.S. Secretary of State Henry L. Stimson cautioned that the situation in Cuba was becoming volatile but preferred not to intervene.[19] U.S. Ambassador Harry F. Guggenheim was being persuaded by the opposition of the Ortodoxo party, particularly ex-President Menocal, to request "preventive intervention."[20] By 1931 Menocal was arrested.[21] During this era many of the Cuban Communists who later would stay in government under Castro became actively involved in the opposition, including Aníbal Escalante, Raúl Roa García (who became Foreign Minister) and Francisco Calderío (who changed his name to Blas Roca Calderío).[22]

Washington had prevented the development of open Cuban politics and thus taught Cuba to rely on U.S. intervention. It was not until 1930 that U.S. President Herbert Hoover reinterpreted the address of President James Monroe asserting that he saw no justification for U.S. intervention in Monroe's words. According to historian Hugh Thomas, "U.S. action, or the threat of action, prevented the seizure or the legitimate capture of power by the liberal party which, through all its evident faults, under José Miguel Gómez, was a genuine popular movement."[23] In 1933 U.S. policy would fundamentally change when Franklin D. Roosevelt came into office and implemented the Good Neighbor policy. But Machado's eight-year tenure left its imprint on Cuban politics. It was under Machado that the Communist, Socialist, and Anarchist parties became involved in opposition politics rather than the actual electoral process. They were to surface again in electoral politics in 1939 when Fulgencio Batista himself accepted the support of the Communist party. As these parties removed themselves from electoral politics, universities became the center of political activity, and the Cuban student organization *A la Izquierda Estudiantil* (AIE) became the major platform for Communist party members such as Carlos Rafael Rodríguez (who later became Cuba's vice-president) to make their positions known.

International Mediation in the 1930s

Cuba's role as a regional negotiator came to light when Cuba joined the five-member peace-making commission during the Chaco War between Paraguay and Bolivia from 1932 to 1935. The commission also included Colombia, Mexico, the United States, and Uruguay. The dispute contested sovereignty over the territory which lay between the two countries; a boundary had not been previously established at the Chaco Boreal, situated at the border of Bolivia and Paraguay.

The Chaco War was internationalized rapidly. Bolivia sought help from Germany. Paraguay sought help from France. Although the dispute lingered and the commission was not able to resolve the dispute, Cuba had established itself as a regional power interested in a leadership role.[24]

Faced with Cuba's increased role in South America, U.S. policy changed. By 1934 Cuba had pressured U.S. officials to abrogate the Platt Amendment. Similarly, legislation was enacted in Panama to attempt to reestablish Panamanian control of its territory. The Western hemisphere nations were beginning to assert a renewed interest in regional unity.

In August 1933 Machado was pressured to resign the presidency. The United States recommended the nomination of Carlos Manuel de Céspedes, Jr., who seemed to have broad popular support, as interim president. After Céspedes was appointed by the Congress of Cuba in August 1933, Roosevelt thought that all would be well. Céspedes lasted only one month in office, however. Every political interest group in Cuba was included in the new cabinet except the army, which Machado had consolidated and politicized.

In September 1933 Céspedes was overthrown by a group of four noncommissioned officers of the army, including Sergeant Pablo Rodríguez, Sergeant José Pedraza, Sergeant Manuel López Migoya, and Sergeant Fulgencio Batista, a court stenographer from Oriente Province. Batista knew the opposition well; as the government clamped down and arrested and tried Machado's opponents (the *Machadato*), the young court stenographer took note of the names of Machado's imprisoned opponents, and with them he forged an alliance.

Much has been written about Batista's domestic influence, but Cuba's foreign policy was also under his direction from 1933 on, and it was markedly different from the policy of his predecessors. The new government formed a five-person directorate, the Pentarquía. It lasted only one month. In September 1933 Ramón Grau San Martín became president; his administration lasted four months. For the next seven years a series of puppet presidents who ruled under the strong arm of Batista followed. Batista himself was elected in 1940.

The Pentarquía was an interesting mix of political perspectives: Rámon Grau San Martín was a doctor who had been out of the country during Machado's rule; Sergio Carbó was a journalist; José María Irisarri was both a lawyer and a professor; Porfirio Franca was a banker. Fulgencio Batista remained head of the army. By all accounts it was a broad-based group. According to Cuba's former Foreign Minister Raúl Roa García, many left-leaning Cubans felt that for once Cuba had an authentic government that was both revolutionary and supported by the Cuban people.

Although the directorate included a broad span of political views, it was regarded as being strongly influenced by Washington. The Cuban people were unhappy with the corruption of the Machado era and not satisfied with Céspedes and the approval he received in Washington. Popular sentiment was becoming more profoundly nationalistic: Cuba should be ruled without U.S. control. U.S. Ambassador Sumner Welles pressed for intervention to prevent the Pentarquía from maintaining power, but Cordell Hull, U.S. secretary of state, was strongly opposed to any intervention.

The position of the U.S. emissaries with regard to Cuba's leadership varied greatly. By 1933, as Machado's support had waned, Sumner Welles openly favored a change of administration. The appearance of Welles's lack of confidence added to the public dissatisfaction with Machado.

In the final days of the Machado administration, "the threat of an American intervention—highly believable in Cuba—hastened the process of disintegration," U.S. Ambassador Philip Bonsal later wrote.[25] It was, however, one of many factors since Machado's resignation was being demanded by most Cubans by August.

U.S. Ambassador Welles described Machado's fall as the "expression of the volition of very nearly the totality of the Cuban people."[26]

As the five-person committee began to fall apart, the predominant role of Batista became obvious. Welles repeated his calls for U.S. intervention, and the United States Congress finally relented, sending thirty warships which stayed in Havana harbor, creating a threat rather than the fact of an intervention. The Pentarquía lost power rapidly. On September 9 power passed to one of the five-member committee, Ramón Grau San Martín. On 10 September Grau became president. Grau's presidency had two of the most well-known Cubans of the 1930s in his cabinet: Eduardo Chibás, who became secretary of public works, and Antonio Guiteras, who became secretary of the interior. Guiteras, who became as important to this administration as Grau, had been one of the leaders of the university group in the 1920s. Grau's first statement of foreign policy in office was to protest the Platt Amendment. As a result, the United States did not immediately recognize the government, dooming it to a short term.

In January 1934 during a union strike, Carlos Hevia, an engineer and former secretary of agriculture in Grau's cabinet, became president. He resigned two days later. Manuel Márquez Sterling's tenure was even shorter. Filling the void left by Hevia on January 18, he became president and resigned the next day. Carlos Mendieta took office and remained until December 1935.

In May of 1934, under Mendieta the Platt Amendment was abrogated because of extreme pressure from Havana, but the provision that established the base at Guantánamo was retained. The United States thought that removal of the Platt Amendment might erase the errors of the past, but Havana's unrest was more deep-seated.

Rise of Cuban Communism

The Cuban Communist party became more powerful during this period. While domestic affairs were in shambles and Batista consolidated his power domestically, Cuba's Communist party representatives traveled worldwide. These party leaders would later take prominent positions in Castro's government.

Strikes against Mendieta began in 1935. Mendieta—on orders from Batista—suspended most civil rights. Many student leaders, including Eduardo Chibás, were arrested. The opposition was being eliminated rapidly.

When Mendieta resigned, soon after the strikes began, his secretary of state, José Antonio Barnet, replaced him as interim president until May, 1936, when Miguel Mariano Gómez was elected. Gómez was impeached in December. His vice-president, Federico Laredo Bru, became president for four years until 1940 when Batista was first elected to the office of president of the republic.

When the Spanish Civil War began in July 1936, Cuba had been divided in its support. Different right-wing factions in Cuba supported the Nationalists; Grau was rallying people in opposition. Ruby Hart Phillips, *New York Times* correspondent covering Cuba at the time, wrote that approximately 100 Cubans went to fight. Most were Cuban Communists who fought for the Republicans in Spain, including Rolando Masferrer (who would later fight with Castro in 1947 at Cayo Confites) and Nicolás Guillén.[27] Blas Roca Calderío, secretary-general of the Communist party, made several public statements of support of the Republicans.

International contacts of the opposition increased in the 1930s and 1940s; while Batista bettered ties with Roosevelt, the Communist party increased relations in Latin America. As a result, the Communist party developed a regional base. Batista also traveled. In 1939 he went to Mexico to visit Mexico's president, General Lázaro Cárdenas.

Batista made peace with the Communist party during these first four years, and according to some accounts, Batista and Blas Roca Calderío made an agreement: the Communist party would support Batista, and Batista would legalize the party and give it the right to organize. (Machado had attempted to make a similar agreement with the Communist party in 1933—legalization in exchange for an end to the strike—to no avail.) Communism as a legal instead of a disturbing force, Batista argued, had become the promoter of democratic formulae.[28] In 1942 Communist party leader Carlos Rafael Rodríguez (vice-president in the 1980s) joined Batista's cabinet.

Cuba in World War II

In 1940 a new constitution was written. Batista won the presidency, pledging a policy of neutrality in World War II, which had begun the year before. Washington began talks through Sumner Welles for collective protection of Latin America in the war. The United States requested that Cuba supply three items in its defense: air fields, financed by the United States (but Cuban-owned); Cuban ports; and surveillance of the waters around Cuba by the government of Cuba. Cuba agreed.

Cuba's foreign policy during this period was shaped by strong bilateral economic and military cooperation with its northern neighbor. Cuba's markets to Europe had been cut off, and Cuba began to rely economically and politically much more on the United States. Cuba also had much to offer.

Ironically, while Batista wished to enter into a formal military agreement with the United States, and although the United States wanted to work in military terms with Cuba, Welles apparently did not favor a formal military alliance. Nonetheless, the Cuban-U.S. relationship flourished during the war, and the United States bought most of Cuba's sugar production. The Soviet Union needed sugar, and as an ally, Cuba sent sugar to Russia for the first time.

The Japanese attack against the United States must be considered "as an attack against Cuba and as against everyone of the American states," Cuba's Secretary of State José Manuel Cortina argued.[29] On 9 December 1941, Cuba declared war on Japan; two days later it declared war on Germany and Italy. In 1942 Cuba established diplomatic relations with the Soviet Union, and one year later the first Soviet embassy was established in Havana. The Cubans even sank a German submarine that was in the Caribbean. In order to better survey the waters, Cuba organized "an FBI, under U.S. training."[30] Cuba, Batista reassured U.S. policymakers, would defend the Caribbean.

Postwar Cuba

To Batista's surprise, Ramón Grau San Martín and the Auténtico party won the 1944 election. While Grau was in office the war ended, and the economy of Cuba felt the positive effects of wartime sugar sales.

In May 1947 Eduardo Chibás founded a new party, the Cuban Peoples party or the Ortodoxos, a reform party that would represent the new reformers, which the Auténticos had set out to be.

In the 1940s the three major opposition groups in Cuba to the two major parties were the Accíon Revolucionaria Guiteras (ARG), the Movimiento Socialista Revolucionaria (MSR), and the Uníon Insurrecional Revolucionaria (UIR) of which Fidel Castro was a member. In the 1948 elections, Carlos Prío Socarrás, an Auténtico, was elected. A Social Democrat, he created and financially supported the Caribbean Legion (La Legión del Caribe) to overthrow dictatorships in the region.

In the 1940s the foreign policy positions of the two principal parties in Cuba were not far apart. The Auténticos, founded by Ramón Grau San Martín in 1937, held power from the late 1940s to 1952. Although the Ortodoxo party was established as a reformist party, denouncing Prío's corruption, the foreign policy posture was much the same. Chibás, a leader of the Ortodoxo party, spoke of forging a new foreign policy, independent from the United States. In addition, a terrorist group was founded, basically by middle-class Cubans, the most prominent of whom were Carlos Saladrigas and Joaquín Martínez Sáenz. Antonio Guiteras had been the secretary of the interior in Grau's previous administration. Because the government of Grau in 1934 did not last long, Guiteras went on to form a new opposition group, *Jóven Cuba*, to fight against Machado.

As the Cold War came to dominate hemispheric politics, Prío suspended Communist newspapers and radio although the party remained legal. Many of its leaders were arrested. The opposition headed by Chibás increased. After an emotional appeal to the Cuban people to end corruption in government, Eduardo Chibás shot himself on his CNQ radio broadcast program. It was an act of defiance and an inspiration to Fidel Castro, which he recalled several times in the years following the revolution.

The cry of anticommunism was being heard throughout Cuba, and the United States was supporting Cuba's anti-Communist crackdowns. The Ortodoxo party continued to oppose Prío, and in 1951 Fidel Castro ran on the Ortodoxo ticket for Congress. In 1952 Batista mobilized the army and ousted Prío. On 10 March

1952, Batista became president for the second time, promising elections which never took place. Economic times were hard. These conditions gave Batista an excuse for a repressive internal rule that was not to end until 1958.

During the next six years, foreign policy was Batista's alone. Foreign policy no longer would include alliances with reform movements in Latin America or Europe. The opposition did attempt to go to the United States to plead for intervention in Cuban affairs; the Ortodoxo party appealed to the Organization of American States (OAS) and to the United Nations. Nonetheless, in March the United States recognized the new government. Student demonstrations followed, the university was closed, and most of Cuba's opposition groups went into hiding or exile.

1953: The Beginning of the Revolution

Many accounts have detailed the strategies and programs of the movement to overthrow Batista. Several years of insurgency and important events mark the major changes: the storming of the Moncada army barracks on 26 July 1953 and the subsequent arrest and imprisonment of Fidel Castro; Castro's release in 1955; the landing of the *Granma* in 1956; and the guerrilla campaign in the mountains of the Sierra Maestra from 1956 to December 1958.[31] Most significant, the opposition to Batista, which coalesced in Castro's Twenty-sixth of July Movement, established close ties with Latin America, Africa, and western Europe.

Notes

1. José Martí, *Our America: Writings on Latin America and the Struggle for Cuban Independence*, ed. Philip S. Foner, trans. Elinor Randall (New York: Monthly Review Press, 1979), p. 440.

2. Interview by the author with Rubén Berríos Martínez, New York, 3 April 1982.

3. Louis W. Koenig, *Bryan: A Political Biography of William Jennings Bryan* (New York: G.P. Putnam's Sons, 1971), p. 273.

4. William Jennings Bryan, statements at a press interview in Savannah, cited in ibid., p. 288.

5. Ibid.

6. For an examination of the origins of the Cuban army, see Louis A. Pérez, Jr., *Army Politics in Cuba, 1898-1958* (Pittsburgh, Pa.: University of Pittsburgh Press, 1976), pp. 3–21.

7. Address to Congress by President James Monroe, 23 December 1823. U.S. Congress, *American State Papers: Documents, Legislative and Executive, Congress of the United States*. Second series, volume five, *Foreign Relations* (Washington, D.C.: Gales and Seaton, 1858), pp. 245-50. See also "The Legacy of Monroe's Doctrine." *New York Times Magazine*, 9 September 1984, p. 46.

8. Report by William Howard Taft and Robert Bacon, U.S., Congress, House, 59th Cong., 2d sess., House Documents 2, series 1505, 1906. Reprinted in 1906 by the Depart-

ment of War as "Cuban Pacification: Report of William H. Taft, Secretary of War and Robert Bacon, Assistant Secretary of State."

9. Pérez, *Army Politics*, pp. 3–21. According to Pérez, a structural weakness in the Cuban army was encouraged by the United States by the creation of the military in the form of a "rural guard."

10. Harold Eugene Davis, John J. Finan, and F. Taylor Peck, eds., *Latin American Diplomatic History* (Baton Rouge, La.: Louisiana State University Press, 1977), p. 193.

11. Ibid.

12. Hugh Thomas, *Cuba: The Pursuit of Freedom* (New York: Harper and Row, 1971), p. 564.

13. Ibid., p. 566.

14. Ibid., p. 577.

15. Bryce Wood, *The Making of Good Neighbor Policy* (New York: Columbia University Press, 1961), p. 51.

16. Carleton Beals, *The Crime of Cuba* (New York: Arno Press and the *New York Times*, 1970), p. 255.

17. Thomas, *Cuba*, p. 586.

18. *New York Times*, 20 September 1929, pp. 1, 23.

19. Robert F. Smith, *The United States and Cuba: Business and Diplomacy, 1917–1960* (New York: Bookman Associates, 1960), pp. 113–136.

20. U.S., Department of State, *Papers Relating to the Foreign Relations of the United States 1930*, vol. 2 (Washington, D.C.: Government Printing Office, 1945), p. 673.

21. *New York Times*, 15 May 1932, p. 9.

22. Thomas, *Cuba*, p. 597.

23. Ibid., p. 599.

24. For a discussion of the Chaco War see Bryce Wood, *The United States and Latin America's Wars* (New York: Columbia University Press, 1966), pp. 19–168; Leslie B. Rout, *Politics of the Chaco Peace Conference, 1935–1939* (Austin, Texas: University of Texas Press, 1970).

25. Philip W. Bonsal, *Cuba, Castro, and the United States* (Pittsburgh, Pa.: University of Pittsburgh Press, 1971), p. 261.

26. Ibid.

27. Thomas, *Cuba*, p. 703, n. 34.

28. Fulgencio Batista, *Cuba Betrayed* (New York: Vantage Press, 1962), pp. 30–31.

29. Thomas, *Cuba*, p. 729.

30. Ibid., p. 731.

31. Several first-hand accounts and analyses detail the period of insurrection of the Twenty-sixth of July Movement. See Antonio Navarro, *Tocayo* (Westport, Conn.: Sandown Books, Shamrock Publishing Company, 1981); Ramon L. Bonachea and Marta San Martín, *The Cuban Insurrection* (New Brunswick, N.J.: Transaction Books, 1976); Jorge I. Domínguez, *Cuba: Order and Revolution* (Cambridge, Mass.: Belknap, 1978).

U.S. Ambassador to Cuba Earl E.T. Smith and Cuban President Fulgencio Batista in Havana after Ambassador Smith presented his credentials, 23 July 1957.

2
Cuba's Relations in the Western Hemisphere

Cuba provided military armed assistance to guerrilla insurgents in every nation of the Western hemisphere except Mexico during the first two decades of revolutionary rule. As a result, although they were small, Cuba's *internationalist* programs of armed assistance to foreign revolutionaries attracted worldwide attention. The number of Cuban soldiers involved in these missions ranged from seven in Falcón, Venezuela, to several hundred in all the nations of Central America combined. Even assuming that, as the U.S. government alleged, five thousand Cuban advisers, teachers, and medical personnel were stationed in Nicaragua after the 1979 Revolution, the total number of Cubans involved in foreign revolutionary movements is relatively small.[1] At the core of the reaction of Cuba's Latin neighbors and the United States is the sophisticated nature of military equipment and training being provided to insurgents in the region and the fact that they can be linked to the Soviet Union.

From the early days of Cuba's revolution, the island has been an example of a small nation that challenged the United States. The image of David fighting Goliath was evoked by José Martí referring to both Spanish colonialism and U.S. imperialism. Cuba's foreign policy since 1958 has sought to promote and extend the policy of internationalism and armed struggle. Foreign policy decisions have been determined by a small group within Cuba's Ministry of Foreign Relations. In its foreign policy, as in its domestic politics, Cuba has not had much experience with democratic procedure. As a socialist nation, its values and practices are very different from those of the United States. Its press does not criticize its policies. Thus, there is no effective way to measure the domestic popularity of its foreign policies.

During the early 1960s, Cuba was excluded from the most important regional organization in the hemisphere, the Organization of American States (OAS), and by the late 1960s its relations with most regional allies had greatly deteriorated. Although there was a brief *apertura* (political reopening) with much of Latin America, in the 1980s Cuba remained on shaky footing with Colombia, Costa Rica, Jamaica, Peru, Ecuador, and Venezuela. Why has Cuba's foreign policy in the region been so unsuccessful? What does Cuba represent to its regional neighbors? Finally, what are Cuba's motivations for foreign policy shifts in its regional bilateral relations?

Cuba's symbolic value to its regional neighbors is complex. Cuba's strong nationalism had enormous importance to the nations of the region, most of which had experienced colonialism by Spain as well as the intervention of the United States. By the 1970s, many had also known insurrection sparked by aid from the Soviet Union. Cuba's neighbors in Central and South America do not reject Cuba's postrevolutionary model solely because it is socialist. They reject Cuba's specific example.

Cuba's motivation for its foreign policy may well be reactive, a reaction to aggression from Spain, then the United States, and ultimately the Soviet Union. In practice, however, its policies are aggressive. The result in the region has been less than overwhelming success. Cuba will likely continue to pursue improved relations and a leadership role in the hemisphere.

The principal reason that Cuba looked first to Latin America in its foreign policy was history; Cuba's historical links to the region, both for geopolitical and economic reasons, were longstanding. In terms of military strategy, Cuba knows the region, speaks the language, and has a similar history: its soldiers had fought with South and Central Americans in many of the battles against Spanish colonial rule. Likewise, philosophical and ideological ties date to Spanish rule. Castro, in addition, had limited experience in fighting revolutions in Latin America during his student days in Havana.

The policies of Cuba in Latin America in the 1960s—even during 1959—may have involved only a small number of Cubans, but they were important to the nations of the region. In the Dominican Republic, Haiti, Nicaragua, and Panama, Cuba implemented policies that were aimed at helping a revolution allegedly already in progress. In Guatemala, Colombia, Venezuela, Peru, and Bolivia, Cuba's foreign policy was devoted to sparking the first flame of revolution. From the first days of the revolution in 1958 through the mid-1960s, Fidel Castro and a small group of guerrilla fighters attempted to assist small radical movements in the hemisphere and, at the same time, to increase Cuba's diplomatic relations. From 1962 when Cuba was suspended from the OAS. Cuba spent much of its time supporting small but symbolically important guerrilla movements. This support continued until the 1967 failure of Che Guevara's Bolivian movement.

After the 1960s, Cuba turned from an emphasis on policies of armed assistance and tried to improve diplomatic relations. By the mid-1970s, Cuba had returned to earlier policies of armed insurrection in Africa, the Middle East, and Latin America.

Stage One: Fidel Castro's Experience

When Fidel Castro was still a student at the University of Havana in the 1940s, one of the first demonstrations he participated in was for the release of Puerto Rican independence leader Don Pedro Albizu Campos. As a student he was active in the independence movement and was a member of the Puerto Rico Pro-Independence Committee.[2] "Historically speaking, political and moral support has always been given to Puerto Rico, always," Castro stated in an interview in 1982. At the university, Cuba supported Puerto Rico's independence fight, which does not mean, Castro qualified, that Cuba "promoted violence."[3]

Puerto Rican independence leader Rubén Berríos Martínez argued that because of the history of close ties between the two independence movements, when the Cuban Revolution gained power, "it's only natural that they continue to support the struggle for Puerto Rican independence in a much more militant fashion."[4]

More significant, however, is the fact that Castro's student days gave him experience as an armed guerrilla in the Dominican Republic and in Colombia. The two most notorious examples of Castro's prerevolutionary activities were in 1947 and 1948.[5] The first expedition involved a plan to overthrow the dictatorship of General Rafael Leonidas Trujillo in the Dominican Republic. As a student in the University of Havana, Castro became a member of the Unión Insurrecional Revolucionaria (UIR), which along with the MSR followed Castro and Dominican leader Juan Bosch to overthrow Trujillo. Castro and one thousand guerrillas gathered at an island off the coast of Cuba's Camagüey Port, called Cayo Confites. Although there are different stories as to why the expedition failed, most accounts agree that Trujillo found out about the plot and forced the Cuban administration of Grau San Martín and the U.S. administration to stop the group.

Significantly, among those with Castro at Cayo Confites in 1947 were Carlos Franqui, who was an editor of *Revolución* (the newspaper of the Twenty-sixth of July Movement) and Enrique Rodríguez Loeches (who became an ambassador); Eduardo Corona; and Feliciano Maderne, a deputy judge of the Supreme Court.[6]

Another student adventure of Castro's prerevolutionary experience took place in Bogotá, Colombia in 1948. In April of that year the Pan-American Conference of American States gathered in the capital city of Colombia; simultaneously, Juan Domingo Perón (later to become Argentina's president) and who paid Castro's fare to the conference, was planning a program to protest the British occupation of the Falkland/Malvinas Islands in the South Atlantic. Ironically, one of Castro's first experiences with regional claims in the hemisphere in 1948 was the rallying point of Latin American regional unity against Britain and the United States.

Along with Rafael del Pino, another member of the UIR, Castro went to Bogotá. While all attendees for the two conferences were in the city, the leader of the Colombian liberal party was murdered during a demonstration. The assassin was killed on the spot by a mob, and three days of killing and violence took place. The incident, known as the *bogotazo*, has been immortalized in the history of Latin America. Although there are several versions regarding whether Castro and Cuba were involved in the insurrection, the most reliable information on the event points to Castro as a participant, though not an organizer.

Castro was not the only member of the Revolutionary Directorate who was establishing international contacts in hemisphere affairs before the Cuban Revolution.[7] In 1957 Carlos Rafael Rodríguez (since 1975 vice-president of the Cuban Council of State and Council of Ministers and since 1960 a member of the Central

Committee of the party) traveled secretly to Latin America. In order to gain support for the guerrilla fight, Carlos Rafael Rodríguez traveled to Latin America, including Brazil, Uruguay, Argentina, Chile, Peru, Ecuador, and Colombia.[8] Although the Communist party had not originally supported Castro, by 1958 Castro had gained the Cuban Communist Party's grudging support.

The 1960s

As the 1960s began, Fidel Castro was keenly aware that his influence in Latin America would have to be based on a two-pronged strategy: First, diplomatic support to progressive regimes in an effort to unify the Latin American left, and, second, assistance to small guerrilla movements throughout Latin America. At no time was one strategy preferred to the other. Latin America was too important and too much of a traditional ally to risk choosing between diplomacy and guerrilla warfare.

In early 1960, there were hints that there would be problems, but on the whole Castro was being received in much of Latin America with enthusiasm. U.S. ambassador to Nicaragua, Lawrence A. Pezzullo, stated, "It looked to most Latin Americans [more] like he was running for office."[9]

The sentiment that unified Latin America in the 1960s and arose again in the 1980s was antiimperialist, anti-American, and nationalist. It was a good time to express these views. Latin America, in a sense, was feeling its oats. It was also the time of the strongest counterforce by the United States. It was not only the United States which opposed revolutionary efforts. There were indigenous forces of reaction in most of the countries of Latin America responding to revolutions of the 1960s. By 1964 Brazil was in the hands of a military administration; in 1968 progressive military governments were established in Panama and Peru. Renewed and strengthened conservative forces in Latin America presented clear opposition to Castro in the early 1960s but did not turn Cuba away from its support of insurgency movements. In 1959 Castro attempted invasions in three Latin American countries. In the 1960s several guerrilla groups—though small—attempted to assist in government revolt in Latin America. In 1962 Cuba launched a significant guerrilla program, Operation Falcón, in Venezuela, and in 1967 the Bolivian *foco* (or small guerrilla insurgency) plan was inaugurated. The policy of promoting revolution both by the expansion of diplomatic relations and armed struggle continued as a principal program in Cuban foreign policy from the early days of the revolution. Castro still has not abandoned it.[10]

Early Military Approaches

Military programs, which included armed attacks by guerrillas from Cuba in 1959, were the first example of Cuban military policy in the hemisphere. According to U.S. newspaper correspondent Tad Szulc, fewer than 100 Cubans attempted to land in Panama to overthrow the government. Both the Cuban and Panamanian governments, however, denied the Cuban participation in the attack.[11] All told, allegations of attacks took place within months in Haiti, Nicaragua, and the Dominican Republic. Of the four armed expeditions in 1959 (Panama, Dominican Republic, Nicaragua, and Haiti), all of which were aborted, Castro only admitted to giving assistance to the invasion of the Dominican Republic.

Early Cuban military and diplomatic overtures focused on Latin America. After the revolutionary government entered Havana in December 1958, Castro toured Latin America in an effort to create a bloc of support for his government. Venezuela was a natural ally since it had fought a revolution in the same year against a military government. In January Castro went to discuss diplomatic matters, with Venezuela's president, Rómulo Betancourt.

Castro visited Caracas on the first anniversary of the ouster of Venezuela's strongman, General Marcos Pérez Jiménez. Castro never established firm footing, however, with the Venezuelans. Castro misread Betancourt. This happened again in the 1970s when he warned Venezuela against U.S. reaction to their oil nationalization. His cautions were not necessary in the case of Venezuela, which successfully proclaimed the nationalization of its oil industry on 1 January 1976.

During his January 1959 trip to Venezuela, Castro spoke often in Caracas. According to interviews by British historian Hugh Thomas with Venezuela's President Rómulo Betancourt, Castro proposed the abolishment of visa requirements; the founding of a Venezuelan military mission in Cuba; and a common market for the region. Betancourt reported that a bizarre conversation ensued: Castro asked Betancourt for a loan of $300 million and oil. Betancourt denied him both.[12] "After Fidel's lightning visit to Venezuela in 1959, Betancourt knew what his role was to be," asserted Régis Debray, a French journalist who spent several months with Cuban guerrillas in Bolivia.[13]

Castro's early experience with Costa Rica was similar. In March 1959 Costa Rica's ex-President José Figueres Ferrer arrived in Havana. He spoke about representative democracy and urged Cuba to side with the United States and the West in the event of any major war. The same day, Castro accused Figueres of being a false friend.

Castro's reaction to Figueres was not surprising. Indeed, the Costa Rican president's trip was unusual for a Costa Rican diplomat. Cuba's foreign policy toward Costa Rica, therefore, has been particularly strained: Costa Rica's government remains strongly anti-Communist, scornful of military development, and democratic.

There might have been reason to believe that Figueres would have been successful during his March trip to Havana. Figueres had led the uprising that took place after the invalidation of the 1948 Costa Rican election. Figueres, after all, was a prominent figure in the National Liberation party, which he had founded after the 1948 revolution. Castro's emphasis on Latin American regional unity, however, was not adequate to overcome the staunch anti-Marxist sentiment of the Costa Ricans.

Other Revolutionary Examples

At the end of the decade, Castro believed he saw two concrete examples—Peru and Panama—"where the military are acting as catalysts in favor of change and in favor of the revolution."[14] Panama had suffered its own coup d'etat in October 1968 when Arnulfo Arías was overthrown for the third time since coming into power in 1941. The military officers who took control, Colonel José Maria Pinilla and Colonel Bolívar Urrútia Parilla, established a provisional junta government.

The Peruvian revolution of 1968 was an interesting dilemma for Cuban foreign policymakers. The 1956 elections in Peru had elected a progressive, Manuel Prado y Ugarteche, backed by the Popular American Revolutionary Alliance (APRA), a radical party founded in 1931 with large popular support. One of its founders, Víctor Raúl Haya de la Torre, moved to the political center over the years to gain a middle-class base and could have been a natural ally of a progressive regime.

Cuba was beginning to withdraw from Latin America when the Peruvian revolution occurred. Before the revolution, Castro stated, "The army was a guardian of the status quo."[15] Castro calculated that the Peruvian military was less repressive than other militaries because it was dominated by an oligarchy. Turbulent economic and political times led these military leaders, Castro argued, to conclude that "what was needed was major structural changes in the country."[16] The military in both Panama and Peru, in the view of Cuban foreign policy, were revolutionary forces. Although Castro had not helped to install these governments, the Cuban government learned several lessons from the revolutions in Peru and Panama.

The Peruvian military administration which had overthrown a civilian government in October 1968 was run by Division General Juan Velasco Alvarado. After Velasco established a military government and suspended the congress of Peru, he introduced fundamental economic changes. His Plan of the Revolutionary Government of the Armed Forces mandated both state ownership and collective management of most enterprises. During its seven-year rule, the Velasco administration nationalized a subsidiary of the Gulf Oil Corporation and assumed title of major electric companies. The experiment, which began soon after the military administration came to power, did not fit either a Communist or free market example; it was a unique experiment in state-oriented growth with a decentralized economy.

The first stage of Peru's economic experiment—and nationalizations—received official support from Fidel Castro. Peru's experiment was very different from that of Cuba's. Its foreign policy, however, emphasized similar goals: sovereignty, local control of natural resources, and, most significant, increased diplomatic relations with eastern Europe, the Soviet Union, and the People's Republic of China. In addition, as relations became more strained with the United States due to expropriation and fishing controversies, Peruvian relations with the Soviet Union and with Cuba improved. In addition to nationalizing oil and electricity, Velasco nationalized Peru's second largest bank, and in 1970 he allowed two of Peru's largest newspapers to be run by Marxists. Also in 1970 Peru received earthquake assistance from Cuba, and by 1974, one year before Velasco was overthrown by Division General Francisco Morales Bermúdez, Peru received Soviet military advisers.

Through the 1960s and 1970s Castro appealed to anti-American sentiment and nationalism in Latin America.[17] Venezuela was moving toward the nationalization of its oil industry, and Castro, as he had done with the Peruvians, warned the Venezuelans against pressure from the United States. He cautioned in 1974 that "when Venezuela nationalizes its iron and oil in the future—as its government has proclaimed—imperialist policy towards Venezuela will probably harden."[18] Venezuela, Castro was sure, would not stand alone as Cuba had to do in 1960. Castro, however, misjudged U.S. policymakers as well as the political power that Venezuela was to hold in Organization of Petroleum Exporting Countries (OPEC). Venezuela would follow a different path after 1958—one that was in marked contrast to Cuba's socialist political and economic system. The United States would continue to support Venezuela—even after its oil nationalization in 1976.

Cuba and Latin American Communism

There was a brief period during which Cuba attempted, with the help of the Soviet Union, to make peace with Communist parties in the hemisphere. Cuba's suspicions, however, were deep-seated and the peace-making effort never occurred on a large scale. In 1964 there was an attempt at reconciliation when a conference of Latin American Communist parties was held in Cuba. The result of the conference was a resolution in which the Latin American Communist parties present endorsed the guerrilla struggles in Colombia, Guatemala, Honduras, Haiti, Paraguay, and Venezuela. For a brief period, roughly between 1962 and 1965, the Soviet Union seemed to be endorsing Cuba's Latin American programs, and the Cubans spoke highly of the Communist party. But Soviet support quickly waned.

The revolutionary theories of Castro and Che Guevara differed. Guevara spoke of achieving "two, three or more Viet Nams."[19] Castro, on the other hand, acknowledged in 1961 that his loud declaration of his commitment to Marxism-Leninism might not have been the best strategy; nevertheless, in 1974 he continued to insist: "There is no future for Latin American countries along the capitalist route."[20] Castro's views of the process by which socialism should be instituted still have not changed. His isolation in the hemisphere did not alter his fundamental belief that socialism could not be achieved through democracy. Chile, Castro argued, was the proof. In 1974 he stated, "The *Unidad Popular* of Chile tested the possibility of making a change by peaceful means and by parliamentary means."[21] Even during the 1970s, isolated from Latin America, Castro felt that the need in Latin America was for armed struggle.

Reaction in Latin America

By the mid-1960s interpreting the Cuban Revolution became the point of definition of most of the Latin American nations and Social Democratic movements that began in the 1930s. Cuba neither began nor stimulated these movements in the 1960s in most of the nations of Latin America. Cuba had been involved in small insurgency programs which had failed in many of them. The question became one of how to react to Cuba's example.

In 1965 Castro referred to the public betrayal of Latin America by Social Democratic movements. He exposed the *false Marxists* and bankruptcy of Social Democratic movements, including those of Peru's Popular American Revolutionary Alliance (APRA), Venezuela's Democratic Action (AD), and Bolivia's National Revolutionary Movement (MNR). By 1967 he turned to the betrayal of the Venezuelan and Bolivian Communist parties.[22] By name he accused Víctor Raúl Haya de la Torre, Rómulo Betancourt, and Víctor Paz Estenssoro of being agents of North American imperialism. It was certainly not the end of Cuba's material and moral support to guerrilla movements, but it was the beginning of a division in support for Cuba within the continent.

At the first Tri-Continental Conference in January 1966, Castro said that "any revolutionary movement anywhere in the world could count on Cuba's unconditional help."[23] The Tri-Continental evolved into a group called Afro-Asian and Latin American Peoples Solidarity Organization (AALAPSO). From then on AALAPSO was headquartered in Havana; its secretary-general was Osmani Cienfuegos.

Latin America's Ideological Direction: Hegel Plus Marx Plus Einstein Equals Haya de la Torre

It was in these early days that Castro through the writing of Régis Debray and in his own practice articulated most clearly the need for the independence of Latin America's ideological direction. Debray stated:

> Not only the independence of Cuba in the Sino-Soviet Dispute, but the whole daily practice of its leaders, both in the Sierra Maestra and in power, indicates that

Latin America is transforming itself into a new center of revolutionary thought, adapted to its own conditions.[24]

At the same time that Latin America's Communist and Social Democratic parties were attempting to discover their own direction, the opposition which was organized politically in response to the Cuban revolution since 1959 successfully benefited imperialism because it was unifying more rapidly than the revolutionary organizations. Debray had lamented the fact that former mass parties had passed "with arms and baggage into the imperialist camp"; the AD in Venezuela, the MNR in Bolivia, and the APRA in Peru had passed out of revolutionary movement.

Nonetheless, these Social Democratic parties were viewed more broadly as progressive movements, and their founders were revered. Debray quoted a Peruvian protege of the APRA leader, "Hegel plus Marx plus Einstein equals Haya de la Torre." The protege's reverence angered Debray.[25] In addition, the Communist parties were unable to mobilize mass parties, and the small Fidelisto movements were unable to maintain themselves because of their lack of experience.

The Cuban revolution was alienated during this period from both the Soviet Union and the United States. It was the period of weakest alliance within the superpowers for the Cuban revolution. As Castro alienated himself and his people from the Communist parties of Cuba, the United States through the Alliance for Progress was forming a real sense of opposition to Cuba within Latin America. According to Debray's account:

> A month before [Douglas] Dillon launched optimistic plans in Punta del Este for transforming Latin America into a "paradise of golden latrines" ... Kennedy submitted to Congress in July 1961 a "special military program designed to guarantee the internal security of Latin America against subversion."[26]

The program allocated approximately $21 million in 1961 alone to help the governments fight internal subversion in Latin America.[27]

At the 1966 Tri-Continental Conference Castro openly supported the idea of armed struggle throughout the continent, and not long after, the major failures of the arms struggle began to be noticed. Because of divisions within the Communist party and among the delegates themselves, it was the first and last conference to be held by the group. The Latin American delegates formed a new organization on the basis of AALAPSO goals, the OLAS, Latin American Solidarity Organization, which held its first conference in Havana in August 1967. The president of the conference was Ernesto (Che) Guevara, although he was in Bolivia not Havana at the time of the first conference. The delegates to the conference backed Castro's appeal for support of Guevara's armed Marxist uprisings in the Western hemisphere.[28]

The revolution was beginning to draw the lines in Latin America between those who were for and those who were against the Cuban model. At the OLAS conference Castro attacked the Venezuelans and the Yugoslavian Communists. In

1968 a trial of party member Aníbal Escalante revealed a profound anti-Soviet sentiment among many party members as well as the defensiveness of Cuba's Latin American policy. Escalante left Cuba in 1962 disillusioned and rebuffed but returned two years later to the government as a splinter group, called a "microfaction" by the government, that condemned armed struggle in Latin America and allegedly considered the guerrilla war in Venezuela an adventure, rather than a true popular movement. More significant, perhaps, Escalante was considered to be pro-Soviet. In 1968 Aníbal Escalante and other Cubans involved in the criticism were tried and imprisoned. The impact was profound; as failures abroad increased, intolerance of criticism domestically seemed to surge.

In October 1968 Cuba denied poet Heberto Padilla permission to receive a prize from PEN International for his poetry.[29] The event exposed internal dissent and revealed the government's intolerance of even veiled criticism.

Che Guevara

In March 1965 Che Guevara returned from an international tour. In the same year, only months after he returned, he resigned as minister of industry. In July 1965 Guevara left for the Congo to fight in the Kinshasa region in one of Cuba's earliest armed assistance programs in Africa. He returned to Cuba, and in September 1966 he left again to begin a guerrilla *foco* in Bolivia. In October 1967 when Che Guevara was killed in Bolivia, his death shook the very premises of Cuba's Latin American policy and left the leadership with a profound sense of betrayal and doubt regarding the motives of and support in Latin America.

What was it that had caused Cuba's hopes for Latin America to be dashed? Was the timing wrong, or the philosophy? Just as Cuba was beginning to feel the impact of its foreign policy failures, an in-depth criticism—from within the ranks— appeared. After traveling through most of Latin America with Guevara, and serving as the quasi-official historian of Cuba's revolutionary travails, Régis Debray wrote *Revolution in the Revolution?*, a critique of Cuba's failures.

Insurgency in Venezuela

Debray's analysis first examined Cuba's aid to guerrillas in Venezuela. Castro's revolutionary assistance in Venezuela had begun with the Venezuelan Communist party in early 1962. The guerrillas were Communists whose purpose was to overthrow the government. In February 1962, two years after Castro's unsuccessful visit with Social Democrat Rómulo Betancourt in Caracas, twenty Venezuelan guerrillas supplied with Cuban arms and led by Douglas Bravo and Teodoro Petkoff set off for Falcón, Venezuela to overthrow the Betancourt government.[30] The insurgents fared poorly. Teodoro Petkoff, a presidential candidate in 1983, was arrested, and the small group, which had been isolated in the mountains, was attacked by the Venezuelan army. After the attack, in May 1962, seven guerrillas became the core of this opposition group. Falcon is a symbolically important state in Venezuelan history because it was the scene of Venezuela's independence battle from Spain in the early nineteenth century. Debray's first essay on revolution in Latin America was entitled, "Report from the Venezuelan Guerrilla."[31] It was an optimistic discussion of the insurgency in Falcon that Debray would evaluate negatively in 1967. From these small roots in 1962, the Communist Party of Venezuela (PCV) grew throughout Venezuela until in 1967 the Communist party split with Douglas Bravo and the guerrillas. In an unusually bitter attack, Castro condemned the Communist party. The party had betrayed the guerrillas, Castro argued; Cuba chose to support Bravo.

By 1962, according to Debray, the United States would attempt to immobilize the guerrillas: an example was the visit of Rómulo Betancourt to President John F. Kennedy in Washington. The strategy of guerrilla warfare articulated by Debray involved three major stages: the first was the *strategic and tactical defense* when resistance consolidates itself and the insurgents are encircled by the army; the second, the *strategic defensive and tactical offense*, in which the imbalance is still in favor of the army but small villages are occupied and in some cases the National Guard attacks; the third, the *strategic offensive*, takes place, when the guerrillas enter the major cities and the revolution is completed. In Venezuela, the third and final stage was never achieved, according to Debray.[32]

Debray's writings and Bravo's political theories took their cue from Castro. The belief in armed struggle was as paramount in 1962 as it appeared to be two decades later in Central America. Bravo argued that the power to be armed and organized is one that cannot stop immediately after the revolution.

> When Fidel entered Havana, this didn't stop the [Carlos] Prío Socarrás, the [Manuel] Urrútias, and others plundering the Ministries, newspapers, and factories. It was just like that here after [Marcos] Pérez Jiménez's flight in 1958.... Why did Fidel win? He won because he hadn't laid down his arms.[33]

It was a theory that Cuba never disavowed. Juan Bosch Gaviño, former president of the Dominican Republic, asserted that the tremendous impact of Debray's book was that he was "expressing the opinions of Fidel Castro."[34] Bosch said the writings of Debray were an indictment of the failures of Communist parties in Latin America. "At the same time *Revolution in the Revolution?* became a weapon in Fidel Castro's struggle to bring about a union of communism and nationalism in Latin America."[35] In a practical sense, Debray's theory was that it was "possible to win power and keep it."[36] This optimistic outlook contrasted with the defeated attitude of the Communist parties of Latin America in the post-World War II period.

Therefore, by 1962 and 1963 Debray, Guevara, and Castro felt that the repression, unleashed as a reaction to the Cuban revolution, also reinvigorated the struggle within Latin America. The only response of the parties could be to arm themselves. Ironically, these Communist parties that had been reinvigorated by the success of the Cuban revolution had by the early 1960s embarked on a new strategy of unity with national bourgeoisies. This was the case with the João Goulart in Brazil; the result was the April 1964 coup d'etat. For theorists of Cuba's revolutionary success, Cuba presented a whole new set of circumstances. Latin America was very different from Europe, China, and the Soviet Union in terms of the method its revolution needed to pursue.

Cuba's clearest divergence from the Soviet Union in terms of its foreign policy was during this period. When Castro broke with all of the South American Communist parties (most notably with those of Bolivia and Venezuela), the differences in the Soviet and Cuban interests in Latin America surfaced. Debray argued that "the old Marxism was no longer any good" because it did not measure up to the standards of class action needed in Latin America. Even theoretical Marxism by European standards could not apply to the social reality of Latin America.[37]

Other Roads to Revolution in Latin America

The Cuban government explained the failures of Venezuela, Peru, and Bolivia as failures of the Communist parties rather than of the programs of Social Democratic parties in the region. For Cuba, two principal lessons could be gleaned from the Chilean failure: first, that developing Latin American countries, such as Argentina, Uruguay, or Costa Rica, could "escape the determinate structure of the continent as a whole," and, second, that Chileans had underestimated the U.S. reaction to "left-wing adventurism." The first defeat for Cuba in Chile was the participation of the Communist party in the 1964 election.

Chile's outlook was, by Castro's accounts, irrational optimism only five years after the Cuban revolution. This disappointment became real when the Communist and Socialist alliance in the 1964 elections (which supported Salvador Allende Gossens) failed. When Eduardo Frei Montalva's Christian Democrat party won the elections in 1964, and relations were already broken by Frei's predecessor, President Arturo Alessandri, Cuba's position in Chile was next to nil until the electoral victory in 1970 of Allende.

Castro deeply felt that Allende's participation in the 1964 elections was naive. Castro's feeling of betrayal was strong; he overlooked the concept and the real possibility of peaceful means to achieve social reform and insisted that Allende had in fact legitimized the electoral process.[38] To Castro, the strategy contradicted a commitment to armed struggle in Latin America and revealed an innocence that would be apparent after the 1970 election. Castro was disheartened by Allende's lack of support in the 1964 campaign. Debray reflected the Cuban mood when he argued, "Chile is the only country in Latin America where the breaking of diplomatic relations with Cuba did not provoke mass demonstrations.[39]

The next opportunity Cuba would have to establish a friend in Chile was in 1970 when Salvador Allende Gossens won the presidential election. It was between 1970 and the military overthrow of Allende in September 1973 that Cuban assistance, which was substantial, was to see its final, failed test in Chile.

In a similar fashion, Debray criticized the strategy of reform in Brazil. The critical error that the Brazilians, like the Chileans, had committed was a serious underestimation of the opposition. The major criticism derived from the fact that the Brazilian Communist party aligned with the national middle-class movement of João Goulart, who was elected in 1961 and overthrown by the military in 1964.[40] Brazil too had its charismatic leaders like Leonel da Moira Brizola, Goulart's brother-in-law, who had great popular support. He was a strident nationalist who had a strong popular backing and who, according to Debray, could "incarnate a Brazilian variety of Fidelism."[41] After a ten-year absence, Brizola was elected governor of the state of Rio de Janeiro in 1982 in the first elections in Brazil since 1964 and became a senior advisor of the 1985 cabinet of Brazil's late President Tancredo Neves.

Cuba in Argentina

Cuba's strong alliance with Argentina dates to the government of labor leader Juan Domingo Perón in the 1950s. Argentina's foreign policy under Perón was consistent with Cuba's. For example, in 1951 Argentina and Mexico voted against a military cooperation proposal to defend South America and the hemisphere at an OAS meeting. In addition, in 1954 Argentina refused to vote for a resolution that condemned Guatemala's regime.[42] The factors that brought Argentina, Mexico, and Cuba together in the 1950s were a strongly nationalist foreign policy and a wariness of U.S. military intervention.

Argentina's President Arturo Frondizi (1958 to 1962) was sympathetic to Cuba and the problems that Cuba experienced as a result of U.S.-Soviet conflicts. In a meeting in April 1961 after the U.S. invasion of Cuba at the Bay of Pigs, Brazil's President Jânio Quadros and Argentina's President Frondizi met to discuss the creation of a power bloc that could mediate between the United States and Cuba on the issue of Cuba's defense.[43] Because Quadros and Frondizi were both out of office by the following year, the South American organization never materialized. Frondizi did meet secretly with Che Guevara in August 1961, and in an effort to bring the United States together with Cuba, Frondizi arranged a secret meeting between Che Guevara and Richard Goodwin, U.S. deputy assistant secretary of state of inter-American affairs under Kennedy.[44] Although the initiative failed, it cemented good relations between Argentina and Cuba. By the Punta del Este meeting, however, Argentina voted with the rest of Latin America, and relations deteriorated between Argentina and Cuba during the subsequent military rule until 1973 when Perón returned to power.

Revolutionary Strategies: The Guerrilla Foco

It is not surprising that Cuba, and Fidel Castro in particular, developed a foreign policy which emphasized support to armed insurgent groups in the hemisphere. Castro was, after all, a guerrilla fighter who had seized power through armed struggle. Indeed, the dual foreign policy discussed earlier of diplomacy with friendly governments and support for revolutionaries in unsympathetic countries, very much reflected the two sides of the Cuban leader's personality: a highly educated lawyer who had won power not by persuasion but by organizing a small band of guerrillas that enjoyed broad popular support. The strategy which emerged was the *foco* program.

According to Debray, the foco theory in its simplest form is an "isolated military detonator organized by itself, independent of any national organization or urban political work."[45] A foco is a very small group "from ten to thiry individuals, professional revolutionaries entirely devoted to the cause and aiming to win power—the 'foco' does not by any means attempt to seize power on its own, by one audacious strike."[46] Their purpose, for example, is not to organize a coup d'etat from the top. A foco was to be a political as well as an armed unit of revolution through which power would be seized by the masses from below. According to Castro's plan, the foco would be a take-off point of a revolution which would extend throughout South America.

Cuba's small presence in Latin America in the 1960s was entirely consistent with its theory of guerrilla warfare. Although the number of Cuban guerrillas in any individual year in the 1960s probably would not have totaled more than sixty or seventy, the foco strategy was to provoke a revolution that could spread.

Debray's *Revolution in the Revolution?* received world attention. His purpose, he later wrote, was to examine the countries in which revolution had failed. He criticized those who would naively think he was presenting Cuba as a model: "The knowing critic who went into battle with spear and shield against this idea would deserve as much respect as the Knight of La Mancha bestriding Rosinante to defy windmills."[47] Debray's analysis, and more important the Cuban effort, made a powerful impression on governments in the Western hemisphere. In the spring of 1967 when Debray traveled with Che Guevara's group of guerrillas in Bolivia, he was arrested by the Bolivian government and sentenced to thirty years in prison. He was accused of involvement in the ambushes which the guerrillas had organized.

In 1964 after five years of Cuban assistance to guerrilla warfare throughout the countries of Latin America, Debray evaluated what was left of *foquismo*. He asked whether it was a valid experience, whether it was a failure or a success? In his assessment, Debray pointed to eleven cases of failure from 1959 to 1964 in Latin America. There had been, of course, many other efforts stopped early in their paths, but these were the eleven principal examples. The survey found "almost total failure everywhere since 1959—the year in which Latin America entered an intensive phase of guerrilla wars—with the single exception of Venezuela." Even by 1964, in Debray's view as in Castro's, most of the efforts at establishing guerrilla focos throughout the hemisphere had failed.[48]

The early 1960s had begun with Cuban efforts to lead Latin America into revolution. By 1964, however, prospects were not good for the small guerrilla movements which faced growing opposition from the United States as well as strong opposition from the military governments in Brazil, Bolivia, and Peru and were further weakened by Communist party opposition.

Notes

1. U.S., Department of State, "Cuba's Renewed Support for Violence in Latin America," Special Report no. 90, 14 December 1981, p. 6.

2. Interview by the author with Dr. Rubén Berríos Martínez, New York, 3 April 1982.

3. Fidel Castro in an interview by Barbara Walters, Havana, 20 May 1977, shown on ABC, 9 June 1977.

4. Berríos Martínez, interview.

5. For detailed accounts of these two expeditions, see Herbert L. Matthews, *Revolution in Cuba* (New York: Charles Scribner's Sons, 1975), pp. 44-45; K.S. Karol, *Guerrillas in Power* (New York: Hill & Wang, 1970).

6. Hugh Thomas, *Cuba: The Pursuit of Freedom* (New York: Harper and Row, 1971), p. 1455.

7. Castro himself had not planned on becoming part of the government after the revolution. He did not have a vision of becoming the president of the republic, he told correspondent Karl Meyer in September 1958. Karl Meyer, *The Washington Post* cited in Thomas, *Cuba*, p. 1057. See also Karl E. Meyer, "Report on Rebel Cuba," 5-part series, *Washington Post*, 14-19 September 1958.

8. He could not travel to Venezuela, he explained in an interview, because he was too well known and his fingerprints were on file. Since he was traveling with a false passport, it would have been unsafe. Later Rodríguez could laugh about the adventure. The passport, he explained, looked nothing like him: "It was the passport of a man who was working in a Havana clinic—they called him King Kong, his face was so different from mine." Interview by the author, New York, 17 June 1982.

9. Presentation by Ambassador Lawrence A. Pezzullo, New York, Center for Inter-American Relations, 23 September 1980.

10. Régis Debray, *Strategy for Revolution* (New York: Monthly Review Press, 1969), p. 95.

11. Tad Szulc, "Exporting the Cuban Revolution," in *Cuba and the United States*, ed, John Plank (Washington, D.C.: Brookings Institution, 1967), pp. 69-97; and Ernesto F. Betancourt, "Exporting the Revolution to Latin America," in *Revolutionary Change in Cuba*, ed. Carmelo Mesa-Lago (Pittsburgh, Pa.: University of Pittsburgh Press, 1971), pp. 105-126.

12. Romulo Betancourt interview by Hugh Thomas, cited in Thomas, *Cuba*, p. 1090.

13. Debray, *Strategy for Revolution*, p. 133.

14. Fidel Castro in Frank Mankiewicz and Kirby Jones, *With Fidel, A Portrait of Castro and Cuba* (New York: Ballantine Books, 1975), p. 171.
15. Ibid.
16. Ibid., p. 170.
17. See Castro at the meeting of the fourteenth anniversary of the committees for the defense of the revolution, Havana, Cuba, 28 September 1974, in ibid., p. 215.
18. Ibid., p. 221.
19. Ernesto Che Guevara, *Obras: 1957-1967*. Havana, Cuba: Casa de las Americas, 1977.
20. Mankiewitz and Jones, *With Fidel*, p. 173.
21. Ibid., p. 169.
22. For a discussion of the failure of the strategies of the Communist parties and the betrayal of the liberal parties of Latin America in the 1960s, see Debray's early essay, "Problems of Revolutionary Strategy in Latin America," written in 1965, in *Strategy for Revolution*, pp. 113-152. It was the APRA movement founded in 1929 in Peru which, according to Debray, "carried out under the name of Marxism the greatest historical betrayal which Latin America has shown these thirty years." Ibid., p. 127.
23. Thomas, *Cuba*, p. 1477.
24. Debray, *Strategy for Revolution*, p. 128.
25. Ibid., p. 127.
26. Ibid., p. 129.
27. *New York Times*, 4 July 1961, p. A1.
28. Thomas, *Cuba*, p. 1478.
29. Much has been written about the case of Heberto Padilla, who was offered the Writers' Union Poetry prize, because his poem entitled "Fuera de Juego" was a tacit criticism of the Cuban government: Lordes Casal, ed. *El caso Padilla: literatura y revolución en Cuba* (Miami, Florida: Ediciones Universal, 1971). In addition Pablo Neruda, the Chilean poet, was scorned in a letter signed by many Cuban writers. Thomas, *Cuba*, p. 1465. See also Jorge Edwards, *Persona Non Grata* (New York: Pomerica Press, 1973), pp. 42-49, 221-242.
30. Debray, *Strategy for Revolution*, p. 95.
31. Ibid.
32. Ibid., p. 96.
33. Douglas Bravo in ibid., p. 103. The guerrilla, wrote Bravo, "is as patient and inexorable as a spot of oil." His theory and optimism revealed what the analogy meant: "He only needs to expand to meet with ever more favorable conditions. It is a question of geography." Soon after, the relationship changed, and in an interview in *Le Monde* (15 January 1970, cited in Thomas, *Cuba*, p. 1479), Douglas Bravo accused Castro of having his own economic interests and being an ally of the Soviet Union.
34. Juan Bosch, "An Anti-Communist Manifesto," in *Régis Debray and the Latin American Revolution*, eds. Leo Huberman and Paul M. Sweezy (New York: Monthly Review Press, 1968), pp. 97-98.
35. Ibid., p. 96.
36. Debray, *Strategy for Revolution*, p. 124.
37. Ibid.
38. Ibid., p. 138.
39. Ibid., p. 138.

40. Interviews by the author in São Paulo, Brazil, 13 November 1982 and 13 April 1983.

41. Ibid., p. 80.

42. Harold Eugene Davis, John J. Finan, and F. Taylor Peck, eds. *Latin American Diplomatic History* (Baton Rouge, La.: Louisiana State University Press, 1977), p. 251.

43. F. Parkinson, *Latin America, the Cold War, and the World Powers, 1945-1973* (Beverly Hills, Calif.: Sage, 1974), p. 106.

44. Ibid.

45. Debray, *Strategy for Revolution*, p. 237.

46. Ibid., p. 38.

47. Ibid., p. 232.

48. Ibid.

Part II
Diplomacy and Insurrection in the Western Hemisphere

Photo by Raúl Corrales/Courtesy Center for Cuban Stud

Symbolic cavalry march at the time of the nationalization of the United Fruit plantations, 1960.

3
Diplomacy and Foreign Policy 1960–1980

By August 1960, a year and one-half after the overthrow of Fulgencio Batista, U.S. officials were increasingly concerned about Cuba's interest in China and the Soviet Union. At the Havana Youth Conference Che Guevara declared that the Cuban Revolution was a Marxist revolution. This speech was the prelude to Castro's own declaration on 1 December 1961 that he had been a Marxist-Leninist since the days of the revolution.

> Do I believe in Marxism? I believe absolutely in Marxism. Did I believe in it on January 1? I did believe in it on January 1. Did I believe in it on July 26? I did believe in it on July 26.... Do I have any doubts about Marxism and do I think that certain interpretations are wrong and should be revised? I have no doubts whatsoever.[1]

Cuba was choosing its path, Castro asserted unequivocally.

Break with the United States

The transformation of private ownership to state ownership had been lightning-quick. Within one and a half years of the revolution, Cuba's private sector was nonexistent. The agrarian reform program Institute of Agrarian Reform (INRA) was the first to nationalize entire segments of the economy. U.S. companies such as United Fruit were offered compensation packages far below their stated value. The land was first confiscated, although sugar mills were not absorbed by the government until 1961.

May 1960 was a landmark month for Cuba's oil industry.[2] On 23 May Texaco and Standard Oil Company were ordered by the government of Cuba to refine a daily planned shipment of Russian crude oil.[3] They responded in less than a month. The U.S. companies flatly refused. On 24 May the National Cuban Bank notified Royal Dutch Shell to prepare to process 300,000 tons, or 2.2 million barrels, annually of Russian crude oil. Nationalization was imminent. Shell Oil Company, along with Texaco and Standard, refused to refine Soviet crude oil.

In reaction to the growing tension, the Council of Ministers met to take wideranging measures to reformulate and alter Cuban law. Encouraged by the refusal on the part of the oil companies, on 5 July 1960, Cuba amended the 1959 Fundamental Law.[4] With the amendment in place the president and the prime minister both had the power to expropriate oil companies and properties owned wholly or in part by U.S. citizens and provide for caretakers to take charge of the properties and to designate the value of the company in order to provide compensation. Contributions to the compensation fund consisted of 25 percent of foreign exchange proceeds of sugar sales to the United States at a price not below 5.75 U.S. cents per pound. Cuban bonds would be given as compensation. There were to be no appeals. All previous laws or regulations were revoked.

The value of the expropriated properties of the oil companies exceeded $750 million. Cuba received more than just the refineries; Cuba expropriated all transportation, storage, and market facilities. Shell was the only company to take steps to test the constitutionality of the seizure in the Cuban courts.[5]

On 28 June, Castro ordered the Texaco oil refinery to refine Soviet crude oil or be expropriated by the Cuban government.[6] The following day, as Soviet oil shipments arrived, the U.S. employees of Esso and Shell Oil left. On 30 June, the Cuban government nationalized the refineries.

Simultaneously, the U.S. Congress heard arguments in favor of a cut in Cuba's sugar quota. In late June, on the same day as Castro's order to the Texaco refinery, the U.S. House of Representatives authorized President Dwight D. Eisenhower to cut Cuba's quotas. One week later the Senate passed the bill. Cuba was already taking action in almost all areas of Cuba's private sector. The grand Havana hotels, including the Hilton and the National Hotel, were expropriated. By the end of the first week in August, all private holdings were taken by the government of Cuba.

At the same time that Guevara made his pronouncement at the Havana Youth Conference, a meeting of the American Foreign Ministers of the OAS convened in August 1960 in San José, Costa Rica. The principal discussion was between the United States and Cuba (which had called the meeting). Christian Herter, the U.S. representative, tried to gather Latin support for a condemnation of Cuba.[7] Before any final decisions were made, however, Cuba withdrew from the meeting and denounced the organization. The final result of the San José meeting was a resolution that condemned intervention in the Americas by non-American states and "declared totalitarian states to be inconsistent with the continental system." Less than a month later, Castro issued a Declaration of Havana to respond to the resolution passed in Costa Rica. Castro, furious at the resolution, declared that Cuba would have no part in U.S. programs established for Latin America.[8]

Castro's response to Eisenhower's Christian Herter, secretary of state, signaled the rupture which ensued. In September 1960 during Castro's second trip to New York since the revolution, he spoke optimistically to the United Nations about the possibility of good relations between the United States and Cuba. Herter offered Castro aid if U.S. companies were protected; Castro refused.[9] By mid-April 1959 relations between Cuba and the United States were good but showing signs of strain. President Eisenhower had not extended an invitation to Castro in April 1959 when Castro accepted an invitation from the U.S. newspaper editors. Eisenhower would not see him and instead left Washington to play golf. Eisenhower later wrote in his memoirs that he would have liked to have denied him a visa. Instead Castro met with Vice-President Richard Nixon. The two had opposite reactions to the meeting. Castro told *Hoy* magazine when he returned that, as far as he was concerned, all had gone well. Nixon had a different reaction: Castro was either naive or was, in fact, a Communist.[10]

Ernesto Betancourt, who had been the Washington, D.C. representative for the Twenty-sixth of July Movement two years before the revolution occurred, was personal adviser to Castro during the trip. In addition to the newspaper visit, Castro addressed the Council on Foreign Relations.[11]

After Washington, Castro traveled to Argentina to attend a meeting of the United Nations Economic Commission on Latin America (CEPAL). He proposed an aid program to Latin America; he repeated this proposal in 1979 at the United Nations in New York.[12]

The White Paper on Cuba

On 3 April 1961, the U.S. State Department issued a report on Cuba. The regime of Fidel Castro, it began, "offers a clear and present danger to the authentic and autonomous revolution of the Americas."[13] The report alleged that Cuba had become "a staging area" for revolutionary activity based on Castro's alliance with international Communism. The report concluded with an urgent call for Cuba to reverse its course and return to the inter-American alliance. While the authors did not intend for the document to be a justification for the invasion which would take place two weeks later, the report called on regional allies to reject "the seizure by Communist movements" of Cuba. Cuba was already sending "large sums of money" to finance pro-Communist student groups plotting to overthrow the government of El Salvador. The "considered judgment of the Government of the United States," the report argued, was that the danger threatened "all the republics of the hemisphere."[14]

On 31 January 1962 at Punta del Este, Uruguay, the eighth meeting of American Foreign Ministers passed a resolution declaring that Cuba had excluded itself from the inter-American organization because of its belief in Marxism-Leninism and, therefore, put itself in a position that was incompatible with the principles of the OAS. Six countries abstained. The provocation of the meeting was Cuba's armed support of insurgency of the guerrillas in Venezuela. The only Latin American nation that refused to comply was Mexico.[15]

Isolation and Internationalism

At the January 1962 meeting of the OAS, Cuba was officially suspended. Abstaining from the vote were Brazil, Argentina, Mexico, Chile, Bolivia, and Ecuador.

Cuba responded by issuing the Second Declaration of Havana in which Castro called on Latin Americans to "rise up against imperialism."[16]

Cuba continued during the 1970s to give military assistance to insurgent revolutionary movements throughout the hemisphere. With the exception of the first two years of the decade when exceptional circumstances prevailed, Cuba never retreated from its policies of *internationalism.*[17]

The decade began with renewed efforts to mend fences in Central America and the Caribbean and to reestablish diplomatic relations in the Western hemisphere generally. The efforts were an overwhelming success. By the end of the decade, Cuba had reestablished relations by opening either an embassy, consulate, or special interest section with seventeen nations of the hemisphere, most of which had broken relations as a result of the OAS sanctions in the 1960s. The two nations of North America which never broke relations with Cuba, Canada and Mexico, continued to enjoy strong economic and diplomatic ties.

During the decade, Cuba would regain several strong political allies. In Chile, Salvador Allende Gossens, despite U.S. resistance, had come to power with a great deal of clandestine Cuban help.[18] Peru's military government, which remained reformist and friendly to Havana, began to increase its ties with the Soviet Union. By 1973 Argentina's Casa Rosada opened its doors to Cuba's diplomats. As Cuba expanded its practice of diplomatic politics, Cuba assisted insurgents in Argentina, Chile, Colombia, Uruguay, Costa Rica, Nicaragua, El Salvador, Guatemala, and Honduras and provided military assistance and training to the governments in Grenada and Jamaica. Rather than abandon guerrilla programs, Cuba merely expanded its methods of foreign relations to include diplomacy and military programs to progressive governments in the region as well.[19]

By 1979 and into the 1980s, Cuba's programs would increase geometrically—with large-scale assistance to Nicaragua and El Salvador. Cuba also seized opportunities in 1975 to engage in military adventures in Africa. Cuba showed both an interest in diplomacy, as it had during the 1960s, and a willingness to employ military means to establish itself in the world community. Although there were minor setbacks, on balance Cuba's efforts to expand its political relationships in the hemisphere made headway; its guerrilla programs, however, had mixed results.

Cuba entered the 1970s on shaky diplomatic footing in the Americas. Many countries feared that clandestine programs by Cuba to assist left-wing opposition movements might prove disruptive to them. In February 1970 at a Caracas Conference of the Inter-American Economic and Social Council (CIES), Cuba suffered from the suspicions that the majority of the member states still had. As the program opened, Venezuela's President Rafael Caldera Rodríguez expressed the hope that Cuba would unite once again with its Latin American family; he was seconded by Sir Eric Williams of Trinidad and Tobago who called for the resumption of trade relations. Caldera's call was taken up in an unanimously adopted resolution condemning Cuba's hostile policies. Nevertheless, Cuba pressed forward with its attempts to persuade its former allies.[20]

In June 1970, despite its precarious domestic economic situation—notably the failure of the Ten Million Ton Harvest and the general collapse caused by overconcentration in sugar—Cuba sent disaster relief to Peru in the wake of an earthquake that had claimed over fifty thousand lives. Such goodwill gestures (repeated in Managua in 1972), began to show results, at least with ideologically sympathetic governments. Thus, in November 1970 the government of Salvador Allende in Chile renounced the OAS sanctions against Cuba.

By the end of 1971, OAS Secretary-General Galo Plaza of Ecuador favored Cuba's request for readmission to the organization. Moreover, Cuba had been invited to join the coalition of developing nations known as the Group of 77, and Cuba became a member of the Caribbean Multinational Shipping Enterprise (NAMUCAR) and the Pan-American Health Organization (PAHO). During the 1970s, Havana's participation in United Nations' specialized agencies increased, giving Cuba a new spotlight on the international stage.

During the following summer, a bill was introduced in the OAS to lift the ban on trade with Cuba and to permit member states to establish diplomatic relations. Although the bill was defeated (seven for, thirteen against, three abstentions), the divided vote reflected the success of Cuba's diplomatic gestures.

Cuba, in fact, was being touted as the successful emissary of regional diplomacy. Mexico's Foreign Minister Emilio Rabasa traveled to Cuba to enlist Cuba's support for his nation's diplomatic initiatives in the Third World. Venezuela and Argentina joined with Mexico and Peru to propose that Cuba be invited to the meeting of Western hemisphere foreign ministers to be held in Buenos Aires in 1975. In Central America, the governments of El Salvador and Honduras expressed their support for lifting the OAS sanctions (which had already been ignored or overridden by Mexico, Argentina, Peru, Panama, Jamaica, Barbados, and Trinidad and Tobago), and in early 1975 Venezuela broke the OAS mandate to establish relations with Cuba. By midsummer 1975, this policy investment by Cuba had paid a sizable dividend. In a decision by sixteen of its twenty-one members, the OAS abolished the economic and political embargo established in 1964.

In 1974 Cuba, along with Mexico and Venezuela, initiated a proposal for the creation of the Latin American Economic System (SELA). Until the end of the decade, Cuba had an active assistance program to Jamaica to improve Kingston's water quality and also sent construction workers, doctors, and fishery experts. When the OAS embargo was lifted in 1975, several nations had already reestablished relations with Cuba. By the 1980s Cuba had relatively normal relations with most of the nations in Latin America and the Caribbean.[21] Examples of normalization of relations include Argentina and Cuba signing agreements on foreign trade, finance, fishing, and technical cooperation, and relations between the chambers of commerce of the two countries. Flavio Bravo, president of Cuba's National Assembly meeting in Mexico arranged exchanges between Cuba's National Assembly and Mexico's Congress.

Within the hemisphere, Cuba was committed to expanding its influence principally by other than military means. Elsewhere in the world, however, Cuba had seized an opportunity to engage in military adventures. New conflicts in Africa offered Cuba a chance to test its military resolve in a region that had a high degree of strategic—and diplomatic—potential. Internationally, an active and successful foreign policy in Africa offered Cuba a chance to regain support of Third World nations, some of which had grown skeptical of Cuba's reflexive conformity to Soviet policy directives. In Africa, Cuba could demonstrate its willingness to protect these newly forming nations from outside aggression.

In January 1976, Brigadier General Omar Torrijos Herrera of Panama visited Havana as did Prime Minister Pierre Trudeau of Canada. Cuba's Latin American and Third World allies continued to open themselves to Cuba. After fifteen years of Cuban participation in the Non-Aligned Movement (NAM) (of which Cuba was a founding member), in 1976 at the summit meeting in Sri Lanka, its members voted unanimously to select Havana as the site for the 1979 Sixth Summit Conference of Heads of State and Government of the Organization, which meant that from 1979 until 1982 Fidel Castro would serve as the organization's chair, presenting its platform to the world at various international forums including the report to the United Nations General Assembly in New York in October 1979.[22] Cuba had never previously had such broad support from the controversial organization with which it had had deep-seated ideological disputes in the 1960s.

Cuba's policy in Angola opened totally new diplomatic channels. The Organization of African Unity (OAU), originally skeptical of Cuba's involvement, lauded Cuba's success. Cuba's Latin American allies, however, were ambivalent. Starting in 1975 Western pressure was building, most noticeably from the United States, and this pressure (in addition to Cuba's domestic economic slump) was reflected in a drop, although not major, in trade within the hemisphere. Cuba's bilateral trade agreements with its Latin American neighbors declined. Between 1975 and 1976 this included a 60 percent drop in trade agreements with Mexico—Cuba's largest trade partner in the region. Ironically, Cuba's trade with Latin America dropped after the abolishment of the OAS sanctions in 1975, while in Central America, Costa Rica and Panama increased trade agreements.[23]

Foreign Policy Activism in 1979: Revolution in Grenada

For Cuban foreign policy, 1979 was a pivotal year. By the end of 1978, Cuba was looking for areas to better its standing since diplomatic support of Cuba's Africa policy was waning steadily. March 1979 marked a victory for Maurice Bishop and the New Jewel movement in Grenada, which ousted former Prime Minister Sir Eric Gairy. Like General Anastasio Somoza Debayle of Nicaragua, Gairy had been a despised dictator. As a result, Maurice Bishop enjoyed great popular support for his revolutionary efforts.

The bloodless revolution occurred in March 1979 when Gairy was away on vacation. A radio station that played reggae music called Grenada's citizens to submit to the New Jewel movement. Within forty-eight hours the revolution had triumphed. No Cuban military assistance was needed.

Cuba's philosophical affinity with Grenada was clear: in 1979 when Castro spoke at the United Nations immediately following his talk to NAM, Maurice Bishop congratulated Castro, giving him a warm bearhug to a resonating sound of applause.[24] Moreover, Grenada and Cuba were the only nations in the hemisphere to vote against the U.N. resolution that condemned the Soviet Union for invading Afghanistan. Soon after the revolution took place in March 1979, Grenada welcomed Cuban military advisers and arms and talked about establishing a people's militia.

In November 1979, in a goodwill gesture reminiscent of the early years of the decade, Cuba sent Bishop's new socialist government three hundred construction workers (highly valued in Cuba where there is a housing shortage) to build a new international airport near St. Georges, Grenada's capital, and offered to pay one-half the estimated $50 million cost.[25] The airport stirred controversy. Having first approached the United States for help in building the airport, Maurice Bishop seemed miffed at the thought that the United States could object to Cuba's assistance in the construction.

The United States alleged that the airport was being built for military purposes. According to U.S. government intelligence, Bishop stated that he had not ruled out possible military use of the airfield. Moreover, some of the more than three hundred Cuban construction workers building the ten-thousand-foot runway at Point Salines were also soldiers.[26]

Cuba's presence in Grenada was limited but real. Throughout the countryside were scattered encampments of people's militia. Although the army was small, by relative standards Grenada's militia followed Cuba's line of domestic surveillance similar to that of the Committee for the Defense of the Revolution (CDR). Cuba sent military and technical advisers to Grenada, but because of their language difference, they were isolated. The airport which, according to U.S. intelligence, would have provided Cuba with a refueling point en route to Africa, would clearly service Grenada's need for an international airport. "Right now," Grenada's foreign minister stated in 1981, "Cuba is a friend and has offered to help."[27] Cuba's alliance with its Caribbean ally all changed in 1983. After Maurice Bishop's assassination on October 19, and Washington's intervention six days later, over fifty Cubans died and Cuba withdrew from the island, embittered by Moscow's weak reaction. "The revolution had committed suicide," Castro said later; "We would have reduced our cooperation."[28]

1980s Shifts

The election of Ronald Reagan in 1980, as well as the exodus of refugees from Cuba, seriously undercut Castro's credibility in the region and strained Cuba's relations with allies such as Costa Rica, Venezuela, and Peru. The election in 1980 of Edward Seaga in Jamaica and the prompt removal of Cuba's attaché signaled that Cuba's advances in the Caribbean would be met with U.S. economic and political counteroffensives. One week after his inauguration, Prime Minister Seaga publicly proclaimed his commitment to eradicate the "pro-Cuban trends" in the region and placed a full page advertisement in the *New York Times* on December 9, 1980 to underscore the point.

In May 1980 Cuban aircraft strafed Bahamian naval vessels, thus aggravating an already tense relationship. By 1980 Cuba had begun to lose much of the ground it had gained in the region during the early 1970s. Diplomatic relations throughout Central America and the Caribbean had been strained. In December 1980 Costa Rica's President Rodrigo Carazo cautioned that the two greatest threats to Central American democracies were "worldwide economic crisis and communist penetration."[29] The United States, he declared, would have to choose between Costa Rica or Cuba.

Carazo and his Christian Democratic administration spoke of Cuba as one of two major threats in the hemisphere. His successor, Luis Alberto Monge (elected in 1982), is similarly anti-Communist. In his election campaign, Monge spoke to the Costa Rican people about protecting the country from the Communist threat, and after his inauguration in May 1982, Monge's Partido Liberación did nothing to reestablish relations with Castro's Cuba.[30] Although the party considers itself strongly Social-Democratic, these anti-Communist sentiments are not inconsistent with the party's history.[31]

According to Monge, Costa Rica has no plans to reestablish relations with Cuba "because it is participating in an expansionist offensive in Central America and the Caribbean." It is not, however, a question of ideology: "We maintain a policy of pluralism in international relations and the fact that we have relations with a country does not mean we approve of their political philosophy."[32]

Cuba and Nicaragua

In July 1979 Nicaragua's president of forty years, General Anastasio Somoza Debayle, was overthrown by the Sandinista National Liberation Front (FSLN). Cuba strongly supported Nicaragua's revolution: Cuba assisted the Sandinistas in their attempt to overthrow Somoza in the 1960s, and Castro himself participated in one of the attempts. Augusto César Sandino, after whom the group named itself, provided intellectual backing and refuge for Cuba's revolution leaders in the 1930s.

Cuba's ties with Nicaraguan leaders were close during the 1950s. One of Nicaragua's revolutionary founders, Carlos Fonesca Amador, participated with Fidel Castro in his unsuccessful attempt to overthrow General Rafael Leonidas Trujillo Molina in the Dominican Republic in 1959.[33] Two years later the FSLN was founded in Havana. General Sandino was murdered in February 1933 by order of General Anastasio Somoza García whose son, General Anastasio Somoza Debayle, won the controlled presidential elections of January 1967.

Nicaragua's fears, like Cuba's, principally focused on U.S. intervention. The United States had occupied Nicaragua between 1912 and 1933 and had been partly responsible for the beginning of the unmerciful Somoza administration. By the late 1970s much of Latin America, especially regional neighbors, was providing moral support to the insurgents against Somoza. As Nicaragua's civil war began to escalate in the late 1970s, it was inflamed by the murder in 1978 of Nicaraguan newspaper publisher, Pedro Joaquin Chamorro. "Cubans have sympathy for the Nicaraguan revolution and its objectives and like any other Latin American nation they feel a duty to aid a progressive, struggling government," Nicaragua's Foreign Minister Miguel d'Escoto stated in 1981. "Cuba's sympathy was not ideological," d'Escoto said. "It is a Latin American sympathy and it is justified."[34] Cuba was one of the many Latin American nations that assisted Nicaragua's opposition with arms. By the time of the final offensive in July 1979, the FSLN was supported by the business group, the Supreme Council of Private Enterprise (COSEP), and the broad opposition front, a center-right political organization. Panama's Brigadier General Omar Torrijos Herrera had welcomed members of the FSLN prior to the revolution in Panama City.

It is understandable why Nicaragua turned to Latin America and Cuba for support, rather than to the United States. After supporting Somoza to the very last minute in 1979, the United States did offer the FSLN military aid, but d'Escoto asked, "How could Nicaragua accept help and aid from a government that had supported the National Guard?"[35] Just weeks before the final offensive, the OAS met to consider a U.S. proposal to send an inter-American peace-keeping force to Managua. The OAS rejected the plan. The United States was losing ground in terms of its diplomatic overtures and attempts to negotiate between the Somoza government and the opposition. What the OAS did approve was a resolution calling for replacement of Somoza. In July as President Jimmy Carter sent several envoys to try to negotiate, U.S. intelligence reports alleged Cuba's arms support of the FSLN.[36]

Although the Cuban government strongly supported the Nicaraguan revolutionaries, it did not supply arms until shortly before the final offensive. According to Cuba's Vice-President Carlos Rafael Rodríguez, Cuba aided Nicaragua "because Somoza was a cancer that had to be removed."[37] The main support for the Sandinistas came from Panama, Venezuela, and Costa Rica. Two years after the revolution, however, the Costa Rican legislature published a report alleging that military equipment was provided to the Sandinistas, mainly from Panama and Venezuela, which was "openly channeled through Costa Rica." Cuba's role, previously undocumented, was discussed in the report as well. Cuba supplied, according to the Costa Ricans, "at least 21 planes carrying raw material between Cuba and Llano Grande and Juan Santamaría Airport."[38] U.S. intelligence sources corroborated the fact that only light weapons were channeled through

Nicaragua. Cuba aided between late 1978 and 1979 in counseling, training, and arming insurgents outside of the country to return to Managua. Nicaragua's Foreign Minister Miguel d'Escoto underscored that fact: "There are no Cuban troops in Nicaragua today, nor have there been at any time. There are no military advisers in Nicaragua."[39] Even according to U.S. intelligence sources, Cuba mainly assisted Nicaragua in setting up a "supply network for channeling arms and other supplies to guerrilla forces."[40]

Cuba understood that the Nicaraguan and the Cuban revolutions were vastly different. According to Cuba's vice-president, Carlos Rafael Rodríguez, Cuba started the revolution with 90 percent support of the population and a very strong organization: "We had the precedent of having trade unions led by members of the Twenty-sixth of July Movement and the Communist Party. So we were deeply rooted in our society and we had great opportunity."[41] For years the Twenty-sixth of July Movement members had been with the Cuban people.

In the fall of 1978, the FSLN orchestrated the first offensive. U.S. sources alleged that Cuba flew arms to Panama, took them overland to Costa Rica, and then delivered them to the guerrillas. Cuba was supplying military advisers to Costa Rica to "train and equip" the Nicaraguan guerrillas with arms.[42] Special U.S. Envoy William D. Bowdler, former ambassador to El Salvador and Cuba, tried to negotiate a compromise between Somoza and the FSLN opposition. In 1979 he met with Sandinista leaders outside of the country.[43] Because this attempt at reconciliation came at a time when victory was near, the United States only engendered resentment.

Only one week had passed after the Sandinista victory in 1979 when an official Nicarguan delegation to Havana met with Castro. According to the account in the *New York Times*, Castro's advice was clear. "He warned us not to repeat Cuba's mistake," said a delegation member.[44] What was that mistake? According to one member of the delegation, Castro's advice was (1) to avoid a confrontation with Washington; (2) not to break with the Catholic Church; (3) to maintain the private sector; and (4) not to implement a system of rationing. Although Havana expressed skepticism about the Sandanista alliance with Nicaragua's bourgeoisie, Cuba was soon to send massive aid to the new government.

Cuba sent teachers, advisers, and medical personnel. According to the U.S. government, 5,000 advisers, teachers, and medical personnel, both military and civilian, were sent in the following two years.[45] Immediately following the revolution, Cuba sent 1,200 teachers and 137 doctors when, according to Nicaragua's foreign minister, Nicaragua needed them most. Twenty-five thousand teachers volunteered from Cuba according to Nicaraguan diplomats.

Immediately following the Sandinista victory, Cuba began to increase arms, supplies, and financial assistance. Between July 1979 and November 1980, Havana sent Managua $10 million according to Nicaragua's foreign minister. The Sandinista government received other aid from eastern European countries, East Germany, and Hungary. In addition, it received clothing and cars from the Soviet

Union.[46] Managua continued to receive aid from West Germany, Holland, Canada, Sweden, Mexico, and Libya.[47] In the next two years, $28 million worth of military equipment came into Nicaragua from Cuba, eastern Europe, and the Soviet Union.[48] According to U.S. intelligence, in the 1980s, sixteen hundred military advisers were providing military instruction and supplying most of Managua's intelligence training from Cuba.

After the revolution was completed in July 1979, the United States was quick to commit Congress to $75 million in aid to Nicaragua, 60 percent of which was to be directed to the private sector. Although it was a massive aid program that could have had a much wider appeal, it took almost one year to approve it, while most other countries were already providing Nicaragua with political and educational training. Just before the Carter administration left Washington, the U.S. Congress blocked the remaining $15 million which had not been disbursed. As the Sandinista directorate waited to see if Washington's decision would be reversed (and the $9.6 million-a-week credit that was offered would begin), Managua was receiving aid from most other Western countries. Although evidence was scant, the aid was not reinstated.[49]

By 1982 Nicaragua was economically deteriorating. "We have not given them advice or counseled moderation," Carlos Rafael Rodríguez explained in 1982, "but we do confide in them and let them know our opinions." Socialism may not be the order of the day in the 1980s, he argued, because of "difficulties, politically, economically and geopolitically." Times had changed, and the Cubans had realized that the 1980s presented a different set of problems for the Nicaraguans. "They are not only ideological questions," Cuba's vice-president cautioned. "They are political ones."[50]

Why was Nicaragua running into so much difficulty? In economic terms, Castro had also given advice to the Sandinistas about the problems of central planning. Cuba had broken up its small farms into plots that were not economically viable and which reduced production. Castro would explain these problems both to Nicaragua and El Salvador in order to guard their land reform programs against making such mistakes. Through 1981 and 1982, Cuba's influence remained strong. Nicaragua had military advisers from Cuba. D'Escoto asserted, "It is a professional army that Nicaragua has today. It is not at war."[51]

Nicaragua mimicked Cuba's literacy campaign of the 1960s with good results. Most important, Cuba's policies in Nicaragua gave Cuba broad public support and enabled Cuba and Nicaragua to celebrate their revolutionary victories together. Each year as the revolution has celebrated its anniversary, Castro has traveled to Nicaragua. Cuban support has also been a mixed blessing. As problems began to occur in 1981 in Nicaragua, and the prospects of a mixed economy and open relations with the West began to diminish, Cuba's support became a hindrance both to Nicaragua and to Cuba. Nicaragua's ties to the Soviet Union began to increase as they did with Cuba, and U.S. relations began to weaken.

Most antagonistic to U.S. interests was Cuba's effort to work with the Nicaraguans to export revolution to the Palestine Liberation Organization (PLO) through its embassy in Nicaragua as well as to El Salvador and Guatemala. According to U.S. sources, Nicaragua has aided in a massive Cuban-directed arms shipment to Salvadoran guerrillas. Although d'Escoto argued in 1981 that the overwhelming majority of Nicaraguans continued to support the achievements of the government, by 1982 widespread criticism became apparent. The Soviet Union was supplying substantial aid after having established its first mission in Managua in October 1979.

In 1980 the comments of Nicaraguan government officials echoed a distress comparable to that of Cuba's with the Soviet Union: "We didn't go for all this in order to exchange American dominance for Soviet influence."[52] Nicaragua like Cuba desperately at first sought a new central ground between the Soviet Union and the United States. In 1981 d'Escoto stated, "We don't expect the Reagan Administration to like our revolution, but at least to accept it as an irreversible reality and to respect it. We want a new relationship of dignity and respect, and not one of docility and servility."[53]

As Nicaragua's relations with Cuba became stronger in 1982, relations with the United States deteriorated. In the summer of 1982, Nicaraguan government officials accused the Central Intelligence Agency (CIA) of backing a right-wing invasion of Nicaragua from Honduras. In the same month, Nicaragua began to buy arms from France.[54]

By June 1982 revolutionary Nicaragua had spawned its own shadow government in exile organized by former Sandinistas of two major divisions of the Revolutionary Democratic Alliance (ARDE) and the Revolutionary Democratic Force (FDN). In April 1982 the FSLN former deputy minister, Edén Pastora Gómez, who during the revolution used the name Comandante Cero, declared his opposition to the FSLN government. For the next few months he traveled through western Europe expressing strong skepticism about the close links between the Nicaraguan government and the Cuban government. With him was a former member of the FSLN junta and businessman, Arturo J. Cruz, a Christian Democrat who resigned from the junta in spring 1982. Cruz's criticism of the FSLN was effective because he had been such an adamant supporter.[55] In July 1982 he wrote, "To insure its control over the nation, the Directorate has set up a powerful secret police apparatus with the help of foreigners, most of whom are East German or Cuban agents." He criticized Nicaragua's foreign policy for following the Cuban line: while it condemned U.S. intervention in El Salvador, it condoned or remained silent regarding Soviet invasion of Afghanistan and the crackdown in Poland. His criticism was all too familiar to Cuba. These inconsistencies, he argued, had "stripped Nicaragua's foreign policy of any credibility and had turned the country into a pawn in the East/West struggle."[56]

To demonstrate its commitment, in June 1983, Cuba had sent Cuba's military commander, General Arnaldo T. Ochoa Sánchez, a trusted former member of the Twenty-sixth of July Movement, to Nicaragua, to supervise its military operations. A member of the Communist Party in Cuba, Ochoa had been engaged in military operations outside of Cuba from 1967 to 1969, and was chief of the Havana Army until 1970. He supervised Cuba's military in Angola and Ethiopia and remains one of the most senior officers in the Ministry of Revolutionary Armed Forces (MINFAR).[57]

By mid-1984, U.S. pressure on the Sandinistas had increased geometrically. A report of Cuban ties to the Sandinistas and FSLN ideology was distributed in July by the U.S. Departments of State and Defense. The report alleged substantial increases in Cuban aid:

> The rapid growth of Nicaraguan military strength could not have been possible without the help of about 3,000 Cuban military-security advisors, some of whom are deeply involved in the decision-making process in Nicaragua. A total of about 9,000 Cubans are in Nicaragua.[58]

Regarding the rebels in El Salvador, the report of the U.S. House Permanent Select Committee on Intelligence reported, "this insurgency depends for its life blood—arms, ammunition, financing, logistics and command-and-control facilities —upon outside assistance from Nicaragua and Cuba. This Nicaraguan–Cuban contribution to the Salvadoran insurgency is longstanding. It began shortly after the overthrow of Somoza in July 1979."[59] Yet the Nicaraguan government continued into mid-1985 to assert that the Cuban military figures that Washington documented were exaggerated. According to Nicaraguan President Daniel Ortega, there were 786 Cuban military advisors in Nicaragua in 1985, "not 8,000, as the United States says."[60] As the debate raged in Congress, and the Nicaraguan economy came to a standstill, the fighting, in 1985, continued, and the U.S. economic embargo began.

Notes

1. Fidel Castro, 1 December 1961, in *Cuba and the Rule of Law*, ed. International Commission of Jurists (Geneva: ICS, 1962), pp. 70–71.

2. See "Castro Does the Expected," *Business Week*, 13 August 1960, p. 104; "Castro's Oil Grab," *National Petroleum News*, August 1960, p. 93; "Cuba's Expropriation Law," *Foreign Commerce Weekly*, 18 July 1960, p. 11; *Wall Street Journal*, 24 May 1960, p. 1; 13 June 1960, p. 1; 24 June 1960, p. 2; 30 June 1960, pp. 1, 3; and 1 July 1960, p. 1.

3. Interview by the author with Dr. Emilio Collado, 14 July 1982, New York.

4. International Commission of Jurists, *Cuba and the Rule*, pp. 98, 99, 103–104. Article 24 was the principal article of the law in question, which referred to the conditions of property expropriation with compensation. On 5 July, Articles 30 and 147 were amended to remove the courts from the expropriation process and broaden the uses of expropriation and the definition of compensation.

5. *Wall Street Journal*, 30 June 1960, p. 3. Texaco: 300 stations, 20,000 barrels per day refinery at Santiago de Cuba. Esso: 800 stations (100 were company owned), 35,000

barrels per day refinery, four ocean terminals, six bulk and packing plants, railroad cars, and fleet of trucks. Royal Dutch Shell Company: 500 stations (most independently owned), 20,000 barrels per day refinery.

6. Hugh Thomas, *Cuba: The Pursuit of Freedom* (New York: Harper and Row, 1971), p. 1289.

7. Ibid., p. 1293.

8. Ibid., p. 1295.

9. John Gerassi, *Fidel Castro* (New York: Doubleday, 1973), p. 93.

10. Dwight D. Eisenhower, *Waging Peace* (Garden City, N.Y.: Doubleday, 1965), p. 523. Castro in *Hoy* (Havana) 16 May 1959. Cited in Thomas, *Cuba,* p. 1211, n. 61. Castro's trip was sponsored by the American National Society of Editors. Castro spoke to the newspaper editors in Washington and at Harvard and Princeton. In New York he met with Henry Luce of *Time* magazine; Frank Bartholomew of UPI; and with the Foreign Affairs Committee of the Senate. He also met with Acting Secretary of State Christian Herter and CIA chief expert on Latin American communism, Frank Droller (who later was in charge of Cuban exile activities). See Thomas, *Cuba,* pp. 210, 1211; Herbert L. Matthews, *Revolution in Cuba* (New York: Charles Scribners Sons, 1975), p. 176.

11. Author interview with Ernesto Betancourt, New York City, 15 February 1983; Washington, D.C., 6 May 1984.

12. Fidel Castro speaking to the Thirty-Fourth General Assembly of the United Nations as Head of the Non-Aligned Movement, 12 October 1979. Author's observation.

13. U.S., Department of State, "Cuba," no. 7171 (White Paper on Cuba), Inter-American series, no. 66, April 1961, p. 2, 26, 28, and 34. Also see U.S. Congress, Senate, Subcommittee on Internal Security, "Communist Threat to the United States in the Caribbean," June 1961, 83rd Congress, 2d sess. See U.S. Congress, Senate, Select Committee to Study Governmental Operations, 94th Congress, 1st session. "Alleged Assassination Plots, Involving Foreign Leaders: An Interim Report of the Select Committee to Study Governmental Operations with Respect to Intelligence Activities." Report #94-465. November 20, 1975. "We have found concrete evidence," the Senate study began, "of at least eight plots involving the CIA to assassinate Fidel Castro from 1960 to 1965." Ibid., p. 71.

14. Wayne Smith, 30 October 1985; and see Spruille Braden, former assistant secretary of state for Inter-American Affairs, former U.S. ambassador to Cuba, before the Cuban Chamber of Commerce, 17 May 1961. Cited in Fulgencio Batista, *The Growth and Decline of the Cuban Republic* (New York: Devin Adair, 1964), p. 267. See also *New York Times,* 4 April 1961, p. 15. According to Batista, the paper was writen principally by White House aides.

15. Harold Eugene Davis, John J. Finan, and F. Taylor Peck, eds., *Latin American Diplomatic History* (Baton Rouge, La.: Louisiana State University Press, 1977), p. 250.

16. Thomas, *Cuba,* p. 1375.

17. U.S. Congress, Senate, Committee on Foreign Relations, "Insurgency in Latin America," by David D. Burks, hearings, 18 September 1967, 90th Congress, 1st sess., pp. 207-219.

18. See John Dinges and Saul Landau, *Assassination on Embassy Row* (New York: Pantheon, 1980).

19. U.S., Congress, Senate, Committee on Foreign Relations, "Insurgency in Latin America," pp. 209-219. See also Jorge I. Domínguez, "Cuban Foreign Policy," *Foreign Affairs* 57, no. 1 (Fall 1978), pp. 83-108.

20. When Rafael Caldera ran again as the COPEI party candidate in 1984 and lost, his skepticism about Cuba had grown.

21. Only Canada and Mexico never broke relations and retained the relations they had before the revolution. By 1982 Cuba had relations with most of the nations it had contacts with before the OAS embargo. Argentina (1973) (reestablished), the Bahamas* (1974), Barbados* (1972), Canada (prior to 1959), Costa Rica (1977) (consular relations only), Dominica* (1980), Ecuador (1979) (reestablished), Guyana (1972), Mexico (prior to 1959), Nicaragua (1979) (reestablished), Panama (1974) (reestablished), Peru (1972) (reestablished), St. Lucia* (1979), Surinam* (1979), Trinidad and Tobago* (1972), United States (1977) (special interests section only), Uruguay (1985), Venezuela (1974) (reestablished).* Ambassadorial level relations; ambassador is housed outside of the country. Source: National Foreign Assessment Center, *The Cuban Economy: A Statistical Review*, March 1981, p. 53; *The Europa Yearbook: A World Survey* (London: Europa Publications Ltd, 1983), pp. 222-223.

22. Author's observations as United Nations representative of the Center for Inter-American Relations attending presentation by Fidel Castro, United Nations, Thirty-fourth General Assembly, October 1979.

23. Jorge Pérez-López and René Pérez-López, "Cuban International Relations: A Bilateral Agreements Perspective," (Northwestern Pennsylvania Institute for Latin American Studies, May 1979).

24. Author's observations at United Nations, Thirty-fourth General Assembly, 12 October 1979.

25. U.S. Department of State, Special Report no. 90, 14 December 1981, p. 10. The U.S. report referred to an interview in *Newsweek* magazine of 31 March 1980 in which Bishop stated that the Grenadian government would not rule out allowing forces opposed to an authoritarian regime in the region use of the new airport to pass through Grenada.

26. Interview by the author with Cuban construction workers, Grenada, February 1981.

27. Interview by the author with Ambassador Caldwell Taylor, Grenada, 5 March 1982. Through its Americas Department, Cuba maintained close ties with most of the Caribbean. When Grenada's prime minister, Maurice Bishop, and ambassador to Cuba, Richard Jacob, traveled to Cuba in March 1980, in addition to Fidel Castro, they met with three representatives of the Americas Department: Manuel Pineiro Losada, Osvaldo Tardenas, and Otto Marrero. *Granma Weekly Review*, 9 March 1980.

28. Fidel Castro to *Newsweek*, 9 January 1984, p. 39.

29. Interview by the author with former President Rodrigo Carazo Odio of Costa Rica, New York, 3 December 1980.

30. Presentation by Luis Alberto Monge, president of Costa Rica, New York, Center for Inter-American Relations, 29 May 1981.

31. Interview by the author with Dr. Constantino Urcuyo Fournier, 4 June 1982.

32. Luis Alberto Monge, presentation at Center for Inter-American Relations, New York, 29 May 1981.

33. Thomas, *Cuba*, p. 1228.

34. Interview by the author with Miguel d'Escoto, New York, 2 October 1981.

35. Ibid.

36. U.S., Department of State, Special Report no. 90, pp. 5-6.

37. *El País* (Madrid), 7 April 1982. Foreign Broadcast Information Service (FBIS), ESE.

38. Costa Rica special legislative commission report of 14 May 1981 as cited in U.S., Department of State, Special Report no. 90, p. 8.

39. Author's interview with Miguel d'Escoto. In 1982 in another interview, d'Escoto did concede that some arms and supplies were passing through Nicaragua to rebels in El Salvador. Stephen S. Rosenfeld, "The Sandinistas Call It War," *Washington Post,* 8 March 1982, p. A13.

40. U.S., Department of State, Special Report no. 90, p. 6.

41. Interview by the author with Carlos Rafael Rodríguez, New York, 12 June 1982.

42. U.S., Department of State, Special Report no. 90, p. 6.

43. Interview with William D. Bowdler, New York, 20 September 1979.

44. *New York Times,* 9 July 1980, p. A10.

45. U.S., Department of State, Special Report no. 90, p. 6.

46. Ministry of Foreign Relations, Government of Nicaragua. Cited in *Latin American Weekly Report* (London), 10 April 1981, p. 1.

47. Ibid.

48. U.S., Department of State, Special Report no. 90, p. 6.

49. *Latin American Weekly Report* (London), 10 April 1981, p. 1.

50. Interview with Carlos Rafael Rodríguez, New York, 12 June 1982.

51. Author's interview with Miguel d'Escoto.

52. Author's interview, ibid.

53. *New York Times,* 13 August 1981, p. A3.

54. Ibid., 13 July 1982, p. A6.

55. Ibid., 14 July 1982, p. A23. Also see presentation by Arturo J. Cruz, New York, Center for Inter-American Relations, 19 November 1981; 26 July 1983; Arturo J. Cruz, "Nicaragua's Imperiled Revolution," *Foreign Affairs,* 61, no. 5 (Summer 1983), pp. 1031-1047. The U.S. fed $80 million to the *contras* in Nicaragua until financing ended in June of 1984, and the FDN numbered 12,000 to 14,000. See David Nolan, *FSLN: The Ideology of the Sandinistas and the Nicaraguan Revolution* (Coral Gables, Florida: Institute of Inter-American Studies, Graduate School of International Studies, University of Miami, 1984).

56. Ibid.

57. U.S. Government, Central Intelligence Agency, *Directory of Personalities of the Cuban Government, Official Organizations, and Mass Organizations.* Report A74-7 (Washington, D.C.: U.S. Government Printing Office, March 1974); *Verde Olivo* (Havana, Cuba: FAR) August 26, 1973, p. 14; "Cuban Commander in Nicaraguan Post," *New York Times,* 19 June 1983, pp. 1, 10; U.S. Department of State and Department of Defense, Report of July 18, 1984, op. cit., p. 13.

58. U.S. Department of State and Department of Defense, *Background Paper: Nicaragua's Military Build-Up and Support for Central American Subversion.* July 18, 1984 (Washington, D.C.: U.S. Government Printing Office, 1984).

59. U.S. Congress, House, Permanent Select Committee on Intelligence, "Report to Accompany House Resolution 2760." 98th Congress, 1st session. Report #98-122, Part I, p. 2.

60. "Ortega Assails Bush," *New York Times,* 20 March 1985.

4
Cuban Assistance to El Salvador and Insurgency through the 1980s

In view of Cuba's successful involvement in Nicaragua, it seemed only natural that Cuba would react favorably to the needs of the opposition forces in El Salvador in 1979. Cuba sympathized with objectives of the guerrilla movement—particularly in 1981 to 1982, with the Farabundo Martí National Liberation Front (FMLN) (a strongly Marxist group) and the Democratic Revolutionary Front (FDR) (a populist coalition of center-left groups which merged with the FMLN)—and the prospects for another military success might have seemed at the time moderately good. For Cuba to assist the guerrillas was entirely consistent with Cuba's two-pronged approach in the region—providing armed assistance to opposition forces in countries where governments were unfriendly, and using diplomatic avenues with friendly regimes.

El Salvador's opposition did not receive help from Cuba in the 1960s. A U.S. congressional report of 1969 concluded, "In the Caribbean area, only Mexico, Costa Rica, and El Salvador have been free of (Cuban) insurgency."[1] But within El Salvador, opposition to the small group of families that ran the country was deep-set. Although the Cubans are by no means late arrivals on the Central American scene, it is important to stress that they alone did not create the conflict in the region. Ambler H. Moss, former U.S. ambassador to Panama, stated in 1981, "The present instability and violence in Central America arise from *internal* factors. Despite Cuba's obvious interest in the area, what we see in Central America today would not be much different if Fidel Castro and the Soviet Union did not exist."[2]

El Salvador's present crisis dates from the 1930s when its few wealthy families (known popularly as the fourteen families, but which actually number over one hundred) assisted the military to protect their landed wealth against growing peasant discontent. The brewing political and economic crisis in the small Central American nation which does not touch the Caribbean Sea began in part because of the nation's reliance on three crops: sugar, coffee, and cotton. Foreign earnings in the 1930s dropped in all of Central America because of the ripple effect of the Depression in the United States. The strength and ruthlessness of the military was amply demonstrated in 1932 when in a matter of weeks, in what became known simply as *Matanza* (massacre), forty thousand Salvadoran peasants were killed.[3]

As in Cuba, opposition groups began to develop in this period. The Communist party (PCS) was formed in 1930, amalgamating many of the unions that had been fragmented before. In May 1930 a workers' strike was supported by over eighty thousand farmers in San Salvador. As in Cuba, both the Mexican Revolution of 1910 and the Russian Revolution of 1917 had an effect on Salvadoran peasants who were excluded from the large land holdings in the country. In 1931 one of the few free elections in Salvador's history was held, and Arturo Araujo was elected president. Although Araujo allowed the Communist party to participate in elections, as Batista had in the 1930s in Cuba, he was not able to deal with growing unrest sparked by economic hard times, and he was overthrown within the year by General Maximiliano Hernández Martínez.

After coming to office, Martínez invalidated the elections that had taken place. Several opposition groups planned a major demonstration for 22 January, to be led by Agustín Farabundo Martí, (from whom the current FMLN takes its name). In order to stop the demonstration, the military police arrested Martí on 18 January. On Martí's orders, the opposition demonstrated without him. After week-long fighting, by the end of January the revolt was quelled and all opposition parties were banned, and on 1 February, Martí was shot. Martínez, with the military's backing, ruled for fourteen additional years.

Agricultural commodities have always been the main source of income in El Salvador; as a result, land ownership and land reform have punctuated Salvador's politics and are the source of most of its unrest.[4] When Martínez came to office he began the first of El Salvador's land reform programs. The program of 1933 redistributed land other than that which produced coffee, affecting approximately 2 percent of El Salvador's farmers. This program also placed a moratorium on debts and devalued El Salvador's currency, the *colón*. Martínez advocated land reform but in effect protected the country's landed gentry. His program would make Salvadorans skeptical of future land reform programs.

In 1948 Lt. Col. Oscar Osorio staged a coup d'etat, and elections in 1950. Soon after Osorio came to power, a party was formed that represented both the military and the landowners, the Revolutionary Party of Democratic Unification (PRUD), and a decade of economic expansion and an ominous political calm followed.

U.S. and Cuban Involvement

In the 1960s many changes occurred in El Salvador. In 1961 PRUD was disbanded by the military in order to bring local business merchants into politics, and in 1961 the Party of National Conciliation (PCN) was formed to resurrect the old alliance and to reunite the military and landowners. In elections in 1962, PCN candidate, Colonel Julio Rivera, became president in an unopposed election and opened the avenues for political opposition parties to function legally. Several opposition parties were established, such as the Christian Democratic party (PDC), the National Revolutionary Movement (MNR), and the National Democratic Union (UDN), which included the Salvadoran Communist party.

In the 1960s the United States began to get involved in El Salvador's development. With support from the United States, the Central American Common Market (CACM) was founded, establishing open trade without tariffs between the countries of Central America.[5] Large amounts of aid were given by the Kennedy administration through the Alliance for Progress to El Salvador's industrialization programs as well as to businesses. Between 1961 and 1968 U.S. aid to El Salvador totaled $53.6 million, which compared favorably to the amounts given to the larger nations in the region such as Mexico (which totaled $76 million).[6]

In 1969 following a soccer match between El Salvador and Honduras, war broke out between the two nations, provoked, clearly, by larger issues: approximately three hundred thousand Salvadorans by the end of the decade were working in Honduras because of the high unemployment rate in El Salvador. Peasants from El Salvador who had migrated to Honduras returned home to a collapsed economy, exacerbating the already difficult conditions. Within months the Central American Common Market folded. Opposition groups and civil unrest increased, and opposition parties began to converge, including the unification of the Christian Democrats, the MNR, and the UDN, forming the coalition called the National Opposition Union (UNO).

The 1970s and the Roots of Present Conflict

Current unrest in El Salvador can be traced most directly to the 1972 elections in which Christian Democrat José Napoleón Duarte won the presidency. The military intervened, and declared the candidate of the National Conciliation party, Colonel Arturo Armando Molina Barraza, to be president. Before Molina could succeed President Fidel Sánchez Hernández, Christian Democrats and other party members (including Duarte himself) opposed to the military revolted. But the revolt failed. Duarte was arrested and exiled to Venezuela where he established close ties to the Venezuelan Christian Democratic party and its president in 1980, Dr. Luis Herrera Campíns. After five years in office, in 1977 Molina was replaced in apparently rigged elections by PCN candidate General Carlos Humberto Romero, who had been Molina's minister of defense.[7]

Provoked by growing violence, opposition parties—this time committed to violence—emerged. In the 1970s several groups were formed including the Popular Liberation Forces (FPL), the People's Revolutionary Army (ERP), and the National Resistance (RN), which included the military section, the Armed Forces of National Liberation (FARN).

Meanwhile, the Roman Catholic church pressed for reform on behalf of the peasants. El Salvador's Archbishop Oscar Arnulfo Romero became a principal spokesperson for the church, arguing for an end to the political repression. The church continued to help different opposition groups, particularly the Christian Peasant's Federation (FECCAS).[8]

While opposition groups increased in strength, support, and numbers, the government of Romero tacitly, and sometimes openly, supported the development of death squads. According to a 1981 report of the Foreign Policy Association, "The government itself organized and armed the largest of the paramilitary rightest groups, ORDEN (Order)."[9] Other armed groups dedicated to murdering opposition party members were formed, such as the White Warriors Union, the White Hand, and the Falange. These death squads, which operated throughout the 1970s and continued through the 1980s, were responsible for thousands of killings of church leaders, opposition groups, and civilians. U.S. Ambassador Deane Hinton stated in an unpublished memorandum that "membership is also uncertain, but in addition to civilians we believe that both on and off duty members of the security forces are participants." This fact was confirmed by ARENA party head Roberto d'Aubuisson, who stated, according to Hinton, that "security force members utilize the guise of the death squad when a potentially embarrassing or odious task needs to be performed."[10]

In October 1979 a group of progressive and centrist army officers overthrew Romero, and a five-person junta was established consisting of two military officers, Colonel Adolfo Arnoldo Majano Ramos and Colonel Jaime Abdul Gutiérrez, and three civilians, Román Mayorga Quiróz, Mario Antonio Andino, and Duarte's running mate in the 1970s elections, Guillermo Manuel Ungo Revelo. The junta was supported by President Carter, who announced a series of social reforms including elections, economic reforms, an ambitious land reform program, and the abolition of ORDEN. Opposition parties which were promised legal status joined the government including many members of the UNO. The junta failed to promote these promised reforms quickly; perhaps most important, the right-wing death squads were not banned.

In January 1980 the three civilian members of the junta resigned. A second junta, again with two military members and three civilians, lasted only until March when a third junta was established and all civilian members resigned. On 3 March 1982, the government announced reforms. Three weeks later San Salvador's Archbishop Oscar Arnulfo Romero was assassinated while saying Mass in the nation's capital.

El Salvador's Opposition and Outside Forces

In the wake of Archibishop Romero's assassination, violence accelerated. Although the origins of the violence were unclear, in April the United States approved more than $5 million in "non-lethal" military aid to the newly constituted junta. Within two weeks a major opposition front took center stage, the FDR, a coalition of Social Democrats, former Christian Democrats, union officials, church members, students, and business people. Organized in April 1980, the FDR was an umbrella organization for almost fifty parties, groups, and unions. When it was first established, the group represented almost every segment of Salvadoran opposition from Marxist Communist party members to large business owners. At the head of the organization was Enrique Alvarez Córdoba, former minister of agriculture, a millionaire coffee grower who became the secretary-general. Outside assistance that was sought by the FDR is illustrative of confusion that has been borne by this crisis. Through 1980 representatives of the FDR travelled throughout western Europe and Latin America to gain international support for a negotiated solution to the crisis.

Alvarez represented the most centrist elements of the FDR coalition. In the 1960s under the administration of General Fidel Sánchez Hernández, he had been deputy agricultural minister, a position he maintained for only a few months because reform was too slow in coming. He returned in 1969 to the Ministry of Agriculture and proposed a land reform program. Finally, after two more stints in the government, he resigned to found the FDR. A *New York Times* account quoted a friend of his, "He was charismatic, like your John Kennedy."[11] Alvarez, who was educated in New York and studied economics at Rutgers University, owned a 145-hectare ranch called *El Jobo* outside of San Salvador. His family's money came mainly from coffee growing, and in 1980 the cattle and dairy ranches that he owned were worth more than $2 million. Dedicated to pluralism and a mixed economy, Alvarez sought widespread international support in opposition to a government junta that had cooperated in political assassinations. In July 1980 he travelled to New York to discuss what the FDR represented: "We are broad-based, as you can see from our group here today.... We want an end to the violence."[12] The State Department, however, would not meet with him and the other representatives of the FDR, including Guillermo Manuel Ungo, former president of the junta. In November 1980 the FDR joined forces with the Farabundo Martí National Liberation Front (FMLN) as the opposition groups that included the FPL, the ERP, the RN, and an additional new group, the Central American Revolutionary Workers' party (PRTC).

On 28 November 1980, the mutilated body of Enrique Alvarez was discovered outside of San Salvador. The FDR would never return to a policy so amenable to the United States. Alvarez's assassination radicalized the opposition. The stage was set for increased Cuban involvement. After returning to El Salvador in March, José Napoleón Duarte was appointed president, and a fourth junta was established. That same month four U.S. church representatives, three nuns and a laywoman, were murdered outside of San Salvador, possibly by the National Guard. The Cuban government began to send arms and assistance to the Salvador Communist party as well as to some of the smaller opposition groups in the FMLN. In addition, the Soviet Union sent arms and advisers to the Communist party. The Soviet Union and Cuba continued to support particular parties in the left opposition. The central FDR remained out on a limb until it merged with the FMLN.

By January 1981 the FMLN and the FDR declared the final offensive with the FDR calling for a general strike. Coordinating the offensive was the military arm of the FMLN/FDR, called the United Unified Revolutionary Directorate (DRU) established in May 1980. It was the organization's most direct link with the Cuban government; indeed, several of the staff members trained in Havana.[13]

The fighting in El Salvador continued to become more polarized. The 1981 swearing in of U.S. President Ronald Reagan did not significantly shift policy, but pressure increased and within a month, the new administration released a White Paper detailing Cuban arms shipments to the rebels.

The White Paper on El Salvador

The White Paper released on 23 February 1981 accused Cuba of large shipments of arms to El Salvador. Even after detailed reports of inconsistencies in the White Paper had surfaced, the Reagan administration continued to accuse Cuba of sending arms. (Even Secretary of State Alexander Haig pointed to "mistranslations and other small errors.")[14] After much of the criticism had waned, in July the Reagan administration announced the discovery of a dramatic increase in Cuba's support. By the end of the month, Haig alleged that Soviet weapons sent by Cuba were arriving in El Salvador. Suddenly, a Latin American civil war had become the staging area for a serious East-West conflict.

The U.S. policy range was evident when Ronald Reagan replaced its ambassador, Robert White, with Deane Hinton. White departed on 2 February; by mid-March 1981 the United States Defense Department had announced that several dozen U.S. military advisers were in El Salvador. Hinton arrived in late May 1981. Moreover, Secretary of State Alexander Haig repeatedly warned that if Cuba did not stop the flow of arms to El Salvador, the U.S. would "go to the source" to solve the problem.[15]

Cuba's response to U.S. warnings seemed out of character. Instead of boasting of Cuban support for the left in El Salvador and soliciting nonaligned support for his position, Castro vigorously denied that Cuba was providing military assistance to El Salvador's guerrillas. Indeed, by 1982 most prominent Cuban leaders had publicly stated that Cuba was not involved in the El Salvador conflict. Cuba's vice-president, foreign minister, and ambassador to the United Nations all stated that Cuba was supplying no arms to El Salvador. The White Papers' incomplete evidence hurt the credibility of both U.S. State Department accusers and the Cuban deniers. The problems in El Salvador after all were not solely caused by Cuba and did not involve an invasion from without; it was an internal political dispute, not a war over territory. Cuban and U.S. involvement have clearly exacerbated problems and clouded issues.

A failure by El Salvador's leaders to meet their promises both to U.S. policymakers and to their own constituencies resulted in miscalculations by the United States. One month before his overthrow in October 1979, General Carlos Umberto Romero had promised free elections. Assistant Secretary of State Viron P.

Vaky told a congressional subcommittee on international affairs that Romero's commitment "to free municipal and legislative elections in March 1980 and to measures to reform and open up the electoral system looked particularly encouraging." Complicating the issue throughout the region, Vaky wrote, was the fact that Castroist/Marxist influence in "extreme insurgent groups have seized upon these legitimate aspirations and unstable situations to advance their own objectives." Romero's promises would never be tested.[16] Cuban aid continued, nonetheless, while Cuba's presence fueled the debate in Congress and in the White House for a U.S. reaction.

The 28 March 1982 elections, however, produced uncertain results. According to U.S. Representative Michael D. Barnes, chairman of the House Subcommittee on Inter-American Affairs, "Properly interpreted, the elections were a success, having accomplished everything they could have been expected to accomplish." Miscalculations of the 28 March vote abound. One month after the election, Barnes wrote:

> The elections were designed to exclude the Left ... There was never any real possibility that the Left would accept its terms on which they were invited to participate, which would have amounted to surrendering a war that they had not lost and placing themselves at the mercy of the Army if they wished to enter the country to campaign.[17]

Barnes concluded that "to interpret the vote as a rejection of the Left ... would be a dangerous delusion."[18] Complicating the issue was the Central Intelligence Agency, whose director, William Casey, bragged of military aid greater than the U.S. government had acknowledged, "which helped it to reduce the supply of weapons from Cuba and Nicaragua."[19]

There are, after all, competing interests in the Caribbean Basin. Ambassador Robert White wrote in 1982, "Those who argue that the peoples of Latin America should be allowed to have their revolutions without any involvement on our part misunderstand both the nature of power and the struggle between democracy and communism."[20] As of June 1982 Reagan's deputy secretary of defense, Frank C. Carlucci, was again warning of Cuban assistance in the region. According to Carlucci, the Soviet Union's shipments of military equipment to Cuba tripled in 1981, which meant that Cuba's military was the largest since the crisis between the United States and Cuba two decades before. According to the Department of Defense, Cuba had two hundred MIG fighters, six hundred fifty tanks, and ninety helicopters. With this enlarged military, Carlucci argued that Cuba continued to shift equipment and arms through Nicaragua to El Salvadoran insurgents. The United States, according to Carlucci, was playing a low-key role, supplying Salvador's armed forces with transport vehicles, helicopters, and communications. Principally, the United States was trying to control the supply of arms to the guerrillas. U.S. technical advisers, he stated, numbered no more than fifty-five. Almost five hundred Salvadoran officers were trained at Fort Benning during the last year. The United States in training these military officers was stressing techniques necessary in a battle of *counterinsurgency*.[21]

Meanwhile the United States increased military aid to the Duarte government. By 1982 several Cuban officials admitted their role in arms supplies to El Salvador. "Yes, we sent arms to El Salvador at one time," Cuba's Vice-President Carlos Rafael Rodríguez conceded in 1982. "It was before the final offensive."[22]

According to U.S. accusations, Cuba was not supplying arms to Salvador's guerrillas directly but through the assistance and coordination of arms deliveries from Vietnam, eastern Europe, and Ethiopia. These arms were then transshipped through Nicaragua. According to the U.S. report, because of the discovery of the arms, the flow was decreased in March and April of 1981. The report alleges that arms flows increased during the guerrilla offensive in August 1980.[23] Between February and June, several analysts found flaws in the report. Its principal author in the U.S. Department of Policy Planning of the State Department acknowledged that there were errors as well as unjustified estimates of the amounts of arms that the U.S. government had made.

The U.S. government's defense of the White Paper was unfortunate. "The premises are correct, even though there are fallacies in the Study," government officials argued.[24] As a result many inferred the opposite conclusion that there was no Cuban interference and arms supplied to El Salvador. That reaction was understandable considering the errors of the report; it was not, however, warranted. A subsequent State Department report claimed that half a million dollars in Iraqi money was laundered through Cuba for aid to the Salvadoran guerrillas.[25] The U.S. government cited an interview in a West German publication with Carlos Rafael Rodríquez, Cuba's vice-president, in which he admitted providing military training to Salvadoran guerrillas on 28 September. Although it is difficult to be precise on the timing and dates of Cuba's arm deliveries, from most accounts there were supplies through August, September, and October of 1980 which increased when Colonel Adolfo Arnoldo Majano Ramos was ousted from the junta in December.

In September 1981 when Castro spoke to the sixty-eighth Inter-Parliamentary Conference in Havana, he asserted that no weapons were being sent to El Salvador: "It is a lie that Cuba's supplying weapons and ammunition to Salvadoran patriots." He insisted that no soldiers were being sent either. "It is a lie," he continued, "and I repeat this here with full moral authority—that there are no Cuban military advisors in El Salvador."[26]

Later in September, Cuba's Foreign Minister Isidoro Malmierca Peoli repeated Cuba's denial of arms supplies to the United Nations General Assembly: "It is a lie that Cuba is supplying arms or supplying any other weapons or ammunition. These are the facts and they are irrefutable."[27] Finally, in early April Carlos Rafael Rodríguez flatly denied supplying arms to El Salvador. "Cuba has not supplied arms to the Salvadoran guerrillas," he told a Spanish newspaper, *El País*, "because the circumstances have just not made it necessary."[28]

"We do not want to talk about what we are doing now," stated Rodríguez, "because our signals are misunderstood."[29] U.S. government intelligence sources continued to argue that Cuba was sending arms to El Salvador across Honduras in trucks or on animals over mountain trails after they were flown to Nicaragua from Vietnam, Ethiopia, and eastern European countries. In July 1982 a cache of arms and equipment was discovered after a battle between military and rebels in Tegucigalpa, Honduras.

But while Cuban support to the Salvadoran insurgents continued through the mid-1980s, their international support waned. Several Western European governments, who had during 1982–83 strongly supported the FDR/FMLN, were impressed by Duarte's June 1984 presidential election victory and offered their support during his 1985 trip to Europe. By mid-1985, Duarte had not only succeeded in overwhelming his opposition internationally, but the March 1985 legislative elections gave Duarte's Christian Democrats a decisive 33-seat majority in El Salvador's 60-seat National Assembly and the support of Salvadorean Defense Minister Carlos Eugenio Vides Cassanova.

With strong Christian Democratic party support internationally, and renewed interest in Duarte by the Socialist International, El Salvador's president became more involved in regional politics, endorsing the Christian Democratic candidate Vinicio Cerezo in Guatemala's 1985 presidential elections.

Latin America and Its Reaction

Panama became involved in the negotiating process soon after the first El Salvadoran coup in October 1979. It continued to participate in negotiations through 1982. With a certain desperation for a prominent position in the peace talks, President Aristides Royo traveled to Havana in June 1982 to discuss negotiations with Fidel Castro. When he returned to Panama City, Royo set up a meeting with Cuban diplomat Ramiro Abreu and Roberto d'Aubuisson.[30]

Royo's diplomatic efforts were not Panama's first. In November 1980 Panama's Brigadier General Omar Torrijos Herrera, who was later killed in July 1981 in an air crash, invited Castro to meet with Majano in an effort to forge an alliance similar to the one attempted two years later. Torrijos had stronger links to El Salvador than did his diplomatic successor, Royo.

Panama, like Mexico, has supported El Salvador's opposition, as have several other nations in the region and in Europe and the Socialist International. However, there has been divided support in the region. When Mexico and France declared their recognition of the FMLN, the FDR, and their joint resolution, Venezuela strongly criticized the government. Venezuela's support of Duarte stems from his strong ties with Social Christian President Dr. Luis Herrera Campíns, ex-President Rafael Caldera, and ex-Prime Minister Aristides Calvani. These ties occurred mainly because of Duarte's seven-year exile in Caracas.

In early June 1982 after discussions with Castro regarding El Salvador, Panamanian President Royo met again with Fidel Castro. Within a week of the public exposure of Royo's diplomatic efforts, he resigned from the presidency a full two years before his term would have expired.[31] Although he cited health reasons, reports from within the military pointed to his difficulties in dealing with the National Guard especially during such controversial negotiations.

Although the guerrillas called for a popular insurrection and a boycott, they admit in retrospect that their calculations were wrong about popular support. After Roberto d'Aubuisson became president of the constituent assembly and a new president, Alvaro Magaña, was appointed, the government suspended the land reform program, until the 1984 elections brought José Napoleón Duarte back to office.

It is likely that Cuba will continue to assist Salvadoran opposition groups because of its philosophical sympathies. Cuba's denial of supplying arms to El Salvador's insurgents damaged its political position only slightly in the short term. In the longer term, Cuban aid and increased guerrilla violence and kidnappings undermined the opposition and Western European support.

Cuba and Colombia's M-19 Movement

Cuba's sympathy with Colombia's insurgents dates to Castro's firsthand view of violence in the Indian nation during the *bogotazo* in 1948 when labor leader Jorge Eliécer Gaitán was assassinated. During the next ten years known as *La Violencia*, more than two hundred thousand people were killed. Castro had seen firsthand the development of opposition to the Colombian government. The opposition was led by Marxist opposition groups which were established in the 1930s in Colombia.

When the National Front came to power in 1958, the same year Castro came to Cuba, its purpose was to bring together liberals and conservatives and exclude the electoral participation of the Communist party. A relatively conservative society, Colombia has had only one military government in the last century. Partly as a result of the exclusion of the Communist party in electoral politics, several opposition groups coalesced as radical opposition and guerrilla factions. The 1960s witnessed the establishment of three guerrilla groups, two of which were sympathetic to Castro, one of them claiming inspiration from Castro's revolution.

Castro's most direct contact in the 1960s was with the Colombian Army of National Liberation (ELN), which was organized in 1964 to 1965 by a group of university students from the Industrial University of Santander. Affiliated with the ELN were principally pro-Castro, non-Communist guerrillas, numbering at most three hundred members. Liberal reform seemed to be the hope of the movement until it became radicalized in the late 1960s with the murder of one of its founders, Father Camilo Torres Restrepo. In keeping with Castro's support of non-Communist parties in Latin America in the 1960s, Castro supported the ELN in 1965.

The second principal guerrilla group, the Colombian Revolutionary Armed Forces (FARC), formed at the same time and was closely affiliated with the Colombian Communist party (PCC). Two other very small guerrilla groups existed in the 1960s: Popular Army of Liberation (EPL) which was oriented to China instead of the Soviet Union, and the Worker, Student, and Peasant Movement (MOEL), which hijacked a Colombian plane in 1967 and took it to Havana.

On 19 April 1970, an election was held and General Gustavo Rojas Pinilla should have been declared the winner. When his victory was denied by the government, the Nineteenth of April movement, known as M-19, was founded. M-19 was formed by members of Rojas Pinilla's party, the National Popular Alliance (ANAPO), which was an outgrowth of the armed radical wing of ANAPO, as well as dissident members of the older Colombian Revolutionary Armed Forces (FARC). Unlike Cuba's Marxist rural guerrillas, Colombia's M-19 was composed mainly of middle-class students unhappy with the increasing decline of the Colombian economy.

Although Cuba continued to support the ELN when Cuba reestablished ties with Colombia in 1975, Cuba's assistance subsided and became clandestine. When in the late 1970s tensions began to increase between Colombia and Cuba, Cuba boasted of its training of Colombia's Nineteenth of April movement during the entire decade, thus further infuriating Colombian officials. The M-19's founder, Jaime Bateman, claimed to have been trained in Cuba. As 1980 began, Cuba's program in Colombia revealed an interest in continuing a guerrilla struggle in an area of the world where opportunity really did not exist.

The issue of Cuba's assistance to nations of the hemisphere became increasingly divisive by the 1980s. Colombia has led the anti-Cuban sentiment. "The interventions of today are of another style," Colombia Foreign Minister Carlos Lemos Simmones stated. "It pits men against their own compatriots."[32] Colombia's emissary was making a point more specific to Cuba's program in Colombia, a nation whose guerrilla activity is the longest continuous opposition to government rule in the hemisphere. In the past, he argued, "when one talked of interventionism in Latin America, it brought to mind the image of marines landing on our beaches."[33] Now, that image had changed; it was Cuba-trained guerrillas who were the aggressors.

Meanwhile, in international forums a position in the United Nations Security Council became available. Similar to the decision they were to make two years later to have a representative of the Third World as the organization's secretary-general, U.S. diplomats agreed informally that the position should be held by a representative from Latin America. As 1979 drew to a close, Colombia and Cuba fought arduously for a seat at the United Nations Security Council. More than eighty ballots ended in a deadlock. Even though Colombia was not a member of NAM, the vote was dividing the organization. Cuba began to gain votes in January, but the Soviet invasion of Afghanistan destroyed Cuba's chance of winning the seat. NAM proposed a compromise solution. Mexico was elected to the seat at the Security Council which was to be led by Mexico's ambassador to the United Nations, Porfirio Muñoz Ledo. The possibility of a seat for Cuba was staunchly opposed by the United States, not only because of its usual opposition to diplomatic successes by Havana but also because the position of president of the fifteen-member Security Council (which is decided on an alphabetical basis, and the letter C would have been next in line) would have given Cuba enormous negotiating power in the midst of the U.S.-Iranian hostage crisis.

As Cuban-Colombian relations continued to be tense, in February 1980 the Colombian M-19 Cuban-trained guerrillas seized the embassy of the Dominican Republic in Bogotá during a diplomatic reception attended by ambassadors of eastern Europe and the Western hemisphere, as well as the U.S. ambassador to Colombia, Diego Asencio. The guerrillas took hostages and kept them for three months until the terrorists were flown to Havana. The mystery of the episode—why several of the eastern European ambassadors had left the embassy just before the hostage crisis—was never solved, and Cuba refused to return the guerrillas. It is interesting to note that the guerrillas themselves seemed to be from the middle class and to be strongly influenced by Cuba. "They were real middle-class kids, not what you would expect in terrorists,"[34] Asencio stated in an interview.

Although Cuba flatly denies training the M-19 guerrillas, as it denied sending arms to El Salvador, several M-19 guerrillas told U.S. Ambassador Asencio during his captivity that they had, in fact, been trained in military techniques and insurgency in Cuba. Although some observers have argued that the group is comprised of other than leftists, all public pronouncements appear to be Marxist, according to Asencio. "Fidel is in the pantheon of saints," he stated.[35] They made it a point that they did not need outside support.

According to U.S. sources, both the ELN and the M-19 received Cuban training. Cuba also encouraged them to unify all opposition forces just as it had consistently advised Nicaragua and El Salvador. Intelligence reports emanating from Washington tell of elaborate training schools such as one in November 1980 in which members of the M-19 traveled to Panama and later to Havana to participate in four weeks of military tactics and training.

In early 1981, Colombia's President Dr. Julio César Turbay Ayala broke relations with Cuba for its role in terrorist activities. "Cuba has turned more active in exporting revolution," Turbay stated.[36] Cuba's assistance to Colombia guerrillas increased, although marginally, in 1981.

In February of that year, 100 guerrillas of Colombia's M-19 attempted an invasion of Colombia. To the surprise of the Colombian police, the guerrillas, who had been trained in Cuba, landed in Ecuador and were *en route* to Colombia when they were apprehended and turned over to the Colombian police.[37]

Cuban officials argued that they had proven conclusively that there was no link between Cuba and the M-19 arms. "That's right," Asencio replied, "if they had done the operation right the link wouldn't have shown."[38] In March of the same year, two failed raids by Colombian guerrillas left 150 killed or imprisoned guerrillas, including M-19 members. Although Colombian authorities had been remotely aware of Cuba's assistance to the guerrillas in rural areas in Colombia in the summer of 1981, Colombia's President Dr. Julio César Turbay Ayala (who left office one year later) was alarmed by the discovery in that summer and pledged to fight Cuba's guerrillas. Cuba did not deny the assistance. On the contrary, Cuba's ambassador to Colombia argued with Turbay that "Cuba was obligated to give its moral support to all leftist guerrilla movements." Turbay was miffed and taken aback: "I didn't take it as an excuse. I considered it a confession." The confirmation to the Colombians that Cuba had, in fact, supported insurgencies against the Colombian government, was characterized as a "Pearl Harbor to Colombians." Dismayed, the Colombian government promptly expelled Cuba's diplomatic community from Bogotá in 1981 and closed its six-year-old Embassy in Havana.[39] Whether Bogotá, as Cuba alleged, provoked Havana is unclear. Along with Chile's President Major General Augusto Pinochet Ugarte, Colombia had several weeks earlier signed an agreement "to combat Cuba's expansionism."[40] Relations after that did not improve.

Again in 1982 Colombia would stand with the United States (along with Chile and Trinidad and Tobago) against Cuba and the rest of Latin America on the crisis in the South Atlantic. Accusations have often been made that the United States pressured Colombia to oppose Cuba in international forums. Both Colombia and the United States deny the charge, insisting that policies are on parallel tracks as U.S. ambassador to Colombia, Thomas D. Boyatt, stated.

Although the M-19 does not have the capability to seriously challenge the government in Colombia, it has a great nuisance value; the FARC—which operates from rural areas—is a much more dangerous organization. There was evidence that Colombia's president elected in 1982, Dr. Belisario Betancur Cuartas of the Conservative party, Turbay's successor, would favor a more lenient approach to insurgencies, although he had not reopened diplomatic relations in 1985, while many regional neighbors did. Betancur did, in fact, repeat Turbay's offer for a general amnesty for all guerrillas—a dream, Asencio stated, of all Colombian politicians for years. Unlike the proposal of Turbay, the 1982 amnesty was more comprehensive, which increased the possibility of its success. "What blew the Turbay objective out of the water was the arsenal raid on New Year's of 1979," Asencio asserted.[41] In addition the major offensive against the guerrillas in 1980 made any compromise unlikely.

Cuba's assistance to Colombian insurgents remained one of its few guerrilla programs in the 1980s. On the whole, Cuba's programs in Colombia had been unsuccessful, but they demonstrated that Cuba was committed to maintaining insurgencies even in light of possible failure and the lack of opportunity. "Cuba's capacity for mischief in the region is infinite," Asencio argued, "but its ability to affect change is low."[42] The future, however, of the guerrillas was unclear. In March, the April Nineteenth movement boycotted presidential elections. Early in the month, two M-19 leaders, Jaime Bateman Cayón and Ivan Marino Ospina, kidnapped *El*

Espectador correspondent Maria Jimena Duzán for nine days. When she returned, she delivered a message from the two guerrillas regarding their new strategy. What Bateman wanted was a direct dialogue and *reincorporation* into civilian life.[43] Four days later, Maria Jimena Duzán revealed what Ivan Marino Ospina, deputy commander of the M-19, told her regarding Cuba. The M-19 would accept collaboration with Cuba. "We do admire other revolutionaries and we accept their teaching," Ospina stated, "but without their help financially or otherwise."[44]

Cuba and Puerto Rico in the 1980s

In other areas, Cuba has pursued a similarly unabated approach to opposition groups. Cuba's support for Puerto Rico's independence movement continued through the 1980s. It is interesting to note that Cuba's position on Puerto Rico has been antagonistic to Washington as well as to Moscow. In 1977 in an interview, Castro stated his position in favor of an independent Puerto Rico. Asked if he would send troops to an independent nation of Puerto Rico, he answered, "If Puerto Rico becomes an independent state and asks us to send advisers, we would have the right to send them if they were willing to receive them."[45] Unlike the Soviet Union, "in Cuba it [support for Puerto Rican independence] is more close to the heart," Puerto Rico's independence leader Rubén Berríos Martínez stated in an interview.[46]

Cuba's support of Puerto Rico, like its support of Jamaica under Michael Manley, is no small issue in Washington. In fact during the United Nations Decolonization Committee's Special Session of the General Assembly in the summer of 1981, the State Department sent the head of the Cuban desk to observe the sessions on Puerto Rico. Cuba's relations in Puerto Rico remained close to the Puerto Rican Socialist party (PSP) rather than the non-Marxist Puerto Rico's Independence Party (PIP). Indeed, at the United Nations Special Session in August 1981, the PIP specifically opposed the Cuban-supported PSP demands.

Cuba's position in Puerto Rico is not new. In September 1975 the Puerto Rican Solidarity Conference took place in Havana. A secret CIA report written on 19 June 1975 and released 5 years later stated:

> Castro may have some explaining to do to Moscow. Before the Solidarity Conference got under way, the Soviets reportedly had expressed concerns about Havana's open support for the Puerto Rico issue and judged that the Cubans had already gone too far.[47]

On the anniversary of the founding of the Puerto Rican Solidarity movement in July 1982, several Cuban delegates attended the festivities in San Juan. Although Cuba viewed its support for Puerto Rico as support for a Latin American nation, it was an interesting way for Cuba to state its opposition to U.S. policies. In an effort more symbolic than substantive, Cuba continued to lend moral support to San Juan's Puerto Rican Socialist Party (PSP), headed by Juan Mari Bras.

Cuba's Role in the South Atlantic Crisis

Cuba's visibility in Latin America surged in 1982. As in El Salvador, Latin America became the center of internationalized crisis when a dispute broke out in the small cluster of South Atlantic islands eight hundred miles off the coast of Argentina which were known as the Malvinas to those who sympathized with Argentina's territorial claim to them and as the Falklands to the British colonists who inhabited the islands.

The crisis in the South Atlantic gave Cuban government officials their first opportunity in almost two decades to stand together with the rest of Latin America. Havana Radio broadcast the government position saying "Cuba repudiates the intolerable aggression and reiterates its solidarity with the Argentine people." Britain, Cuban government officials said, was "interrupting the negotiation process" with Argentina.[48]

In April 1982 the government of Argentina invaded the Malvinas/Falkland Islands. The islands, long claimed by Argentina as part of the mainland, had been taken by the British in 1833. Castro's early introduction to the conflict in 1948 at the *bogotazo* gave him credibility as a leader who recognized the Argentine insistence on sovereignty over the islands.[49]

Cuba quickly offered military assistance. Soon after the outbreak of the crisis, Cuba's Vice-President Carlos Rafael Rodríguez stated in an interview in *Le Monde* that Cuba would support Argentina "by every means, including military."[50] It was a rare time of unity within the southern half of the hemisphere. For Cuba it was a time in which other nations of Latin America were expressing the same virulent anti-imperialism that Cuba had expressed so often during the years. Cuba's open offer of assistance went largely unnoticed, however. A meeting of NAM's Coordinating Bureau was held in Havana on 5 May 1982. It was the first time a representative of the government of Argentina had traveled to Cuba in twenty years.

Argentina had maintained a relatively low profile in NAM. Its uneasy posture changed on 2 April. At the NAM meeting on 5 May, Argentina's representative informed the coordinating bureau about the developments that had taken place since the first meeting of the bureau on 26 April: tension had gravely increased, peace was endangered, and security was endangered in the region and in the world.[51] As head of NAM's coordinating bureau, Cuba issued the declaration after the first meeting on 26 April. As spokesperson for the movement, Cuba had higher visibility than any other nation in the crisis. The declaration read as follows:

> The Government of Cuba in conjunction with the Movement of Non-Aligned Nations and in agreement with the resolution of the General Assembly of the United Nations, has always recognized and proclaimed the sovereign rights of Argentina of the Malvinas Islands. Cuba also urgently requests the immediate

ceasefire of "all hostile military and economic acts, and all actions against this fraternal Latin American country and non-aligned nation," and warns of the consequences for security and peace in the region.[52]

At the 5 May meeting, the coordinating bureau issued a declaration asserting five principal points, the strongest of which was the reaffirmation of support for Argentine sovereignty over the Malvinas Islands. The principle of Argentine sovereignty had been repeated several times by NAM, including at the ministerial meeting in New York in September 1981.[53] By 2 May 1982, Havana was using stronger language. The declaration by the Cuban government itself stated that the "colonial arrogance of the British Government—which now has the brazen backing of U.S. imperialism—" was repudiated by Cuba.[54] In the face of this attack on a Latin American country, the declaration continued, the United States is joining with the aggressors. Cuba was appealing in its most blatant way to the sense of regionalism that the conflict was arousing. Havana stated that "this is the hour of Latin American solidarity. The cause of the Malvinas is the cause of the Argentine people—and therefore the cause of Latin America and the Caribbean."[55] Whatever support would be necessary, the statement continued, Cuba and the rest of Latin America would provide.[56]

When the United States decided to openly back Great Britain, Argentina's foreign policy had little incentive to continue to support U.S. policy in Central America, or perhaps more significantly with respect to the Soviet Union, a shift was likely by Argentina to a foreign policy of nonalignment. Moscow's opinion was clear in its statement that Argentina had a legitimate claim to sovereignty of the islands and that the British should withdraw: "Britain stubbornly opposed decolonization of the Islands and invariably delayed negotiations with Argentina on the issue."[57] Argentina's appeal to NAM was not unprecedented. Since the elections of 1973, Argentina had opened its trade and political relationship with NAM. During the decade, Argentine-Cuba trade had increased substantially. Even prior to the OAS removal of the embargo, Argentina traded with Cuba. From the presidency of Dr. Héctor J. Cámpora through the presidency of Juan Domingo Perón and continuing during the military regimes that followed, Argentina maintained strong economic and political ties with Cuba and the Soviet Union.[58] Indeed, Argentina's relationship with the Soviet Union was not new to the crisis in the South Atlantic. When Perón came to power after World War II, he renewed relations with the Soviet Union after a twenty-year break. In 1952 Perón negotiated a major trade agreement, the first Latin American country to negotiate commercial arrangements with the Soviet Union.[59]

On 3 June 1982, Cuba signed a $100 million trade agreement with Argentina in an apparent reaction to the crisis in the South Atlantic. At the June NAM meeting of ninety-four nations in Havana, Argentina's foreign minister, Nicanor Costa Méndez, acknowledged only diplomatic and commercial relations. In previous trade policies, Cuba and Argentina have maintained ties. The magnitude, however, of the 3 June trade agreement underscored the sense of regional unity that both Castro and Costa Méndez brought to Havana. In his comments at the conference, Argentina's foreign minister praised Cuba among other nations for its struggle for liberation.[60]

What was unusual about the treaty and the warm relations between Castro and Costa Méndez was not the trade agreement, since Cuba and Argentina had been strong trading allies for decades, but the strong show of support for Argentina by Castro's antifascist government and the strong support by Costa Méndez's anti-Communist government for Castro. Speaking to reporters, Castro stated that Havana has been a supporter of Argentina's claim to the islands for more than three decades and that he admired the "very clean and elegant way" that the islands were seized by Argentina.[61]

U.S. Reaction to Cuba and the Falklands/Malvinas

The U.S. reaction to Cuba's promotion of regional unity during the South Atlantic crisis was one of alarm. The Defense Department analyzed the damage that could come to U.S. interests in Latin America in a report prepared in late May 1982 but not published. The report recommended that the United States "broaden regional military-to-military contacts and seek active military cooperation of key countries, such as Argentina, Brazil, Chile, Mexico, Venezuela, and Colombia."[62] A U.S. official stated that the only benefits from the crisis would be reaped by the Cubans and the Soviets, referring to fears of East-West conflicts being renewed in the region. The Defense Department study went on to recommend that the United States increase military ties with nations of Central America and the Caribbean, including Panama, Honduras, Jamaica, and the Dominican Republic.

Cuba in the 1980s

In his brief statement to NAM Castro reiterated his call for regional unity. The conflict, he stated, was going to be "a lesson for all the Third World countries that no matter what their political and social systems, [they] are defending their sovereignty and territorial integrity."[63]

Signs of solidarity within Latin America began to increase in May. On 11 May, Aristides Royo, the president of Panama, sent a message to the U.N. secretary-general asking for a suspension of aggression against Argentina. In addition, Peru's Foreign Minister Javier Arias Stella stated in an interview that the Rio Treaty ought to be applied in this instance.[64] Calling for an emergency meeting of foreign ministers of Latin America, ex–Foreign Minister Simon Alberto Consalvi of Venezuela said that the seriousness of the situation demanded it.

On 2 June, Cuba denounced the United States for its support of England in the South Atlantic crisis and offered "all necessary help." In the Cuban government discussion led by Foreign Minister Isidoro Malmierca Peoli, criticism was heard about U.S. policy in the Middle East, Central America, and South America. Wayne Smith, the head of the U.S. Interest Section in Havana, who would resign one month later, walked out of the talks, labeling Malmierca's speech "unacceptable and insulting."[65] The meeting of the NAM nations in Havana (which forty-two foreign ministers attended) was called not for the South Atlantic crisis but as a meeting of the coordinating bureau to prepare for the meeting scheduled in Baghdad, Iraq in September. However, since Argentina requested the discussion, the program focused on the crisis. Malmierca accused both the United States and Britain of "typical colonial arrogance."[66]

Two months after the resolution of the crisis, the OAS Argentine Secretary-General Alejandro Orfila would send a signal of openmindedness to Havana. Speaking to a New York audience, he argued that subversion from outside continued to menace the democracies of the region, obliquely referring to Soviet aid. When asked about Cuba's membership in the organization, he replied, "Cuba was never asked to leave the OAS; it was merely suspended."[67] He said that the thirty-one members could vote tomorrow to reinstate Cuba, and then it would be Havana's choice.

Although Argentina enjoyed strong trade relations with Cuba before the crisis, the two nations' political philosophies remained markedly different. With these contradictions so apparent, political tensions and public pronouncements of distrust insured that a comfortable distance would exist between Buenos Aires and Havana. Only weeks before the crisis erupted, the Cuban government referred to the Argentine military junta as fascist. As the crisis was nearing an end, a *New York Times* editorial wrote of the NAM meeting in Havana regarding the crisis: "Fidel Castro can finally throw away that tiresome tract about how the OAS is only a rubber stamp for Yankee Imperialism." Cuba, the editorial continues, "sees in the Falkland conflict a way to end its regional isolation—even if that requires embracing the generals who made thousands of revolutionaries 'disappear.' "[68] That relationship changed when Nicanor Costa Méndez (who would resign soon after the crisis) traveled to Havana. That trip cost Costa Méndez a great deal, Orfila argued, but NAM carried great weight, and it was the only diplomatic option left to Argentina. According to Argentina diplomats, the purpose was not to embrace Castro but to seek support of NAM.

Cuba's Latin American Regionalism

Cuba's perception of Latin America and the Caribbean in the 1980s was articulated in a speech given in April 1982 by Jesus Montane Oropesa, head of the Central Department of Foreign Relations of the Central Committee of the Communist party and member of the Secretariat. In a speech at the opening of the International Theoretical Conference in the International Conference Center, he argued that among the first areas of interest in the liberation of nations in Latin America one must look at the case of Puerto Rico, "a Latin American and Caribbean nation because of its historic roots, language and cultures . . . now threatened with annexation by the United States." The speech also reflected the fact that Havana's analysis is that the present crisis in Latin America and the Caribbean is not merely economic but political, "encompassing all spheres of society."

The South Atlantic crisis had a profound impact on inter-American relations but did not cause irreparable damage to relations with nations in the hemisphere and the United States as many diplomats initially feared. Instead, it opened many bilateral relationships of nations within Latin America which had been closed for decades, and it rekindled old friendships. However, Cuba now presents a very different challenge to governments in the region than it did in 1959 and 1960 when it invaded Nicaragua, the Dominican Republic, and Panama. U.S. Ambassador Diego Asencio argued:

> When [the Panamanians] led a group of Cubans and they got lost in the jungle, it was "comic opera" style. They (the government of Panama) had to go and find them. It was a "Three Stooges" operation. But they have become more sophisticated since then, along with their societies.[69]

In May 1982 Argentine economist Raúl Prebisch, founder of Economic Commission for Latin America (ECLA), met with Fidel Castro and Carlos Rafael Rodríguez in Havana. Dr. Prebisch was in Cuba at a conference of the National Association of Economists of Cuba (ANEC) to commemorate Mexican economist Juan Noyala who was active in Cuban politics.[70] Prebisch pointed to two factors today that diminished the interest in global talks. The first was that the developed countries have never seen the need to change the international economic order. The second was that the international recession would influence these countries to take an unfavorable stand on global talks. When he addressed the problems of trade, Prebisch recommended continued trade with the Soviet Union, which, he said, would prove fruitful for Cuba.

In 1982, twenty years after Cuba's initial foreign policies of armed struggle, Cuban government officials were openly speaking again of the need for armed struggle in Latin America. Manuel Piñeiro, a member of the Communist party Central Committee, stated:

> In those countries where the extreme right rules, using forms of armed fighting . . . it is a virtually inescapable imperative.[71]

Piñeiro's advice is particularly telling in light of the fact that he is the head of the Americas Department of the Communist party Central Committee. His comments were made in Havana at a conference of Latin American left-wing groups.

The idea of a Latin American regional organization did not begin either with the theories of Castro, as articulated by Régis Debray, or with the Argentine generals in 1982. In fact, a probable reason for the popularity of the concept of unity was the region's history: Simón Bolívar (between 1815 and 1830) strongly advocated a league of states of Hispanic nations that would serve several purposes: arbitrate disputes, provide military cooperation in defense of South America, and negotiate with England, aims similar to those articulated by Latin American and Cuban diplomats during the dispute a century and a half later.[72]

Many regional policymakers point to Cuba's role in the South Atlantic crisis as the reemergence, and most significantly, the acceptance, of Cuba in Western Hemisphere diplomatic circles. Particularly with South America's social democratic governments—in Brazil, Uruguay, and Argentina—relations with Cuba began to improve as they did with Ecuador two years after the crisis.

Notes

1. U.S., Congress, Senate, Committee on Foreign Relations, Subcommittee on American Republics Affairs, report by David D. Burks, "Insurgency in Latin America," 91st Cong., 1st sess., 29 April 1969, p. 207.

2. Presentation by Ambassador Ambler H. Moss at the Center for Inter-American Relations, New York, 2 October 1980.

3. Robert Armstrong and Janet Shenk, *El Salvador: The Face of Revolution* (Boston, Mass.: South End Press, 1982).

4. Lawrence R. Simon and James C. Stephens, Jr., *El Salvador Land Reform 1980–1981: Impact Audit* (Boston, Mass.: Oxfam America, March 1981). See also Armstrong and Shenk, *El Salvador*, pp. 5–7.

5. U.S. Congress, Committee on Foreign Relations, Subcommittee on American Republics Affairs, *Survey of the Alliance for Progress*, 91st Cong., 1st sess., 29 April 1969, pp. 148–162.

6. Ibid., p. 856.

7. See Walter LaFeber, "The Burdens of the Past," in *Central America: Anatomy of Conflict*. Edited by Robert S. Leiken. New York: Pergamon Press/Carnegie Endowment for International Peace, 1984.

8. Alan Riding, "The Cross and the Sword in Latin America," *New York Review of Books*, 28 May 1981, pp. 3–8.

9. Foreign Policy Association, "El Salvador and the United States," edited by Nancy Hoepli (New York: Foreign Policy Association, 1981), p. 3.

10. Ambassador Deane Hinton, unpublished airgram memorandum to U.S. Department of State from the U.S. Embassy in San Salvador, "A Statistical Framework for Understanding Violence in El Salvador," 15 January 1982.

11. Raymond Bonner, "In Salvador, The Unmaking of an Oligarch," *New York Times*, 14 December 1980, p. 2E. See also Raymond Bonner, *Weakness and Deceit: United States Policy and El Salvador* (New York: Times Books, 1984).

12. Interview by the author with Enrique Alvarez Córdova, New York, Center for Inter-American Relations, 28 July 1980, and with Guillermo Manuel Ungo Revelo, New York, 9 October 1980.

13. Foreign Policy Association, "El Salvador," op. cit., p. 4.

14. Alexander M. Haig, Jr., *Caveat: Realism, Reagan and Foreign Policy*. New York: MacMillan Publishing Co., 1984, pp. 138–140; Jonathan Kwitney, "Tarnished Report?" *Wall Street Journal*, 8 June 1981, p. 14; James Petras, *Nation*, 28 March 1981, p. 9.

15. Briefing by Secretary of State Alexander Haig to representatives of NATO, Austria, New Zealand, Japan, and Spain, *New York Times*, 21 February 1981, p. A6. "With Cuban coordination," Haig argued, "the Soviet bloc, Vietnam, Ethiopia and radical Arabs are furnishing at least several hundred tons of military equipment to the Salvadoran leftist insurgents." As the *New York Times* printed it, Haig stated, "Off the record, I wish to assure you we do not intend to have another Vietnam and engage ourselves in another bloody conflict where the source rests outside the target area."

16. Viron P. Vaky, former assistant secretary of state, in testimony before the Subcommittee on Inter-American Affairs, Committee on Foreign Affairs, U.S. House, 11 September 1979.

17. Michael D. Barnes, chairman, Subcommittee on Inter-American Affairs, U.S., House, "The United States and Central America," before the National Committee on American Foreign Policy, 19 April 1982.

18. Ibid.

19. William J. Casey, Director of Central Intelligence, letter to the editor, *New York Times*, 30 July 1982, p. 24A.

20. Robert E. White, "Central America," *New York Times*, 18 July 1982, p. 22.

21. Presentation by U.S. Deputy Secretary of Defense Frank C. Carlucci at Washington Conference of the Council of the Americas, 21 June 1982.

22. Interview by the author with Dr. Carlos Rafael Rodríguez, Republic of Cuba, 17 July 1982, New York City.

23. U.S., Department of State, *Communist Interference in El Salvador*, Report no. 80, 23 February 1981; see also Thomas O. Enders, assistant secretary for Inter-American Affairs, before the Subcommittee on Security and Terrorism of the Senate Committee on the Judiciary, 12 March 1982; U.S., Department of State, *Cuba's Support for Terrorism in the Western Hemisphere*, Current Policy no. 376; and Luigi Einandi, presentation at the Center for Inter-American Relations, 6 January 1981. U.S., Department of State, *Cuba's Renewed Support for Violence in Latin America*, Special Report no. 90, 14 December 1981, p. 7.

24. Jon Glassman, presentation to the Center for Inter-American Relations, New York, 20 May 1981.

25. U.S., Department of State, *Cuba's Renewed Support for Violence in Latin America*, Special Report no. 90, 14 December 1981, p. 7.

26. Fidel Castro at the Sixty-eighth Inter-Parliamentary Conference, Havana, Cuba, 15 September 1981 (Havana: Editora Politica, 1981).

27. H.E. Isidoro Malmierca Peoli, statement to the General Debate of the Thirty-sixth Session of the U.N. General Assembly, 24 September 1981.

28. *El Pais* (Madrid), 7 April 1982, Foreign Bureau Information Service.

29. Interview by the author with Dr. Carlos Rafael Rodríguez.

30. *New York Times*, 11 July 1982, p. 3.

31. Ibid., 31 July 1982, p. 11.
32. *New York Times*, 13 August 1981, p. A3.
33. Ibid.
34. Telephone interview by the author with Ambassador Diego Asencio, U.S. Department of State, 30 July 1982.
35. Ibid.
36. *New York Times*, 13 August 1981, p. A3.
37. U.S., Department of State, Special Report no. 90, p. 11.
38. Interview with Asencio.
39. *New York Times*, 13 August 1981, p. A3.
40. Ibid., 18 August 1981, p. A4.
41. Interview by the author with Asencio.
42. Ibid.
43. *Carisol Newswork* (Bogota), 3 March 1982, cited in *Foreign Bureau Information Service*.
44. Ibid.
45. Fidel Castro in an interview with Barbara Walters of ABC, 20 May 1977, Havana.
46. Interview by the author with Rubén Berríos Martínez, New York, 3 April 1982.
47. U.S., Central Intelligence Agency, *National Intelligence Daily*, 19 June 1975, cited in *Miami Herald*, 6 August 1980, pp. 1E-2E.
48. Declaration of the government of Cuba on the crisis in the Malvinas. Issued in Havana, 2 May 1982. Distributed by *Prensa Latina* by International Telex.
49. For a thorough discussion of the Malvinas Island crisis, see *Latin America Regional Reports*, Southern Cone, 9 April 1982, pp. 1, 6, 7; *Latin American Weekly Report* (London), 30 April 1982, p. 1; *Time*, 10 May 1982, pp. 18-28; *Newsweek*, 10 May 1982, pp. 28-37; interview with Alexander Haig, "The High Stakes for US in the Falklands," *U.S. News and World Report*, 10 May 1982, pp. 26-28. The crisis itself in April 1982 brought to the fore several issues lurking in Latin American politics which Cuba sought to exploit. The first was an issue of territorial sovereignty. There were several nations within Latin America which had territorial battles either with neighboring nations of Latin America or with Europe. The position many of these nations took, although apparently reflecting unity, also revealed domestic concerns of their own territorial disputes. There were several nations at that time that were involved in disputes: Gibraltar, the point in southernmost Spain, remained a British dependency claimed by Spain since its seizure in 1704; Guyana and Venezuela also continued to fight over the Essequibo region, where oil had recently been discovered, and the Port of Spain Protocol regarding the territorial dispute was set to expire in two months. A third territorial debate which was continuing at that time concerned the area of Belize, recently independent from Britain, still claimed by Guatemala, and protected by British troops. In addition, the Beagle Channel, the islands south of Chile's Tierra del Fuego, had been claimed both by Argentina and Chile. Argentina's strong stand in the Falkland/Malvinas Islands laid the groundwork for a possible claim by Argentina to the Beagle Channel. Finally, Spain withdrew from the Western Sahara, the former Moroccan colony, which is now claimed both by the government of Morocco and a guerrilla force backed by Algeria. The strength of regional unity was reflected most strongly in the vote by the OAS in May: 17 to 0 to recognize Argentina's sovereignty; the vote (Chile, Colombia, the United States, and Trinidad and Tobago abstained) passed a resolution supporting sovereignty of Argentina in the Falklands. It did, however, qualify the vote with insistence on the application

of the United Nations' Security Council resolution no. 502 which states: Troops must withdraw from the Islands and a negotiated settlement be passed." In the process of negotiations several proposals were made—by the United Nations' Secretary-General Javier Perez de Cuellar, by the Irish Government, and by the Peruvian Government.

The United States attempted to propose a compromise settlement—a plan rejected by Buenos Aires. On 29 April 1982 the U.S. House of Representatives passed a resolution expressing "full diplomatic support for Great Britain in its effort to uphold the rule of law." On 30 April, the U.S. Senate approved a resolution declaring that the United States "cannot stand neutral." Reluctantly, the United States decided to back Great Britain openly. Argentina, disheartened by U.S. support of Britain, began to look toward NAM during the days of the dispute. In a closed-door session of the group on 5 May in New York, the United States was denounced by the Argentine delegation (*New York Times*, 6 May 1982, p. 17). Eduardo Roca, the Argentine delegate to the United Nations, stated that "the United States is now helping the colonialist aggressor." Although Cuba was playing a minor role in the dispute, the crisis gave Cuba a platform for agreeing with the rest of Latin America on an issue perceived as central to regional nationalism.

50. *New York Times*, 6 May 1982, p. 17. Cited from interview in *Le Monde* (Paris), 5 May 1982, p. 3.

51. Communique adopted by the Coordinating Bureau of NAM, 5 May 1982. Issued by the Permanent Mission of Cuba to the United Nations, New York City.

52. Declaration by Cuba on the crisis in the Malvinas Islands. *Prensa Latina*, 2 May 1982, released by International Telex, New York. Translation by the author.

53. The statement of NAM conformed to the August 1975 declaration of the Conference of Ministers of Foreign Affairs held in Lima, Peru (paragraph 87).

> The non-aligned countries, without prejudice to ratifying the validity of the principle of self-determination as a general principle for other territories, strongly support in the special and particular case of the Malvinas Islands, the just claims of the Argentine Republic and urge the United Kingdom to actively continue the negotiations recommended by the United Nations in order to restore the said territory to Argentine sovereignty, and thus put an end to that illegal situation which still persists in the southern part of the American continent.

Communique issued by the NAM coordinating bureau, distributed by the Cuban Mission to the United Nations.

54. Declaration of the government of Cuba on the crisis in the Malvinas. Issued in Havana, 2 May 1982. Distributed by *Prensa Latina* by International Telex.

55. Ibid.

56. *Granma* (Havana), 9 May 1982.

57. *Latin American Weekly Report* (London), 9 April 1982, p. 1.

58. See James Nelson Goodsell, "Why Cuba Can't Break Loose from Soviet Aid, Influence," *Christian Science Monitor*, 10 May 1982, pp. 1, 12.

59. Harold Eugene David, John J. Finan, and F. Taylor Peck, eds., *Latin American Diplomatic History* (Baton Rouge, La.: Louisiana State University, 1977), p. 251.

60. *New York Times*, 5 June 1982, p. A5.

61. Ibid.

62. Richard Halloran, "U.S. Officials Fear a Prolonged War," *New York Times*, 5 June 1982, p. A5.

63. Statement by Fidel Castro to the heads of state of Non-Aligned Movement, June 1981. Distributed by the Cuban Mission to the United Nations.

64. *Granma* (Havana), 23 May 1982.

65. *New York Times*, 3 June 1982, p. A14.

66. Statement of Isidoro Malmierca Peoli, minister of external relations, Republic of Cuba, to the United Nations, General Assembly, Thirty-sixth Sess., 24 September 1981.

67. Statement by Alejandro Orfila, former secretary-general of the OAS at the Foreign Policy Association, New York, 2 August 1982.

68. *New York Times*, 3 June 1982, p. 22.

69. Interview by the author with Ambassador Diego Asencio, U.S., Department of State, 30 July 1982. (Former U.S. Ambassador to Colombia, Asencio was assigned to the State Department's Department of Consular Affairs after the hostage crisis, and became U.S. Ambassador to Brazil in 1983.)

70. *Granma* (Havana), 23 May 1982.

71. Manuel Piñeiro, from *Prensa Latina*, cited in *Miami Herald*, 29 April 1982, p. 17.

72. Harold A. Bierck, Jr., ed., *Selected Writings of Bolivar*, vol. 1 (New York: The Colonial Press, 1951).

Part III
Cuba's New Frontier: African Assistance Programs

Cuban and Angolan troops, members of the MPLA, in a weapons practice session at the training center of St. Vincente, near Cabinda, Angola, 1976.

5
Cuba's African Assistance Programs

Cuba's African policies in the 1970s—particularly toward Angola and Ethiopia—signalled the commencement of an era of active international involvement for Cuba. Although Cuba had had a policy of providing support to Africa since the early years of the revolution, including aid to Algeria in 1963 and Zanzibar in 1964, the assistance programs of the 1970s represented a marked escalation.

Cuba was frustrated by the minimal gains achieved in the 1970s through a program of slow and steady diplomacy. Africa presented a new opportunity. It was an area of the world that had been exploited and colonized for several decades. In addition, there was little likelihood that the United States would retaliate for Cuban initiatives since Africa was not considered to be in an Eastern or Western sphere of influence. Africa also offered future economic opportunities.

By the end of 1977, Cuba had more than twenty thousand troops in Angola. At the height of Cuba's involvement, more than thirty-five thousand troops were stationed throughout Africa. Cuba's foreign assistance policy had changed dramatically. The Cuban leadership's commitment to *internationalist solidarity* had remained firm as had its decision to aid developing African nations on the road to independence. However, Cuba's economic and military assistance program to Africa took on greater proportions, the consequences of which the Cuban government itself probably did not foresee.

To understand Cuban foreign policy in Africa it is helpful to examine Cuba's assistance programs to the socialist regimes of Dr. Antônio Agostinho Neto in Angola since 1975, and to Lieutenant Colonel Mengistu Haile Mariam in Ethiopia since 1977. These policies contrasted both ideologically and strategically with each other, and their overall costs were dramatically different.

Angola, 1974 to 1976: Operation Carlota

History of the Conflict

African nationalist sentiment in Angola culminated in the Angolan Civil War of 1975–76. Independence sentiment had begun to develop soon after World War II and was reinvigorated by the demise of Portuguese colonial rule. In 1961 the colonial government of Antônio de Oliveira Salazar had opened Angola's economy to foreign investment. The Portuguese government began to show signs of the strain of financing the fight against African liberation movements. By the early 1960s, key portions of the economy were controlled by Belgian, British, U.S., and South African monopolies, most noticeably in the oil industry.[1] Wars of independence were waged by three separate African factions during the early 1960s against Portuguese rule and foreign investment.

In April 1974 a significant blow was felt by the Portuguese leadership when a military coup by the Armed Forces Movement ousted Antônio de Oliveira Salazar's successor, Marcello Caetano, in Lisbon, Portugal. In early 1975 the new Portuguese leadership signed an agreement that transferred power to a transitional government composed of three political parties that had serious ideological divisions. Each party quickly sought and obtained significant amounts of economic and military assistance from different foreign governments. The three political parties had grown out of factions loosely divided along tribal and ethnic lines, and they reflected language, cultural, and political differences. In the 1950s and 1960s, they evolved into the Popular Movement for the Liberation of Angola (MPLA), mainly of Mbundu and small urban groups; the National Front for the Liberation of Angola (FNLA), mainly Bakongo; and the National Union for the Total Independence of Angola (UNITA), which was made up of the Ovimbundu population.

During the 1950s and 1960s, the MPLA (the party that had Cuban support and was the only legal party recognized by the government of Angola in 1979) was the weakest of the three factions in terms of both military strength and popular support. Its popularity grew in the 1960s from a small group of mestizos and urban intellectuals in Luanda who were politically active.[2] The party's organizational strength was a contributing factor in its ultimate consolidation as Angola's leading revolutionary party.

The MPLA declared its intentions officially in December 1956 when the leaders circulated a manifesto that stated the doctrine that held the rival factions together until the fall of the Salazar regime. The manifesto announced the formation of a coalition government united by a single goal—the overthrow of Portuguese colonialism. The MPLA would fight for an independent Marxist Angola, governed by a democratic and popular government of the working people, "irrespective of racial distinction, social origin, religious belief and the individual make-up."[3]

The FNLA was the outgrowth of the Angolan People's Union founded in 1954 by Holden Roberto. Supported strongly by Zaire, Roberto and the FNLA party gained the support of several Western sources and forged a strong revolutionary party in the early 1970s.[4] UNITA was founded in 1966 by Dr. Jonas Savimbi, who shifted from an early socialist orientation to an emphasis on Western ideas. As the leader of the numerically largest faction in Angola, he attempted to bring foreign investors to Angola. Like the FNLA, UNITA sought and gained the support of a neighboring African country, Zambia. The driving force behind all three factions was the goal of overthrowing Portuguese colonial rule, specifically that of Antônio de Oliveira Salazar. The fifteen years between the first major protest in Luanda in February 1961 and the beginning of the civil war among the three major factions witnessed a dramatic increase in the amount of foreign investment in the nation and foreign assistance to the warring factions that fueled the conflicts. The levels of foreign assistance are of paramount political importance in the Angolan conflict. Certain foreign actions, no doubt, sparked action and reaction.

Timing is important for an accurate understanding of the Angolan civil war. Different chronologies paint radically differing pictures of the conflict. Regardless, by the climax of the fighting in early 1976, all three factions in the civil conflict were receiving outside funding: the MPLA, from Cuba and the Soviet Union; the FNLA, from Zaire, China, and the United States; and UNITA, from the United States and China. While China discontinued most of its support after 1974, the United States, the Soviet Union, and Cuba continue to have deep stakes in the fighting. U.S. resistance to involvement in the civil war in Angola in the 1960s was based principally on strong agreements with the Portuguese colonial government. President Richard Nixon, in 1971, effective retroactively to 1969, had signed an executive agreement with Portugal that exchanged U.S. use of the Azores for the authorization of a U.S. Export-Import Bank credit/loan to Portugal for $436 million.[5] By 1974, foreign involvement in the internal affairs of Angola included military assistance and troops and mercenaries from the United States, Spain, Belgium, Cuba, China, South Africa, and the Soviet Union. Reflecting the international concern for the conflict, various United Nations pronouncements assessed the war and made suggestions for its resolution.

Cuban Involvement

Cuban identification with the plight of the Angolan MPLA dates to the mid-1960s. Cuba's earliest assistance occurred in Cuba when several MPLA officers studied guerrilla tactics in Havana. Cuba escalated its assistance in response to the heavy civil conflicts between 1974 and 1976.[6] As 1975 began, Portugal's new government met with the three factions (MPLA, UNITA, and FNLA). After the fall of the Caetano regime, Portugal had little interest in spending resources and effort on a civil war so far from home. On 10 January, in Alvor, Portugal, the Portuguese commitment was formalized. The agreement was signed, setting the date of 10 November—ten months from the time of the signing of the agreement—to give the Portuguese colony its independence and calling for an immediate ceasefire by all forces.

The fighting began long before Angola ever reached its formal day of independence. The declarations made by each of the factions after Independence Day, however, had been scheduled in advance. On 11 November, the MPLA declared the independence of the People's Republic of Angola. Two weeks later, on 23 November, UNITA and the FNLA declared the independence of the Democratic People's Republic of Angola.

In addition, the Alvor Agreement established a tripartite transitional government to govern alongside a Portuguese high commissioner. The leaders of the three guerrilla factions would, according to the agreement, constitute a Presidential Council, whose leadership was controlled by each of the three leaders on a rotating basis.[7]

By March 1975 the first signs of dissension were visible. Reportedly, Soviet aircraft landed in the People's Republic of the Congo to bring arms to the MPLA, which later fought and won access to the port of Luanda.[8] Within months increasing numbers of Angolan medical doctors and technical experts of Portuguese descent began leaving Angola. Approximately eighty-five thousand refugees a month fled during August, September, and October.[9] On 22 August, UNITA formally declared war on the MPLA, and in September the Portuguese government recognized the suspension of the Alvor Agreement and announced the withdrawal of all troops by 11 November 1975.

According to John Stockwell, the former chief of the CIA Angola Task Force, the National Security Council established the "Forty Committee" to aid sympathetic rebel groups in Angola.[10] Stockwell's chronology alleges that the United States helped the FNLA and UNITA to violate the Alvor agreements with massive infusions of CIA funds to both the FNLA and UNITA. During the course of Congressional hearings called by U.S. Senator Dick Clark, the CIA reported to have spent over $31 million in military equipment and related assistance to the FNLA and UNITA in order to defeat the MPLA. The Forty Committee allocated $300,000 to Holden Roberto individually for political action, according to reports.[11]

During 1973 and 1974, the Chinese began to fund both the FNLA and UNITA, sending advisors to Zaire in May 1974 and arms to the FNLA. Washington's initial aid in July 1974 to Holden Roberto was formally approved in January 1975 by the newly formed Forty Committee—only ten days after the signing of the Alvor Agreement. By mid-year the committee had stepped up its support to $14 million for the two rebel factions combined.

In 1984–85, while over 15,000 Cuban troops remained, UNITA, the principal remaining force in Angola, continued rebel attacks. What began as a foreign program expected to last a few years after the victory of the MPLA had turned into a permanent assistance program, a thorn in the side of continued negotiations regarding Namibia's independence. By some accounts, the United States violated the promise of the agreements by deploying massive arms and advisors to both the FNLA and to UNITA in March 1975, and both the Soviet Union and the Cubans responded. Washington argues that it responded to the increase in Soviet aid in May and April. Most important, Peking, Moscow, Washington, and Havana focused on the strategic and economic importance of Southern Africa. Economically and strategically, U.S. interests were great in Angola. Economically, in addition to the U.S. oil refineries in Cabinda, mineral wealth in Angola is substantial. "Both Angola and Mozambique secure the strategic flanks of South Africa," according to David M. Abshire, current Ambassador to NATO, writing of the 1960s, "the wealthiest and most powerful area in Africa." It had been the importance of the Azores and the access to the West Indian Ocean and the South Atlantic that reinforced U.S. close ties to the Portuguese colonial governments of Salazar and Caetano.[12]

The Cuban Decision to Send Troops

According to Fidel Castro, the decision to send Cuban troops to help the MPLA came in November 1975 after five thousand South African troops intervened in the conflict on October 23 by entering Angola from its Namibian border. Whether this invasion, named Operation Zulu, was the first occasion for the MPLA leader Dr. Antônio Agostinho Neto to request Cuban help is in dispute. During the previous May, Neto had met with Cuban military officer Flavio Bravo in Brazzaville to request that the Cubans increase the shipment of arms, military aid, and training officers. On 16 July 1975, a request for additional aid was issued by the MPLA.[13] In August South African troops had entered Angola for the purpose of protecting a hydroelectric plant that was being threatened by guerrillas, and in August 1975 a delegation of Cuban civilians led by Raúl Díaz Arguellas arrived in Luanda.[14]

Curiously, the *Vietnam Heróica*, one of three Cuban supply ships to embark on the military assistance program to Angola, had departed from Cuba in September 1975. According to eyewitness reports, the first Cuban ship arrived at Punta Negra, Angola, with five hundred to six hundred Cubans aboard.[15] Soon after, two additional supply ships, the *Coral Island* and the *La Plata*, arrived in Angola carrying vehicles and medical supplies.[16] In October the first contingent of Cuban combat troops arrived. Evidence to suggest that significant numbers of Cuban troops landed before the October 23 invasion is not conclusive. Three accounts of Cuban involvement before October, however, include a statement by a Cuban prisoner (of the FNLA) that troops had come from the Congo in August 1975, a statement by FNLA sources that fifty Cubans had arrived in Brazzaville (the Congo) in July, and a UNITA statement that the first Cubans were seen in the middle of August 1975. None of the testimonials are from disinterested sources. U.S. government accounts of the incident refer to September 1975 as the date of first arrival of Cuban combat troops.[17]

Cuban government officials do acknowledge that several hundred military advisers were stationed in Angola at the time of the South African invasion of October 1975. These advisers were sent to serve emergency combat duty but were not originally sent on a combat mission, according to Oscar Oramas Oliva, director of Subsaharan Africa policy at the Ministry of Foreign Relations (MINREX), who served as the Cuban ambassador to Angola and was in Luanda at the time of the invasion.[18] One indication of the possibility of Cuban military presence in Angola prior to 23 October was the statement of a Cuban prisoner at a UNITA press conference who said that he and thirty-two other Cubans had flown to Angola in August 1975.[19] By all accounts, Cuba was not a reluctant intervenor: Castro was ready to extend his military support to distant shores.

Military training in Angola itself had been visible for some time, and a report indicated that the MPLA military force received formal military instruction, including political and military training, at least four hours a day.[20] In October 1975 the full complement of troops of the Cuban Expeditionary Force began to arrive in Angola. According to Gabriel García Marquéz, the Cuban military mission, called Operation Carlota, was named after a black slave killed in a rebellion in 1843. November was the month of the heaviest fighting, and on 5 November, airborne UNITA and FNLA troops met MPLA and Cuban troops at the Bengula port, and the first Cuban prisoners were taken.[21] The largest clash of the civil war was fought directly between Cuban and South African troops on 9 December 1975. The Bridge Fourteen battle had high costs. Approximately two hundred Cubans and two hundred MPLA soldiers died in three days.[22]

In December 1975 Cuba and the MPLA signed a treaty of assistance for Cuban aid in education, agriculture, and transportation. At that time, four hundred Cuban combat troops were arriving weekly in Angola. By January the number of soldiers had increased to one thousand per week.[23] The MPLA, aided by an experienced Cuban team, including Cuba's ambassador in Angola, Oscar Oramas Oliva, who was stationed in Luanda, Angola in 1976 and had extensive African experience, was beginning to take key cities. By February 1976 Cuba's combat troops assisting the MPLA totalled fifteen thousand.[24]

Between the arrival of the first Cuban combat troops in October 1975 and the conclusion of the conflict, approximately twenty thousand Cuban soldiers had been deployed.[25] Most analysts agree that this massive deployment of Cuban troops was critical to the victory by the MPLA. Neither the FNLA nor UNITA received foreign assistance in levels that matched Cuba's assistance to the MPLA.[26]

In February 1976 the Organization of African Unity recognized the MPLA as the government of Angola, and by November the MPLA had captured twelve of sixteen provincial capitals. When the Portuguese government left the capital of Luanda on 11 November, the MPLA proclaimed itself the only official authority in Angola: it had already received recognition by many countries.[27] The future of MPLA rule in Angola was not questioned when Angola's first president, Antônio Agostinho Neto, died in September 1979. His successor, José Eduardo dos Santos, however, is likely to attempt a settlement with the rival factions, according to Jonas Savimbi, head of UNITA. Dos Santos, former minister of planning in the Council of Ministers of the Neto government, visited the Soviet Union in January 1980 to sign a bilateral cooperation agreement. The Angolan-Soviet communique called for strong ties between the two nations.[28]

Involvement since 1976

Since the end of the Angolan Civil War, the MPLA has remained the only party recognized by the de facto government of Mengistu. Between 1975 and 1977, Angola's gross domestic product (GDP) and growth rate decreased by 15 percent, mainly as a result of the crop damage incurred during the first two years of civil war, although the Neto government had inherited a national budget surplus of $740 million in 1975.[29]

Cuban troops remained in Angola in 1979 to 1985. Castro stated that Cuban troops would be removed from Angola when the MPLA is able to control Angola with its own force.[30] Cuba offers three principal reasons to explain the continuing Cuban presence: (1) Angola's organizational problems, that is, a lack of trained personnel in middle- and low-level positions of the MPLA have hindered the installation of a progressive government; (2) lack of training in the use of sophisticated military equipment; (3) continued guerrilla opposition by the FNLA and UNITA; and (4) South African invasions.

As of 1982 both UNITA and FNLA continue to seek a government of national unity and claim that the dos Santos government like that of Neto constitutes a foreign-dominated minority faction and does not represent popular participation. Tribal affiliations remain strong. Jonas Savimbi and his UNITA forces have maintained their strong support among the Ovimbundu population which continues to oppose the MPLA government. The FNLA has kept the support of the Bakongo people. Both factions periodically wage guerrilla attacks against the MPLA which, according to Fidel Castro, is another reason why Cuba keeps troops in Angola.

In March 1976 Cuban troops began to leave Angola. Approximately two hundred Cuban soldiers were scheduled to leave weekly until early 1977 when twelve thousand troops would remain.[31] For several reasons Cuban troop withdrawal was halted. First, guerrilla attacks by the FNLA and UNITA continued. Both factions were supported by arms from Western and South African sources. Second, an invasion in Zaire in early 1977 caused suspicion among Angola's neighbors. This created a renewed security problem in Angola.[32]

In 1977 as Cuban troops continued to withdraw from Angola, a small group of MPLA soldiers led by MPLA officer Nito Alves unsuccessfully attempted to overthrow Antônio Agostinho Neto. Since Alves was himself considered pro-Soviet, there was speculation that the Soviet Union, which had continuous disputes with Neto, might want to establish a more Moscow-oriented government. Although the event may have produced a degree of tension between Havana and Moscow, the allegations of Soviet aid were never substantiated. But as a result, in June 1977 Cuban troops were increased to twenty-five to thirty thousand and have remained at that level.[33]

Cuba's large-scale military policy in Africa, beginning in 1975 in Angola, had thrust Cuba's foreign policy into a larger military scale than had been undertaken during the 1960s. As a military program, Cuba's policy in Angola exemplified the high risks that Cuba would run in the 1970s. Cuba's policy in Africa was successful on several fronts: its rapid response to an invasion of Angola brought Third World support; it gave Cuba added credibility for supporting socialist movements; and most important, it gave Cuba access to Africa, a continent of potentially strong allies.

By 1982 Cuba's programs in Angola had become expensive politically and economically. Repeating the commitment made by the Angolan foreign minister in May 1981, Cuba and Angola signed a joint communique in February 1982, expressing the intention that Cuban troops will be withdrawn from Angola "as soon as all signs of possible invasion have ceased." Several conditions were made. The Angolans asked Cuban troops to leave if South African troops would withdraw at least to the border between South Africa and Namibia, drawn usually as the Orange River. Other conditions were the establishment of a SWAPO (South West Africa People's Organization) government in Namibia and a guarantee of an end to South African invasions of Southern Angola.

As the 1980s began, according to U.S. government sources, Cuba had twenty thousand troops in Angola, fifteen thousand in Ethiopia, and a total of one thousand military advisers throughout the Congo, Guinea-Bissau, Mozambique, and Namibia. In addition to military forces, Cuba provided scholarships and technical advice: more than ten thousand students study in Cuba from Angola, Ethiopia, and several other nations in Africa, at a school located in the Isle of Youth. In addition, approximately six thousand five hundred technical advisers are in Angola.

Angola continued to be a popular issue for Cuba among the nations of NAM in the 1980s. In testimony before the General Debate of the United Nations' General Assembly, thirty-sixth session, Cuba's Minister of External Relations Isidoro Malmierca Peoli stated, "The aggression against Angola seeks to extend apartheid's frontiers. It is an aggression not only against Angola, but against the whole of black Africa, and especially against the countries of Southern Africa." In his statements of 24 September 1981, Cuba's minister of external relations argued that the purpose of Cuban troops was to protect against aggression from outside, when he stated:

> The visit of Under Secretary [William] Clark (of the United States) to South Africa and the meeting between [Ronald] Reagan and [P.W.] Botha (of South Africa) opened for them the possibilities of stepping up their military and subversive actions against the frontline states and particularly against Angola and Mozambique.[34]

Malmierca outlined the three areas of focus of Cuba's foreign policy: "[a]ssistance of those struggling against apartheid in South Africa . . . against Zionism in the Middle East . . . [and] against the dictatorships of Central America." In

Africa, he continued, there are several areas of concern. The first is the protection of the SWAPO government, the "sole and legitimate representative of the people of Namibia." Second, the goal of the Cuban government was to protect the Angolan and Mozambiquen troops against what Cuba has always considered an outside invasion. In Western Sahara, Cuba also stated its support for self-determination and independence. By the mid-1980s China's interest in the region had waned, and Portuguese aid to UNITA had increased.

Cuba's assistance to Angola was popular as long as it was framed as protection from outside aggression. Cuban troops in Angola appeared to take on an additional purpose: leverage in the negotiations for the independence of South-West Africa, or Namibia, which were hampered by a September 1985 South African invasion of Angola.

"The two questions are very closely interrelated," Chester Crocker, Reagan's assistant secretary of state for African affairs, argued in 1982. "Movement on one would make a decisive contribution to movement on the other."[35]

Notes

1. Oleg Ignatyev, *Secret Weapon in Africa*, trans. David Fidlon (Moscow: Progress Publishers, 1977), p. 20. Specific investments of foreign capital included: U.S. Gulf Oil ownership of the Cabinda oil fields, Belgian control of coffee production, and iron ore mining by West German Krupp. Under the Salazar government, approximately 12 percent of government assets were taken out of the country (ibid., p. 19).

2. Dr. Antônio Agostinho Neto gained prominence during this period as a poet in Luanda. Ernest Harsch and Tony Thomas, *Angola: The Hidden History of Washington's War*, Malik Miah, ed. (New York: Pathfinder Press, 1976), p. 26.

3. Ignatyev, *Secret Weapon*, p. 7. The MPLA was formed by a merger of the 1955 Communist party of Angola (PCA) and the African party of Angola (PLUA) in 1956. Harsch and Thomas, *Angola*, p. 26.

4. Zaire was a strong supporter of the FNLA. Some attribute this connection to the fact that President Mobutu Sese Seko of Zaire and Dr. Holden Roberto were brothers-in-law. Ian Greig, *The Communist Challenge to Africa: An Analysis of Contemporary Soviet, Chinese, and Cuban Policies* (London: Foreign Affairs Publishing Company, Ltd., 1977), p. 214. In addition, much has been written about Holden Roberto's possible connection to the U.S. Central Intelligence Agency. Ignatyev, *Secret Weapon*, pp. 23–82; Harsch and Thomas, *Angola*, pp. 21, 97.

5. *National Security Study Memorandum 39: The Kissinger Study of Southern Africa*. Edited and introduced by Mohamed A. El-Khawas and Barry Cohen. Original text of National Security Council Interdepartmental Group for Africa: Study in Response to National Security Study Memorandum 39: Southern Africa. August 15, 1969. Westport, Conn.: Lawrence Hill & Co., 1976, p. 47.

6. The circumstances and dates of the commencement of Cuban involvement in the Angolan conflict are debated at length, and there are as many dates given for the initial deployment of Cuban troops as there are analysts of the crisis. There is good reason for the debate. Different dates lead to different analyses of the Cuban government's motivations for

intervention. Certain dates question the veracity of testimony by Cuban leaders. Since the Cuban leadership explains Cuban intervention on the basis of the defense of Angola in the wake of a foreign attack, it would be significant if Cuban troops landed on Angolan soil before the attack took place.

7. This agreement also provided for a twelve-person ministry cabinet to be proportionately chosen from the factions, and the agreement was to be enforced by a joint militia of Portuguese and guerrilla troops. See Greig, *Communist Challenge*, pp. 211-236. Interview by the author with Oscar Oramas Oliva, director of sub-Saharan Africa policy at the Ministry of Foreign Relations, 24 January 1980. Oramas served as the Cuban ambassador to Angola and was in Luanda at the time of the invasion. He is also author of *Angola: ha nacido una nueva generación* (Havana, Cuba: Editorial de Ciencias Sociales, 1978).

8. Greig, *Communist Challenge*, p. 215.

9. Ibid., pp. 216-217.

10. John Stockwell, *In Search of Enemies: A CIA Story* (New York: W.W. Norton & Co., 1978). Also see Jonathan Kwitney, *Endless Enemies: The Making of an Unfriendly World* (New York: Congdon & Weed, 1984), pp. 132-151; Michael A. Samuels, et al., *Implications of Soviet and Cuban Activities in Africa for U.S. Policy* (Washington, D.C.: Georgetown University Center for Strategic and International Studies, 1979); Wayne Smith, unpublished manuscript, 1985.

11. El-Khawas, op. cit., pp. 183-186. Appendix A, "Extracts from the Presidentially Censored House Report on the CIA, January 19, 1976; John Stockwell, op. cit., pp. 183-186.

12. David M. Abshire, pp. 435-436, in *Portuguese Africa: A Handbook*. Edited by David M. Abshire and Michael A. Samuels (New York: Praeger Publishers, 1969). Cited in El-Khawas and Cohen, op. cit.

13. Gabriel García Márquez, "Operation Carlota: Cuba's Role in Angolan Victory," *Cuba Update*, no. 1 (April 1977), p. 2.

14. According to Cuba's delegate to the Afro-Asian People's Solidarity Conference in Luanda (Peralta). From the *Financial Times* (London), 4 February 1976, cited in Colin Legum and Tony Hodges, *After Angola: The War in Southern Africa* (London: Rex Collins, 1976), p. 18. Two months earlier, in June, a delegation of approximately 250 Cuban instructors had arrived, which may account for some of the confusion. See García Márquez, "Operation Carlota," p. 1. This Colombian writer was one of the first to document the Cuban role and was officially recognized by the Cuban government which released parts of the story to *Prensa Latina*, the Cuban news agency, before it was published.

15. According to Ian Greig, the *Vietnam Heróica*, a Cuban warship, arrived in Punta Negra with five to six hundred Cubans aboard in September. On 9 October, over two weeks before the South African invasion, four additional ships carrying three hundred Cubans arrived in Luanda. Three days later, another Cuban ship unloaded tanks, trucks, and crates. Greig, *Communist Challenge*, pp. 219-220. According to the García Márquez account, three Cuban ships arrived on 4, 7, and 11 October carrying 480 Cuban instructors, a medical brigade, and 115 unspecified vehicles.

16. Greig, *Communist Challenge*, pp. 219-220; U.S., Department of State, *Background Notes: Angola*, October 1976, p. 4.

17. U.S., Department of State, *Background Notes*, p. 4.

18. Interview by the author with Oscar Oramas Oliva, 24 January 1980, Havana.

19. Legum and Hodges, *After Angola*, p. 20. The statement by the Cuban prisoner was cited from AZAP (Kinsasha), 20 December 1975, and *Times* (London), 8 January 1975. Greig, *Communist Challenge*, p. 227. Still another account argues that in September 1975 Cuba committed its first combat troops which numbered one thousand, the largest overseas deployment by the Cuban Armed Forces. Edward González, "Complexities of Cuban Foreign Policy," *Problems of Communism*, 26, no. 6 (November-December 1977):1-15.

20. Sometimes the training was given by Cuba's Young Pioneers. Greig, *Communist Challenge*, p. 226.

21. Ibid., p. 235. The Cuban column was given the code name *Zulu* after succeeding in holding the important coastal city against more heavily armed South African FNLA/UNITA unit.

22. Ibid. *Foxbat* was the code name for the Cuban unit in this battle. Reports of the incident do not record casualties of South African troops.

23. William LeoGrande, "Cuban-Soviet Relations and Cuban Policy in Africa." (Paper prepared for presentation to the annual meeting of the International Studies Association, Toronto, Canada, 22-26 March 1979), p. 20.

24. Oscar Oramas Oliva had previously served in Guinea and Mali. Greig, *Communist Challenge*, p. 219.

25. In January 1976, two hundred Cuban troops entered Angola daily for over two weeks, and the total strength reached 10,500 troops. At this time the Cubans were heavily equipped with Soviet artillery. The most comprehensive cataloguing included: one hundred 122mm rocket projector lorries, or Stalin Organs; twelve thousand single barreled 122mm rocket projectors; thirty thousand rifles; four hundred 60mm mortars; three thousand heavy machine guns; one thousand four hundred grenades and antitank grenade launchers; 82mm and 76mm recoiless rifles; one thousand 82mm mortars and antitank and antipersonnel mines. U.S. Pentagon, cited in ibid., p. 229.

26. LeoGrande points to the fact that the U.S. Congress prohibited further aid to South African troops, and they were forced to retreat. LeoGrande, "Cuban-Soviet Relations," p. 20.

27. Ibid.

28. *Granma Weekly Review*, 6 January 1980, p. 6.

29. GDP in 1977 was $2.8 billion. U.S. Central Intelligence Agency, *National Basic Intelligence Handbook* (Washington, D.C.: Government Printing Office, July 1978).

30. In 1979, 791,000 Angolans out of a population of 6.5 million were considered fit for military service.

31. LeoGrande, "Cuban-Soviet Relations," p. 23.

32. For a detailed discussion of the Katanga invasion of the Shaba province of Zaire, the history of Kantanga independence movement under Moise Tsombe, and a discussion of Cuban involvement, see ibid., pp. 24-26.

33. An additional threat to Angolan security was presented by a second attack by Katangan nationalists in May 1978 under Kantangan-captured Kolwezi.

34. Isidoro Malmierca Peoli, minister of external relations, Republic of Cuba, address to the United Nations, General Assembly, Thirty-sixth Session, 24 September 1981.

35. Interview with Chester A. Crocker, assistant secretary of state for African affairs. Mimeo. 12 February 1982, carried on the Africa wireless file for 23 February 1982.

Cuban artillery private with two Somali insurgent soldiers in village of Tug Wajale, Ethiopia, 1978.

6
Ethiopia and the Costs of Cuba's African Assistance

Ethiopia, 1977 to 1979

Cuba's involvement in Ethiopia is more difficult to assess than its prior involvement in the Angolan Civil War. In the late 1960s Cuba trained Eritrean rebels to help them in their insurgent struggle against Haile Selassie I. Today, however, having subsequently allied with Lt. Colonel Mengistu Haile Mariam in the Ethiopian conflict with Somalia, Cubans are now financially supporting Mengistu against the Eritreans. Cuba's role in Ethiopia is thus further complicated. The change of policy is a source of bitter fighting by the Eritrean and Tigrean rebels: Cuba first supported Eritrea against Selassie and later helped Mengistu fight the Eritreans. The change was Marxism, or the Brezhnev doctrine of the limtied sovereignty of socialist states. Cuban officials describe it as *territorial integrity,* according to Ramón Sánchez Parodi, head of the Cuban Interest Section in Washington.[1]

In terms of military expenditures and troop commitment, Cuban involvement in Ethiopia between 1977 and 1979 was similar to Cuba's assistance program to Angola three years earlier. Cuba entered the Ethiopian conflict with more experienced, institutionalized armed forces, as a result of the military victory in Angola. Otherwise, the military dimensions of the two policies were similar. The nature of the conflict in Ethiopia, however, was markedly different. The combined effects of Cuban assistance in a dispute that, in world opinion, was less clear-cut than the Angolan dispute, and the added impact of a second military commitment and its costs, affected Cuba's domestic economic picture.

History of the Conflict

The Ethiopian dispute actually involves two separate conflicts. First, it involves a border dispute between Ethiopia and Somalia over the Ogaden region, and the invasion into Ethiopia by Somalia during this conflict. Second, it involves the conflict between the central government of Ethiopia and the Eritrean People's Liberation Front (EPLF), a separatist group demanding independence for the region of Eritrea.

Ethiopia's modern history begins with the defeat of the Italians in the last years of the nineteenth century by Menelik II, the history of which the Ethiopians remain proud. Contemporary political tradition may be traced more directly to the succession to the throne of regent Ras Tafari Makonnen in 1916, who became emperor in 1930, taking the name of Haile Selassie I.[2] Ethiopia was invaded in 1935 by Italian forces and occupied until 5 May 1941 when the British reconquered the capital city of Addis Ababa. Between 1941 and 1952, Eritrea was ruled as a colony under British administration.

In 1952 at Selassie's request, the United Nations General Assembly decided that the colony of Eritrea, formerly Italian, would be joined to Ethiopia as an autonomous area within the federation of Ethiopia and Eritrea. In 1962 Eritrea became a part of the nation of Ethiopia and all vestiges of a federal state disappeared.

In February 1974 protests over low wages erupted into a revolt against the emperor. The revolt was led by Ethiopia's Second Army Division. On 12 September 1974 (Independence Day), Emperor Haile Selassie was taken prisoner. He died in prison on 22 August 1975. The new government declared a socialist state in December of that year. It eliminated most vestiges of Haile Selassie's half-century of royal rule. It suspended the 1955 Constitution, dissolved the Parliament, and abolished all royal titles.

The revolution was led by the military, known during the conflict as the Armed Forces Coordinating Committee, also known as the Dergue or committee. This military coalition government, which consisted of more than 100 members at the time of the revolution, established a Provisional Military Government (PMG) headed by Lt. Gen. Aman Andom.

Disputes within the military quickly surfaced. On 24 November 1974, Gen. Aman Andom was shot, and the PMG was replaced by the Provisional Military Administrative Council (PMAC) directed by Brig. Gen. Teferi Banti. To increase his power, Teferi Banti reorganized the PMAC in December 1976, reducing the control of the PMAC vice-chairmen, Lt. Col. Mengistu Haile Mariam and Lt. Col. Atnafu Abate.

In February 1977 a second coup took place. The result: Teferi Banti was shot, leaving Mengistu and Atnafu as vice-chairmen. According to the U.S. Department of State, Mengistu encourages the story that he personally fired the shot that killed Banti, although documentation is difficult. In November Atnafu too was shot. By year's end, Mengistu was head of state and the uncontested chairman of the PMAC. With each coup, Ethiopia's leadership became more radicalized.

Economic Problems and Signs of Discontent

Under socialist leadership, Ethiopia initiated programs that included social reforms as well as the nationalization of land and industries. One of the first major reform programs, entitled Ethiopia First, was established in December 1974. It nationalized most banks, major industries, and holdings and schools. It established worker's councils, farm cooperative programs, and a land reform program that continues in the mid-1980s. In 1975 a massive literacy campaign, similar to

Cuba's literacy campaign of 1961, employed more than sixty thousand students in rural areas.[3] By the end of 1975, however, signs of worker discontent became widespread. The Confederation of Ethiopian Labor Unions (CELU) called a general strike which paralyzed production. The PMAC quickly declared a state of emergency and replaced the CELU with the All-Ethiopia Trade Union.

For several reasons the government of Mengistu and the ruling Dergue have been under attack since 1976. The opposition comes from right-wing opponents of the socialist land reform and nationalizations, from Marxist guerrillas demanding more radical government distribution, and from several secessionist groups including the Eritreans. Another major objection to the Dergue leadership, cutting across ideological divisions, is the government's counterinsurgency programs in which, during 1977 to 1978, the government imprisoned many opponents.[4] In an interview, Hailu Kebede, the chargé d'affairs of the Ethiopian embassy in Cuba, boasted, "In four years of difficult struggle we have defeated both the internal and foreign enemy forces."[5]

The Somali Conflict

In 1960, when Somalia became independent, according to *New York Times* reports, it appealed to the United States and other Western nations for support but accepted Soviet aid when Western support was not forthcoming. The agreement was clear: military equipment from the Soviet Union in exchange for use of Somalia's port, airfield, and missile-storage facilities.

The unusual change of alliance came in 1975, when Haile Selassie I, who had strong military ties to Washington and had received help for several years in his battle with Somalia over the Ogaden desert region and against the Eritreans, was overthrown by socialist military commanders. The new government was immediately successful in its request for Soviet military assistance. Within a year, the United States would offer to supply, but not deliver, arms to Somalia, establishing a substantial increase in the Horn of Africa. President Jimmy Carter and Secretary of State Cyrus Vance responded to Somalia's request. The U.S. would evaluate assistance to "states which are threatened by buildup of foreign military equipment and advisors on their borders in the Horn and elsewhere in Africa."[6]

In 1977 Somali forces backed by Saudi Arabia entered the Ethiopian Ogaden region and took the towns of Jijiga and Harar. Cuba sent approximately fifty military advisers to Ethiopia in response to the attack by the combined forces of Somalia and the Western Somalia Liberation Front (WSLF). Responding to promises of U.S. and Saudi support, the Somali army increased the number and frequency of attacks, and in July 1977, forty thousand Somalis entered the Ogaden. In January 1978 Ethiopia launched a counteroffensive, and it took Jijiga in the beginning of March. Guerrilla activity continued through 1978 and into 1979, but the recapturing of Jijiga marked a major victory for Ethiopian forces. In addition, the Somali forces were no longer being supported by the United States.

Moreover, the United States had even politically blocked the transfer of U.S. arms from Saudi Arabia and Egypt.

By the time of the major Somali attack, most of Africa supported the central government of Ethiopia against Somali aggression. By March, Cuban troops sent to Ethiopia numbered thirteen thousand, and they increased to approximately seventeen thousand by April when the Somali army withdrew.[7]

For several decades since the Ogaden was first claimed by Somalia, it has been an area of conflict. The major force within Ethiopia which supports Somali aggression is the WSLF, founded in 1975 and headed by Secretary-General Abdullahi Hassan Mahmud. Its guerrilla forces of approximately three thousand are often assisted by forces provided by the central government of Somalia. A smaller and insignificant secessionist group that also advocates a united Ogaden and Somalia is the Somali Abo Liberation Front (SALF).

In March 1978 Castro said of the Ethiopian-Somali dispute, "The critical situation created by the invasion in late November [1977] led the Ethiopian Government to make an urgent request that we send tank, artillery and aviation specialists to help the army, and to help the country, and we did so."[8] Castro explained that Cuban specialists started arriving in Ethiopia in mid-December and early January. "Why did it become necessary for us to send fighters?" Castro continued. "Because of the scope and magnitude of Somalia's aggression."[9]

Ethiopia—Eritrean Conflict: Cuban Involvement

The independence struggle in Eritrea is one that parallels many Latin American struggles for separation from a colonial neighbor. Culturally and politically, Eritrea and Ethiopia are worlds apart. Ethiopians and Eritreans speak over 70 languages and 200 dialects. Eritreans principally speak Arabic, Galligna, and Tigrigna; Ethiopians speak Amharic and English. Eritrean colonial history of conquest and rule by Italy at the turn of the century contrasts sharply with Ethiopia's Portuguese past.

Ethiopia's interest in retaining control over its northern province parallels several historical insurgent independence struggles on another front. Ethiopia cannot afford to allow Eritrea to secede. Eritrea occupies most of the coastline that gives Ethiopia access to the vital parts of the Red Sea. As a result, 50 percent of Ethiopia's industry is located in Eritrea. The central government of Ethiopia has not gained much international support for its fight against Eritrean separatists. As of late 1979, the PMAC was supported only by Kenya, the People's Democratic Republic of Yemen, Libya, and Cuba.

The separatist conflict in Eritrea has remained serious although the groups calling for independence are divided. One of the three major parties involved is the Revolutionary Council (ELF-RC), known as the ELF until 1978, which is headed by Ahmad Muhammad Nasser and is the oldest of the three parties, founded in 1958. The party is Marxist although its principal support is from Moslem groups. It supports the Eritrean Liberation Army. The EPLF is the largest of the three separatist groups. Headed by Secretary-General Ramadan Muhammad Nur, it was founded in 1970 as a splinter group of the ELF.[10] The EPLF also maintains a guerrilla army (approximately thirty thousand soldiers), called the Eritrean People's Army (EPLA); unlike the EPLF, it is composed of both Christian and Moslem Marxists. The third group, established as a splinter group of the ELF, is the Eritrean Liberation Front-Popular Liberation Front (ELF-PLF). It is headed by Secretary-General Osman Saleh Sabbe. It has guerrilla forces of approximately four thousand soldiers.

Eritrean separatism became strongest after 1962 when Eritrea lost its separate status and was annexed by Ethiopia. By 1978 after more than fifteen years of conflict between the three Eritrean separatist factions and the government of Ethiopia, the Eritrean groups controlled more than 80 percent of the province.[11] Ethiopia, on the offensive in 1978, however, regained several key cities.

Eritrean Popular Liberation Front leader, Ahmad Muhammad Nur, referred to Cuban and Soviet forces in November 1977, as "democratic forces."[12] Fidel Castro first became involved in the Ethiopia-Somali dispute in March 1977. At that time, Castro proposed "the creation of an anti-imperialist federation composed of South Yemen, Ethiopia, Somalia, an autonomous Ogaden, and an autonomous Eritrea."[13] In 1978 Mengistu signed a treaty with the Soviet Union to supply military aid and advisers. The Soviet Union established a naval base in the Dahlak Islands, owned by Ethiopia, in the Red Sea. The Red Sea is vital to the Suez Canal and strategically important to oil routes and other commercial shipping. The Soviet Union previously had a naval base before it was asked to leave Somalia in 1978. The United States subsequently established a naval base in Berbera, Somalia. Mengistu has held a tight rein on domestic affairs.

Cuban sympathy for the Eritrean struggle, however, lessened after Castro's diplomatic effort at a settlement failed. At the time of the Ethiopian struggle with Somalia, Castro explained in a speech on 15 March 1978, "Ethiopia had to struggle all over the country against groups of counter-revolutionary bandits, aided from abroad and directed by feudal elements, and *against secessionist movements in the north.*"[14] The difference, as the Cubans see it, is the difference in the central government of Ethiopia. The Cuban government sent assistance and aid to the EPLF when it was fighting what the Cubans considered the oppressive and exploitive government of Haile Selassie in the 1970s.

Ethiopia's War Economy

Ethiopia is one of the world's ten poorest nations, according to 1979 United Nations ratings. In a nation whose per capita income was $100, the costs of revolution, civil strife, and war have been dramatically high. From the late 1960s until 1973, Ethiopia's economy grew at a slow but sustained rate of 4 percent. By 1975 Ethiopia's growth rate had fallen to zero.[15] Agricultural production and communications systems suffered most from continued fighting, especially in port areas. Coffee exports (which constitute 70 percent of export revenues) were cut by almost 30 percent.[16]

Although Ethiopia depends heavily on external financing of development plans, the economy was considered self-sufficient in agricultural production in 1975.[17] Since 1977, however, Ethiopia's principal problem has been severe food shortages. There has been development of the largest existing gold mine near Addis Ababa with the help of the Soviet Union, Ethiopia's economy does not seem in the short or long run to promise economic development or trade.[18] Between 1977 and 1978, Ethiopia's balance of payments had deteriorated sharply. In 1977 exports equaled $329 million (U.S.) and imports $348 million (U.S.), bringing Ethiopia's balance of payments to a deficit of $19 million (U.S.). By 1978, however, Ethiopia's deficit totaled $319 million (U.S.).[19]

In November 1979 Ramón Sánchez Parodi, head of the Cuban interest section in Washington, D.C., the highest Cuban government official in the United States, repeated the sentiment expressed by Vice-President Carlos Rafael Rodríguez, at the Non-Aligned Conference in 1978: "Cuba wishes to maintain the territorial integrity of Ethiopia."[20] Before 1974, other Cuban leaders such as Rogalado Blanco argued, there was a class struggle that does not exist today.[21] Although Cuba has expressed the sentiment that Eritrean problems should be peacefully negotiated and has even expressed its concern over the aggression by Ethiopia, the Dergue continues to launch major offensives in Eritrea with arms provided to them by Cuba and the Soviet Union.

At the same time, however, Ethiopia increased military spending. In 1978 when foreign exchange was vitally needed for food imports, Ethiopia spent its hard currency to purchase Soviet military equipment worth over $1 billion (U.S.).[22] Ethiopia's military budget rose during the decade of the 1970s from 14.3 percent of central government budget in 1970 to 33 percent in 1979.

Ethiopian Technical Assistance

In September 1978 the Cuban-Ethiopian memorandum on technical and economic cooperation was signed. In October the Soviet Union and Ethiopia signed several economic, technical, and trade agreements.[23] In 1977 a three hundred-member Cuban medical team arrived as part of an economic, scientific, and technical cooperation program.[24] In six months the medical team had treated 150,000 patients. The plan also predicted a 1979 assistance program including university medical teaching by Cuban physicians at the University of Addis Ababa. In addition, Cuban engineers were sent to the Ethiopian Sugar Corporation to assist in the management of sugar mills.[25]

After Ethiopian President Mengistu visited Havana in April and September 1978, Cuba and Ethiopia signed an economic, scientific, and technical cooperation memorandum on 28 September 1978. The memorandum outlines Cuban assistance in agriculture, livestock breeding and raising, irrigation, and trade and physical and economic planning. In the memorandum of 1978, according to Mengistu, the aid was given free of charge to the Ethiopian government, and several hundred Cuban specialists were sent to Ethiopia.[26] A total of twelve hundred Cuban medical personnel were sent to more than a dozen African nations, directed and organized by Cuba's Ministry of Public Health (MINSAP).[27]

A nation must pay for its program of foreign aid and must consider the international dimensions of such a program; political analysts argue that "international politics lie at the heart of foreign aid."[28] Cuba's African aid programs have taken their toll on the domestic development of Cuba, but they have also served as an international political strategy of the Cuban government.

Other Medical and Technical Assistance in Africa

Cuban medical teams situated in the People's Republic of the Congo treated more than thirty-nine thousand patients in 1978 alone.[29] The two teams, working in Gambona and Ncayi, were each composed of four doctors, three nurses, an anesthetist, and laboratory and x-ray technicians.[30] Medical aid to the Congo began in 1974.

In October 1978 Cuba signed an agreement sending six hundred Cuban technicians to Mozambique to aid national reconstruction, including technicians trained in education, agriculture, industry, and civil reconstruction. It also provided twenty-nine hundred scholarships for workers and high school students.[31]

As with technical and medical assistance programs to Angola and Ethiopia, medical assistance programs throughout Africa by the Cuban government have been substantial. In 1979, for example, one-third of Cuban workers in Angola were doctors.[32] Cuban economic analysts were also sent to Angola to assist in the reformulation of the Angolan revolutionary regime; Cubans have assisted at the Ministry of Finance, the Bank of Angola, the Ministry of the Interior, the Directorate of Intelligence and Security.[33] In total, by 1979 there were between ten thousand and eleven thousand civilian Cuban technicians in Africa.[34]

Cuban technical assistance programs have varied greatly in size and duration. In 1975, 250 Cuban construction workers built three Tanzanian secondary schools. The construction materials, including cranes and bulldozers, were paid for by Cuba as a gift to the Tanzanian people.[35] The major technical assistance given by the Cubans to Ethiopia was in the fields of agriculture, industry, cattle breeding, commerce, physical planning, economic planning, education, medicine, and the training of military soldiers.[36] This aid was explained by Hailu Kebede, the Ethiopian chargé d'affaires of the Ethiopian Embassy in Cuba, in an interview in 1979 when he stated that the major Ethiopian issue in 1979 is economic development.[37]

However, both natural disasters (locusts and drought) and the war in the Ogaden have caused great economic hardship in Ethiopia. As a result, the aid

Ethiopia solicited has been in the form of machinery, scientific and technical aid, and specialized personnel. By increasing agricultural productivity and the size of state farms run by the All Ethiopia Farmers' Union (AEFU), the Ethiopian leadership hopes to stimulate economic development.[38]

Costs of Cuba's African Policies

Cuba's foreign policies in both Angola and Ethiopia have proven costly for Cuba. In neither country has the fighting ceased. On the contrary, in Angola, Jonas Savimbi's forces numbered over 40,000 by 1985 and were given an added boost by the repeal in both the U.S. Senate and House of the 1976 Clark Amendment, which banned aid to Angolan rebels. Cuban troops in support of the MPLA government numbered 25,000–30,000. In Ethiopia, the fighting in the Tigre and Eritrean regions appeared to subside due to a severe drought followed by widespread famine and world attention. Allegations by several observers and journalists that the Mengistu government was routing relief away from the Northern rebel regions resulted in a provision in the 1985 U.S. foreign aid bill that allowed for the suspension of trade with Ethiopia "if the President determined that the Ethiopian Government was deliberately starving its people."[39] In both aid programs, Cuba's foreign policies were becoming increasingly vulnerable.

The Soviet Union: The "Proxy" Debate

Cuban officials argue that the military assistance program was motivated in 1977 in Ethiopia by the same goals as was the 1963 aid to Algeria: (1) ideological affinity; (2) a desire to aid socialist regimes; and (3) the view that the nations assisted were being attacked by foreign powers. At the height of the Angolan Civil War in January 1976, Russian military aid to Angola amounted to $200 million.[40] The parallel aid by Cuba and the Soviet Union raises serious questions about Cuba's principal motivations in Africa and its possible involvement as a Soviet proxy. Many analysts believe that Cuba is paying a high price for its international adventures because of the drain on its technical and medical personnel. Joint military exercises, both on the ground and in the air, by the Soviet Union, Cuba, Ethiopia, and South Yemen attest to the coordination of policy by Cuba and the Soviet Union in the region. In 1980 the United Front of South Yemen reported joint exercises of training in desert warfare in a desert strip which extends from South Yemen to Saudi Arabia, known as the Empty Quarter desert.

The increase in the levels of assistance and military training have been sparked by changes in the international environment and facilitated by Soviet security protection to Cuba itself. Cuba has been able to carry out the policy of aid to the Third World, in part, because Cuba does not have to worry about its own defense, as it had to in the first half of the decade. As a result of this greater domestic security, the increase of the number of troops in both Angola and Ethiopia was possible, as was the shift in Cuban aid from aid to guerrilla movements to aid to progressive governments.[41]

The Soviet interest in both nations is strong and visible and Cuba's role as a loyal ally of the Soviet Union in Africa is at the forefront of Cuba's programs. In June 1985, African affairs writer Colin Legum reported in the *Christian Science Monitor* that a document was released in London that details the Soviet assistance to the Mengistu government in Ethiopia. "The establishment of a Leninist party and the success of socialism in Ethiopia," the report stated, "will be a source of moral inspiration . . . for the revolutionary class struggle being waged in Africa." The report written by the Ethiopian Ministry of Justice and Legal Affairs, calls the Eritreans, "reactionary," and proposes to "indoctrinate" the armed forces of Ethiopia.[42]

Leadership: The Political Decision to Intervene

During 1975 Cuba never officially informed its people of the intentions or facts of Cuban troop intervention in Angola. Cuban involvement in the Angolan Civil War, however, was reported by the French, British, African, and U.S. news agencies before Fidel Castro announced the Cuban program officially in January 1976.[43] It is likely that international events such as the meeting of Non-Aligned Nations, which many Cuban delegates attended, and the World Youth festival as well as the foreign press agencies in Cuba such as Agence France-Presse (AFP) might have brought this information to Cuban attention before official government notification.[44] The international financial community was not visibly distressed by either the Cuban government's African assistance program, or its troop involvement in Angola since Eurocurrency loans to Cuba peaked during this period; $375 million (U.S.) was loaned to Cuba in Eurocurrency loans and $1.3 billion (U.S.) was loaned by Argentina. On the other hand, the slow progress in relations between the United States and Cuba was abruptly halted as a result of Cuba's involvement in Africa. Although the U.S. government's position was greatly antagonistic to Cuba's new Africa program, U.S. corporations, through foreign subsidiaries, continued to trade with Cuba in amounts that surpassed $345 million (U.S.) between August 1975 and December 1976 alone, at the height of the Angolan conflict.[45] In fact, some observers argue that at first Cuba's involvement in Angola improved its position in the international commercial market.

Castro stated that the decision to intervene to assist the MPLA in the civil war in Angola was to prevent a foreign invasion, namely by South Africa. Most important, in January 1976 at the height of the conflict, a high level Cuban official stated that Cuba would not discontinue troop deployment even if the Organization of African Unity requested an end to foreign intervention.[46] Cuba's decision to intervene in Africa reflected a shift in Cuban assistance programs from aid to guerrilla movements, which Cuba had assisted more frequently in Latin America in the 1960s. Castro stated in 1977:

We are supporting African governments that have requested our cooperation; they are duly constituted governments, and revolutionary and progressive governments at that. Our military advisors are not lending their services to any fascist government anywhere in the world... Our military advisors are assisting governments that help their own peoples, support their own peoples, and are either revolutionary or progressive governments.[47]

In 1979 at the ministerial conference of heads of state and government of the countries of NAM in Belgrade, Yugoslavia, Castro explained Cuba's reasons for Cuba's 1978 African assistance program: Cuba's "international combatants" were stationed in Africa at the request of the governments of the nations involved in order to "contribute to the struggle against backwardness and the aggression of the racists, annexationists and the pawns of imperialism."[48]

Economic Effects

Some Western nations withdrew their loan arrangements to Cuba because of Cuba's African involvement. Canada, for example, withdrew development aid on the basis of Cuba's programs in Africa. In June 1978 Canada cancelled $4.4 million (U.S.) in technical assistance and $10 million (U.S.) in trade credits.[49] In addition, in February 1976 the West German minister for economic cooperation banned economic aid to Cuba on the basis of Cuba's foreign policy in Africa. No development aid, he stated, would "be given to nations that intervene in other nations."[50] West Germany was nevertheless giving aid to Angola, Minister Egon Bahr explained, since a nation is not denied economic aid merely because it is Communist, according to the criteria of the Organization for Economic Cooperation and Development.

Although Cuban-African relations have been confined to Cuban military and technical assistance to African nations—with no immediate reciprocal benefits—there are several possible explanations of Cuba's motivations for its African policy. The economic advantage of improved relations with Africa is one possible explanation. Africa is a continent rich in natural resources—particularly minerals, diamonds, and oil. In the 1970s African nations, like many Third World nations, have been confined to agricultural, primary-product exports. Because of the low cost of African labor, foreign investors earned high profits from commercial agreements.

Angola, for example, is rich in minerals with deposits of 80 to 100 million tons of manganese. In addition, diamonds were produced in the early 1970s at an annual production rate of 1.5 million carats, and oil output was 130,000 barrels in 1972. Angolan industrial development in the 1970s has been improving rapidly; hydroelectric power plants have increased Angolan electricity output, and the industries of tobacco, chemicals, and plastics have also been growing. Iron ore, oil, and other raw materials are an extremely important source of essential products in the West—a source which will increase in importance in the 1980s.

Prior to the civil war, annual export earnings were high; the most important products included oil ($450 million), coffee ($20 million), diamonds ($80 million), and iron ore ($75 million), as well as a diversified agricultural and production base which included cotton, fish, and cement.[51] During the mass refugee exodus of August to October 1975, almost all agricultural production ceased.[52] In 1979 the Angolan economy was in a state of collapse. In the short run, the war undoubtedly had a devastating effect on the economy particularly since it is a country which relied on foreign investment for the development of light industry in urban areas. Agricultural mainstays such as tobacco, rice, coffee, sisal, and timber have been damaged. Moreover, the MPLA had no access to oil in Cabinda in view of the problem of separatist sentiment in the region. Despite these problems, oil production in Cabinda has made Angola the third largest producer of oil in Africa, south of the Sahara.[53] Oil production in Cabinda accounts for the bulk of Angola's oil production, according to U.S. congressional testimony. Moreover, of $170 million (U.S.) in direct U.S. investment in Angola, $150 million (U.S.) was in oil exploration costs which amounted to 6.3 percent of total U.S. investment in Africa at that time.[54]

In the short term, there is little reason to believe that Cuba will benefit economically from better relations with Angola. As a result of the war, production of diamonds has diminished dramatically, coffee exports were reduced by 25 to 30 percent, and iron ore exports were halted altogether. Labor problems also have decreased productivity, and raw materials in all sectors were short throughout the late 1970s. Finally, foreign trade has decreased enormously. Oil production, in fact, is the only productive sector that has remained fairly stable. Thus, it seems unlikely with regard to either Angola or Ethiopia that economic incentives would be at the core of Cuba's foreign policy programs. In the short term, both economies have been damaged severely by the prolonged fighting. Ethiopian coffee exports were reduced by approximately 30 percent and in Angola copper production was one of several industries seriously affected, thus damaging close to 18 percent of world copper production.[55] Another motivation for Cuban involvement in Angola is that of the strategic benefits, including, first, the access it provides for surveillance of Western communications in the Southern Atlantic Ocean, and, second, Angola's proximity to Namibia at a time when the security and administration of Namibia (South-West Africa) is in question.[56]

While the 1975 victory in Angola was Cuba's, the ultimate success of Cuba's strategy in Angola will continue to undergo strain, as the fighting enters its second decade and prohibitions to U.S. aid to the Angolan rebels are challenged. In mid-June 1985, the U.S. Senate voted to repeal the Clark Amendment, which barred funds to assist the Angolan insurgents, who were fighting the MPLA government of dos Santos.[57]

The continent must be viewed as a whole, however, in order to understand the international dimensions of the conflicts in Africa. The U.S. position on Africa's economic troubles, like that of the Soviet Union, is that they are a threat to vital security interests.

Ideological and Political Motivations

The reasons for Cuba's pursuit of a foreign military policy of international solidarity are complex. The most prominent reason cited in speeches by the Cuban leader during the 1970s is race.[58] In his 1976 speech, "We Stand with the People of Africa," Castro stated:

> Racial discrimination existed in our country . . . Is there anyone who has forgotten that racial discrimination was prevalent in all aspects of work and study? . . . In keeping with the duties rooted in our principles, our ideology, our convictions and our very own blood, we shall defend Angola and Africa![59]

Cuba's ideological affinity to the Marxist regimes of Agostinho Neto in Angola and Mengistu Haile Mariam in Ethiopia is apparent. The programs of distribution and social reform in Ethiopia were similar to those initiated in the 1960s in Cuba.

Ideological strength domestically, however, may also be the inspiration of a policy posture, and two possible explanations of Cuba's policy in Africa are the following: first, Cuba's involvement in Africa provided a sense of revolutionary spirit to the younger generation, who had not experienced life in prerevolutionary Cuba and the economic and political hardship of Fulgencio Batista, and who did not remember clearly the Bay of Pigs invasion. The conflict in Angola, Castro stated in 1976, "was the twin sister of the victory at Giron."[60] Second, the policy in Africa strengthened Cuba's domestic popular support among the generation for whom fighting was a way of life in the late 1950s, and who have had to suffer the restrictions of the Revolution.

In his first public assessment of the extent of Cuba's programs in a closed session before the National Assembly in Havana on 27 December 1979, Fidel Castro spoke to the delegates about Cuban troops in Angola and in Ethiopia. At the height of Cuban involvement, he stated, thirty-six thousand troops were stationed in Angola and twelve thousand in Ethiopia—soldiers who "spent entire months in trenches." In December 1980 Cuba's second party congress was held. In a speech to the two thousand delegates gathered from 140 nations, Castro confirmed Cuba's socialist commitment, "We simply say never will Cuba abandon Communism."[61]

Cuba's policy in Africa in the mid-1980s presents very different dilemmas from those presented in 1975 when Cuba's African commitments expanded significantly. In both Angola and Ethiopia, Cuba—as well as the United States and other major powers in the region—is in a military stalemate. Moreover, what was seen as assistance programs necessary in the short term have ended up with an unanticipated extended duration and high costs for the Cuban government.

Notes

1. Interview by the author with Ramón Sánchez Parodi, Washington, D.C., 16 April 1980.

2. The throne of the kingdom of Ethiopia had been occupied from 1889 to 1913 by Emperor Menelik II. In 1913 Menelik II's grandson inherited the throne but was overthrown by the Christian governing forces because of his Muslim ties. Menelik's daughter became empress and was succeeded by Haile Selassie I (Ras Tafari Makonnen) in 1930. The religious cleavages still play a part in present-day Ethiopia.

3. U.S., Department of State, Bureau of Intelligence and Research, 10 June 1985.

4. The Marxist resistance comes mainly from the guerrilla-based Ethiopian People's Revolutionary party. The Ethiopian Democratic Union constitutes the strongest centrist opposition.

5. *Granma Weekly Review*, 8 October 1978, p. 10.

6. Graham Hovey, *The New York Times*, 27 July 1977, p. 3.

7. William LeoGrande, "Cuban-Soviet Relations and Cuban Policy in Africa." Paper prepared for presentation to the Annual Meeting of the International Studies Association, Toronto, Canada. 22–26 March 1979, p. 44.

8. Fidel Castro, 15 March 1978, Santiago de Cuba, in *Granma Weekly Review*, 26 March 1978. Also see ibid., 14 March 1978 for military operations in Ethiopia.

9. Ibid.

10. The ELF and the EPLF announced they would unite in early 1979. A study financed by the U.S. Department of Defense and published in 1977 stated that both the Soviet Union and Mengistu requested Cuban military aid to stop the secessionist movement in Eritrea. The Cuban government objected, stating that the Eritrean cause might in fact be a legitimate one. *Washington Post*, 22 September 1979, pp. A1, A27. When Mengistu succeeded in the Ogaden conflict with Somalia and then turned to quell the Eritrean separatists with military equipment and financing from the Cuban government, another study argued, the Cuban government did not object, stating that it was an internal political question of Ethiopia alone. See LeoGrande, "Cuba-Soviet Relations," p. 47. Also stated in comments by Sánchez Parodi, head, Cuban Interest Section, Washington, D.C. at "Open Panel on Cuba's Foreign Policy," National Conference on Cuba, Center for Cuban Studies, New York, 3 November 1979.

11. *The Europa Yearbook: A World Survey* (London: Europa Publications Ltd., 1979), p. 309.

12. Roger W. Fontaine, "Fidel Castro Front and Center," *Washington Quarterly*, spring 1979, p. 80.

13. LeoGrande, "Cuban-Soviet Relations," p. 42.

14. *Granma Weekly Review*, 26 March 1978.

15. U.S. Central Intelligence Agency (CIA), *National Basic Intelligence Handbook* (Washington, D.C.: Government Printing Office, July 1979).

16. *Europa Yearbook*, "Ethiopia," 1979. Industrial development in Ethiopia has now shown substantial drops since industry accounts for less than 6 percent of GDP, p. 310.

17. U.S., Department of State, *Background Notes: Ethiopia*, (Washington, D.C.: Government Printing Office, December 1975).

18. *Europa Yearbook*, p. 310.

19. U.S., Central Intelligence Agency, Intelligence Handbook, 1979. In the fiscal year 1977-78, exports were reduced to $193 million (U.S.) and imports had increased to $512 million (U.S.).

20. Comments by Ramón Sánchez Parodi at National Conference on Cuba, Center for Cuban Studies, New York, 3 November 1979.

21. Comments by Rogalado Blanco at National Conference on Cuba, Center for Cuban Studies, New York, 3 November 1979.

22. *Europa Yearbook*, p. 310.

23. *Granma Weekly Review*, 8 October 1978, p. 10.

24. Ibid., 22 October 1978, p. 9.

25. Ibid.

26. Ibid., 8 October 1978, p. 3.

27. Gail Reed, "Cuba's Medical Brigade in Ethiopia," *Granma Weekly Review*, 18 April 1979, p. 5.

28. John D. Montgomery, *The Politics of Foreign Aid* (New York: Praeger, 1962), p. 4. There is extensive literature on foreign aid in the United States and specifically by the United States to Latin America. In fact, it is in this literature that much of the discussion of international and domestic linkages takes place. See Albert O. Hirschman, *The Strategy of Economic Development* (New Haven: Yale, 1958); Hans J. Morganthau, "Preface to a Political Theory of Foreign Aid," *Congressional Record*, 13 March 1962, pp. A1886-A1890; Walt W. Rostow, *The States of Economic Growth* (Cambridge: Cambridge Press, 1960); Denis Goulet and Michale Hudson, *The Myth of Aid* (New York: Orbis, 1971); Riordan Roett, *The Politics of Foreign Aid in the Brazilian Northeast* (Nashville, Tenn.: Vanderbilt, 1972).

29. *Granma Weekly Review* (Havana), 29 April 1979, p. 10.

30. The four doctors include highly trained medical specialists such as a surgeon, a pediatrician, an internist and an orthopedist.

31. *Ganma Weekly Review* (Havana), 5 November 1978, p. 12.

32. *Third World*, p. 16. Of all workers in 1979 in both Ethiopia and Angola, the study entitled "The Medical Brigades" documented the numbers of medical personnel relative to all Cuban technicians in Africa.

33. Greig, *Communist Challenge*, p. 108.

34. *Third World*, p. 108.

35. Ibid., p. 8.

36. *Granma Weekly Review*, 18 February 1979.

37. Ibid.

38. The AEFU is similar in goals and organization to the Cuban National Association of Small Farmers, *Granma Weekly Review*, 18 February 1979.

39. Alan Cowell, "Reporter's Notebook: Angola's Children of War," *New York Times*, 10 June 1985, p. 2; Blaine Harden, "No Amount of Aid Will End Hunger in Ethiopia," *Washington Post* (National Weekly Edition), 17 June 1985, p. 23; Bernard Gwertzman, "Foreign Aid Bill May Be Vetoed Over Strictures," *New York Times*, 12 July 1985, p. A7.

40. Amount of Soviet aid is cited from a statement by Henry Kissinger in Colin Legum and Tony Hodges, *After Angola: The War in Southern Africa* (London: Rex Collins, 1976), p. 20.

Ethiopia and the Costs of Cuba's African Assistance • 109

41. This foreign policy change in the 1970s was also due to the failure of the guerrilla movements of Latin America, the perception that the United States would counter efforts in Latin America, and the collapse of the Portuguese colonial rule in Africa. William LeoGrande, "Cuban-Soviet Relations and Cuban Policy in Africa." Paper published for presentation to annual meeting of the International Studies Assoc., Toronto, Canada, 22-26 March 1979, p. 2.

42. Colin Legum, "Document Spells Out Alleged Soviet Role in Ethiopia," *Christian Science Monitor*, 3 June 1985, p. 1, 15.

43. Legum and Hodges, *After Angola*, p. 20.

44. Other foreign press bureaus in Havana include: *Agence France-Presse (AFP)*, *Agencia EFE* (Spain), *Agentstvo Pechati Novosti (APN)* (USSR), *Agenzia Nazionale Stampa Associata (ANSA)* (Italy), *Allgemeiner Deutscher Nachrichtendienst (ADN)* (German Democratic Republic), *Bulgarian Telegraph Agency (BTA)*, *Československá tisková kancelář (CTK)* (Czechoslovakia), *Magyar Távirati Iroda (MTI)* (Hungary), *Novinska Agencija Tanjug* (Yugoslavia), *Polska Agencja Prasowa (PAP)* (Poland), *Reuters* (UK), *Telegrafnoye Agentstvo Sovietskogo Soyuza (TASS)* (USSR), *Viet-Nam News Agency (VNA)*, *Xinhua (New China News Agency)* (People's Republic of China).

45. See Rosemary Warrett, *Cuba: At the Turning Point* (New York: Business International Corp., 1977), p. 109; and Pamela S. Falk, "Viewpoint" in the *Stamford Advocate* (Connecticut), 20 January 1979, p. A5.

46. *Guardian*, cited in Ian Greig, *The Communist Challenge to Africa* (Richmond, Va.: Foreign Affairs Pub., 1977), p. 40.

47. Fidel Castro, "Address to the Second Period of Sessions of the National Assembly," 24 December 1977 (Havana: Political Publishers, 1978), pp. 61-62.

48. *Granma Weekly Review* (Havana), 3 June 1979, p. 10.

49. LeoGrande, "Cuban-Soviet Relations," p. 51.

50. *Journal of Commerce*, 26 February 1979, p. 7.

51. U.S., Department of State, *Background Notes: Angola* (Washington, D.C.: Government Printing Office, October 1976).

52. Greig, *Communist Challenge*, p. 216.

53. Ibid., p. 212.

54. U.S., Congress, House, Committee on Foreign Affairs, testimony by Sheldon Gitelman at the hearings before the Subcommittee on Africa, 91st Cong., 2d sess., 20 May 1970, pp. 167-189.

55. *Journal of Commerce*, 2 February 1976, p. 7.

56. Greig, *Communist Challenge*, p. 211.

57. Steven V. Roberts, "Reagan Letter Presses Latin Rebel Aid," *New York Times*, 12 June 1985, p. 3.

58. The great majority of Cuban troops sent to Angola were black. Legum and Hodges, *After Angola*, p. 20. See Jorge I. Domínguez, "Racial and Ethnic Relations in the Cuban Armed Forces: A Non Topic." *Armed Forces and Society* 2, no. 2 (February 1976): 273-290. The study, however, deals with the role of the armed forces and the racial composition of the armed forces before the beginning of the major African military assistance programs of the late 1970s.

59. Fidel Castro, address to a rally in Havana at the end of the First Congress of the Communist Party of Cuba, 22 December 1979 (New York: Venceremos Brigade, 1976), p. 9.

60. Speech by Fidel Castro at the Fifteenth Anniversary of the Bay of Pigs attack, Havana, 19 April 1976. Translated by Edicioines Políticas, Havana, 1976.

61. Fidel Castro, Main Report to Second Congress of the Committee of the Communist Party of Cuba (New York: Center for Cuban Studies, 1981).

Part IV
International Economic Policy and International Decision Making

Members of a Cuban health delegation arriving in Managua, 25 July 1979.

7
Cuba's International Presence

Sino-Cuban Relations

Cuba's relations with the People's Republic of China were established before Castro's revolution and have never been broken. However, Havana's relations with Peking experienced severe strains culminating in Castro's bristling characterization of Mao Zedong as a "senile idiot."[1] A trade and political thaw began in 1985 with the signing of several trade accords and the upgrading of diplomatic missions.

China had welcomed the 1959 Revolution. Although Castro did not come to power as a Communist, his anti-American, anti-imperialist language was appealing to Chinese leaders. In this early period, Chinese leaders were on more friendly terms with Latin America as a whole than they would be during the 1970s and early 1980s. In an editorial of 4 January 1959, a People's Republic of China (PRC) newspaper carried an analysis praising Castro's victory and characterizing it as the "national, democratic movement of the Cuban people."[2] The same month ex-President Lázaro Cárdenas of Mexico was told at a rally in China that the people of China understood Cuba's plight because China too had been a victim of imperialism.[3]

In November 1960 Che Guevara travelled to Peking to tell several audiences that China's 1949 Revolution had inspired Cuba's guerrillas.[4] Although the Soviet Union hesitated to fully support Cuba, China praised Cuba openly and often. As Cuban diplomatic envoys made trips to Peking—some of whom were received by Mao—Chinese delegations were visiting Cuba on a regular basis, and Peking daily newspapers reflected only praise for Fidel Castro and the workers' revolution.

On 2 October 1961, Cuba and China issued a joint communiqué attesting to their friendship.[5] Relations improved in 1962, and Chinese Foreign Minister Ch'en Yi praised Castro for his method of dealing with the affairs of dissident Communist party member Aníbal Escalante.[6] In 1962 Sino-Cuban relations continued to improve. In fact, relations with Peking were significantly better than those with Moscow because of tensions which resulted from the missile crisis in October 1962. As Cuba's economy continued to plummet, Castro began to negotiate with both the Soviet Union and China for aid programs. Although relations with Peking had steadily improved while communication with Moscow deteriorated, in 1963 Cuba signed a major trade accord with the Soviet Union, the terms of which Peking could not meet.[7]

When Castro visited Moscow in 1963, in the light of Sino-Soviet antagonism, according to one historian of China, the "Chinese suspected that he had used their endorsement of him as the model for Latin America to gain more leveraging in his bargaining with the Russians."[8]

But in 1964 a schism developed in Sino-Cuban relations, principally due to Cuba's increasing ties with Moscow. Castro's comments in Moscow and at the Havana Conference of Latin American Communist Parties condemned factionism within the socialist nations, clearly referring to the Chinese, infuriating Mao.[9]

In 1966 China and Cuba had locked horns over a series of conflicts including China's reversal of its 1966 trade protocol providing rice to Cuba and an increase in propaganda for Peking.[10] Finally, in 1966–67 the publication of Régis Debray's writings, which were viewed as pro-Soviet, seemed to affirm the break. No single event exacerbated the divisions as much as the Angolan Civil War, which by 1974 had placed Cuba and China on opposite sides of the war.

Since the Revolution, Cuba has had normal diplomatic relations with China. By 1982 Cuba was seeking to increase economic ties and to improve relations in the political sense with China, according to Cuba's vice-president. It is easier, he argued, "as they change their point of view."[11] As distant as the Far East is to Cuba, Cuba's diplomatic relations are surprisingly good. In addition to the People's Republic of China, Cuba's relations with Japan, which were established before the Revolution, continued through the 1980s, as did its relations which were established with Mongolia in 1960 and with North Korea in 1960.

Cuba's International Diplomacy

Cuba remained active in several of the regional organizations within the hemisphere including the Caribbean Multinational Shipping Enterprise (NAMUCAR), the Pan-American Health Organization (PAHO), and the Latin American Economic System (SELA). During the 1980s as in the 1970s, Cuban foreign policy put a great deal of emphasis on the United Nations where Cuba could express itself in a world arena. It became active in sixteen United Nations' committees and made its voice heard in many of these, including: United Nations Educational, Scientific, and Cultural Organization (UNESCO), United Nations Development Program (UNDP), United Nations Conference on Trade and Development (UNCTAD), and General Agreement on Tariffs and Trade (GATT). Most important, Cuba maintained its membership in Economic Commission for Latin America (ECLA).

In the summer of 1980, Cuba's leadership in NAM slumped—not to be revived again until the 1982 South Atlantic crisis. The decision was announced from New Delhi, India in August 1980 that the next meeting of NAM would be held in January 1981 instead of June and would take place in New Delhi rather than Cuba, which would have been the natural location since Castro is the current chairperson of the movement. The stated reason was the split in the vote at the United Nations regarding the Soviet invasion of Afghanistan. Cuba had been elected chair of the movement in 1980 to serve for three years until 1983, which is also the cycle of nonaligned summit meetings. (Meetings of the coordinating bureau are more frequent.) The issue of Afghanistan had polarized the organization, with India arguing that no initiative of the organization was preferable to divisions and that instead bilateral contacts should be made. Yugoslavia, on one other hand, believed that NAM should take a position in opposition to great power intervention.

Cuba's Relations with Western Europe and Southeast Asia

With few exceptions, Cuba maintains relations in the 1980s with all of western Europe, nations which never broke relations with Cuba at the time of the Revolution. Cuba has maintained relations since before 1959 (and continues them today) with Austria, Belgium, Denmark, Finland, France, Greece (which upgraded their diplomatic relations and exchanged ambassadors in July 1982), Iceland, Italy, Luxembourg, Netherlands, Portugal, Spain, Sweden, Switzerland, the United Kingdom, and the Vatican. Immediately following the Revolution, Cuba established relations with Cyprus and Yugoslavia in 1960. Cuba later established relations with Malta (established in 1977), Norway (reestablished in 1968), and West Germany (reestablished in 1975).

By the 1980s Cuba's relations in western Europe began to improve, especially with the Socialist governments of Prime Minister Andreas Papandreou in Greece and President François Mitterrand in France. Less than one month before the European, Japanese, and U.S. foreign policymakers met in France at the Versailles Summit Conference in 1982, Cuba's Vice-President Carlos Rafael Rodríguez concluded a three-day official visit to France with French President François Mitterrand.[12] Included in the delegation were Prime Minister Pierre Mauroy and Claude Cheysson, minister of foreign affairs. Although France hoped to be the mediator between the United States and Cuba, other issues between Washington and Paris took first priority.

Cuba's relations in Southeast Asia became a sore point between the United States and the Soviet Union in the 1970s. Generally, Cuba's assistance to Vietnam, with which Cuba had relations from 1960, was a thorn in the side of the United States during the 1960s. In 1982 Cuba maintained relations with most of the nations of Southeast Asia, including: Kampuchea (reestablished in 1975), Laos (1974), Malaysia (1975), Thailand (1963), and Vietnam (1960).

Cuba reopened relations with most of South Asia in the 1970s. It had strong relations with Sri Lanka from 1960. In 1980 Cuba maintained relations in South

Asia with Afghanistan (1975), Bangladesh (1972), Burma (1976), India (prior to 1959), Maldives (1977), Nepal (1975), and Sri Lanka (1960).[13]

Cuba's Relations in the Middle East

Cuba's relations in the Middle East are extensive, principally in the Arab countries, and particularly with the Palestine Liberation Army (PLO). Cuba's relations with most Arab nations in the region were cemented when Cuba sent a combat mission to fight alongside Syria in the 1973 Yom Kippur War with Israel. Cuba's relations in the region include relations with Iran (reestablished in 1979), Iraq (1960), Jordan (1979: ambassadorial relations—ambassador resides outside of country), Kuwait (1974), Lebanon (1960), South Yemen (1972), Syria (1965), Turkey (prior to 1959), and Yemen (1982).[14]

Cuba's relations with the Arab nations continued through the 1980s. In May of 1982, Guillermo García Frías met with the general-secretary of the Polisario Front, president of the Command Council of the Revolution of the Sahara Arab Democratic Republic, Mohamed Abdelazziz. García, vice-president of the Council of State and the Council of Ministers, repeated the need to recognize the Sahara Arab Democratic Republic, which had been admitted to the Organization of African Unity by the Foreign Ministers' Conference only months before.[15]

Cuba's choice of allies in the 1980s also provoked criticism. Cuba's work with the PLO in the Middle East and in the Sahara Desert fighting Morocco alongside guerrillas of the Polisario lost Cuba several partners. Cuba's diplomatic maneuvers in 1980 were not limited to Africa. In March of 1980 Cuban Foreign Minister Isidoro Malmierca Peoli visited Pakistan on behalf of the Cuban president to offer his services as mediator in the Afghan dispute. The objective of the trip was to mend fences with Pakistani president Mohammad Zia ul-Haq, who led the Islamic delegation of foreign ministers in January to condemn the Soviet invasion of Afghanistan and to begin a boycott of the Afghanistan government. In meetings with Pakistani president Zia and foreign policy adviser Agha Shahi during a two-day trip to Islamabad, the Cuban government sought to reverse the decision of the Moslem organization to ban Afghanistan's membership in the Islamic foreign ministers group.[16]

Across the Red Sea from the Horn of Africa, Cuba also began in 1980 to support the regimes of Yemen and Oman. In early 1980 a Soviet ship carried twelve hundred soldiers to South Yemen, a small Marxist nation at the entrance of the Red Sea. The Egyptian newspaper *Al Akhbar*, which reported the incident, stated that the ship started from Havana.[17] According to reports, Cuba sent military advisers to South Yemen in response to a friendship treaty signed by South Yemen and the Soviet Union in 1979. Cuba's assistance in the Arabian Sea and Indian Ocean area is strategically important because the Gulf of Aden at Yemen's border and the Gulf of Oman at Oman's northern tip are the ports of entrance to the Red Sea and Persian Gulf, respectively.

Both the Red Sea and the Persian Gulf are oil rich and have been areas of Western investment for several decades. The stated fear of several countries of the West, including the United States, is that Cuba's assistance programs and troops in southern Yemen will be used against neighboring Oman. That fear was articulated by Ronald Reagan in a press conference when he stated that "the Cuban intervention forces are being trained in armed warfare and will likely be deployed from southern Yemen against neighboring Oman." There is a link, he continued, between "Soviet moves in the Middle East and the role of Cuban mercenary forces in the service of Soviet strategic objectives."[18] In May 1982 Cuba and the Yemen Arab Republic established diplomatic relations at the embassy level.[19]

How Foreign Policy Is Made

The Structure of Foreign Policy: Cuban Constitutions of 1902, 1940, and 1975

In Cuba's two prerevolutionary constitutions, foreign policy decision making was not as centralized as it is under Castro's rule. Cuba's 1940 Constitution was promulgated only six months after Fulgencio Batista was elected and lasted until the government issued a new constitutional code in mid-1953. The opposition to Batista in 1952 (after the elections of Ramón Grau San Martín and Carlos Prío Socarrás) unified over the need to reinstate the 1940 document, which was considered balanced and just.

Although the 1940 Constitution was short lived, it established a basis of constitutional law which received wide public approval. The structure divided Cuba's government into three branches with a bilateral house in the legislature which by request of the president's cabinet could declare a state of national emergency. The executive branch had aspects of a European parliamentary system as well as the U.S. presidential structure.

After Batista's 1952 coup the Constitution was suspended, and the Constitutional Act of April 4 was enacted, to which Castro, leading the opposition, objected. The Constitution was reinstated for only a brief two years in 1955. Ironically, the suspension of the 1940 Constitution became a signal of Cuba's lost democratic values. In his defense at trial in October 1953, Castro staunchly criticized the principles of Batista's April 4 act, Article 118, which provides that the president is nominated by the Cabinet, thus circumventing Cuba's democratic process and the 1940 Constitution. It was this same contradiction which would also exist in Castro's first 1959 Fundamental Law and the Constitution of 1975.

In the early 1970s while Cuban foreign policy programs were changing, Cuba's leaders and the Cuban people were immersed in discussion and debate about the proper structure of domestic political institutions. By mid-decade, however, Cuba's foreign assistance programs had taken on an international dimension which Cuba's leaders (according to previous government predictions) had evidently not foreseen, and which had a lasting impact on the evolution of domestic government structures. Specifically, Cuba's increasing African involvements coincided with a significant retrenchment in the level of planned popular participation in the new government institutions: the fledgling and theoretically more democratic plan to institutionalize and democratize the revolution was reoriented to reinforce the more centrally controlled foreign policy program.

The original plan for Cuba's civil government called for the establishment of a "socialist revolutionary democracy" with a written constitution, the decentralization of government and the distribution of responsibility to different branches and levels of government, as well as a high degree of popular participation in all government decision making. Yet, while the military grew in importance and became more professional; plans for Poder Popular became less ambitious. Ironically, the 1970s were a decade of little outside threat; relative to other periods, Cuba's survival was not in question.

By the end of the decade, Cuba's assistance policies in Angola and Ethiopia caused identifiable changes in the Cuban military, including doubling the defense budget by 1979 and tripling it by 1982 as well as an increase in the number of military officials in the civilian government. Politically, the continuation of Cuba's Africa policy beyond its original scope created a need to maintain and strengthen government's decision-making authority at the expense of the decentralization plan. Although popular participation was formalized in the 1975 Constitution, it was confined to local issues; decisions on foreign policy and national development policy were left outside the legislative process. Cuba's legislature and judiciary stand as dependent branches of government, subordinate to the executive branch.

Background of the Adoption of the Constitution of 1975

After sixteen years under the rule of the provisional Fundamental Law of 1959, and the passage of several pieces of interim legislation, the Cuban government drafted a comprehensive constitution. Over the next year, it was widely circulated, submitted to the Communist party leadership at the meeting of the First Party Congress, and then presented for adoption by popular referendum. Significant changes, however, were made after popular approval which, in practical terms, left important decision making, particularly in the area of foreign policy, in the hands of the central government.

The process of drafting the Constitution began on 22 October 1974 when a constitutional committee was formed under the directorship of Blas Roca Calderío (an officer in the Political Bureau of the Cuban Communist Party Central Committee). Six months later a proposed draft of the new Constitution was published in the Cuban newspaper, *Granma*. For eight months thereafter, even before the Constitution was presented to the First Party Congress, 6.2 million people participated in discussions of the proposed Constitution and recommended changes.[20] Changes were then recommended by Fidel Castro (acting as first secretary of the Political Bureau of the Communist party) and by party officers; the Central Preparatory Commission incorporated many of these changes into the draft. In December 1975, three thousand party delegates met at the First Congress of the Communist party to approve the new document.[21]

In its approved form, on 15 February 1976 the Cuban Constitution was ratified by direct secret national referendum. Of Cuba's 5.5 million voters, 97.7 percent favored the Constitution, which took effect on 24 February 1976. As finally enacted, Cuba's new Constitution established a three-tiered legislative system, known as Poder Popular, which creates 169 municipal assemblies, 14 provincial assemblies, and 1 national assembly.[22] Legislators on the municipal level were designed to be elected by direct popular vote and appointed on the provincial and national levels. In addition, the new Constitution created a formal national government, including a Council of Ministers, the highest ranking executive body; a Council of State, whose members are elected by the National Assembly; and a Judiciary. The judiciary is, according to the Constitution, subordinate to the executive branch of government. The temporary Revolutionary and Popular Tribunals, established soon after 1959, were eliminated in the 1970s with the establishment of a court system.[23] Finally, the Constitution formalized the role of the Communist party in government.

The Continuation of Centralized Power: The Party and the State

A crucial question which was resolved only after the popular ratification process was the method of electing members to the National Assembly. The first draft of the Cuban Constitution, which defined the manner of implementing the prototype experiment in local elections that had taken place in Matanzas in 1974, and extending to all fourteen provinces of Cuba, had left one question unanswered: how would the National Assembly be elected?

The Cuban government had two distinct choices. On one hand, the deputies of the National Assembly could have been elected directly to their positions by the general public. On the other hand, the delegates to the municipal assemblies could elect the deputies to the National Assembly based on nominations from both within their ranks as well as by government and party officials. The difference between the two methods was particularly significant in areas which were not open to the public view, such as national development plans and foreign policy. Direct popular elections would have made legislators more accountable to public opinion for national policy decisions. Election by municipal assembly delegates, on the other hand, would not only insulate the National Assembly from direct accountability but also consolidate financial and policy power within the central government since municipal assembly delegates were unlikely to challenge foreign policy decisions for fear of alienating the national leadership.

The first draft of the Constitution was published in *Granma* on 11 April 1975. Article 69, Chapter VIII, entitled "Supreme Organs of People's Power," states: "The National Assembly of People's Power is elected according to the way and number established by law." The widely circulated draft, therefore, left the crucial question unanswered. This draft did contain the following provision:

> All Cubans 16 years of age and over in elections for deputies to the National Assembly and those for delegates to the Municipal Assembly . . . have the right to vote. (Chapter XI, Article 135.)

Clearly, the original plan presumed that the registered population would elect members of the National Assembly directly.

In the final draft, however, after the Constitution had been ratified by popular referendum, Article 69 of Chapter VIII was changed by the Central Preparatory Commission presided over by Fidel Castro to read, "The National Assembly of People's Power is composed of deputies elected by the Municipal Assemblies."[24] Article 135 of Chapter XI correspondingly deletes the reference to the National Assembly in its declaration of voting rights.

Another significant difference between the draft and final Constitution concerns the ratification of international treaties. Under the Constitution, the Council of Ministers must first approve a treaty. In the Constitution as originally drafted, the treaty would then be submitted to the National Assembly for ratification (Article 96(d)). In the final form, however, the National Assembly was stripped of this power, which was transferred to the Council of State (Article 96(ch)). The power to renounce treaties was also removed from the National Assembly (Article 73(i)) and remained in the hands of the Council of State (Article 88(m)). Additional changes in the draft Constitution include the addition to the final form of the power of the president of the Council of State to "sign the decree—laws of the Council of State," (Article 91(h)), and the power of the Executive Committee of the Council of Ministers to "in emergency cases . . . rule on matters normally under the jurisdiction of the Council of Ministers" (Article 95).

Foreign Policy Decision Making since 1975:
The Overlap of the Government and the Military

The balance between government concern for domestic development and concern for military matters has been uneasy since 1975. Its delicacy is most evident in the area of foreign policy decisions and political institutions. Specifically, there appears to be a split of opinion within the Council of Ministers regarding the proper role and function of Cuban foreign policy and, more particularly, the role of the military leadership in the decision-making process: Fidel Castro favors political aid and small arms programs; Carlos Rafael Rodríguez, a vice-president of the Cuban republic, emphasizes economic development; and Raúl Castro, first vice-president and until recently head of the armed forces, strongly supports increased military progress.

Role of the Cuban Armed Forces

One domestic political cost of Cuba's foreign policy is the increase in number and sophistication of Cuba's military establishment. As Cuba's defense budget doubled, the Cuban armed forces (Fuerzas Armadas Revolucionaria—FAR) acquired much more sophisticated weaponry in the mid-1970s than it had previously possessed. Between 1970 and 1974, the FAR changed significantly, setting the stage for a massive military involvement in Africa. Cuba's Africa policy, however, had effects on the domestic military establishment, which Cuba probably had not anticipated—effects which once formalized were difficult to reverse. Cuba's military, during this four-year period, changed from being labor intensive to capital intensive. While the numbers of standing military forces diminished from approximately 250,000 in 1970 to 100,000 in 1974, the costs doubled.[25]

Curiously, the history of the military in Cuba prior to the Revolution was one of upheaval and collapse. The role of the military in the sixty years from Cuban independence to Cuba's modern Revolution shifted. In the 1930s the army became a political force, more cohesive and stronger than any political institutions; in the 1940s the army began making policy decisions on a national level. With the 1933 Revolution, Batista turned the army into a vehicle for personal power, thus breaking all traditions of training requirements. Two weeks after Castro came to power, the government suspended the army, navy, and National Police Force and created the Revolutionary Armed Forces.

In a report published by the Cuban government on Cuban security in *Granma Weekly Review*, "The State Security Agencies: 20 years in defense of the Revolution," Cuba's contemporary military defense systems are outlined. "No revolution is worth anything unless it is able to defend itself," appeared as the cover quote by Lenin, emphasizing the importance of the military in the defense of the Revolution.[26]

The Cuban leadership and its power remain about the same as they were in the 1960s before the Constitution was ratified. Meanwhile, in the absence of truly democratic political institutions, civilian quasi-military groups similar to the postrevolutionary Committees for the Defense of the Revolution (CDRs) were established on 28 September 1960 as "groups to protect the Revolution and spread information about it."[27] In his 1980 May Day address, Castro called for the establishment of a civilian militia.

Shortly before the call for a civilian militia, Castro took a major step to further consolidate the power of the central government and, specifically, his own power. On 11 January 1980, *Granma* announced a decision by the Council of State to terminate twelve ministry-level positions and to consolidate nine government agencies.[28] The most significant shift involved ministry supervision: high-ranking members of the Executive Committee of the Council of Ministers each assumed direct supervision of several major ministries. Fidel Castro took charge of the armed forces (subordinating Raúl Castro in the process) and the ministries of health, interior, and culture. Carlos Rafael Rodríguez was named supervisor of foreign affairs, trade, and economic cooperation.

As Cuba enters its third decade of revolutionary rule, the institutional strength of the military is increasing. The military is the principal contender with the PCC for foreign policy decision-making power. Although government leaders had always agreed that the military should play a strong defensive role if the Revolution was to survive both foreign and domestic threats, there was no such consensus on the question of military involvement in domestic planning and administration. Raúl Castro, for example, reportedly favored the strengthening of the Ministry of the Armed Forces, while Fidel Castro reportedly favored limited military involvement in the institutionalization process.

The original government plan for the 1970s was to institutionalize the Cuban Revolution along broad, democratic lines. Despite the debate about its proper role, the military appeared to have been relegated to a back seat at the outset of the institutionalization process. The major theme of the Cuban leadership was to encourage participation by the Cuban people in both the planning and administration of all phases of government. In October 1974 the Cuban leadership embarked on its plan for institutionalization. The leadership of the party (the Political Bureau) and the leadership of the state (the Executive Committee of the Council of Ministers) established the Joint Party and Government Commission to draft a Cuban Constitution. In order to test the participatory legislative body which would be established in the Constitution, the joint commission proposed a small-scale experiment by local levels of direct election of the constituent assembly.

Thus, in 1974 the first experiment in popular participation and local decision making was initiated in the province of Matanzas to establish the basis of a participatory legislative branch of government. Massive educational campaigns accompanied the experiment, preparing the Cuban population for the first democratic elections in twenty years of revolutionary rule, during which most of the population had never once voted. The goals of Cuba's institutionalization process were ambitious. The objectives, according to the Cuban government, were to democratize the electoral process, decentralize the state apparatus, and reduce the government bureaucracy. On the local level only, the summer of 1974 experiment was an unqualified success.

In a national referendum, 97.7 percent of registered Cubans voted in favor of the draft Constitution. The ratification process of the Cuban Constitution was a long and thoughtful one. It began in October 1974 when the Joint Party and Government Commission was created to write a draft constitution.

This change in plans coincided with the rapid increase in Cuban involvement in Angola. In November 1975 Cuban forces entered the Angolan conflict in earnest.

By December Cuban troops were entering Angola at the rate of four hundred per week. In January the rate surged to one thousand weekly. In February 1976 while Cubans were going to the polls to approve their first Constitution, the number of Cuban soldiers in Angola totalled fifteen thousand. The rapid escalation of Cuban military support to Angola required a strong central government with full authority to make quick, binding foreign policy commitments. The changes in the Constitution were contrary to the original spirit of the draft Constitution. The experience since the adoption of the Constitution and the ostensible success in Angola suggest that military concerns have preempted concerns for popular participation in the mind of the Cuban leadership.

Notes

1. Fidel Castro's speech of 2 January 1966, published in *Granma*, was a harsh reply to China's cut in sugar purchases. In the following weeks, several accusations were made including Castro's characterization of Mao as a senile idiot and his call to Cubans "not to put up with leaders who had passed the sixty mark." Cited in K.S. Karol, *Guerillas in Power*, trans. Arnold Pomerand (New York: Hill and Wang, 1970), p. 305.

2. Survey of the China Mainland Press, no. 1930, cited in Cecil Johnson, *Communist China and Latin America, 1959-67* (New York: Columbia University Press, 1970, p. 130). For a discussion of the early skepticism of Chinese leaders of Castro see Donald S. Zagoria, *The Sino-Soviet Conflict 1956-1961* (Princeton, N.J.: Princeton University Press, 1962).

3. At the welcoming rally, a member of the Chinese Communist party's Political Bureau of the Central Committee emphasized China's close ties with the Western hemisphere, stating, "The Chinese people and the Latin American people have common aspirations . . . in their striving for national independence." Statement by P'eng Chen, 22 January 1959. Cited in Johnson, *Communist China*, p. 134.

4. Ibid., p. 136.
5. Ibid., p. 144.
6. Ibid., p. 148.
7. For a discussion of the Cuban-Soviet trade agreement signed in February 1963 and the Chinese agreement of April 1963, see Andres Suaréz, *Cuba: Castroism and Communism* (Cambridge, Mass.: MIT Press, 1967), pp. 156-164, 179-182, 199.
8. Johnson, *Communist China*, p. 154.
9. Ibid., p. 163.
10. Ibid., p. 165.
11. Interview by the author with Carlos Rafael Rodríguez, Vice-President of Cuba, New York City, 17 June 1982.
12. *Granma*, 16 May 1982.
13. National Foreign Assessment Center, *The Cuban Economy: A Statistical Review*, March 1981, p. 53.
14. Ibid.
15. *Granma*, 9 May 1982.
16. *Washington Post*, 28 March 1980, p. 33.
17. *Miami Herald*, 4 February 1980, p. 20A.

18. Ibid., 8 February 1980, p. 20D.
19. *Granma*, 23 May 1982.
20. The discussion concerning the proposed Constitution occurred at meetings of the Communist party (PCC), trade unions, Committees for the Defense of the Revolution, the Federation of Cuban Women, the National Association of Small Farmers, the Federation of University Students, the Federation of Students of Intermediate Education, military units, and Cuban missions abroad. Fidel Castro, "Address to the First Congress of the Communist Party," Havana, 17 December 1975.
21. The 1976 Constitution eliminated the role of prime minister of the Republic of Cuba. The president of the Council of State under the new Constitution is also the head of state and the head of government.
22. The original experiment in the province of Matanzas, which Cuba entitled Poder Popular, would have established a four-tiered system with municipal, regional, and provincial assemblies, and a proposed National Assembly for legislative representation. When the new Constitution was established, a new politico-administrative system was instituted—for the purpose of decentralizing power within these legislative bodies and enabling the bodies to function more effectively—in which the number of provinces was increased from six to fourteen, the number of municipalities decreased from 407 to 169, and the regional level of Poder Popular was eliminated altogether. For a discussion of the Cuban judicial system, see Harold J. Berman and Van R. Whiting, Jr., "Impressions of Cuban Law," *The American Journal of Comparative Law* 28, no. 3 (Summer 1980). The framework of Cuban criminal law is similar to U.S. and Western European law insofar as the right to counsel and the presumption of innocence.
23. The Central Preparatory Commission which aided in the drafting of the Constitution and recommended changes to it consisted of Fidel Castro, presiding, Raúl Castro, Osvaldo Dorticós, Juan Almeida, Guillermo García, Armando Hart, Ramiro Valdés, Sergio del Valle, Blas Roca, Carlos Rafael Rodríguez, Raul García Palaez, Isidoro Malmierca Peoli, Pedro Miret, Antonio Perz Herrero, and Jorge Risquet.
24. There is some dispute about when the changes were made. One account is that the draft constitution was published in *Granma*; the final draft approved by the party in December was published in final form first in the *Gaceta Oficial* and then in *Granma* in January, and thus submitted in final form for popular referendum and proclaimed on 24 February 1976. See Jorge I. Domínguez, *Cuba: Order and Revolution*, appendix D, "Textual Changes in the Draft Constitution of 1976 and the Draft Family Code" (Cambridge, Mass.: Belknap Press of Harvard University Press, 1978). A second account is that the draft Constitution was published in *Granma* on 11 April 1975 approved by the First Party Congress, and submitted to the *Official Gazette* on 27 December. The referendum, held on 15 February 1976 then asked the question: "Do you approve the draft Constitution and the draft Law on Constitutional Transition—Yes or No?" The Cuban population voted, therefore, on the draft Constitution. The Central Preparatory Committee then incorporated the recommendations that were made in public discussion and submitted the final form of the Constitution to the *Official Gazette* on 24 February 1976. (See appendix J, "Resolution on Approval of the Constitution".) See Pamela S. Falk, "Cuba, 1974–1978," in *Constitutions of the Countries of the World*, eds. Albert P. Blaustein and Gisbert H. Flanz (Dobbs Ferry, N.Y.: Oceana, 1979), pp. 4–13. In either case, the Constitution that was widely circulated for public consumption, both authors agree, was the draft version, which provided for

broad public participation, and the Constitution which was officially proclaimed retained strong centralized power.

25. Jorge I. Domínguez, "The Cuban Operation in Angola: Costs and Benefits for the Armed Forces," *Cuban Studies* 8, no. 1 (January 1978):12. See Jorge I. Domínguez, "The Cuban Armed Forces and International Order." (Paper delivered at the Center for International Studies, Harvard University, January 1977.)

26. Ana Maria Radaelli, *Granma Weekly Review* (Havana), special supplement, 9 December 1979.

27. Castro described the CDRs in an address to the First Congress of the Communist Party, as "a crushing and militant response by the masses to counterrevolutionary terrorism." Fidel Castro, Report to the First Congress, Department of Revolutionary Orientation of the Central Committee of the Communist Party of Cuba (Havana, 1977).

28. The Cuban Constitution stated (article 93) that the "number, denomination, and functioning of the ministries and central agencies making up the Council of Ministers are determined by law." Pursuant to that mandate, on 30 November 1976, Law 1323 was enacted, which named the previously mentioned state agencies.

Leonid Brezhnev, Nikita Khrushchev, and Fidel Castro.

8
The Dollars and Cents of Cuba's Foreign Economic Policies: The Cost of Soviet Aid

Foreign trade, for developing and developed nations alike, is considered essential for economic autonomy, economic growth, and development planning. International commercial agreements are often regarded as the nexus between domestic development and foreign policy, and most analysts of Cuba's development during the two decades since the 1959 Revolution agree that Cuba's foreign economic policy plays a large part in determining Cuba's future domestic course. In general, the influence of a nation's foreign trade on its domestic economy is direct and obvious: foreign trade creates the export earnings, which feed back into the economy and provide the fuel for development programs. The choices of foreign commercial arrangements determine a nation's trade partners and ultimately affect its international political relations. A successful foreign trade policy may form a surplus balance of payments; an unsuccessful program creates a deficit.

Cuba's economy, analysts argue, is exceptionally open to the fluctuations of the international market place. Four basic characteristics of the Cuban economy are primarily responsible for Cuba's vulnerability: (1) Cuba's overreliance on sugar as its primary export commodity; (2) Cuba's dependence on the Soviet Union for favorable trade subsidies, a guaranteed market for its sugar products, and loan agreements; (3) the vulnerability of sugar to international market pressures; and (4) the disparity between Cuban urban and rural standards of living.[1] These factors make Cuba's position in the international market place (a product of international perceptions of Cuba as well as the terms of commercial agreements) of paramount importance for domestic development.

These commercial agreements will be discussed with regard to (1) the importance of sugar exports in Cuba's commercial agreements of the last decade; (2) the effects of a single-export economy on balance of payments and future plans to industrialize or diversify agriculture; (3) the Cuban government's stated desire to diversify foreign trade partners; and (4) the effect of Cuba's socialist trade, that is, trade with the Soviet Union, and Cuba's membership in the Council for Mutual Economic Assistance (CMEA) on the future of Cuba's trade. The commercial agreements may be separated into three categories: Cuba's trade with socialist countries (the Soviet Union and the CMEA); Cuba's trade with nonsocialist countries (Latin America, Europe, Canada, Japan); and multinational agreements, such as the U.N.-sponsored International Sugar Agreement and the U.N. General Agreement on Tariffs and Trade (GATT).

In the early 1960s, Edward Boorstein, a U.S. economist who was invited to Cuba to participate in the early planning programs of the National Bank of Cuba and the Ministry of Foreign Commerce, stated, "Little of anything in Cuba can be understood unless the parts are related to the whole."[2] It is within the context of this constant interaction between foreign trade and Cuban government decisions regarding development programs that foreign trade must be analyzed. In short, Cuban foreign trade policy is a major factor in the Cuban government's foreign policy.

Cuba's early foreign trade agreements (1960–63) were influenced and in part directed by the transition from a capitalist, market economy to a socialist, centrally planned economy. Additional influences during this period include the economic blockade by the United States, the sanctions imposed on Cuba's trade with Latin America by the OAS, and the favorable terms of trade offered by the Soviet Union. During the next period, from the mid-1960s to 1970, Cuba's foreign trade and domestic economic strategies were affected by other pressures. Limited by the U.S. and OAS embargoes, Cuba's economic planners experimented with different policies and were themselves divided as to the most advisable course. From 1963 to 1970, Cuba concentrated all energies on the sugar industry, diverting labor and capital from early industrialization plans. The Cuban policy emphasized its comparative advantage in sugar production; it established strong credit and trade relations with the Soviet Union; and it remained fairly isolated from other potential international trade partners.

Cuba's International Trade: An Overview

In Cuba, foreign trade dominates the domestic economy. This was true before the Revolution and continues to be true today—typical, some analysts state, of an island economy. In the 1970s and 1980s, according to the Cuban government, foreign trade accounted for 25 to 30 percent of Cuba's gross national product.[3]

The 1970s began an era of contradictory trade policies and domestic development strategies. Cuban leaders stated their desire to industrialize and diversify agriculture, but concentrated development in the sugar industry. Internationally, in the early 1970s Cuba diversified trade partners. Significantly, in 1972 Cuba joined the CMEA, whose terms of trade have provided an incentive for an increase in Cuba's sugar export reliance.

The period from 1970 to the mid-1980s presented new policy dilemmas to Cuba's foreign economic advisers. Cuba had been unsuccessful in the domestic pursuit of establishing a trade surplus through sugar production and was more vulnerable to the international financial forces (because of the concentration on its sugar infrastructure) than during any previous era. Cuban government leaders had now experimented with entirely different development strategies—one of rapid and sustained industrialization and another of concentration in agriculture production. Both failed for domestic reasons.

Cuba's 1985-90 goals are cautious. While export promotion is a priority, Cuba presented the national economic goals to its Western creditors with an emphasis on restrictions of domestic consumption, increases in productivity, and minimal increases in "quality of life" expenses such as wages and benefits to workers.[4] While Cuba's trade remained 86 percent tied to socialist countries, Cuba increased imports totaling $334 million in capital and intermediary goods in order to lay a better foundation for export promotion during 1985-90.[5]

Most significant, Cuba's return to market mechanisms (or its program of material incentives—simply stated, the introduction of profit in the Cuban economy), has expanded since the distribution of surplus goods in the retail market was first introduced as the "free market" in 1980. In large part, the ability of the Cuban economy to resell two-thirds of its oil imports is based on austerity measures imposed on the Cuban population, while the "free" or open parallel market has increased salaries of the Cuban population. As a result, Cuba planned to introduce additional market incentives in its proposed 1985-90 economic program. These include bonuses for increased exports to workers, special bonuses for savings of fuel and electricity, and further planned increases in the "free markets," which increased by 45 percent in 1984, resulting in the increase of salaries (including wages, benefits, and bonuses) by 8.2 percent.

Cuba's *trade composition* has not changed significantly since 1958. Sugar, as of 1976, remained the principal export commodity, accounting for 86 percent of export earnings. Most studies place Cuba's sugar export ratio at between 74 and 82 percent of total exports in 1958. Nickel and other minerals constituted 8 percent of exports, and tobacco and shellfish another 24 percent each. Although there was a substantial increase in the structure of imports from 1966 to 1970 (from consumer goods to capital goods and spare parts), the structure of imports has not changed significantly during the 1970s. This represents an initial conversion of the economy to a centrally planned socialist economy. The lack of significant shifts in the 1970s represents the failure of Cuba's import substitution policies.

Cuba's foreign trade since 1961 has grown at an average annual rate of 10 percent, which includes exceptionally high growth years such as 1974 when the volume of foreign trade grew by 14 percent.[7] The composition of Cuban imports in the 1970s, moreover, has not shifted significantly, and the major imported goods continue to be crude petroleum and transportation equipment. In 1978 Cuba's most important imports included capital goods, industrial raw materials, food, and petroleum.[8]

The direction (or *partner composition*) of Cuban trade changed fundamentally in 1960 but has not shifted significantly during the last fifteen years, according to the Cuban government; 83.5 percent of Cuban trade has been conducted with the same trading partners during this period.[9] The proportion of socialist trade declined from 71 percent of total trade to 66 percent during the first four years of the 1970s and increased again in the last four years. In the 1970s a period of internationalization of the Revolution began in which bilateral agreements with different trade partners increased. According to a study of Cuba's trade, bilateral agreements signed during this period "suggest a deliberate Cuban policy to legitimate its system by creating links with other nations."[10]

Inflation and other international monetary shifts in capitalist trading began to affect Cuba's trade with Western nations in the mid-1970s.[11] In part, this accounts for Cuba's 1975 trade deficit of $650 million (U.S.). "External debts and balance-of-payments difficulties increase," the Cuban ambassador to the United Nations, Raúl Roa Kourí stated in 1979, "while purchasing power deteriorates and access to Western markets becomes more and more limited." Specifically, Cuban imports of capital goods (for investment in agriculture and industry) have increased enormously "exerting a negative influence in the existing terms of trade between developed and underdeveloped countries."[12]

Foreign trade crises in Cuba, which first occurred during the early period of revolutionary growth and later during the 1963 to 1970 period, laid the groundwork for the ensuing years of difficulty in the 1970s. The decisions that Cuba made in the mid-1970s deepened the negative effects of this international economic crisis. Cuba's 1970s trade commitments with socialist nations and the resultant structure of the Cuban economy left the Cuban economy vulnerable to the fluctuations of the international market place.

In 1975 world market prices of sugar fell. High prices in 1974 to 1975 had caused world consumption to drop and resulted in lower prices and an increase in global sugar-stock reserves for the first time in several years.[13] Although Cuba remains the largest sugar exporter in the world, internationally Cuba has dropped to fourth place in world production. Soviet subsidies of Cuban sugar exports and oil imports have been vital to the growth in the economy. By Cuba's calculation, each metric ton of sugar exported to market economies during 1983–85 cost Cuba $116 in hard currency because of the low price of sugar in the world market.[14]

Additionally, Cuba is dependent on the improved technologies and trade of the advanced capitalist countries, whose economies are today in crisis.[15] The international monetary crisis in Western markets today, and above all the crisis of the U.S. dollar, have "gravely affected the economy of the developing world," the Cuban Ambassador Raúl Roa Kourí argued in 1979.[16]

Cuba's first rescheduling of its foreign debt to the West came in 1982, due, by Cuba's calculations, to the drop in the price of world sugar prices and the amount of sugar exported. But by Cuba's own calculations, the loans to Cuba from the West have had a limited impact because they have been principally restricted to trade financing. The Cuban National Bank reported in 1985:

> The rescheduling, most of whose causes were alien to the debtor country, has made it possible to soften temporarily the debt service, but its benefits have been considerably limited by being restricted to strictly financial criteria rather than extended

to the broader context required by the process of economic development and the long-term equilibrium of the balance of payments.[17]

Cuba's Trade with Socialist Countries, 1970 to 1985

Cuba's economy is a centrally planned stated-owned economy in which the "state organizes, directs, and controls the economic life of the nation."[18] Foreign trade, according to the Constitution, is "the exclusive function of the state" (Article 18). The Ministry of Foreign Trade was created in 1961 to be the only state agency authorized to conduct foreign trade.[19] All trade is conducted by the ministry through its forty foreign trade enterprises, each responsible for a specific product. The central planning agency, the Junta Central de Planificación (JUCEPLAN), established in 1961, formulates the direction of long-range economic planning, and in 1970 it became the highest agency of Cuban economic policy.[20] Annual budgets of individual agencies and economic enterprises are submitted to JUCEPLAN. After conferring with members of the National Bank where it compiles Cuba's central budget, JUCEPLAN then submits a recommended budget to the Council of Ministers. The budget today is based on a system of cost accounting and calculated by computer and data collection systems introduced since 1970. Cuba's state bank, the National Bank of Cuba, in addition to aiding JUCEPLAN in the formulation of the annual budget, issues all currency and finances all imports. The Ministry of Foreign Trade (MINCEX) directs the movement of the enterprises such as CUBAZUCAR (sugar and sugar products); CUBAEXPORT (oil, cement, chemicals); CARIBEX (seafood); CUBATOBACO (tobacco); CUBANIQUEL (nickel); and CUBARTESANIA (textile garments). Until 1975 the Cuban enterprises did not retain their earned income; nor did they fulfill cost accounting and profitability measures. The new 1975 Economic Management System requires each enterprise to balance its budget. Since all elements of the economy are state owned, trade and specific commercial agreements rely heavily on Cuban government policies of (1) budgetary accountability, (2) profitability, (3) diversification of trade partners, and (4) domestic development.

As a result, the implementation of the Economic Management System (Sistema de Dirección Económica) also affects Cuba's foreign trade. Foreign trade in the 1970s, Cuba's choice of foreign trading partners, and the terms of foreign trade agreements have together had a forceful impact on Cuba's balance of payments, its ability to increase trade with different nonsocialist nations, and its choice of domestic economic development programs. Ultimately they have been the most significant factors in the determination of the direction of the domestic economy. The Cuban economy must absorb the entire shock of its foreign trade arrangements. In sum, the levels of development indicate that Cuba's trade is as vulnerable on the international financial market as it was in prerevolutionary days.

Membership in the Council for Mutual Economic Assistance and Integration and Specialization Policies: Trade with the Soviet Union

In January 1949 the Council for Mutual Economic Assistance (CMEA) was established in Moscow with the objectives of improving the economic development of socialist nations, exchanging technological and economic information, and counteracting the Marshall Plan assistance program from Western nations.[21] In 1969 the CMEA charter was written, and it listed the aims of the organization as follows: (1) to contribute to advanced economic and technical growth of member countries, (2) to achieve a higher level of industrialization in the less developed countries of the organization, (3) to increase labor productivity through efficiency, and (4) to insure continual progress in the welfare of member states.[22]

A significant aspect of CMEA agreements is the link between foreign trade and national development plans which is implicit in its policy of "international socialist division of labor," which was adopted by CMEA members in June 1962. At that time, the organization enunciated the goals of *coordinated development* of the economies of member nations as well as a policy of specialization of their export products.

The trade policies most significant to Cuba's involvement in CMEA are those of integration and specialization. Planning of integration and specialization in CMEA countries is based on the principles of socialist development. This definition, which orients CMEA accords, applies several tenets of Marxist economic theory to policies of distribution. The realization of the Communist welfare state is a major objective of development based on the principle of "to each according to their needs, from each according to their ability." Each society, according to its resources and production capability, must achieve as high a rate of growth as possible with the maximum possible diversification of products. A second tenet applied in these socialist trade agreements is the law of planned proportional development. The application of a proportional development strategy requires an economy which is state owned and centrally planned and which follows a growth strategy which considers social as well as political and economic objectives. By definition, planned proportional development includes socially progressive programs such as education. This policy is sometimes referred to as unbalanced since it seeks, at times, to deemphasize rapid growth in certain sectors in favor of the policy of distribution and social reform. Finally, economic development along socialist lines requires the deemphasis of the importation of capital goods in order to emphasize self-sufficient production and reduce consumer product imports.

The CMEA policy of specialization derives from the simple trade maxim that concurrent expansion of trade within a region or alliance enables the region to expand trade and production at a faster rate than the domestic production in each member nation individually. This policy is established by eliminating overlapping and duplicate production among participant countries.[23] A 1960s study of intraregional coordination policies within CMEA illustrated that a 50 percent increase in production specialization would increase their labor productivity by 20 percent.[24] The result, CMEA planners insisted, would be mutual interdependence.[25]

The major problem with a policy of specialization in theory (and one which has been responsible for the lack of development within certain key sectors of Cuba's economy) is that it increases trade dependence. Among the beneficial effects of regional cooperation is the resultant increase in regional labor productivity and trade relations which are interdependent not dependent.

CMEA trade is organized on the basis of two types of trade agreements: first, trade protocols or annual accords which fix prices and quantities, and, second, middle-term (five-year) trade agreements.[26] Two international organizations which serve as extensions of CMEA trade organizations (and are tangentially important to Cuba's membership) are the two banks of the council: the International Investment Bank (IIB) and the International Bank for Economic Cooperation (IBEC).[27] Both banks were established to serve the member nations with intraregional trade: IBEC provides short-term capital credits in nontransferable currency, the transferable ruble; the IIB provides long-term capital for members and has an endowment of both transferable rubles as well as hard currency.[28]

In 1954 CMEA established the policy which linked *specialization* to the coordination of member countries' national economic plans.[29] A CMEA handbook, published in 1972, defined the policy of specialization as follows:

> The idea of international division of labour, which is one form of social *division of labour*, is that countries should specialize in the production of particular goods for subsequent exchange. *Transcending national borders*, it has drawn all peoples into the process of social production.[30]

Although this process guarantees the most efficient use of natural, economic, and manpower resources, there are significant problems with the policy.

CMEA: Trade Policy

Since the 1960s, CMEA has adopted the principles of international socialist division of labor. In the early 1970s, CMEA had other serious economic problems. Among those were the following: (1) the Eastern bloc had a hard currency debt to the West, estimated at $45.8 billion (U.S.) at the end of 1976; (2) global inflation and the international recession increased prices of imports to CMEA countries; (3) there was less demand since reduced aggregate growth in developed nations of the West had reduced imports; and (4) oil prices were higher with eastern Europe paying $3 billion (U.S.) for oil supplies.[31]

Even more significant, the major problem within CMEA trade is the regulation of prices. In the past decade, CMEA has produced a market in which the prices paid for machinery and equipment are higher than the world market prices and the prices paid for primary products with the exception of sugar are lower.[32] Since Cuba's trade in 1974 was 52 percent with CMEA in addition to the fact that this trade was done as a semibarter negotiating process, the amount of convertible currency in Cuba was (and is) low. CMEA agreements or annual trade protocols establish the prices and volume of each nation's trade quotas with the council and are based on political considerations and foreign policy decisions in addition to economic factors.

Cuba's trade with the CMEA has accounted for a significant proportion of Cuba's foreign trade since its membership in 1972. Exports to CMEA countries tripled between 1973 and 1976, from $781 million (U.S.) to $2.3 billion (U.S.) in 1976. Imports from CMEA countries almost doubled during the same period, from $1.2 billion (U.S.) in 1973 to $2.2 billion (U.S.) in 1976. In 1974 after two years of trade under the CMEA agreements, Cuba's trade concentration with member nations of the CMEA and other socialist nations combined did not exceed Cuba's trade concentration with the United States in 1958. By 1976, however, trade concentration with socialist nations was at approximately the equivalent to Cuba's prerevolutionary U.S. trade. At that time, Cuban exports of sugar to CMEA countries reached 64 percent of total sugar exports.

CMEA trade agreements offered Cuba additional subsidies to those that Cuba received from Soviet trade. Cuba joined CMEA because it provided incentives even greater than Cuban-Soviet trade had, with no reduction in Soviet assistance. In fact, Cuba entered the CMEA on terms far more favorable than all other nine members.

In December 1979 Fidel Castro emphasized the problems of CMEA trade when he addressed the National Assembly. Trade with CMEA member nations, he stated, is unable to provide Cuba with essential supplies. Wood, for example, was a product that Cuba needed, and it had an agreement to buy five hundred thousand cubic meters from the Soviet Union. The contract was not honored, however, and only three hundred thousand cubic meters were delivered, which had a severe impact on Cuba's troubled construction industry. A second socialist trade agreement for chickens was cancelled, thereby forcing Cuba to slaughter more cattle in order to fulfill domestic food needs. However, subsidies from the Soviet Union for sugar exports in December 1979 were thirty cents above the world market price (of fourteen cents per pound). Oil sold below world market prices (of twenty-five to thirty dollars [U.S.] a barrel).[33]

Subsidies by CMEA nations by 1980 were high, and in the short term Cuba could not find as favorable trade agreements on any other market. Although Cuba's domestic production has been low and domestic economic problems prevail, Cuba does not have the viable option of diversifying trade partners or reducing trade concentration in CMEA nations for the foreseeable future. Cuba's membership in CMEA offered Cuba, at a minimum, a continuation of subsidized sugar prices and favorable terms of trade on capital goods imports from the Soviet Union. The additional advantages included greater efficiency with less labor necessary as a result of the CMEA policies of labor division and plan coordination.

The significance of Cuba's export structure in the early 1970s has become more apparent since the close of the decade. Higher levels of productivity did occur in the late 1970s, and the volume of Cuban exports did not increase. Rather, Cuba's membership in the CMEA has resulted in a static policy of comparative advantage and expanded production in Cuba's single principal sector—sugar. Clearly, the costs of Cuba's membership in the CMEA have been and continue to be extremely high.

It is too simple an answer to point only to pressures from the Soviet Union for an understanding of Cuba's motivation to join the council. Cuba's debt to the Soviet Union in 1972 was high, but Cuba during this period had substantial economic and political assets to offer to both council member nations and the Soviet Union. First, Cuba's membership added political credibility to the organization. Second, and more important, Cuba's economy in 1972 was beginning to gain steadily—though slowly—and all indications were that the Cuban economy was in the beginning of a period of sustained growth. This prospect was evident in 1973, and it culminated in 1974 in high sugar prices, consequent high revenues, and a surplus balance of payments.

Cuba joined the CMEA in 1972 because the Soviet Union provided Cuba with strong incentives to do so. In addition, Cuba had options in the 1970s; perhaps they were restricted relative to the economic prospects of a developed market nation. Nonetheless, Cuban economic planners and political leaders had a choice, and the promise of an economically sound future. As Cuba entered its third development decade, Cuban planners had a narrower range of options. According to the Cuban government, the economy has grown as an annual average of 4.7 percent during the last 25 years. However, other sources point to growth rates as low as -0.2 percent during the same period. The 1985 plan cited the growth of gross social product from 4.5 percent to 5 percent; a 3.5 percent increase in productivity; a 1.5 percent increase in wages; and maintenance of the present "standard of living".[34] At this point, with an infrastructure firmly tied to sugar production, and record world market inflation, Cuba has little choice but to retain the trade alliances which it made slightly more than a decade ago.

There had been several incentives for Cuba to enter the CMEA, including high subsidized prices for Cuban commodities, low prices for necessary capital goods and oil, and perhaps most significant, the promise of more efficient production through policies of coordinated planning. Membership, however, necessitated that Cuba emphasize production which required the least immediate investment—sugar. Cuban economic planners reluctantly acknowledge the fact that Cuba's trade with the CMEA encouraged Cuba's sugar production and trade.[35] The second term Cuba accepted was one which all member nations must accept—the *barter trade* based on nonconvertible currency, the result of which is the restriction of Cuba's trade partners due to a shortage of currency with which to trade on the open market.

Trade with the Soviet Union

In addition to Cuba's trade with the Soviet Union through CMEA agreements, Cuba and the Soviet Union maintain substantial separate commercial arrangements. A sign of increased Cuban-Soviet relations were the five Cuba-USSR 1972 Economic Agreements, signed on 23 December 1972. The first two agreements concern the repayment of Cuba's foreign debt and the establishment of credits. The first agreement, regarding Cuba's debt to the Soviet Union incurred from 1960 to 1973, postpones repayment of the credits which the Soviet Union granted to Cuba to compensate for an unfavorable balance of trade until 1 January 1986 (Article 1). Thereafter, they are to be paid over a period of twenty-five years (Article 2) with interest suspended (Article 3). The second agreement reschedules the debt incurred by Cuba to the Soviet Union for the years 1973, 1974, and 1975. It too is deferred until 1986 for a period of twenty-five years with no interest. The third agreement specifies the commodities which would be exchanged in the 1973 to 1975 period by both countries. The most significant agreement, however, is the fourth agreement, concerning economic and technical cooperation during this three-year period. In Article 1 of this agreement the Soviet Union and Cuba agree to cooperate in the development of the textile, nickel, electric power, and oil-refining industries and to discuss such projects as mechanization of the sugar harvest, introduction of computers in the national economy, automobile repair plants, military training, and irrigation project cooperation.

The fifth agreement establishes a floor price of sugar at approximately eleven cents (U.S.) per pound and a floor price of nickel at approximately five thousand U.S. dollars per ton. This agreement is an attempt, according to Fidel Castro, "to create conditions to promote the production of sugar and nickel to Cuba and eliminate the influence of wavering world market prices."[36]

Soviet subsidies in the form of loans, credits, and commodity subsidies have been substantial. The Soviet Union assisted Cuba in the maintenance and modernization of Cuba's sugar industry.[37] Cuba's debt to the Soviet Union for military assistance totaled $1.7 billion (U.S.) for the 1981–83 period.[38] Economic support from the Soviets had risen to $13 million (U.S.) per day by 1983, or $4 billion a year in addition to $600 million annually in military assistance.[39]

An additional subsidy supplied by the Soviet Union in the mid-1980s was the increasing supply of fuel, which the Cuban government was permitted to export for hard currency, if domestic consumption was limited and surpluses were available.[40] By 1983, Soviet exports of oil to Cuba totaled 225,000 barrels daily.[41] In 1984, Cuba resold approximately two-thirds of the total oil imported from the Soviet Union.[42]

Cuba's Trade with Nonsocialist Countries, 1970 to 1985

The purpose of the U.N. sponsored International Sugar Agreement (ISA) of 1977—which went into effect on January 1, 1978 for a period of five years (1978 to 1983)—

was to create an equilibrium between *supply* and *demand* in the world sugar market.[43] In theory, this equilibrium is created by stabilizing the price levels, quantities, and stocks of sugar, thus making sugar prices profitable for producers and fair to consumers. The agreement establishes a *price stabilization mechanism* which combines a quota system for the sale of sugar on the world market with a system of special stocks which are managed at the international level but maintained on a national level.[44] The price scale in the agreement establishes a floor price of eleven cents a pound and a maximum of twenty-one cents a pound. Cuba received the highest quota endowment of 2.5 million tons during 1978 to 1979. Article 31 of the ISA outlines the "exports by Cuba to Socialist countries" stating that Cuba may export to socialist countries which are CMEA members, but is limited to exporting 650,000 tons annually to non-CMEA socialist nations, after which any exports are deducted from the quota that Cuba is given.

Although world market prices have occasionally risen to far above this level, on the average this price is favorable. An analysis by the Cuban government in 1975 argued that if the price of sugar had been stabilized at ten cents per pound during the first two decades of the revolution, Cuba's trade balance during those years would have been in the black.

In 1976 to 1977 world sugar prices fell as a direct result of the ratification of the ISA. The market was glutted since sugar-exporting nations, fearing problems with the quota restrictions with surplus sugar stocks, sold large quantities before the finalization of the agreement on 1 January. World sugar prices were low in 1976 to 1977 (because of a rise in world production), thus creating a surplus on the world market. The tripling of import duties by the United States in 1976 slowed trade in Western markets. As a result there was an even greater imbalance of trade.[45] In July 1976 the world price of sugar plummeted to 13.2 cents per pound; the price fell to less than 10 cents per pound in August 1976; and it ranged from 7.1 to 10.0 cents from September to December 1977. In addition, the prospect of increased production in 1977 to 1978 caused prices to drop. As anticipated, the world sugar production rose to 90 million tons in 1977 to 1978, an increase of 5.2 percent over 1976 to 1977.[46]

On 2 January 1980, the United States ratified the ISA, adding substantial weight to the international impact of the agreement. In April of the same year, the U.S. Senate approved legislation which allows the United States to become a full member. As of 1980, the only major sugar-trading region that had not signed the agreement is the European Economic Community.

The agreement provides in chapter IX for the special arrangement "which Cuba has with the Soviet Union to provide a guaranteed market for sugar and higher than world market purchase price."[47] The ISA gives Cuba the largest export quota of 2.5 million tons although Cuba's actual 1978 shipment was limited to 2.1 million tons, providing Cuba with hard currency earnings of $450 million (U.S.) in 1978.[48] The agreement stabilized a market whose fluctuations had ranged from 65.5 cents per pound to 7.5 cents in twenty-two months, at a time when

Cuba had been hit with three years of severe drought.[49] The world price fluctuations were now regulated to some extent by the agreement. Minister of Foreign Trade Marcelo Fernández Font emphasized the importance of the ISA, given Cuba's marked dependency on sugar exports.[50] He cited three reasons for the importance of the agreement: (1) it ratified Cuba's position as the leading world sugar exporter, (2) it gave Cuba special arrangements that favor Cuba and acknowledge Cuba's trade arrangements with the Soviet Union, and (3) it created favorable export prices which had currency exchange.[51] Due to Cuba's harvest problems in 1980, the increased world sugar prices and the lifting of sugar quotas were not particularly helpful to the Cuban market.

Cuba's trade with Western markets diminished significantly in 1975 to 1976 and began to increase again in 1977. However, the high levels of debt—based on loans and negative balances of payment during these years—has forced Cuba to cut back on trade with these nations in 1978. Whereas Cuba's imports from Western markets equalled $1.6 billion (U.S.) in 1977, they were reduced to $1.3 billion (U.S.) in 1978. Exports rose only slightly (by 10 percent) in 1978 to total $780 million (U.S.).[52]

Although Cuba's trade with Latin America has not risen significantly since the OAS embargo was lifted in 1975, Cuba does maintain leadership in Latin American trade alliances, such as the Latin American Economic System (SELA). Cuba contributed 7 percent, or $133,000, to the 1977 SELA budget. A budget of $1.9 million was determined for SELA at the meeting of the Latin American Council held in January 1976. The amount contributed was determined by the level of economic development.[53]

Future of Cuba's International Trade Agreements

The principal impediment to a program of diversification of Cuba's foreign trade is Cuba's sugar agreements and the perpetuation of Cuba's sugar infrastructure. The second problem is Cuba's agreements with the socialist nations to supply quotas of export production. The third and significant block to Cuba's trade diversification is Cuba's lack of convertible currency. Without surpluses of hard currency, Cuba cannot enter the market.

The 1979 International Sugar Agreement held out promise for Cuba's hard-currency surplus. A troubled sugar harvest restricted the anticipated hard-currency earnings thus far. There is, however, another major source of hard currency for Cuba—the loan market.

Cuba is not a newcomer to the loan market. The Cuban government has borrowed consistently from Western markets since the early days of the Revolution—and has a growing debt-servicing bill to prove it. Between 1973 and 1975 Cuba was able to borrow substantial sums in Western international financial markets. This not only gave Cuba additional revenues, but it also gave Cuba much needed hard-currency reserves.

Hard-currency transfers increased substantially from the Soviet Union in 1975 to $515 million (U.S.). In June 1975, it was announced that Cuba had raised a 200 million deutsche mark loan at the Eurocurrency loan market in London. The loan was granted for a period of five years with a period of two years grace, and an interest rate of 1.25 percent above the rate of London interbank level.[54] The Eurocurrency loan was signed on July 25, 1975 by the National Bank of Cuba; the final amount came to approximately $100 million (U.S.). The loan, which was procured mainly for the purpose of importing capital goods, demonstrates Cuba's creditworthiness in international financial circles. This procurement of convertible currency—which has been estimated at between $238 and $250 million (U.S.) in 1975, and $83 million (U.S.) in 1976—provided added income in a year when the drop in sugar prices and a low 3 percent growth rate in agriculture could have destabilized Cuba's economy just as, at least in terms of export revenue, the Cuban economy was gaining strength.[55] The income reports for the period from January to September 1975 alone revealed a trade surplus of $268 million (U.S.), an increase in the gross national product of 9 percent.[56]

In addition, several credit lines were extended to Cuba. Although they did not represent hard-currency reserves since they may only be used to finance imports from the nations involved, they signified additional trading in Western markets. These substantial credits included $1.2 billion (U.S.) from Argentina and $900 million (U.S.) from Spain.

In November 1979 Cuba was refused a Swiss bank-backed Eurocurrency loan (that had been approved and announced in the press) on the basis of Cuba's foreign involvement in Africa.[57] Cuba had hoped to borrow $18.2 million (U.S.) in a twelve-year Swiss government note.[58] The manager, Singer and Friedlander, decided to withdraw the loan because of press criticism.[59]

The first decade of Cuba's foreign trade (after the Revolution) was characterized by isolation from Western markets and a concentration of trade with Communist countries (between 75 to 80 percent of total trade). This corresponded to Cuba's domestic programs of distribution and the literacy and social welfare programs which focused the attention of Cuban policymakers on domestic development. Additionally, the mobilization for sugar production in 1970 reduced Cuba's ability to export commodities from other sectors.

By 1970 Cuban trade began to branch out. In 1970 Cuba's exports to Communist countries totaled 71.6 percent of total exports. By 1974 Cuba's trade concentration with Communist countries had fallen to 54 percent of total exports. Exports to the Soviet Union were down to 34 percent from almost 50 percent in 1970, and from significantly higher percentages during the previous decade.

Although Cuba's trade with CMEA members (including the Soviet Union) still represented the major portion of Cuban trade, Cuba's trade with nonsocialist countries, however, began to expand significantly (relative to Cuba's postrevolutionary trade history). Cuba's trade with Japan increased from 10 percent to 16 percent during this period, and Cuba's trade with Spain doubled. The proportion of trade with Western markets increased substantially from 24 percent in 1970 to 45 percent in 1974.

Internationally, this period paralleled Cuba's increased creditworthiness in financial agreements reflected in loans and credit extensions from nonsocialist markets. On the domestic front, this period corresponded to increased hard-currency surpluses, financial solvency (reflected in a surplus balance of payments), and a bright year in sugar production including productivity and world prices. Internationally and domestically, 1974 was a dramatically successful year for the Cuban economy. Although Cuba's domestic economy was as closely tied to sugar as it had ever been, the Cuban government was on the road to achieving one of the fundamental objectives of Cuba's foreign trade—diversification of trade partners.

Unrelated to the domestic setbacks that the Cuban economy began to experience between 1975 and 1977, Cuba's foreign trade direction began to shift in late 1975. In fact, Cuba's financial agreements with Western markets began to deteriorate on several fronts during that year. Cuba's bilateral trade agreements with Western markets dropped markedly, and several hard-currency loan applications were refused.

After Cuba's bilateral agreements with the West had almost quadrupled between 1970 and 1974 (and increased by another 64 percent in 1975), they dropped significantly in 1976. Cuba's bilateral trade agreements with its Latin American neighbors also dropped by almost 60 percent in the case of Mexico, Cuba's largest trading partner in the region. This shift coincided with an increase in Cuban agreements with the CMEA and other socialist nations in 1976.

Cuba's sugar exports to the West also decreased in 1976. Japan, which had been Cuba's largest Western sugar importer in 1974, cut its sugar imports to one-third in 1975 and reduced them by another one-third in 1976.[60] Other Western nations, including Spain, also reduced imports of Cuban sugar by 1976. Cuba's overall trade with Japan decreased substantially in 1975 and plummeted in 1976 from a high point of approximately $450 million (U.S.) in 1974, to $50 million (U.S.) in 1976.[61]

There are several aspects of Cuba's financial and trade shifts away from the West in 1975 to 1976, apparently not by the Cuban government's choice, which cannot be explained by the terms of Cuba's trade agreements or Cuba's domestic production. The most glaring change that took place in Cuba during these two years was political.

The relation of Cuba's trade accords, bilateral commercial agreements, and creditworthiness in financial markets to its foreign policy is sometimes direct (as in the case of Cuba's 1979 Swiss Bank Eurocurrency loan application) and sometimes indirect (as trade with Latin America and the Western market nations). The impact of Cuba's foreign policies during these years, in political and economic relations, certainly varies in degree. It is clear, however, that Cuba's foreign policy during these years has had an influence on the development of its domestic and international economic relations.

International economic forces have had an enormous effect on the direction of Cuba's economic development. Both economic forces of the international financial market beyond Cuba's control and the international trade agreements that the Cuban leadership negotiated have directed Cuba's domestic development programs. In part, this magnified effect is due to the ripples that Cuba would logically feel as a developing nation in a time of international recession, protectionist policies, and export-oriented growth by many developed countries which themselves are fearful of the impact of a worldwide economic crisis. The evidence in this chapter, however, suggests more than this; it suggests that Cuba's international commercial agreements of the past decade, and their consequences, have contributed to the speed and direction of Cuba's development plans.

In December 1977 Fidel Castro stated, "In a word, we need to have an awareness of exporters rather than of importers, especially with regard to convertible currency countries."[62] Cuba's commercial agreements, particularly with socialist countries, since the 1972 decision to join CMEA have had four major consequences: (1) as part of the international socialist division of labor and production defined by CMEA, Cuba's position as the world's leading exporter of sugar has been reaffirmed; (2) due to a slump in world sugar prices in 1976, Cuba's GNP increased only 3.8 percent, and the Cuban economy remained strongly import oriented; (3) because of the necessity to maintain levels of trade commensurate with CMEA trade agreements (and a slowdown in production), Cuba's trade agreements restricted the diversification of trade partners, that is, Cuba's nonsocialist trade partners; and (4) as a result of this concentration of trade with CMEA and the barter trade, the levels of Cuba's convertible currency have remained extremely low.[63]

The reason Cuban planners might have chosen such a problematic trade policy may be understood in light of domestic events. The early 1970s were the hardest times that Cuba had witnessed since the early days of the Revolution, both psychologically and economically. The failure of the 1970 sugar harvest put Cuba in a shaky position both domestically and internationally. Exports were down since Cuban planners had diverted all energy to that sector. The anticipated morale boost was absent. Trade with CMEA, and in particular with the Soviet Union, offered, no doubt, high subsidies, a guaranteed market for Cuba's sugar, and an extremely generous debt-servicing agreement. In other words, it offered Cuba an opportune short-term solution to severe economic woes; what it did not offer was a chance for Cuba's economy to change "its structure with all the strength, experience and soundness that [our] Revolution has acquired."[64]

Cuba's decision, domestically, to emphasize sugar production was directed by the belief that the Cuban economy had a comparative advantage in sugar; sugar could produce the highest export earnings with the least immediate investment.

As a result Cuba, in theory, would have been able to channel the surplus earnings into industrialization and agricultural diversification programs. Cuba's decisions, internationally, were made for similar if not identical reasons. Cuba would take advantage of favorable international agreements for economic and technical cooperation and trade with the Soviet bloc. In time, Cuba could diversify trade partners and shift the emphasis of its domestic production. The agreements which Cuba signed, however, did not produce that result; Cuba's position within the economic integration unit of socialist countries provided only for the expansion of Cuba's sugar production—albeit with excellent terms of trade—and only minimal allocations for development of other industries.[65] There is a real possibility that Cuba will remain the major supplier of sugar and nickel and little else.

The direction of Cuba's development and the growth of its economy are traceable to a complex mix of international economic trends and the choices made by the Cuban government through its foreign trade agreements. Cuba's economy is likely to experience the effects of the international financial crisis for the foreseeable future. According to a United Nations study, the disequilibrium in the economies of the developed market economies will continue, as will the global economic tendencies that follow suit—protectionism, export promotion, and slowed rates of growth acceleration. The same is expected in the developed centrally planned economies. Economic growth in these nations for the remainder of the 1970s, the study concludes, will emphasize external balance and international improvement by means of a slowdown in aggregate demand.[66]

Because of a deepening world economic crisis, coherent and unified programs of international development policy are of great concern to developing nations. At the core of a policy of international development, a United Nations Industrial Development Organization (UNIDO) study asserted, should be a system of major financing from advanced developed nations.[67]

In 1979 Cuba's desire to industrialize key productive sectors of the economy remained a priority of economic planners. In fact, Cuba's investment in industrialization projects increased more than one-fifth between 1978 and 1979, with $377 million (U.S.) invested in industrialization projects between January and July 1979.[68]

While Soviet subsidies increasingly tied Cuba's economy to the Soviet Union, lengthy explanations were given in Cuba's 1985 National Bank report to Western creditors. During the 1983–85 period, were Cuba to have exported its sugar to the market economies, Cuba would have lost more than $640 million, based on the 1977 standards established by the International Sugar Agreement. In order to offset the losses, Cuba traded less with the market economies, according to the report. The result: trade with market economies dropped from 22 percent of total trade (1977–80) to 13 percent (1982–84). In addition, Cuba's debt service to the Soviet Union begins in 1986. Moreover, Cuba anticipates earning $1 billion during the 1986–90 period in nonsugar convertible currency exports.[69]

However, a key investment sector of the Cuban economy since 1975 has been in the military. Military finance programs, like economic development programs, have inevitable political and psychological effects. More difficult to assess, they are important and influential aspects of a nation's ultimate development direction. "Agriculture and industrialization are only two aspects of development," Castro stated in his speech to the General Assembly. "Development involves attention to human beings, who should be the protagonists and goal in all development efforts."[70] However, in 1977 when Cuba's GNP was approximately $12 billion (U.S.) and per capita income about $1,200, Cuba's total armed forces totaled 189,000: 160,000 in the army, nine thousand in the navy, and twenty thousand in the air force, with an additional ten thousand paramilitary people's militia.[71]

In total, Cuba's African assistance program involved over fifty thousand Cuban soldiers and technicians in 1979. Of fifty thousand Cubans, approximately twenty thousand fought in Angola, ten thousand in Ethiopia, ten thousand in the Congo and Rhodesia, and five thousand were medical, educational, and engineering technicians throughout the continent.[72]

In dollar figures, Cuba's military budget in 1979 surpassed $1.1 billion (840 million pesos) which accounted for 8.9 percent of Cuba's national budget and a 3.5 percent increase over any pre-1975 budget.[73] The military service required of Cuban citizens is three years for all citizens over the age of seventeen. Service in Africa, however, is voluntary. In January 1976, 10 percent of Cuba's total army strength had been committed to Angola in that volunteer army.[74]

One of the principal proposals of Castro's 1979 address to the United Nations General Assembly was a program to reduce the "persistent channeling of human and material resources into an arms race."[75] Quoting the NAM resolution written in Havana, he demanded that a substantial part of these resources be channeled into economic and social development. In a similar report, the office of the United Nations secretary-general proposed a program by which the five permanent members of the United Nations Security Council would reduce military expenditures by 10 percent and establish a development fund for Third World nations.[76]

"Arms expenditures are irrational," Castro stated in his address to the U.N. General Assembly. "They should cease, and the funds thus released should be used to finance development."[77]

According to Castro's 1979 figures, that sum, if channeled to Cuban domestic development, would build two thousand two hundred schools (with capacity for 1.5 million students); construct two hundred twenty thousand homes (for 11 million people); build one hundred ten hospitals (and provide sixty-six thousand beds); build seventy-three factories (and employ seventy-three thousand workers); and build an irrigation system that (with the application of technology) could feed 3.7 million people. The social welfare costs of Cuba's military adventures remain high.

Regardless, Cuba was able to reschedule its debt to the West again in February 1985. The debt totaled $3.43 billion at the time of the agreement with the Western banks. The portion rescheduled was the $750 million in debt due in 1985 to both private and public lenders from the United Kingdom, France, Spain, West Germany, Austria, Canada, Japan, and Switzerland.

Most important, in a good-faith effort to its creditor countries, Cuba presented a comprehensive report by its central bank, the National Bank of Cuba, arguing that Cuba's purpose was to "reach a stage of more mature industrial growth and achieve a broad diversification of its exports" through an increase in trade. In order to achieve that goal, Cuba presented a list of items from honey and grapefruit for Japan to coffee for Switzerland, which Cuba hoped to exclude from those nation's import tariffs.[78] In 1982, Cuba's National Bank reported a net outflow of $115 million; in 1984, it reported that "a balance was finally achieved between foreign credits and debt service."[79]

In reporting to its Western creditor countries, the central bank's report outlined the measures that Cuba was requesting to improve its terms of trade including a broadening of the Generalized System of Preferences, to include new products; the elimination of several areas of nontariff restrictions; improvement of tourism; increased importation of new technology; and a fund for research of new areas of export promotion.[80] Cuba's five-year plan 1985-90 emphasized the reduction of energy consumption, an increase in imports to 20 percent from market economies, continuation of exports to socialist countries, limitation of austerity measures on the Cuban population, and maintenance of export priorities while investing in domestic production.[81]

Notes

1. Sergio Roca and Roberto E. Hernández, "Structural Economic Problems," in *Cuba, Castro and Revolution*, ed. Jaime Suchliki (Coral Gables, Florida: University of Miami Press, 1972) are the main proponents of the argument that unemployment and the disparities in rural and urban living standards contribute to the vulnerability of the Cuban economy. A study by Jorge I. Domínguez, entitled "Cuba: Domestic Bread and Foreign Circuses," *The Washington Quarterly* (Spring 1979), pp. 68-74, emphasizes the urban economy's dependence on the production of sugar for 80 percent of Cuba's export earnings. He examines the implications of this dependence in an international market where sugar prices have been as low as seven cents per pound in recent years, and when Cuba's foreign trade accounts for almost 50 percent of the gross material product.

2. Edward Boorstein, *The Economic Transformation of Cuba* (New York: Monthly Review Press, 1969), p. vii.

3. Lawrence Theriot, "U.S.-Cuba Trade: Question Mark?" *Commerce America*, 24 April 1978, pp. 2-5. In the mid-1950s, Theriot's evidence shows, imports equaled 32 percent of GNP (gross national product), slightly lower than the 1970s but not significantly different. For a discussion of the 1985 development program, see National Bank of Cuba, *Economic Report, 1985*, National Bank of Cuba: Havana, Cuba, 1985, pp. 7-8.

4. Ibid., p. 7.
5. Ibid., p. 13.
6. Ibid., pp. 7–8, 16–17.
7. Republic of Cuba, National Bank of Cuba, *Development and Prospects of the Cuban Economy* (Havana: Cuban Book Institute, 1975), p. 30. The 1974 figures do not include the import of capital goods and replacement parts.
8. U.S., Central Intelligence Agency (CIA), *National Basic Intelligence Handbook* (Washington, D.C.: Government Printing Office, July 1979).
9. National Bank of Cuba, *Development and Prospects*, p. 36.
10. Jorgé Pérez-López and René Pérez-López, "Cuban International Relations: A Bilateral Agreements Perspective," (Pa.: Northwestern Pennsylvania Institute for Latin American Studies, May 1979), p. 37. Their study illustrates Cuba's increase in agreements with Latin American and African Third World nations during the early years of the 1970s.
11. National Bank of Cuba, *Development and Prospects*, p. 36.
12. Presentation by Ambassador Rául Roa Kourí at the Center for Inter-American Relations, New York, 9 February 1979.
13. If not for the drop in sugar prices and world consumption, an increase in the amounts of sugar stocks would have been advantageous. The extreme effect of the weather on sugar was due to the year-end stocks of sugar since the early days of the Revolution that had been kept extremely low. The irregularity of production, therefore, is seen in the export amounts, and Cuba's sugar production becomes a hand-to-mouth affair. G.B. Hagelberg, "Cuba's Sugar Policy," in *Revolutionary Cuba in the World Arena*, ed. Martin Weinsten (Philadelphia, Pa.: ISHI, New York University, CLACS, 1979), pp. 31–51.
14. National Bank of Cuba, op. cit., p. 28.
15. Edward González and David Ronfeldt, *Post-Revolutionary Cuba in a Changing World* (Santa Monica, Calif.: Rand Corporation, December 1975), p. 50.
16. Roa, comments, 9 February 1979.
17. National Bank of Cuba, *Economic Report*. Havana: National Bank of Cuba, February 1985, p. 1. The report went on to say that, "Nor does the gradual restitution of credit that has taken place in the past two years serve these purposes, since it involves only indispensable trade financing facilities." Ibid., p. 1.
18. Article 16 of the Constitution defines the purposes and general direction of the Cuban economy: "The state organizes, directs, and controls the economic life of the nation in accordance with the *central plan of socio-economic development* in whose elaboration and execution the workers of all the branches of the economy and of the other spheres of social life have an active and conscious participation. The development of the economy serves the purpose of strengthening the socialist system, cultural needs of the society and of the citizens and of promoting the flowering of human personality and serves the progress and the security of the country and the national capacity to fulfill the internationalist duties of our people." Pamela S. Falk, "Cuba, 1974–78," in *Constitutions of the Countries of the World,* eds. Albert P. Blaustein and Gilbert H. Flanz (Dobbs Ferry, N.Y.: Oceana, 1979). Monograph.
19. Created by Act 964, 1961. Fidel Castro, "Report to the First Party Congress," Havana, December 1975.
20. Although JUCEPLAN was established in the early years of the Revolution, its authority to institute economic plans was taken away in 1966, and its economic policy decentralized. Both its early plans of 1962 to 1966 and annual plans from 1965 to 1970 were

reviewed but not instituted. See Jan Knippers Black et al., *Area Handbook for Cuba* (Washington, D.C.: Government Printing Office, 1976), p. 379.

21. Membership included the founding nations: Bulgaria, Czechoslovakia, Hungary, Poland, Rumania, and the Soviet Union. Present membership also includes: German Democratic Republic (1949), Mongolia (1962), Cuba (1972), and Vietnam (1949). Observer status countries include Yugoslavia and Finland. Albania was a former member (1949-62).

22. A study by Edward A. Hewett argued that the CMEA in the 1970s pursued a policy of rapid growth following more rigid policies of integration and specialization in order to achieve larger gains from trade. This policy of "static comparative advantage" of the less developed member nations was fought by the Rumanian government, which argued that the program was similar to capitalist trade patterns that resulted in long-term primary product economies in developing nations. Edward A. Hewett, "Cuba's Membership in the CMEA," in *Revolutionary Cuba in the World Arena*, p. 62. See also Marie L. Lavigne, *The Socialist Economies of the Soviet Union and Europe*, translated by T.G. Waywell (White Plains, N.Y.: International Arts and Sciences, 1974).

23. Josef M.P. Van Brabant, *Essays on Planning, Trade and Integration in Eastern Europe* (Netherlands: Rotterdam University Press, 1974), pp. 43-63, 83-103.

24. Ibid., p. 270.

25. Van Brabant points to the fact that often the member nations develop a dual technology: sophisticated methods of production in key sectors (large capital-to-labor ratios), and they pay less attention to other sectors, which must be operated on the basis of old and existing technology (with low capital-to-labor ratios), ibid., p. 47.

26. Specific terms of CMEA agreements are not often published. For a discussion of this problem see Hewett, "Cuba's Membership," p. 52.

27. See Lavigne, *Socialist Economies*, pp. 297-299, for an extensive discussion, and B. Poklad and E. Shevchenko, *COMECON* (Handbook) (Moscow: Novosti, 1973).

28. Funds for the IIB are from members and international financial institutions.

29. Lavigne, *Socialist Economies*, p. 303. The example that Lavigne gives is the 1957 specialization projects in Poland—Poland was to become the main supplier of coal in CMEA. In 1957 Poland cut back the coal supplies because of internal difficulties. This threatened the economic equilibrium in other countries, and the GDR and USSR could not adequately supplement supplies. In 1977 CMEA financed and opened the coal mines in Poland.

30. Poklad and Shevchenko, *COMECON*, op. cit., p. 33.

31. Ibid.

32. Hewett, "Cuba's Membership." CMEA prices are calculated by the council and are supposed to be related to world market prices. In fact, they differ significantly with this example of the relative costs of machinery and primary products, one of the more blatant examples. It is common, Hewett argues, however, for trade agreements within CMEA to deviate from the agreed upon central prices. Ibid., p. 63.

33. Trade with the capitalist world at world market prices at the time of Castro's speech, he emphasized, would be catastrophic. His estimates, according to the report of revenues, were that 7 million tons of sugar at world market prices would earn Cuba only $2 billion (U.S.) and purchase of oil at world market prices would cost $2.5 to 3.0 billion (U.S.). *Latin American Weekly Report*, 8 February 1980, p. 3. See also Edward Hewett, *Foreign Trade in the Council for Mutual Economic Assistance* (Cambridge: Cambridge University Press, 1974).

34. Castro's figures were cited in a 1984 interview with *Newsweek* magazine, "Castro's Challenge to Reagan," interview with Patricia J. Sethi, *Newsweek*, 9 January 1984, pp. 38–41; Castro cited similar figures in the *Second Congress of the Communist Party of Cuba*, (Havana: Political Publishers, 1981). The Third International Round Table Discussion on Rural Development sponsored by the FAO Regional Office for Latin America and the Caribbean estimated an average annual growth of 3.4 percent from 1970 to 1981 and 4.2 percent between 1975 and 1976. In *Cuba Update*, January-February 1984, p. 5. U.S. government World Bank statistics showing the 1960 to 1978 per capita annual rate of growth as —1.2 percent. In *Cuba's Renewed Support for Violence in Latin America*, Special Report 90, 14 December 1981, p. 3.

35. Interviews by the author with Felix Loaces and Alejandro Romero, Ministry of Foreign Commerce (MINCEX) Havana, 25 January 1979. See also Lawrence Theriot and Linda Droker, *Cuban Trade with the Industrialized West 1974-1979*, Office of East-West Planning, Department of Commerce (Washington, D.C.: Government Printing Office, May 1981); Lawrence Theriot and John Gibbon, *Cuban Trade with CMEA 1974-1979*, Office of East-West Planning, Department of Commerce (Washington, D.C.: Government Printing Office, April 1981).

36. Fidel Castro, *Granma*, 14 January 1973, pp. 2-3.

37. Theriot, "U.S.-Cuba Trade," p. 554. See also Lawrence Theriot and Linda Droker, *Cuban Trade with the Industrialized West 1974-1979*, Office of East-West Planning, Department of Commerce (Washington, D.C.: Government Printing Office, May 1981); Lawrence Theriot and John Gibbon, *Cuban Trade with CMEA 1974-1979*, Office of East-West Planning, Department of Commerce (Washington, D.C.: Government Printing Office, April 1981).

38. U.S., Department of Defense, *Soviet Military Power*, Washington, D.C., April 1984, p. 123.

39. *Financial Times* (London), 14 November 1979, p. 7.

40. Cuban dependence on sugar export earnings range from 81 percent to 95 percent of its total export earnings. Sugar constituted at least 80 percent of Cuban exports prior to the revolution. According to Raúl León Torras, minister-president of Cuba's National Bank, "The crisis on the sugar market is as dramatic as at the worst moment of the Great Depression of the '30's." Cited in *Business Week*, 20 September 1982, p. 56–57.

41. National Bank of Cuba, op. cit., p. 1.

42. National Bank of Cuba, *Economic Report*, Havana: National Bank of Cuba, February 1985, pp. 1–10; *New York Times*, "Cuban Economic Report Is Candid on Economic Burdens," by Clyde H. Farnsworth, p. D1. For an earlier assessment of Cuba's rescheduling of foreign debt with the banks, see Elaine Fuller, "Cuba Negotiates Rescheduling of Foreign Debt," *Cuba Update*, 5, no. 2 (March/June, 1984), pp. 5–6; *New York Times*, 25 December 1983, p. A12; *Wall Street Journal*, 3 August 1984, p. 20.

43. For the full text of the agreement see United Nations, Conference on Trade and Development, *United Nations Sugar Conference, 1977* (London, 1977).

44. Ibid., p. 3.

45. José A. Benítez, *Granma*, 14 November 1976.

46. United Nations, *World Economic Survey* (New York: United Nations Publications, 1977), pp. 1–8. Although world prices increased in 1977 to 1978, the overall increase in the developing countries was 3 percent, with increases recorded in Latin America in Barbados,

Belize, Bolivia, Brazil, Ecuador, Honduras, Panama, and Venezuela, and decreases in Chile, Colombia, Cuba, Guyana, Jamaica, Mexico, Peru, Trinidad and Tobago, and Uruguay. United Nations, ibid., pp. 1–9.

47. Hagelberg, "Cuba's Sugar Policy," p. 34. The Soviet price for sugar under the 1975–80 agreement is 30 cents per pound free on board (FOB). National Bank of Cuba, *Development and Prospects*, p. 32.

48. Theriot, "U.S.-Cuba Trade," p. 4.

49. Fidel Castro, *Granma*, 28 September 1976.

50. Interview with Marcelo Fernández Font, Minister of Foreign Trade, Ministry of Foreign Commerce (MINCEX) February 1976. Cited in the *Center for Cuban Studies Newsletter* 3, no. 4–5 (Winter 1976) from *Granma*.

51. Ibid.

52. *Financial Times* (London), 14 November 1979, p. 7.

53. *Documentación básica sobre el Sistema Económico Latinoamericana: SELA*, p. 411. Cited in Robert D. Bond, *International Organization* 32, no. 2 (Spring 1978), pp. 44–45.

54. *Latin American Economic Report* 3, no. 23 (1 August 1975), p. 120.

55. Ibid., 3, no. 48 (5 December 1975), p. 192.

56. Ibid.

57. *Miami Herald*, 10 November 1979, p. 28A.

58. *Financial Times* (London), 9 November 1979, p. 44.

59. *Latin American Weekly Report*, 16 November 1979, p. 30. There were other recent loans granted from the West (90 million deutsche marks from West Germany) at the same time. The public policy was a significant blow to Cuban prestige in international financial markets.

60. In 1974 Cuba exported 21 percent of total sugar exports to Japan, not significantly lower than Cuba's 35 percent exports to the Soviet Union in 1974. Jan Knippers Black et al., *Area Handbook for Cuba* (Washington, D.C.: U.S. Government Printing Office, 1976), p. 419.

61. *Latin American Regional Reports Caribbean*, 23 November 1979, p. 5.

62. Fidel Castro, Address to the Second Period of Sessions of the National Assembly of People's Power, Havana, 24 December 1977 (Havana: Political Publishers, 1978), p. 24. "So far," Castro stated in the same speech, "an importer's mentality has prevailed in our country and among our cadres—we must import this, this and this—and not an exporter's mentality. Everybody spoke of what he needed, what was good and what was required. Everybody talked about importing from here and there, from socialist or capitalist countries. Nobody talked about exporting."

63. Ibid.

64. Ibid.

65. The important exception to these favorable subsidies was in 1974 when the CMEA price was below the world market price of sugar.

66. United Nations, *World Economic Survey*, p. 5.

67. Castro referred to the Lima meeting of the United Nations Industrial Developed Countries (UNIDO) Conference, which suggested an annual level of development financing between $450 and 500 billion (U.S.) by the end of the century, of which one-third would be financed by external sources. Fidel Castro, Address to the Thirty-fourth Session of the General Assembly, 12 October 1979. Official government translation by the Permanent Mission of Cuba to the United Nations.

68. Ibid.
69. National Bank of Cuba (1985), op. cit., pp. 2-4.
70. Castro, 12 October 1979, op. cit.
71. A. Blake Friscia, "Cuba's Potential for U.S. Business," *International Finance* (New York: The Economic Groups of The Chase Manhattan Bank), 23 January 1978, pp. 7-8. Cuba's GNP (although not the national-accounts statistic that Cuba uses) was based on estimates derived from Cuban Central Bank data. See also The International Institute for Strategic Studies, *The Military Balance, 1977-78* (London: ISS, 1977).

Courtesy Center for Cuban Studies Archives

Havana.

9
Conclusions

Regardless of future shifts in Cuban national philosophy, Cuba is likely to retain a highly visible, independent-minded, and interventionist foreign policy. Any interpretation of Cuban foreign policy that focuses solely on Cuba's post-1959 ideological commitment to Marxism fails to understand the complex and subtle interplay of the currents that feed both this foreign policy and Cuba's ideological commitment to Communism. Such a narrow focus ignores Cuba's strong loyalties to the Soviet Union, Castro's own brand of Western defiance and nationalism, and the international visibility and leverage that a controversial foreign policy gives Cuba. Washington too often forgets Cuban history; Cuban-American writers and Cuban politicians both recall the legend of a vehemently nationalistic José Martí.

Cuba's fundamental foreign policy premises have not changed much since Cuba's independence in 1898. Cuba has tried to be an independent and autonomous state that can exert international influence. This effort, which is articulated in the work of Cuba's nineteenth-century political philosophers, and is repeated by Cuban historians, has persisted through eras of dependence on three colonial and neo-colonial powers: first Spain, then the United States, and the Soviet Union.

Cuban foreign economic and political policies have been built on a commitment to national defense (resulting from a long-standing fear of invasion), military and economic assistance programs in the Third World, and concern for domestic development. Cuba's ties to the Soviet Union, during the two decades following the 1959 Revolution, are based both on an ideological commitment to Marxism but also on a pragmatic commitment to the country that subsidizes its economic existence and supports its military and overseas programs. While Cuba's foreign policy adequately suits its ideology, its ideology does not necessarily determine and shape its foreign policy. Cordial foreign policies with Franco Spain and Argentina during the latter's military government, and Cuba's tireless efforts to remain creditworthy with the Western banks point, at least in part, to a foreign policy that is determined, rather, by the desire to project Cuba into an internationally visible position in world affairs and the enduring frustration of Cuba's leadership to reshape its image of dependence on a superpower benefactor.

Although José Martí died before Cuba finally achieved independence, his warning about Spanish colonialism and his foresight regarding U.S. control are often cited. Not surprisingly the philosophy of Martí is evoked by Castro frequently in his discourses on Cuban leadership in international affairs—as well as by Castro's adversaries both in the exile community (such as Abdala, a name taken from his epic poem) and in "Radio Martí," the anti-Castro U.S. radio broadcast of Voice of America.[1] In 1891, Martí wrote,

> Whoever says economic union, says political union. The nation that sells, serves. The nation that buys, commands. The nation eager to die, sells to a single nation.[2]

Cuba has to date, not been able to escape the single-crop, single-partner dilemma.

Modern Cuban Foreign Policy: The Break with Spain

Spain did not give Cuba independence easily, and as Spain's hold on the hemisphere weakened, America's sphere of influence (as reflected in the Monroe Doctrine) grew.

Cuba's first experience with the United States was the military occupation of Cuba at the conclusion of the war with Spain. Cuba's long fight against any military government ended in the appointment by the United States of General Leonard Wood. The nation's first Constitution was written in 1901 during the U.S. occupation. Appended to the Constitution was the Platt Amendment which flatly established Washington's right to intervene in Cuba's internal affairs. Indeed, Washington and Madrid signed the Treaty of Paris without a single member of the Cuban delegation present. Until its abrogation in 1934, the Platt Amendment stood as a constant reminder to Cubans that true independence had not been fully achieved. The Paris Treaty had given the United States the naval base at Guantánamo, and thus a lasting presence in Cuba.

From the time of President William McKinley, through President Dwight Eisenhower, the neo-colonial relationship, including several military occupations, continued. While U.S. officials tried to quell the opposition to Cuba's first President, Tomás Estrada Palma, the majority of Cubans opposed the government, perceived to have been placed in office from outside. The U.S. Secretary of War and the Assistant Secretary of State reported back:

> We cannot maintain the Palma government except by forcible intervention against the whole weight of public opinion in the island.[3]

William H. Taft and Robert Bacon concluded, "if the insurrectionary habit persists, if again the Cubans divide into armed forces, the strong hand of our Government will have to be imposed."[4]

But Cuba's foreign policy continued to strive to present an independent posture of international prominence. When World War I broke out, Cuba was among the first Latin American nations to become involved in the war by supplying sugar to the allies. During the 1920s and 1930s, Cuba asserted foreign policy prominence first through the international student movement led by Julio Antonio Mella, and later through its international mediation in the Chaco war between Bolivia and Paraguay. Prior to 1929, during the early years of the 1920s, Cuba experienced unprecedented prosperity including full employment and a per capita income higher than most of Latin America. Domestically, however, during the same period, Cuba was experiencing brutal repression by the dictatorship of General Gerardo Machado, who subverted democratic processes from 1925 to 1933.

The children of this era ultimately revolted, led by the quiet court stenographer, Fulgencio Batista, who had recorded the names and addresses of those rebels sentenced to jail for their role in opposing Machado. Corruption and moral deterioration were deep by the 1930s and the revolution to oust Machado was well received.

Batista's first government was comprised of a broad-based coalition of Cuban political currents including labor unions and the Communist party. When Pearl Harbor came, Cuba willingly declared war on Japan. Gradually, however, as U.S. money poured into Cuba, corruption became widespread. Cuban politicians of the 1930s had depleted Cuban reserves and major increases in tourism and aid became necessary.

By the 1940s, Cuba's revisionist historians, such as Emilio Roig de Leuchsenring and Ramiro Guerra, began to write a new Cuban history cast in terms of "stolen destiny" and frustrated national direction. Cuba's 1959 revolution was created and supported by the children of the 1930s, who blamed Washington's continuous intervention for the deep-seated political corruption. Finally, the Great Depression caused economic instability. What the United States had given in previous years, the Depression snatched away in the 1930s. Cuba's economic contribution to the war effort and heavy foreign investment in tourism in the 1940s only partly alleviated the fundamental economic insecurity brought on by the post-depression years. The World Bank wrote in 1950:

> Cuba enjoys a level of income and a standard of living among the highest in Latin America and probably the highest of any tropical country. However, the productive basis of this was mainly established before 1925, in the upbuilding of the agricultural and industrial phases of sugar-producing. Since then, the Cuban economy has made relatively little progress. Cuban incomes have fluctuated with the world market for sugar—affected strongly by trade cycles, tariffs and quotas, and wars—but have shown little, if any, over-all tendency to advance. Instead of dynamic development, there has been stagnation.[5]

Thus, long before Castro, U.S. investors had difficulties and complaints about investment in the Cuban economy. In a confidential quarterly report on the "Operation and Status of Programs under the Mutual Security Act of 1951," U.S. Ambassador to Cuba Willard L. Beaulac argued in July 1953:

> Cuba's economic development has been retarded principally by corrupt and demagogic government and by nationalistic and restrictive laws and practices which discourage foreign and domestic private capital from making the contribution they otherwise might be willing to make.[6]

Far from laying a foundation for autonomy and world or even regional influence, post-colonial Cuba had become dependent on the U.S. for economic growth and political power.

Constitutional governance and the rule of law has rarely existed in Cuba. In over eighty years as an independent republic, and through three Constitutions, Cuba's rule under Constitutional protections totals approximately twelve years. The 1940 Constitution (promulgated in an independent Cuba) took effect four decades after the 1901 constitution had been written by American governors. The July 1940 Constitution, which reportedly "united and harmonized all opposition groups," took effect during Fulgencio Batista's first term. Little in history explains the anomaly between Batista's first and second term which some have described in terms of a total personal transformation. Whatever the cause, Batista's second term in office, beginning with the March 1952 coup d'état, lacked even a veneer of constitutional authority.

Only one-and-a-half years into the second administration of Fulgencio Batista, the economy was in a nosedive and the political climate unsteady. "The political difficulties of the Batista regime," U.S. Ambassador Willard Beaulac argued, "have been increased by a sharp decline in Cuba's economy due to a world sugar surplus which developed shortly after the Government came to office."[7] The government, he argued, had little support outside the armed forces and Batista's own party. "Because of the unsatisfactory political situation," Beaulac cautioned, "our armed forces are enjoined to give the least possible publicity to the aid they are giving the Cuban armed forces."[8]

All reports that the U.S. government received from the Cuban ambassador to Washington were laudatory. "Batista has a very good record for fair supervision of elections," reports read optimistically from the Office of Middle American Affairs the Department of State.[9] Although many nations of Latin America established relations with Cuba shortly after the 1952 coup d'état that brought General Fulgencio Batista y Zaldívar back to power, and deposed President Carlos Prío Socarrás, Washington was worried. U.S. Secretary of State Dean Acheson wrote to President Harry S. Truman:

> While Batista when President of Cuba in the early '40's tolerated communist domination of the Cuban Confederation of Workers, the world situation with regard to international communism has changed radically since that time, and we have no reason to believe that Batista will not be strongly anti-communist.[10]

Nonetheless, the pressure was on Washington and Havana's allies to isolate Batista.

As the economy deteriorated, and as the opposition to Batista mounted, the U.S. government quickly decided to take a hands-off approach. By June 1952, the Assistant Secretary of State for Inter-American Affairs, Edward G. Miller, Jr., wrote to U.S. Ambassador Beaulac with new directives. "The Cubans," he stated, "seem to be headed for a terrific mess both politically and economically, and as you say, our ability to limit these developments is almost non-existent."[11] The Constitution of 1940 was reinstated in early 1955 but lasted only one-and-a-half years, until Batista suspended constitutional guarantees. Indeed, the unifying force in Cuba became the prospect of reestablishing the Constitution. Yet after 1952, until December 1958, rule in Cuba was Batista's alone.

Break with the United States: Alliance with the Soviet Union

Between February and April 1959, administrative reform, literacy campaigns, land expropriation, and political bickering between political parties dominated Cuba's work force and energies. The new revolutionary government under the presidency of Manuel Urrutia-Lleó (a jurist during the Batista era who distinguished himself for his defenses of political liberties to the chagrin of the Batista government), attempted to negotiate with the United States. However, Urrutia-Lleó resigned in mid-July. He had defended Castro to the press and to the politicians during these early months of the new government. Confident that Castro was not a Communist, Urrutia-Lleó had condemned the Communists vociferously, hoping to establish a more defined distinction to the United States and to his own public. By July his pronouncements angered Castro, who on 17 July denounced Urrutia-Lleó, questioning his appointments as president and attacking his political commentary as creating an unnecessary Communist scare.

Constitutional authority had never seen the light of day in Cuba, Urrutia-Lleó argued, and the Cuban popular resentment for U.S. support of the old guard was hard to overcome. The equation was drawn in the early days, he lamented, between support for Washington and the anti-Communist theme: "Constitutional protections were a subtlety that the Cuban people were not allowed to afford."[12]

Despite a promise of new government the Constitution was never again implemented and the Fundamental Law of 7 February 1959 was in force until the promulgation of a new Constitution in 1975.

By May 1959, when Castro's sweeping Agrarian Reform Law took effect and American properties were seized, U.S.-Cuban relations were characterized by strong mutual distrust. Accusations became inflamed confrontations. The new vocabulary of the Cuban government was anti-American and nationalistic, and was beginning to sound increasingly leftist. However, the Cuban Communist party's lack of enthusiasm for Castro, its refusal to endorse the Twenty-sixth of July Movement, and Castro's official proclamations about the new democracy, had given early assurances to the international press and to Washington that Castro was not a Communist. His later actions however, belied the promise.

As early as 1959, the Cuban government began to aid small revolutionary brigades in Venezuela, the Dominican Republic, Panama, and Haiti. Cuba's involvement in the Venezuelan opposition angered the new Venezuelan government, which, in the same month as Cuba, had thrown out a military government, and was now committed to democratic elections and processes. Washington had serious problems with Caracas and Eisenhower hoped to reverse the negative impression left by Venezuelan criticism of Vice President Richard Nixon's 1959 trip. Cuba's Venezuela-based operation *Falcón* gave the Venezuelan's adequate reason to condemn Cuba.

As relations worsened, Havana appeared to brazenly reject Washington's offers to compromise, and Washington made its own set of antagonistic demands. Eisenhower and Castro were in conflict and an increasingly hostile public on both sides reinforced the inflexibility at the bargaining table.

When the Agrarian Reform Law took effect on 17 May 1959, Castro offered compensation to protesting U.S. property holders. He offered to pay the assessed value which the property owners themselves had reported on their tax returns, an evaluation far below market value. The offer was unacceptable and communication deteriorated. When Castro visited the United States in mid-April of that year, President Eisenhower would not see him. Accompanied by economist and advisor Ernesto Betancourt, National Bank Director Felipe Pazos, and an entourage of over sixty other government officials, Castro had requested no aid and no loans from the United States.

Thus, well before Washington's antagonistic programs of 1960–61, U.S.-Cuban relations had worsened. Both Washington and Havana must share the blame for allowing antagonisms to become irreversible. As 1960 began, a cycle of reactions set the two nations on a course of conflict. Eisenhower sought congressional authority to cut Cuba's sugar sales to the U.S. Cuba then swapped sugar with Moscow for crude oil. By 29 June, all U.S.-owned sugar mills were nationalized. Within a week, Eisenhower had received the congressional authorization to cut Cuba's sugar quota. The sugar was immediately purchased by the Soviets.

During the following eight months all U.S. property was nationalized by Castro. The April 1961 invasion of Cuba at the Bay of Pigs and the February 1962 trade embargo by the United States guided U.S.-Cuban relations to a point of active hostility. Cuba's regional neighbors expelled Cuba from the OAS in 1964. Castro responded with the "Second Declaration of Havana," signed by future Chilean President Salvador Allende Gossens and Mexico's past President General Lázaro Cárdenas.

The October 1962 missile crisis exposed the Soviet Union vividly as Cuba's new benefactor. Only nine months earlier Kennedy had offered to restore relations, on condition that Cuba would sever relations with Communist countries. At this point the die was cast. Cuba would not turn back. When the bridges to the United States were burned, however, Cuba was neither isolated nor independent.

Cuba's Foreign Policy of Internationalism: "Bonapartismo" and Sovietization

Economic ties with the Soviet Union were completed in April 1963, and Castro visited Moscow to sign comprehensive trade accords.[13] Between 1964 and 1965, Cuba's economic dependence on the Soviet Union became enormous, including trade agreements, sugar subsidies, and credits. The economic relationships culminated in Cuba's 1972 decision to join the socialist bloc Council for Mutual Economic Assistance (CMEA). This decision, made to a large degree by economic necessity, left Cuba with less independence but a greater opportunity to influence world affairs.

All Western Hemisphere nations except Mexico joined in the sanctions imposed by the Organization of American States in 1964. Cuba's foreign policies in the 1960s involved only small numbers of Cubans but Cuba's message was clear. In the Dominican Republic, Haiti, Nicaragua, and Panama, Cuba helped revolutions which Cuba perceived to be already in progress. By contrast, in Guatemala, Colombia, Venezuela, Peru, and Bolivia, Cuba sent small guerrilla bands to spark the flame of revolution. The failure of Che Guevara's Bolivian movement was a severe shock to Cuba's overseas adventures. Between 1970 and 1978 Cuba turned to policies of improving diplomatic relations in the Western Hemisphere.

In the 1960s Cuba's policies reflected a two-pronged strategy: diplomatic support to progressive regimes in an effort to unify the left in the hemisphere, and assistance to small guerrilla groups opposing centrist and right-wing governments. Castro's relations within Latin America in the 1960s vacillated greatly. Initial approval of the Revolution in 1959 by Latin America became problematic for Cuba as U.S.-Cuban tensions rose and pressure mounted on both fronts. Castro's failed visit to Rómulo Betancourt in Caracas in January 1959 (resulting in a rupture with Venezuela) and his misreading of Costa Rica's President José Figueres in March (resulting in Castro accusing Figueres of being a "false friend") were early signs that the revolution would not enjoy smooth sailing among Latin America's social democrats. By mid-decade, Castro was becoming disillusioned by the lack of support of even leftist fringe groups in Latin America. Pressure from the United States, he understood, was responsible for the OAS vote. But why were not the more progressive social democratic movements more supportive?

When Che Guevara was killed in Bolivia in October 1967, Cuba's Latin America policy was profoundly shaken and the Cuban leadership was left with a deep sense of betrayal and a need for reevaluation. The 1970s began with renewed effort by Cuba to mend fences in Latin America and to establish diplomatic relations. These efforts were an overwhelming success. During the decade Cuba regained several political allies, and by 1979, Cuba had reestablished relations with over seventeen countries of the hemisphere. In Chile, Allende's support was strong; he had come to power with a large amount of covert Cuban assistance; Peru's military government was friendly to Havana and Moscow; and by 1973

Argentina had reestablished relations. By 1975, the OAS embargo was lifted against Castro.

Even as Cuba was making friends in the hemisphere, it began to broaden the scope of foreign involvement and perhaps to overreach for international influence. Cuba's aid programs took on a new dimension when in 1975, Cuba sent thirty-six thousand troops to Angola to resist an invasion by South Africans from Namibia and to help the Marxist MPLA maintain power, and in 1978, when twelve thousand Cuban soldiers were sent to Ethiopia. For Cuban foreign policy, 1979 was a pivotal year. The March 1979 "golpe" marked a victory for Maurice Bishop's New Jewel Movement in Grenada. By the end of 1979, Cuba's programs to Nicaragua and El Salvador had increased enormously but Cuba's backing of the Soviet invasion of Afghanistan left Cuba once again a suspicious partner to its renewed Latin American neighbors, most of which had improved relations with Cuba since the OAS ban was lifted in 1975. Understanding the extent of Soviet ties to Cuba is essential to understanding Cuba's foreign policy. One must ask whether Cuba is really acting as a proxy of the Soviet Union in Africa and in Central America. How much do Cuba's ties to the Soviet Union constitute a threat to U.S. security?

Cuba's aid to the Latin American revolutionary movements in the 1980s is a continuation of its past programs. Cuba continues to aid left-leaning and Marxist governments in the region or insurgent opposition to reactionary governments. A new factor, however, changes the overall picture. By the 1980s, Cuba's army was significantly enlarged. Today its political institutions which determine foreign policy are no more democratic: small groups of policy makers from the original Twenty-sixth of July Movement continue to decide foreign policy, unimpeded by popular democratic institutions, and a new generation of political leaders in neither government nor the military, has emerged. In the 1960s, when Cuba was aiding Venezuelan and Bolivian guerrillas, Cuba was less able to increase its aid or continue in light of any major opposition.

Massive economic and military programs from Washington during the 1960s and from Cuba since the 1970s have tipped El Salvador's delicate political apple cart. The result has been the radicalization of the social democratic political opposition, increased support of the left, and an overall increase in guerrilla forces—all this even in the face of mounting counteroffensives. Neither the March 1982 elections, which produced a right-wing constituent assembly to the chagrin of American policymakers, nor the May 1984 return of former Presidential candidate José Napoleón Duarte, signaled the restoration of peace to El Salvador.

Cuban aid to Central America has been significant in the 1980s, including its deliveries of rifles and armament in addition to the deployment of eight thousand Cubans in Nicaragua as advisors and military personnel. This aid cannot be considered unimportant by any standards. Moreover, Cuba's early denial that it was providing armed aid, and its subsequent reversal in public statements by its vice president and foreign minister, undermine its credibility in world affairs. Just as

U.S. policymakers have learned in Cambodia and later in Nicaragua, secret wars and secret weapons shipments, regardless of the rationale, violate rules of international convention and global responsibility.

In the short term, however, Cuba's recanting has done only slight harm. But it has made Cuba's subsequent and more publicized overtures of peacekeeping more suspect. For although Cuba's overtures to seek a negotiated settlement in El Salvador and Nicaragua are noteworthy, Cuba is far too involved in the issue to be a reliable negotiator.

While Havana's relations deteriorated with Washington in the mid-1980s over Cuba's Central American and Grenada policies, Cuba's diplomatic relations in the hemisphere have grown steadily. Cuba added to its list of Western Hemisphere partners in January 1984, when Ecuador and Cuba elevated the level of diplomatic representation to ambassador from the level of chargé d'affaires, and Ecuador's new President, León Febres Cordero visited Cuba in 1985. New ambassadors from the Peoples Republic of China, Mozambique, and Yemen were welcomed by the Cubans in early 1984, as were elections of social democrats José Sarney in Brazil, Julio María Sanguinetti in Uruguay, Raúl Alfonsín in Argentina, and Jaime Lusinchi in Venezuela, which opened doors to Cuban diplomats.

Dominance and Divergence

Ideology

Ever since 1961, the year of Castro's ideological self-baptism as a Communist, Cuba has become an advocate and active partner of the Soviet side of the Cold War and what is, in contemporary terms, known as the East–West conflict. As a result, the status of superpower conflict vis-à-vis coexistence shapes the U.S. view of Cuban affairs. Very few nations have been able to make a dent in international affairs, and yet avoid the international ideological feud between Moscow and Washington since World War II. The countries which have to some extent been able to achieve that unique status have done so either by keeping a relatively low profile or because they have the resources or other bargaining chips to be able to get away with it. The Non-Aligned Movement has failed miserably in its attempt to create an independent third force representing the interests of the developing world. Cuba's role as chair of the Movement in 1979 further eroded the already doomed institution's credibility.

In the inflexible political definitions of postwar international relations, Cuba has unquestionably and vigorously assumed the role of Third World spokesperson for the Soviet bloc. Not surprisingly, relations between the United States and Cuba improved during the 1970s, when the Nixon administration adopted a policy of détente with the Soviet Union, which lasted approximately a decade. But the Soviet invasion of Afghanistan in December 1979 refueled the Cold War, and U.S.-Cuban relations continued a downward plunge.

The most apparent areas of Cuban-Soviet cooperation are in economic, political, and military affairs. The principal concern to the United States is the area of military accord, specifically, the danger of Soviet placement of offensive weapons systems in Cuba.

Economic Aid

Cuba's economy is dominated by Soviet aid. Cuba's dependence on Soviet aid, in 1984, amounts to $4 billion (U.S.) annually, or 25 percent of Cuba's gross national product. That Soviet subsidy (of $13 million daily) includes only the combined cost of price supports for the purchase of sugar and nickel and subsidies for the sale of petroleum, which provide approximately 95 percent of Cuba's oil intake. Assistance from the Soviet Union has totaled approximately $40 billion since Cuba's 1959 Revolution.

While Cuba was able to reschedule approximately one-half of its $3.5 billion debt to Western banks and several governments, Cuba's economy suffers, woes similar to other developing countries in the mid-1980s. Lines remain long and rations short, at the same time that Cuba's need for hard currency to service its debt to the West falls short by several hundred million dollars annually.

Difficulties of economic expansion are principally blamed on Cuba's monocrop economy and the lack of foreign investment. To alter the pattern, in 1982 Cuba's joint ventures law was introduced to encourage foreign industries to invest at favorable rates although the program never was very popular with Western investors. Due to Cuba's perceived risk, however, most of the banks lending to Cuba charged two percentage points over European London Inter-Bank Official Rate (LIBOR), bringing Cuba's interest rate to approximately 12 percent annually in early 1984.

Not all is gloomy, and Cuba was able to increase its trade with Caribbean neighbors and open limited trade with Switzerland in the early 1980s. In fact, the Cuban government cites a 4.7 percent annual economic growth rate as an annual average for the past twenty years, a figure challenged by U.S. government sources. Moreover, Cuba's efforts to stem the black market have had limited success but have, in essence, undercut corruption and hoarding. Cuba's trade with the West dropped by half during the last two years from its 1977–80 level, but regardless of the negative impact of the embargo, Cuba is able to secure substantial amounts of hard currency from two sources. The resale of two-thirds of Soviet petroleum exports to Cuba on the world market generated over $400 million in 1984 alone and tourists, numbering 200,000 in 1984, contributed to Cuba's hard currency savings.

Contrary to Cuba's desire to diversify its economy, Cuba remains tied to sugar as its principal export. Sugar accounts for 85 percent of all exports—a figure virtually unchanged since 1959. It is unlikely that Cuba's economic picture will brighten in the late 1980s, and it may become more troubled, if predictions of difficulties in Soviet oil exports prove accurate. In addition, a scaling down of troops in Angola would prove costly, if Cuba actually receives the $300-$500 million in hard currency for this participation, as Washington has alleged.

Cuba's ability to continue its foreign aid programs, indeed to grow politically in the future, will depend in large part on whether Cuba's decision making—particularly foreign policy leadership—depersonalizes its structure and recognizes the differences between power and philosophy in foreign affairs.

Military Aid

Since 1980, when the Soviet Union dramatically increased its shipments of military supplies and advisors to Cuba, Cuba has become the most militarized society in all of Latin America. In terms of troops and equipment, Cuba in 1984 is the most militarily prepared nation, with the capability of mobilizing more troops than any Latin American nation, or for that matter, Canada.

The Soviet military subsidy of Cuba's military programs is staggering, with the Cuban contribution adding approximately 10 percent of its own central budget to defense. Starting in 1981, the Soviet Union increased shipments of military equipment, totaling over $5 billion during the three-year period to 1984, and $2.5 billion in the previous twenty-year period.[14]

On May Day, 1984, Cuba's Politburo member Roberto Veiga Menéndez addressed the Cuban people at the Plaza of the Revolution in downtown Havana. The Peoples Militia had doubled, he announced, from 500,000 to one million Cubans in 1984. The Peoples Militia had been established in 1980 to mobilize Cubans who because of age and sex were unable to enter the armed forces. The force had been established in late 1980 as relations grew tense with Washington, in order to defend against outside attacks while Cuba's active forces were involved off of the island.

By 1984, the active armed forces numbered 225,000 and reserves, 190,000; making Cuba's combined military forces larger than the United States' total number of National Guard and reserves, according to the U.S. Defense Department. By that account, Cuba's active military forces account for 2.3 percent of its population and combined with the Peoples Militia, the total was approximately 15 percent.[15]

In addition, the Cuban government organized several mass organizations since the early days of the revolution. These function as "watchdogs" of the community, and sometimes are on active armed duty. The oldest of these institutions is the Committees for the Defense of the Revolution (CDRs) which have been the most active monitors of community antigovernment activities, with a membership of 5.3 million Cubans, not all of which are active participants in the program.

Soviet military shipments by sea also increased substantially during the 1981-82 period, expanding from an average of twenty thousand metric tons between 1976 and 1980, to between 66 and 69 thousand metric tons in 1981 and 1982, or $600 million annually. The Soviets have also supplied Cuba's Air Force with over 200 MIG-23 jet fighters. During the five-year period from 1975 to 1980 membership in Cuba's Communist party doubled to 434,000 members, expanding Cuba's elite. Soviet academic grants aided seven thousand students in 1984, up from four hundred students in the 1960s.

Political Emulation

Without proximity to its mentor, Cuba's political institutions have evolved into an interesting mix of Soviet bureaucracy, Western liberal democratic philosophy, and Castro's own weltanschauung, often called *Fidelismo*. While Cuba's constitution contains remnants of U.S. and French constitutional tradition, it mainly reflects classic socialist tenets such as government control of finances, resources, and press.

In reality, no real democratic roots are evident in Cuban government institutions. There is no free press as a matter of government policy. "We don't believe in a free press," the Director of Radio Havana argued, "not when our security and the future of socialism is at stake." Cuba's Vice-President Carlos Rafael Rodríguez echoes the director's remark; "We do not believe in the majority of one. That is not our view of the press."[16] The daily newspaper *Granma*, the weeklies *Bohemia* and *Verde Olivo*, and Radio Havana are all government owned and controlled. The newspaper closest to being a critical journal is the popular weekly published by the Institute of Internal Demand, one of the most controversial and powerful institutions in Havana, because of the mass polls it conducts for the government. Its president, Eugenio Balari, publishes the weekly *Opina*, which, between love stories, exposes its readership to Western fashions and ads for parallel market goods. Most importantly, it runs comics, which are often mildly mocking of Fidel.

Although Cuban nationalism and foreign policy views are anti-American, the country has a strong pro-American element if one can judge from the mass exoduses in 1965 and 1980, as well as by public statements by government officials and observations by most visitors.

Divergences

Cuba is clearly a member of the Soviet Bloc in all economic and political aspects; however, serious signs of strain exist. On several occasions, Cuban and Soviet paths have diverged.

As early as 1962, the outcome of the Missile Crisis angered Castro. His exclusion from the final resolution caused Castro to refuse United Nations supervision of the withdrawal of the intercontinental missiles, thus creating the current confusion about whether the U.S. and the Soviet Union are still tied to those agreements.

According to Wayne Smith, former head, U.S. Interests Section in Havana, the United States continues to be tied to the 1962 accord. He argues that the interpretation

> that Cuba's refusal to allow on-site U.N. verification rendered the agreement null and void is simply wrong. Leaving aside the matter of Soviet removal of the

missiles as uncovered deck cargo, which we accepted *nolo contendere,* and our subsequent insistence on U-2 overflights since the on-site verification hadn't been granted, *en lieu* thereof, the fact is that American administrations have for over twenty years stated that the understanding was binding. The Nixon administration based itself on the understanding in 1970 in demanding the Cienfuegos facilities be dismantled. Carter indicated our continued adherence to the understanding in 1978 when he reviewed the introduction of MIG-23s. Thus, we can hardly now say, twenty-two years later, "We never regarded it as valid."

However, evidence on the Missile Crisis agreements is far from conclusive. Former Kennedy aide and counsel, Arthur M. Schlesinger, Jr., argues that the Kennedy-Khrushchev agreement on Cuba was dependent on the acceptance by Fidel Castro of the U.N. inspection program which had been proposed by Khrushchev. Since Castro refused that inspection, Schlesinger argues, the agreement never went into effect.[17]

Cuba's Interest/Soviet Interest

Soviet financing for Cuba's Central American policy reflects a desire to both gain allies in a U.S. sphere of interest, and by so doing to embarrass the United States. Cuba's programs, while financed by Moscow, serve Cuba's interest, often called "Bonapartismo," Cuba's foreign policy empire-building.

Nevertheless, while strains have existed between Moscow and Havana, the evidence on balance reflects more overlap than divergence in Cuban and Soviet interests. On the other hand, the financing of Cuba's adventures does not make Cuba a Soviet proxy; this is a simplistic definition which underestimates Cuba's own commitment to Fidelist expansionism. After all, foreign policy diverts attention from the lack of independence in domestic affairs. The perceived threat from outside serves to consolidate domestic feeling in favor of Cuban efforts.

While Cuba's gratitude for Soviet patronage is evident, there can also be little doubt that Castro's alliance is regarded by Castro as the result of having had no choice. Undeniably, Castro went for the best deal: U.S. policymakers have never offered to subsidize Cuba as the Soviet Union is doing. Today, the United States would not consider paying Cuba $4 billion a year to be an ally.

Cuba's support for revolutionary movements in El Salvador has not gained it many friends. Latin Americans may also find it hard to believe that Cuba started the problems of the region, since they know poverty can spark instability. Faced with the evils of political polarization, Communism, and poverty in Central America, many Latin American nations look to neither the United States, the Cubans, nor the Soviets for a center ground.

Contemporary U.S. Policy

Ever since Cuba followed the Soviet shepherd the United States has waged unsuccessful efforts to lure, attack, and frighten Cuba from the Soviet fold.

Although the military accord between the United States and the Soviet Union appeared to prompt both superpowers to back away from the brink of nuclear war, danger has arisen—although not at all on a comparable scale—twice since: in the 1970s and in 1979. And while the Soviet Union appears ready to test U.S. resolve, confrontation appears unlikely, since both parties have much to lose.

Through seven administrations and five separate strategies U.S. policy has failed to alter the policies or the fundamental nature of the Cuban government. Each President has sought his own concessions from the Cubans and has succeeded only in partially isolating Cuba from the Western Hemisphere democracies. To be sure, the U.S. embargo on trade with Cuba has inflicted economic damage, but only in discrete areas such as technology and Western consumer products. In short, Cuba has paid a price for being a Soviet ally, but U.S. interests have not advanced accordingly.

Following the rocky and confrontational Kennedy years, Lyndon Johnson pursued similarly aggressive covert programs, without a parallel attempt to negotiate changes in relations with Castro. On six different occasions, U.S.-supported assassins attempted to kill Castro: they were dropped from planes supplied with all manner of deadly paraphernalia, including poison pens and poison food. The Cubans responded with an open door, creating the first mass exile exodus in 1965, allowing several thousand Cubans to leave from the port of Camarioca.

The Nixon administration did speak with the Cubans. The principal goal of the Kissinger discussions with Cuba was to pull Cuba as far out of the Soviet orbit as possible. But the administration's negotiations with the People's Republic of China angered the Soviets, who in 1970 secretly attempted to deliver nuclear missiles to Cuba's submarine base at Cienfuegos, on Cuba's southwestern coast. Whether it was an effort to test American resolve or Washington's intelligence capacity, the incident represented Cuba's first major provocation since 1962. Although Kissinger succeeded in secretly persuading the Cubans and the Soviets to force the Soviet submarine to change course, the prospects for any improved relations dimmed. Cuba became a low priority for Washington and proceeded to increase its diplomatic relations with Latin America.

When the possibility of the construction of a Soviet naval base at Cienfuegos came to the attention of the Department of State in September of 1970, U.S. Secretary of State Henry Kissinger opened discussions directly with Soviet Ambassador Anatoly Dobrynin. Although the Cuban government officials in the United States reacted with surprise when the information was first leaked to the press on 25 September, they confined both public and private statements to the fact that only a naval support facility was being built at Cienfuegos harbor and that no major submarine base was in any stage of being built. This argument was substantiated by U.S. Defense Intelligence Agency analysts such as Colonel John Bridge.[18]

Whether or not the United States felt the threat of a nuclear base on Cuban soil existed, Kissinger negotiated directly with Dobrynin, and Dobrynin with Castro, and the issue never became a serious confrontation for either the Cubans or the American public. Even though Cuba had become involved in a distant war in Africa, Cuba's acceptance in the West was increasing. In 1975, when the Organization of American States lifted the regional embargo of Cuban goods, President Gerald Ford adopted a policy of slow rapprochement with Cuba, allowing subsidiaries of U.S. companies to resume trade with Cuba despite the embargo.

President Jimmy Carter continued the approach, but with markedly different objectives. By offering a series of concessions to Cuba and accords on diplomatic initiatives, and commercial agreements leading directly to the reestablishment of limited diplomatic relations, the Carter administration expected the Cubans to scale down their foreign policy adventures.

The first agreement that the Carter administration made was one in the spring of 1977 to regulate the fishing industry. In addition, Washington halted reconnaissance flights. Two months later, diplomatic contact, through interest sections (the U.S. Interest Section in the old Embassy building in Havana, and the Cuban Interest Section in the Czech Embassy in Washington) was established. Additional negotiations were under way on health and medical exchanges. The Cubans, in turn, released four thousand political prisoners and created the "Dialogue", a series of negotiations with the Miami-based Cuban exile community, including a family reunification program.

The Carter administration was sorely disappointed when, in 1977, Cuba sent in excess of twenty thousand soldiers to aid the Marxist government of Mengistu Haile Mariam in Ethiopia. Irked by this affront to the spirit of cooperation, the United States responded with hostile public remarks. When Katanganese rebels from the region of Shaba entered Zaire in May 1978, the Carter administration became outraged. Relations deteriorated rapidly. In August 1978, the Soviet Union delivered Cuba's first shipment of MIG-23 fighter planes; a Soviet brigade was discovered on the island in 1979, and Cuba released over 125,000 Cubans from the port city of Mariel during the spring and summer of 1980, including over four thousand criminals. U.S.-Cuban relations plummeted to an all-time low. The sense of betrayal in Washington was strong and evident in charges and policy changes.

By the fall of 1979, the Carter administration had changed direction. A week before leaving office, the administration increased military aid to El Salvador dramatically because of suspected Cuban covert aid, and cut off its $75 million aid package to Nicaragua basing its decision on congressional stipulations regarding the aid. All commercial accords were suspended. The assumption that Castro would be flexible in foreign policy had been unfounded. By January 1981, when the administration of Ronald Reagan took office, Cuban-U.S. relations did not have hope of improving. In March 1981 President Reagan released the White Paper on El Salvador. Cuba, it alleged, was the "source" of strife in Central America. Yet, administration representatives Secretary of State Alexander Haig and special envoy Vernon Walters traveled to meet with Cuban Vice-President Carlos Rafael Rodríguez and Fidel Castro on separate trips in 1982.

During July 1984, Cuba and the United States began the first official negotiations between the two countries since the election of Ronald Reagan. The discussions involved immigration issues and agreements were made to "return" over 2,700 of the "excludable" Cubans who had been sent to the United States during the Mariel exodus in exchange for the gradual processing of over 24,000 Cuban applications for visas to move to the United States.

The agreement, made in late 1984, was quickly overturned by the Cuban government, when Washington began its radio broadcast, "Radio Martí," in May 1985.

U.S. Policy Interests

Although Cuba decisively left behind its dependence on the United States in the early 1960s the interrelationship of Cuba and U.S. interests which has existed since colonial times continues. Judging from its conduct toward Cuba, the United States has five distinct areas of concern regarding the island: U.S. security, hemispheric relations, broader international Cuban influence, U.S. trade with Cuba, the divisive effect of U.S. Cuban policy on the American public, and encouraging political *apertura* in Cuba. To date, U.S. policy has failed to make steady progress on any of these fronts.

Cuba remains a potential, albeit small, security threat to the United States. With Cuba's military buildup in 1981 and 1982, Cuba has become a highly militarized society. More important, the danger that Cuba would host offensive Soviet missile bases has been shown to be real. Although the United States may well have exaggerated the security threat which Cuba poses (and by so doing left Cuba feeling justifiably threatened), some U.S. concern is warranted.

Cuba's export of revolution to regional neighbors is undeniable. Cuba has actively supported the destabilization of authority in El Salvador and has played a significant role in the Nicaraguan revolution. The United States should be concerned about Cuban guerrilla and military involvement, particularly in view of the source of Cuba's military patronage. It is, more likely, Cuba's familial alliance with the Soviet Union and not its ideological commitment to Communism that angers Washington, as warmer relations between Washington and Beijing illustrated in 1984. As for Cuba's broader internationalism, the United States—as a major world power—has reason to hope that Cuba or any other nations will refrain from inflaming and then exploiting civil conflicts around the globe.

On the positive side, the United States has a genuine interest in establishing good working relations with Cuba and working toward communication. Not only would such an achievement illustrate U.S. diplomatic strength and enhance U.S. standing in the developing world, it might diminish the relative strength of the Soviet Union in the Americas.

The United States has a clear domestic interest in improved relations with Cuba. While public opposition is vociferous, particularly in the exile community, it is far from united. Finally, if indeed the principles articulated in the U.S. Constitution and the U.S. commitment to human rights inform U.S. foreign policy at all, improved relations might lead to political *apertura* in Cuba.

Strategies for U.S. Policymakers

Despite a history of difficulties with Cuba, U.S. policymakers could implement specific strategies which would further the U.S. interests outlined above. A national policy must take Cuban concerns—the need for autonomy and international influence—into account. The United States, in short, should set realistic goals for limited benefits. Perhaps most important, U.S. policy should be consistent over the long term.

The closest model for U.S.-Cuban relations is the present U.S. relationship with Mexico. Although Mexico was never an ally of the Soviet Union—perhaps the greatest thorn in the U.S. side—Mexico has an economy—including a nationalized oil industry—which is highly socialized relative to the U.S. economy and frequent tensions in the relationship show that allies can disagree and the alliance remain strong. Foreign Minister Bernardo Sepúlveda has refused to bend Mexican foreign policy. In April 1984, Sepúlveda—a leader of the region's *Contadora* initiative in Central America—dismissed the report that U.S. President Reagan had demanded support of Washington's Central American policy in exchange for economic assistance, saying that it would underestimate Mexico's historic role in international affairs. Indeed, some antagonism strengthens the domestic consensus in Mexico, giving its leaders greater strength in bridging the gulf between Latin America and the United States. Despite good relations, Mexico holds a view which is widely held in the region including Cuba: "The U.S. never remembers, and Latin America never forgets." The policy of accommodation and cautious engagement reflects a sober and sensible recognition of current realities and offers stability and hope for greater success.

To arrive at a similar result with Cuba, the United States must initiate a series of slow moves aimed at improving channels of communication. Even conservative analysts who favor military approaches concede that speaking first is appropriate.

Reagan's April 1984 trip to the People's Republic of China illustrated that relations with Communist nations would not be impossible. Why, then, does the United States have such difficulty with the ideological aspects of relations with Havana? In part, improved relations with the Chinese illustrate the seriousness of the hostilities between the United States and the Soviet Union—the creation of post-World War II Cold War tensions, and the divisions between East and West. It is not Moscow's internationalism, but Soviet military might which has been at the core of U.S. antagonism toward Cuba.

For negotiations to be effective between the United States and Cuba, initial discussion must begin without preconditions. Previously, Cuba had insisted that the embargo be lifted before talks begin. Last year, Castro offered to talk without preconditions. Most important, Washington must recognize the limits to a relationship with Havana during a Castro government. Forging a national U.S. policy requires the commitment to a long-term view based on realistic options and limited benefits.

The first subject of negotiations would be the mutual withdrawal of Cuban and Soviet forces from Angola and South African forces from Namibia, in accordance with United Nations observations, in addition to Cuba's scale-down of military forces in Ethiopia.

Negotiations with Cuba regarding Southern Africa and Angola are particularly feasible since Southern Africa and Namibia's independence became an issue of intensified international debate. Castro's visit to Angolan President José Eduardo dos Santos in March 1984 served to underscore the agreements which Cuba and Angola had designed two years earlier. The joint communiqué, issued in March, did not commit Cuba to withdrawal of the twenty-five thousand Cuban troops stationed in Angola, but opened the door to further negotiations with the United States and South Africa. The communiqué served to merely reinforce Cuban resolve to support the Namibian opposition—South West Africa People's Organization (SWAPO)—that is wedged in between heavily militarized South Africa and Angola. The agreement, signed two months after publicized accounts of Cuban withdrawal of seven thousand troops from Addis Ababa, Ethiopia, signaled a shift in Cuban resolve if South African invasions ceased.

Because the fundamental antagonism appears to be rooted in Cuba's relationship with the Soviet Union, and not solely on ideology, improvement in relations with the United States would logically pull Cuba, at least to some degree, away from the Soviet Union. Finally, many smaller bilateral issues could be negotiated along the way: antihijacking agreements, fishing and maritime accords, medical assistance, and even tourism.

With the resolution of key issues, such as Cuba's export of revolution in the Caribbean Basin and South America, military bases in Cuba, and pending economic differences, the United States could have a Cuban neighbor whose ideology it disliked but whose existence was not threatening. The United States could reaffirm the now-disputed commitment of 1962 not to invade Cuban territory in exchange for a treaty which delineated a ban of offensive Soviet weapons and bases in Cuba and which stopped Cuba's export of insurgencies to the region.

If military issues were in hand, the United States and Cuba might well be able to confront economic and financial issues. Pending bilateral issues involve compensation to U.S. businesses expropriated in 1959, and the migration of criminals from Cuba, on the Cuban side, offset by Cuba's claims of damages relating to the Bay of Pigs, the economic embargo, as well as the territorial claim of Guantánamo base. Moreover, the $2 billion expropriation cost seems manageable. Underlying any negotiation must be a willingness to tolerate Cuba's present commitment to Eastern European socialist doctrine.

Assuming such accords could be reached, the bargaining could next focus on matters closer to home, and negotiations might begin to end Cuba's export of revolution in the Western Hemisphere as an area of perceived strategic interest to the United States. Ironically, during 1983, Nicaragua offered to ban both Soviet bases and its own hemisphere arms transfers. Although Washington doubted Sandinista sincerity at the time, the concessions illustrate the willingness by Cuba's closest regional ally to concede to fundamental tenets of U.S. regional security.

Indeed, the successes and failures of Cuban foreign policy are judged by Cuba's own objectives as well as by international perceptions. To many of Cuba's Latin American neighbors, the Cuban model of a developing nation is definitively not one to follow—yet it is one they admire in limited areas.

Cuba's successes are noted by many regional leaders, primarily in terms of the independence that Cuba has been able to establish from the United States. Though Cuba's dependence on Moscow is evident, Cuba's ability to successfully withstand pressure from Washington is without parallel. Deep resentments among Third World nations toward the foreign policies of Washington and Moscow appear to accrue to Havana's benefit. Washington's attempts to overthrow and assassinate Castro have helped Castro win allies. As Castro attempts to build alliances in Africa, Washington and Moscow struggle to explain their bizarre switch of sides in the Ethiopian–Somalian dispute. How does Castro react to being entirely dependent on Moscow in military, economic, and political terms? In 1985, he echoed his words of 1965: "We are the most independent country of the world because we do not depend, not even the slightest, on the United States. And what country at present depends less on the United States than us?"[19]

In economic terms, the success of Cuban foreign economic policy is measured in Cuba's continued ability to distribute its resources equitably except for a relatively limited degree of corruption. Although the strong commitment to full employment began to waiver with an economic crisis in 1980 and Cuba's first unemployment compensation program, in 1985, employment continued, nonetheless, at 96 percent. Although all Cuban government officials cite the multibillion dollar harm that they estimate the embargo has inflicted, Cuba has been able to survive without its former trading partner to the North, and with limited Western financial sources.

Policies of the Council for Mutual Economic Assistance (CMEA) of specialization that oblige Cuba to maintain high levels of sugar production have thwarted Cuba's ability to shift from an 86 percent dependence on sugar—a dependence equal to that of 1959. The introduction of domestic capitalist programs such as the farmers free market, which allows for a profit and free-market sale of surpluses, and the 1980 joint venture law, have produced few positive results because most Western Hemisphere and African developing nations are U.S.-oriented.

During the 1960s and through the 1980s, Cuba's massive military assistance programs in Central and South America and in Africa were on a par with those of the Soviet Union. Cuban leaders reluctantly admitted that, metaphorically, they were working with the same compass. Simultaneously, Cuba's international agreements began to shape Cuba's options. Trading accords with the socialist CMEA restricted Cuba's ability to trade in the future with the West by fundamentally limiting Cuba's ability to diversify its exports, to import technology, and to borrow more extensively in Western financial markets.

Thus, the common perception of Cuba's coordination with the Soviet Union on foreign policy programs is real, even if labeling Cuba a pawn misses the subtleties of the relationship. Both in Africa (previously considered a neutral region) and Central America (traditionally viewed as in the Western sphere of influence), Cuba placed itself by choice in the middle of a conflict explicitly characterized by Washington and Moscow as East versus West.

To the developing world, Cuba's greatest foreign policy failure is in not establishing a third alternative to the superpower conflict—in failing to encourage a truly nonaligned organization of nations. Rather, for the third time in Cuba's history the nation has strongly aligned with a major developed nation. Along with Cuba's new alliance and the foreign programs in which Cuba was now more equipped to engage came the liabilities that prominence on the world stage implies: contradictions, compromise, and realpolitik. Cuba fell short of establishing and maintaining a consistent set of values and a rule of morality, as it had set out so firmly to do in its domestic politics. In Czechoslovakia, Cuba acquiesced; in El Salvador Cuba deceived world leaders; and in Nicaragua, by Cuba's own assessment, Cuba prevented the new revolutionary junta from establishing better ties with Washington. Though Cuba's defiance has brought Cuba some regional respect, Cuba's ability to toe the line politically in strategically important United Nations votes (such as those on the Soviet invasion of Afghanistan) undermine Cuba's role as a model of either ideological purist or David fighting its northern Goliath.

To understand Cuban behavior in world affairs, one must keep in mind both aspects of Cuban yearnings: to be independent, and to have world influence. This seems to be reflected even in the most anti-Castro Cuban-Americans. "He gave us our dignity in those early days," a leader of the exile community sighed, "and only later did he take it away."[20] Admittedly, Cuba exerts international influence. But this power flows from its alignment with the Soviet Union. Thus, although Cuba is independent and autonomous in a technical sense, it is not recognized internationally as being either. Whether Cuba would relinquish some international leverage for increased political and economic autonomy remains a key question for policymakers.

Cuba's foreign policy has changed only in scope and in allegiance during the eighty years since its independence from Spain. Particularly since the 1959 Revolution, Castro has attempted to channel the Cuban perception of national interest—of frustrated independence, international leadership, and world recognition—into a foreign policy that suits his personal ambitions, fosters Cuban unity and nationalism, and, by and large, suits the Soviet Union. Above all, the effort has been to create a foreign policy that would project strength and a vision.

For three different political eras—first with Spain, later with the United States, and finally with the Soviet Union—Cuba has expressed its sense of frustrated national identity through its foreign policy. Until Cuba finds a way to break the cycle of political and economic dependency, Cuba's foreign policy will not have achieved that fundamental goal. Little doubt remains, however, that Cuban foreign policy will continue to be highly visible in the years ahead.

Notes

1. Radio Martí was approved by the U.S. Congress in fall 1983, to serve as a "consistently reliable and authoritative source of accurate, objective and comprehensive news" for those living in Cuba. Budgeted by Congress at $25 million for a two-year period, Radio Martí is gradually expected to broadcast over thirteen hours a day on the 180 kilohertz AM radio frequency from Voice of America facilities at Marathon, Florida. See U.S. Department of State, Current Policy No. 392, "Radio Martí and Cuban Interference," 10 May 1982. Statement by Thomas O. Enders, Assistant Secretary of State for Inter-American Affairs before the Subcommittee on Telecommunications, Consumer Protection, and Finance of the House Committee on Energy and Commerce; *New York Times*, 5 August 1984, p. A14; 26 September 1983, p. A20; 30 September 1983, p. A10; *Newsweek*, 28 February 1983, p. 13.

2. José Martí, *Our America: Writings on Latin America and the Struggle for Cuban Independence*. Edited by Philip S. Foner. New York: Monthly Review Press, 1977, pp. 33-34.

3. Report of William H. Taft, secretary of war, and Robert Bacon, assistant secretary of state, *Cuban Pacification*, Appendix E to the Annual Report of the Department of War. Washington, D.C.: Government Printing Office, 1906, p. 470.

4. Ibid., p. 468.

5. *Report on Cuba: Findings and Recommendations of Economic and Technical Mission*. Organized by the International Bank for Reconstruction and Development in collaboration with the Cuban government in 1950. Washington, D.C.: International Bank for Reconstruction and Development, 1951, p. 65.

6. *Foreign Relations of the United States, 1952-1954. Volume IV, The American Republics*. Ed., William Z. Slany. Washington, D.C.: U.S. Government Printing Office, 1983, p. 893.

7. Ibid., p. 893.

8. Ibid., p. 895.

9. Ibid., p. 896. Confidential memorandum of conversation by Harvey R. Wellman regarding "Political Situation and Possible Political Settlement in Cuba" with Ambassador Aurelio F. Concheso.

10. Ibid., p. 871. Secret memorandum by the Secretary of State to the President. March 24, 1952. Within two weeks of the coup, fourteen Latin American countries had recognized the new government. Ibid., p. 872.

11. Ibid., p. 875. Secret letter from Assistant Secretary of State for Inter-American Affairs Edward G. Miller, Jr., to Ambassador Willard Beaulac. June 10, 1952.

12. Interview by the author with Manuel Urrutia-Lleó, New York, June 1975; also see Hugh Thomas, op. cit., pp. 1232–33; Manuel Urrutia-Lleó, *Fidel Castro & Company*, op. cit., p. 46.

13. Tad Szulc, "Friendship is Possible, But," *New York Daily News Parade Magazine*, 1 April 1984, pp. 4–6.

14. United States, Department of Defense, *Soviet Military Power*, 3rd edition. Washington, D.C.: Government Printing Office, April 1984, p. 123; U.S., Department of State, *Cuban Armed Forces and the Soviet Military Presence*, Special Report 103, August 1982, p. 22. Also see U.S. Department of State and Department of Defense, *The Soviet-Cuban Connection in Central America and the Caribbean*, March 1985, Washington, D.C.: Government Printing Office, 1985.

15. U.S., Department of Defense, *Soviet Military Power*, op. cit., p. 123; U.S., Department of State, *Special Report 103*, p. 2.

16. Interview by the author with Olga Fernández, Havana, 23 January 1980; interview by the author with Carlos Rafael Rodríguez, 17 June 1982.

17. Arthur M. Schlesinger, Jr., *Robert Kennedy and His Times* (Boston: Houghton Mifflin, 1978), pp. 550–556. See also his discussion of the Atwood negotiations. Wayne Smith, 18 September 1984. The 1962 Missile Crisis agreement is a source of great debate. The agreement was informal and between Soviet Premier Nikita Khrushchev and U.S. President John F. Kennedy and involved a commitment by Washington not to invade and a commitment by the Soviet Union not to place offensive missiles in Cuba. The disagreement on historical data involves whether or not the proper verification was allowed by the Soviet Union to the United States to permit the United States to determine if all offensive weapons had been removed from Cuba in 1962, since Fidel Castro ruled out on-site verification. The debate has significant consequences since improper verification would render the agreement null and void. For extensive discussion, see Seymour M. Hersh, *The Price of Power*, pp. 251, 255; Theodore C. Sorenson, op. cit.

18. Seymour M. Hersh, *The Price of Power: Kissinger in the Nixon White House*, New York: Summit Books, 1983, pp. 250–257; United States, U.S. Naval Institute, "Soviet Submarine Visit to Cuba," *Proceedings*, September 1975, Washington, D.C.: U.S. Government Printing Office, pp. 30–39; Cyrus Sulzberger, *Age of Mediocrity*, New York: Macmillan, 1973, pp. 655, 660; Elmo Zumwalt, *On Watch*, New York: Quadrangle, 1976, pp. 310–313. For a discussion of Carter administration policy, see Wayne Smith, "Dateline Havana: Myopic Diplomacy," *Foreign Policy*, no. 48 (fall 1982), pp. 157–174. While no major base was being built, the Soviet Union did send barges for submarine support to operate out of Cienfuegos, according to Wayne Smith, 30 October 1985.

19. Fidel Castro. Interview by Dan Rather for *60 Minutes*, March 17, 1985. Transcript distributed by CBS News, Volume XVII, No. 27, p. 3.

20. Confidential interview with Cuban exile leader, 1984.

Factsheet
The Republic of Cuba, 1985

I. Population and Land

Population

10 million: 67% urban, 30% rural
Capital: Havana, 2 million
Average annual growth: 1.2%
Ethnic divisions: 51% mulatto; 37% white; 11% black; 1% Chinese
Language: Spanish
Literacy rate: 90–95%[3]
Labor force: 3 million; agriculture, 30%; services, 20%; industry, 20%; construction, 11%; commerce, 10%; government, 5% [1,3]

Area

44,200 square miles; 14 provinces, 169 municipalities[2]

II. Economy

Peso: $.88 (1985)[6]
Current account deficit (hard currency): $108 million[6]
Debt (to West): $3.4 billion (1984); $750 million due 1985
Debt (to Soviet Union): $22 billion[8]
Reserves: (1984) $179 million[6]
GNP: $15 billion; per capita, $1,534; real growth rate 1.4%.[3] (Also, calculated in gross social product: [1983], 5.2)[7]
Agriculture: sugar, tobacco, rice, potatoes, citrus, coffee
Fishing[2]
Industries: sugar milling, petroleum refining food and tobacco processing, textiles, chemicals, metals, cement. *Exports:* $6 billion (f.o.b.);[2] sugar, nickel, shellfish,

tobacco. *Imports:* $6.6 billion (c.i.f.); capital goods, industrial raw materials, food, petroleum[3]
Oil imports: 225,000 barrels daily from USSR[9]

III. Trade

Exports: USSR, 70%; other CMEA countries, 18%; Western Europe, 13%.[6] *Imports:* USSR, 70%; other CMEA countries, 23%; other, 7%[3]
Foreign aid: Current: $8 million daily from USSR in subsidies on petroleum imports and sugar exports ($4.1 billion annually).[10] *Previous:* U.S. (1946-61), $41.5 million (loans $37.5 million, grants $4.0 million); USSR economic (1960-79), $5.7 billion credits, $11 billion subsidies; military (1960-79), $2.3 billion[3]

IV. Budget

$12.5 billion[3]
Unemployment: 3%[1]
Tourism: 200,000[6]

V. International Organizations

Membership: Council for Mutual Economic Assistance; Economic Commission for Latin America; Food and Agriculture Organization; Group of 77; General Agreement on Tariffs and Trade; Inter-American Defense Board (nonparticipant); International Atomic Energy Agency; International Civil Aviation Organization; International Fund for Agricultural Development; International Hydrographic Organization; International Labor Organization; International Maritime Organization; International Rice Council; International Sugar Organization; International Telecommunication Union; International Wheat Council; Non-Aligned Movement; Caribbean Multinational Shipping Line (NAMUCAR); Organization of American States (nonparticipant); Pan American Health Organization; Permanent Court of Arbitration; Postal Union of the Americas and Spain; Latin American Economic System; United Nations; United Nations Educational, Scientific, and Cultural Organization; United Nations Industrial Development Organization; Universal Postal Union; World Federation of Trade Unions; World Health Organization; World Intellectual Property Organization; nonparticipant member Inter-American Development Bank.[3,4]

Sources

1. Committee on Population and Demography, *Fertility Determinants in Cuba*, Report #26. By Paula E. Hollerbach and Sergio Díaz Briquets. Washington, D.C.: National Academy Press, 1983

2. Republic of Cuba, Junta Central de Planificación (JUCEPLAN), *Anuario Estadístico de Cuba*, 1981. Havana, Cuba: Comité Estatal de Estadísticas

3. Central Intelligence Agency, *The World Factbook*. Washington, D.C.: U.S. Government Printing Office, April 1984

4. U.S. Department of State, "Background Notes: Cuba." Washington, D.C.: U.S. Government Printing Office, April 1983

5. *Political Handbook of the World: 1982-1983*. Edited by Arthur S. Banks and William Overstreet. New York: McGraw-Hill, 1983

6. National Bank of Cuba, "Economic Report." Havana: National Bank of Cuba, February 1985.

7. Economic Commission on Latin America and the Caribbean, "Preliminary Overview of the Latin American Economy during 1984." New York: United Ntions/CEPAL, #409/410, January 1985, Table 2,3.

8. *New York Times*, "Cuban Report Is Candid on Economic Burdens," by Clyde H. Farnsworth. 5 June 1985, p. D1.

9. CIA, cited in Ibid.

10. *Washington Post*, "Cuba Resells Cheap Sugar to Soviets," by Joanne Onang, 5 June 1985, p. 30.

Appendix A:
Cuban Heads of State

January 1, 1899– December 23, 1899	John Brooke (U.S. Military Governor)
December 23, 1899– May 20, 1902	Leonard Wood (U.S. Military Governor)
1902–1906	Tomás Estrada Palma
September 29, 1906– October 13, 1906	William Howard Taft (Provisional U.S. Governor)
October 13, 1906– January 28, 1909	Charles Magoon (Provisional U.S. Governor)
1909–1913	José Miguel Gómez
1913–1921	Mario García Menocal
1921–1925	Alfredo Zayas
1925–1933	Gerardo Machado Morales
August 12, 1933– September 5, 1933	Carlos Manuel de Céspedes
September 5–10, 1933	The Pentarquía– Ramón Grau San Martín Porfirio Franco José Miguel Irisarri Sergio Carbó Guillermo Portela
September 10, 1933– January 15, 1934	Ramón Grau San Martín
January 15–18, 1934	Carlos Hevia
January 18, 1934	Manuel Márguez Sterling
January 18, 1934– December 11, 1935	Carlos Mendieta Montefur

December 11, 1935–May 20, 1936	José Antonio Barnet y Vinageras (Provisional President)
May 20, 1936–December 24, 1936	Miguel Mariano Gómez Arias
December 24, 1936–October 10, 1940	Federico Laredo Bru
1940–1944	Fulgencio Batista y Zaldívar
1944–1948	Ramón Grau San Martín
1948–1952	Carlos Prío Socarrás
1952–1959	Fulgencio Batista y Zaldívar
January 2, 1959–July 17, 1959	Manuel Urrutia-Lleó (President)
January 1, 1959–February 13, 1959	José Miro Cardona (Prime Minister)
July 17, 1959–December 3, 1976	Osvaldo Dorticós Torrado (President)
February 13, 1959–February 14, 1976	Fidel Castro Ruz (Prime Minister)
February 14, 1976–present	Fidel Castro Ruz (President)

Appendix B: Cuban Ambassadors to the United Nations and Representatives to Washington, 1959-Present

United Nations (New York)

	Appointed	Credentials Presented	Departed
H.E. Mr. Emilio Núñez-Portuondo	4/52	5/52	1/59
H.E. Mr. Manuel Bisbé-Alberni	2/59	2/59	3/61
H.E. Mr. Mario García-Inchaustegui	4/61	6/61	11/62
H.E. Mr. Carlos Lechuga	10/62	11/62	7/64
H.E. Mr. Fernándo Alvarez Tabío	11/64	11/64	10/65
H.E. Miguel J. Alfonso Martínez Chargé d'Affaires		11/65	7/66
H.E. Dr. Ricardo Alarcón-Quesada	7/66	9/66	4/78
H.E. Dr. Raúl Roa Kourí	4/78	4/78	7/84
H.E. Dr. Oscar Oramas Oliva	8/84	8/84	present

United States (Washington)

Ernesto Dihigo Ambassador to the United States	1959
Ramón Sánchez-Parodi Head, Interest Section	1977–present

Appendix C: Treaty of Paris between Spain and the United States, 1898

Concluded at Paris December 10, 1898; ratification advised by the Senate February 6, 1899; ratified by the President February 6, 1899; ratifications exchanged April 11, 1899; proclaimed April 11, 1899.

ARTICLES

I. Relinquishment of Cuba.
II. Cession of Porto Rico, Guam, etc.
III. Cession of Philippine Islands.
IV. Spanish trade with the Philippines.
V. Return of Spanish soldiers from Manila; evacuation of Philippines and Guam.
VI. Release of prisoners.
VII. Relinquishment of claims.
VIII. Property relinquished and ceded.
IX. Property and civil rights of persons in ceded territory.
X. Religious freedom.
XI. Legal rights in ceded or relinquished territory.
XII. Determination of pending judicial proceedings.
XIII. Privileges of copyrights and patents preserved in ceded territories.
XIV. Consular privileges.
XV. Mutual privileges of shipping charges.
XVI. Obligations of Cuba.
XVII. Ratification.

The United States of America and Her Majesty the Queen Regent of Spain, in the name of her august son Don Alfonso XIII, desiring to end the state of war now existing between the two countries, have for that purpose appointed as plenipotentiaries:

The President of the United States,

William R. Day, Cushman K. Davis, William P. Frye, George Gray, and Whitelaw Reid, citizens of the United States;

And Her Majesty the Queen Regent of Spain,

Don Eugenio Montero Ríos, president of the senate, Don Buenaventura de Abarzuza, senator of the Kingdom and ex-minister of the Crown; Don José de Garnica, deputy to the Cortes and associate justice of the supreme court; Don Wenceslao Ramirez de Villa-Urrutia, envoy extraordinary and minister plenipotentiary at Brussels, and Don Rafael Cerero, general of division;

Who, having assembled in Paris, and having exchanged their full powers, which were found to be in due and proper form, have, after discussion of the matters before them, agreed upon the following articles:

ARTICLE I.

Spain relinquishes all claim of sovereignty over and title to Cuba.

And as the island is, upon its evacuation by Spain, to be occupied by the United States, the United States will, so long as such occupation shall last, assume and discharge the obligations that may under international law result from the fact of its occupation, for the protection of life and property.

ARTICLE VI.

Spain will, upon the signature of the present treaty, release all prisoners of war, and all persons detained or imprisoned for political offences, in connection with the insurrections in Cuba and the Philippines and the war with the United States.

Reciprocally, the United States will release all persons made prisoners of war by the American forces, and will undertake to obtain the release of all Spanish prisoners in the hands of the insurgents in Cuba and the Philippines.

The Government of the United States will at its own cost return to Spain and the Government of Spain will at its own cost return to the United States, Cuba, Porto-Rico, and the Philippines, according to the situation of their respective homes, prisoners released or caused to be released by them, respectively, under this article.

ARTICLE VII.

The United States and Spain mutually relinquish all claims for indemnity, national and individual, of every kind, of either Government, or of its citizens or subjects, against the other Government, that may have arisen since the beginning of the late insurrection in Cuba and prior to the exchange of ratifications of the present treaty, including all claims for indemnity for the cost of the war.

The United States will adjudicate and settle the claims of its citizens against Spain relinquished in this article.

ARTICLE XIII.

The rights of property secured by copyrights and patents acquired by Spaniards in the Island of Cuba and in Porto Rico, the Philippines and other ceded territories, at the time of the exchange of the ratifications of this treaty, shall continue to be respected. Spanish scientific, literary and artistic works, not subversive of public order in the territories in question, shall continue to be admitted free of duty into such territories, for the period of ten years, to be reckoned from the date of the exchange of the ratifications of this treaty.

Article XVI.

It is understood that any obligations assumed in this treaty by the United States with respect to Cuba are limited to the time of its occupancy thereof; but it will upon the termination of such occupancy, advise any Government established in the island to assume the same obligations.

Article XVII.

The present treaty shall be ratified by the President of the United States, by and with the advice and consent of the Senate thereof, and by Her Majesty the Queen Regent of Spain; and the ratifications shall be exchanged at Washington within six months from the date hereof, or earlier if possible.

In faith whereof, we, the respective Plenipotentiaries, have signed this treaty and have hereunto affixed our seals.

Done in duplicate at Paris, the tenth day of December, in the year of Our Lord one thousand eight hundred and ninety-eight.

[SEAL]	William R. Day
[SEAL]	Cushman K. Davis
[SEAL]	William P. Frye
[SEAL]	Geo. Gray
[SEAL]	Whitelaw Reid
[SEAL]	Eugenio Montero Ríos
[SEAL]	B. de Abarzuza
[SEAL]	J. de Garnica
[SEAL]	W R de Villa Urrutia
[SEAL]	Rafael Cerero

Source: *The Consolidated Treaty Series* Vol. 187 (1898–1899), pp. 100–105, Clive Parry, Editor (Dobbs Ferry, New York: Oceana Publication, Inc., 1979).

Appendix D: The *Platt Amendment*

Treaty between the United States and Cuba Embodying the Provisions Defining the Future Relations of the United States with Cuba Contained in the Act of Congress

56th Congress, Session II, Ch. 803

Signed at Habana, May 22, 1903.
Ratification advised by the Senate, March 22, 1904.
Ratified by the President, June 25, 1904.
Ratified by Cuba, June 20, 1904.
Ratifications exchanged at Washington, July 1, 1904.
Proclaimed, July 2, 1904.

I. Treaties with foreign powers.
II. Public debts.
III. Intervention to maintain independence.
IV. Acts during military occupation.
V. Sanitation of cities.
VI. Island of Pines.
VII. Coaling stations.
VIII. Ratification.

BY THE PRESIDENT OF THE UNITED STATES OF AMERICA.

A PROCLAMATION.

Whereas a Treaty between the United States of America and the Republic of Cuba embodying the provisions defining the future relations of United States with

Cuba contained in the Act of Congress approved March 2, 1901, was concluded and signed by their respective Plenipotentiaries at Habana on the twenty-second day of May, one thousand nine hundred and three, the original of which Treaty, being in the English and Spanish languages is word for word as follows:

Whereas the Congress of the United States of America, by an Act approved March 2, 1901, provided as follows:

Provided further, That in fulfillment of the declaration contained in the joint resolution approved April twentieth, eighteen hundred and ninety-eight, entitled, "For the recognition of the independence of the people of Cuba, demanding that the Government of Spain relinquish its authority and government in the island of Cuba, and to withdraw its land and naval forces from Cuba and Cuban waters, and directing the President of the United States to use the land and naval forces of the United States to carry these resolutions into effect," the President is hereby authorized to "leave the government and control of the island of Cuba to its people" so soon as a government shall have been established in said island under a constitution which, either as a part thereof or in an ordinance appended thereto, shall define the future relations of the United States with Cuba, substantially as follows:

"I. That the government of Cuba shall never enter into any treaty or other compact with any foreign power or powers which will impair or tend to impair the independence of Cuba, nor in any manner authorize or permit any foreign power or powers to obtain by colonization or for military or naval purposes or otherwise, lodgement in or control over any portion of said island."

"II. That said government shall not assume or contract any public debt, to pay the interest upon which, and to make reasonable sinking fund provision for the ultimate discharge of which, the ordinary revenues of the island, after defraying the current expenses of government shall be inadequate."

"III. That the government of Cuba consents that the United States may exercise the right to intervene for the preservation of Cuban independence, the maintenance of a government adequate for the protection of life, property, and individual liberty, and for discharging the obligations with respect to Cuba imposed by the treaty of Paris on the United States, now to be assumed and undertaken by the government of Cuba."

"IV. That all Acts of the United States in Cuba during its military occupancy thereof are ratified and validated, and all lawful rights acquired thereunder shall be maintained and protected."

"V. That the government of Cuba will execute, and as far as necessary extend, the plans already devised or other plans to be mutually agreed upon, for the sanitation of the cities of the island, to the end that a recurrence of epidemic and infectious diseases may be prevented thereby assuring protection to the people and commerce of Cuba, as well as to the commerce of the southern ports of the United States and the people residing therein."

"VI. That the Isle of Pines shall be omitted from the proposed constitutional boundaries of Cuba, the title thereto being left to future adjustment by treaty."

"VII. That to enable the United States to maintain the independence of Cuba, and to protect the people thereof, as well as for its own defense, the government of Cuba will sell or lease to the United States lands necessary for coaling or naval stations at certain specified points to be agreed upon with the President of the United States."

"VIII. That by way of further assurance the government of Cuba will embody the foregoing provisions in a permanent treaty with the United States."

Whereas the Constitutional Convention of Cuba, on June twelfth, 1901, adopted a Resolution adding to the Constitution of the Republic of Cuba which was adopted on the twenty-first of February 1901, an appendix in the words and letters of the eight enumerated articles of the above cited act of the Congress of the United States;

And whereas, by the establishment of the independent and sovereign government of the Republic of Cuba, under the constitution promulgated on the 20th of May, 1902, which embraced the foregoing conditions, and by the withdrawal of the Government of the United States as an intervening power, on the same date, it becomes necessary to embody the above cited provisions in a permanent treaty between the United States of America and the Republic of Cuba;

The United States of America and the Republic of Cuba, being desirous to carry out the foregoing conditions, have for that purpose appointed as their plenipotentiaries to conclude a treaty to that end,

The President of the United States of America, Herbert G. Squiers, Envoy Extraordinary and Minister Plenipotentiary at Havana,

And the President of the Republic of Cuba, Carlos de Zaldo y Beurmann, Secretary of State and Justice,—who after communicating to each other their full powers found in good and due form, have agreed upon the following articles:

ARTICLE I.

The Government of Cuba shall never enter into any treaty or other compact with any foreign power or powers which will impair or tend to impair the independence of Cuba, nor in any manner authorize or permit any foreign power or powers to obtain by colonization or for military or naval purposes, or otherwise, lodgment in or control over any portion of said island.

ARTICLE II.

The Government of Cuba shall not assume or contract any public debt to pay the interest upon which, and to make reasonable sinking-fund provision for the ultimate discharge of which, the ordinary revenues of the Island of Cuba, after defraying the current expenses of the Government, shall be inadequate.

Article III.

The Government of Cuba consents that the United States may exercise the right to intervene for the preservation of Cuban independence, the maintenance of a government adequate for the protection of life, property, and individual liberty, and for discharging the obligations with respect to Cuba imposed by the Treaty of Paris on the United States, now to be assumed and undertaken by the Government of Cuba.

Article IV.

All acts of the United States in Cuba during its military occupancy thereof are ratified and validated, and all lawful rights acquired thereunder shall be maintained and protected.

Article V.

The Government of Cuba will execute, and, as far as necessary, extend the plans already devised, or other plans to be mutually agreed upon, for the sanitation of the cities of the island, to the end that a recurrence of epidemic and infectious diseases may be prevented, thereby assuring protection to the people and commerce of Cuba, as well as to the commerce of the Southern ports of the United States and the people residing therein.

Article VI.

The Island of Pines shall be omitted from the boundaries of Cuba specified in the Constitution, the title thereto being left to future adjustment by treaty.

Article VII.

To enable the United States to maintain the independence of Cuba, and to protect the people thereof, as well as for its own defense, the Government of Cuba will sell or lease to the United States lands necessary for coaling or naval stations, at certain specified points, to be agreed upon with the President of the United States.

Article VIII.

The present Convention shall be ratified by each party in conformity with the respective Constitutions of the two countries, and the ratifications shall be exchanged in the City of Washington within eight months from this date.

In witness whereof, we the respective Plenipotentiaries, have signed the same in duplicate, in English and Spanish, and have affixed our respective seals at Havana, Cuba, this twenty-second day of May, in the year nineteen hundred and three.

         H. G. SQUIERS. [SEAL.]
         CARLOS DE ZALDO. [SEAL.]

COPYRIGHT.

BY THE PRESIDENT OF THE UNITED STATES OF AMERICA,

A PROCLAMATION.

Whereas, it is provided by section 13 of the act of Congress of March 3, 1891, entitled "An act to amend title sixty, chapter three of the Revised Statutes of the United States, relating to copyrights", that said act "shall only apply to a citizen or subject of a foreign state or nation when such foreign state or nation permits to citizens of the United States of America the benefit of copyright on substantially the same basis as its own citizens; or when such foreign state or nation is a party to an international agreement which provides for reciprocity in the granting of copyright, by the terms of which agreement the United States of America may, at its pleasure, become a party to such agreement";

And Whereas it is also provided by said section that "the existence of either of the conditions aforesaid shall be determined by the President of the United States by proclamation made from time to time as the purposes of this act may require";

And Whereas satisfactory official assurances have been given that in Cuba the law permits to citizens of the United States the benefit of copyright on substantially the same basis as to the citizens of Cuba:

And Whereas the said Treaty has been duly ratified on both parts, and the ratifications of the two governments were exchanged in the City of Washington, on the first day of July, one thousand nine hundred and four:

Now, therefore, be it known that I, Theodore Roosevelt, President of the United States of America, have caused the said Treaty to be made public, to the end that the same and every article and clause thereof may be observed and fulfilled with good faith by the United States and the citizens thereof.

In testimony whereof, I have hereunto set my hand and caused the seal of the United States of America to be affixed.

Done at the City of Washington, this second day of July, in the year of our [SEAL.] Lord one thousand nine hundred and four, and of the Independence of the United States of America the one hundred and twenty-eighth.

              THEODORE ROOSEVELT

By the President:
 ALVEY A. ADEE
  Acting Secretary of State.

SUPPLEMENTARY CONVENTION BETWEEN THE UNITED STATES AND CUBA EXTENDING THE PERIOD WITHIN WHICH MAY BE EXCHANGED THE RATIFICATIONS OF THE TREATY OF MAY 22, 1903, BETWEEN THE UNITED STATES AND CUBA, EMBODYING THE PROVISIONS DEFINING THEIR FUTURE RELATIONS.

Signed at Washington, January 20, 1904.
Ratification advised by the Senate, January 27, 1904.
Ratified by the President, June 25, 1904.
Ratified by Cuba, June 20, 1904.
Ratifications exchanged at Washington, July 1, 1904.
Proclaimed, July 2, 1904.

BY THE PRESIDENT OF THE UNITED STATES OF AMERICA.

A PROCLAMATION.

Whereas a Supplementary Convention between the United States of America and the Republic of Cuba, extending the time within which may be exchanged the ratifications of the treaty signed May 22, 1903, embodying the provisions defining the future relations of the United States with Cuba, contained in the Act of Congress of the United States approved March 2, 1901, was concluded and signed by their respective Plenipotentiaries at Washington, on the twentieth day of January one thousand nine hundred and four, the original of which Supplementary Convention, being in the English and Spanish languages, is word for word as follows:

The United States of America and the Republic of Cuba, considering it expedient to prolong the period in which, by Article VIII of the treaty signed by their respective plenipotentiaries on May 22, 1903, embodying the provisions defining the future relations of the United States with Cuba, contained in the act of Congress of the United States approved March 2, 1901, the exchange of ratifications of the said treaty shall take place, have for that purpose appointed their respective Plenipotentiaries, namely:

The President of the United States of America, John Hay, Secretary of State of the United States; and

The President of Cuba, Gonzalo de Quesada, Envoy Extraordinary and Minister Plenipotentiary of Cuba at Washington;
who, after having communicated to each other their respective full powers, found in good and due form, have agreed upon the following additional article to be taken as part of said treaty.

SOLE ARTICLE.

The respective ratifications of the said treaty shall be exchanged as soon as possible, and within six months from January 21, 1904.

Done in duplicate at Washington, in the English and Spanish languages, this 20th day of January A. D. 1904.

JOHN HAY [SEAL.]
GONZALO DE QUESADA [SEAL.]

And whereas the said Supplementary Convention has been duly ratified on both parts, and the ratifications of the two governments were exchanged in the City of Washington, on the first day of July, one thousand nine hundred and four;

Now, therefore, be it known that I, Theodore Roosevelt, President of the United States of America, have caused the said Supplementary Convention to be made public to the end that the same may be observed and fulfilled with good faith by the United States and the citizens thereof.

In testimony whereof I have hereunto set my hand and caused the seal of the United States of America to be affixed.

Done at the City of Washington, this second day of July, in the year of our Lord one thousand nine hundred and four, and one thousand nine
[SEAL.] hundred and four, and of the Independence of the United States of America the one hundred and twenty-eighth.

THEODORE ROOSEVELT

By the President:
ALVEY A. ADEE
Acting Secretary of State.

Sources: *Treaties Between the U.S. and Other Powers 1771-1909.* Vol. 1. Committee on Foreign Relations, U.S. Senate, 60th Congress, 2nd Session. Washington, D.C.: GPO, 1910, pp. 362-366; *Papers Relating to Foreign Relations of the U.S.*, Washington, D.C. Dept. of State: GPO, 1905, pp. 243-247; transmitted to Congress Dec. 6, 1904; *U.S. Statutes at Large*, Vol. 31 (Washington, D.C.: GPO, 1901), pp. 897-898.

Appendix E: Guantánamo Bay Lease Agreements

Guantánamo Bay U.S. naval base was established at a constitutional conference held in Havana from December 1900 through May 1901.[1] An agreement was signed by the U.S. and Cuba written as Article VII of the Appendix of the Constitution of Cuba (approved May 20, 1902), and Article VIII of the act of the U.S. Congress (approved March 2, 1901), that "the United States . . . maintain the independence of Cuba, and protect the people thereof, as well as its own defense, (to enable the U.S. to do so) the Cuban Government will sell or lease to the United States the lands necessary for coaling or naval stations, at . . . specific points, to be agreed upon with the President of the United States."[2] During November 1902, the United States suggested that the bases to which it was entitled, in order to fulfill the "guarantee of independence" assumed under the Platt Amendment (see appendix D) should be Guantánamo, Cienfuegos, Bahía Honda and Nipe. President Tomás Estrada Palma persuaded the U.S. to cut their demand to Guantánamo and Bahía Honda, and for the bases to be leased rather than actually sold.[3]

The stated provisions according to the agreed-upon lease:

Article I: The payment of $2000 per year in gold coins by the United States to the Republic of Cuba for the leasing of said area. All private lands within the areas shall be bought by the U.S. and accepted by the Republic of Cuba.

Article II: The area shall be bounded, and the fees incurred for bounding shall be paid by the United States.

Article III: No industries, commercial or otherwise shall enter, maintain or establish within the said area.

Article IV: Fugitives of either country shall be returned to the respective country.

Article V: Specific duty laws and regulations.

Article VI: The U.S. may place no obstacles upon vessels entering or departing except in time of war. All vessels are subject to specific regulations as described in Article VI.

Article VII: The specific regulations relating to the ratification of the said lease.

The area included within the Guantánamo Bay naval base is 45 square miles of land and water. Most significant to the agreement, the lease was written in perpetuity. The original request for usage by the Department of the Navy was submitted to Congress on 20 January 1904. Although the land was already under the United States' lease, there had not yet been a formal plan approved. This plan included hospital facilities necessary for the care of seamen and marines stationed at, or visiting the base in navy vessels.

Following the 1959 Revolution, Foreign Minister Raúl Roa García stated that the 1903 contract was not valid because Cubans were not on "an equal footing with the United States." Roa also argued that Cuba did not agree to the lease "because the Cuban people were coerced by a system of government imposed upon them from abroad."[4]

On 16 March 1961, it was reported that Cuban workers within the confines of Guantánamo believed that the Cuban government would forbid them from working there any longer. However, the U.S. government stated that this was a fairly remote possibility since Castro needed the American dollars received from the Cuban employment within the base to aid his sagging foreign exchange.[5] February 1964 brought drastic change. Cuba cut off the water supply to protest against U.S. government actions. Washington retaliated by ordering the reduction and replacement of Cuban employees at Guantánamo. They also began installation on a desalting plant (which was completed in 1965) to free workers from dependence on Cuba for water supplies. In 1984 the Cubans working at Guatánamo Bay totalled 89 as opposed to over 3,000 in 1961.

Guantánamo Bay is the only U.S. naval base located in a Communist country and the only base by which Soviet ships pass. Within the base there are 452 marines and 300 armed navy sailors permanently stationed. Annually, over 40,000 sailors are trained within the 45-square-mile radius.

Washington's rental of the base has increased due to the change in the price of gold. In 1983, the United States paid an annual rental of over $4,000.[6] As U.S. relations with Cuba became more tense in 1984, Washington initiated "Ocean Venture I" a military exercise involving 350 ships and 30,000 U.S. soldiers in a three-week maneuver aimed at protecting the United States "national interests by projecting military power."[7]

Notes

1. Hugh Thomas, *Cuba: Pursuit of Freedom*. New York: Harper and Row, 1971, p. 449.

2. *Papers relating to the Foreign Relations of the United States*, Washington, D.C.: Government Printing Office, 1904, pp. 350-353.
3. In 1912 Bahía Honda was cut out while the size of Guantánamo Bay was increased.
4. *Current Intelligence Weekly*, Washington, D.C.: Central Intelligence Agency, Office of the Current Intelligence Weekly, *Summary*, February 9, 1961. Released to the public on March 7, 1976, pp. 9-10.
5. Ibid., March 16, 1961. Released to the public in 1977.
6. *New York Times*, 1 May 1984, p. A2.
7. Ibid.

Source: H.R. Documents 449, U.S., Congress, 58th Congress, 2nd Session, Washington, D.C.: Government Printing Office, 1903.

AGREEMENT FOR THE LEASE TO THE UNITED STATES OF LANDS IN CUBA FOR COALING AND NAVAL STATIONS.

Signed by the President of Cuba February 16, 1903 and by the President of the United States February 23, 1903.

ARTICLES.

I. Lease of land. III. Jurisdiction.
II. Waters.

AGREEMENT

Between the United States of America and the Republic of Cuba for the lease (subject to terms to be agreed upon by the two Governments) to the United States of lands in Cuba for coaling and naval stations.

The United States of America and the Republic of Cuba, being desirous to execute fully the provisions of Article VII of the Act of Congress approved March second, 1901, and of Article VII of the Appendix to the Constitution of the Republic of Cuba promulgated on the 20th of May, 1902, which provide:

"Article VII. To enable the United States to maintain the independence of Cuba, and to protect the people thereof, as well as for its own defense, the Cuban Government will sell or lease to the United States the lands necessary for coaling or naval stations, at certain specified points, to be agreed upon with the President of the United States."
have reached an agreement to that end, as follows:

Article I.

The Republic of Cuba hereby leases to the United States, for the time required for the purposes of coaling and naval stations, the following described areas of land and water situated in the Island of Cuba:
   1st. In Guantánamo. . . .
   2nd. In Bahía Honda. . . .

Article II.

The grant of the foregoing Article shall include the right to use and occupy the waters adjacent to said areas of land and water, and to improve and deepen the entrances thereto and the anchorages therein, and generally to do any and all things necessary to fit the premises for use as coaling or naval stations only, and for no other purpose.

Vessels engaged in the Cuban trade shall have free passage through the waters included within this grant.

Article III.

While on the one hand the United States recognizes the continuance of the ultimate sovereignty of the Republic of Cuba over the above described areas of land and water, on the other hand the Republic of Cuba consents that during the period of occupation by the United States of said areas under the terms of this agreement the United States shall exercise complete jurisdiction and control over and within said areas with the right to acquire (under conditions to be hereafter agreed upon by the two Governments) for the public purposes of the United States any land or other property therein by purchase or by exercise of eminent domain with full compensation to the owners thereof.

Done in duplicate at Habana, and signed by the President of the Republic of Cuba this sixteenth day of February, 1903.

[SEAL]   T. Estrada Palma.

Signed by the President of the United States the twenty-third of February, 1903.

[SEAL]   Theodore Roosevelt

Source: *Treaties between the U.S. and Other Powers, 1776–1909.* Vol. 1. Committee on Foreign Relations, U.S. Senate, 60th Congress, 2nd Session. Washington, D.C.: GPO, 1910, pp. 358–59.

Appendix F:
Report of the Secretary of War, 1906: *Cuban Pacification*

Excerpts from the Report of William H. Taft and Robert Bacon

We have the honor hereby to submit to you a report of what was done by us under your direction in assisting to bring about peace in Cuba . . . after the provisional government of the Republic of Cuba, in the meantime established under the "Platt Amendment," had been, by your direction, turned over to Governor Magoon. . . .

DEPARTMENT OF STATE
Washington, September 10, 1906.

STEINHART, *Habana:*

Two ships have been sent, due to arrive Wednesday. The President directs me to state that perhaps you do not yourself appreciate the reluctance with which this country would intervene. President Palma should be informed that in the public opinion here it would have a most damaging effect for intervention to be undertaken until the Cuban Government has exhausted every effort in a serious attempt to put down the insurrection and has made this fact evident to the world. At present the impression certainly would be that there was no real popular support of the Cuban Government or else that the Government was hopelessly weak. As conditions are at this moment we are not prepared to say what shape the intervention should take. It is, of course, a very serious thing to undertake forcible intervention, and before going into it we should have to be absolutely certain of the equities of the case and of the needs of the situation. Meanwhile we assume that every effort is being made by the Government to come to a working agreement which will secure peace with the *insurrectos*, provided they are unable to hold their own with them in the field. Until such efforts have been made we are not prepared to consider the question of intervention at all.

BACON, *Acting Secretary.*

DEPARTMENT OF STATE, *September 11, 1906.*
STEINHART,
   American Consul-General, Habana:

Your letter of September 5th has had the careful consideration of the President, who, for your private information, believes actual, immediate intervention to be out of the question. We are considering, however, and would like your opinion, as to whether or not to send a word of emphatic warning as to the certainty that intervention will come in the end unless the people of Cuba, for the sake of their country, find some way to settle their difficulties, irrespective of personalities, cease their contentions, and live in peace. This you may convey confidentially to President Palma, but not for publication. You will urge President Palma to use in the most effective manner all the resources at his command to quell the revolt.

BACON.

Hon. ROBERT BACON, *Acting Secretary of State.*

You described the dreadful disaster imminent in Cuba and the evil of anarchy into which civil war and revolutionary disturbances would assuredly throw her, and pointed out that the only way in which Cuban independence could be endangered was for the Cuban people to show their inability to continue in their path of peaceful and orderly progress; and that our intervention in Cuban affairs would come only if Cuba herself showed that she had fallen into the insurrectionary habit. You solemnly adjured all Cuban patriots to band together, to sink all differences and personal ambitions, and to rescue the island from the anarchy of civil war. You said that under the treaty with Cuba, as President of the United States, you had a duty in the matter which you could not shirk; that the third article of the treaty explicitly conferred upon the United States the right to intervene for the maintenance in Cuba of a government adequate for the protection of life, property, and individual liberty; that the treaty conferring the right was the supreme law of the land, and furnished you with the right and means of fulfilling the obligation that you were under to protect American interests; that your information showed that the social bonds throughout the island had been so relaxed that life, property, and individual liberty were no longer safe; and that in your judgment it was imperative for the sake of Cuba that there should be an immediate cessation of hostilities and some arrangement which would secure the permanent pacification of the island. You closed (the letter) as follows:

I am sending to Habana the Secretary of War, Mr. Taft, and the Assistant Secretary of State, Mr. Bacon, as the special representatives of this Government, who will render such aid as is possible toward these ends. I had hoped that Mr. Root, the Secretary of State, could have stopped in Habana on his return from South America, but the seeming imminence of the crisis forbids further delay. . . .

OYSTER BAY, N. Y., *September 26, 1906.*

TAFT, Habana:

It is undoubtedly a very evil thing that the revolutionists should be encouraged and the dreadful example afforded the island of success in remedying wrongs by violence and treason to the Government.

If the Palma Government had shown any real capacity for self-defense and ability to sustain itself and a sincere purpose to remedy the wrongs of which your telegrams show that they have been guilty, I should have been inclined to stand by them, no matter to what extent, including armed intervention, but as things actually are we do not have the chance of following any such course.

Before you and Bacon went down we had been notified that Palma would resign; that the vice-president and cabinet would refuse to go on with their Government, and now you inform me that this is their definite intention; in other words, that they absolutely decline either to endeavor to remedy the wrongs they have done or to so much as lift a hand in their own defense or make an effort to secure the stability of their Government or the overthrow of the insurrectionists.

Under such circumstances, as the least of two very serious evils, it seems to me that we must simply put ourselves for the time being in Palma's place, land a sufficient force to insure order, and notify the insurgents that we will carry through the programme in which you and they are agreed—keeping control simply until this programme can be carried through.

I do not have much hope that with the example before them of such success in an insurrection the people who grow discontented with the new government will refrain from insurrection and disturbance some time in the future, but there is a slight chance and in my opinion we should give them this chance. Then if the new government sooner or later falls to pieces under the stress of another insurrection, not only will our duty be clearer but the conception by our people and by the people of other nations of our duty will be clearer, and we will have removed all chance of any honest people thinking that we have failed to do our best to establish peace and order in the island without depriving it of its independence.

It seems to me that by following this course—that is, by avoiding any threat or warning to the insurgents unless they refuse to carry out the agreement which they have already made—we shall put ourselves in a strong position in case any of the insurgents refuse to carry out the agreement.

From what you say it is possible the insurgents may not act together, and in that case it would be an advantage to us to have a portion of them with us in case a struggle should ever come.

I feel, therefore, that in ordering the troops to land or insuring any proclamation in my name, which, of course, I hereby authorize you to do, you should base your action upon the ground that organized government had disappeared and that order must be kept, and should avoid issuing the ultimatum to the insurgents or the use of any phraseology saying that they are in revolt against the United States until you have seen whether they will not in good faith carry out the agreement they have already made with you, you on your part carrying out so much of the agreement as you had intended to have Palma carry out.

Of course there may be circumstances known to you which make this plan of mine futile, and I am giving my views with the understanding that they come from a man at a distance who does not know the facts as you do on the ground.

If possible, cable me fully, but if a crisis comes and has to be met I hereby authorize you to do whatever in your discretion you deem best.

THEODORE ROOSEVELT.

OYSTER BAY, N.Y., *September 26, 1906.*

TAFT, *Habana:*

Just received your telegram of today. Immensely pleased with it and am delighted with the way you are handling the situation. You are doing just what I hoped would be done.

Avoid the use of the word "intervention" in any proclamation or paper of yours and if possible place the landing of our sailors and marines on the grounds of conservation of American interests, emphasizing the temporary character of the landing and the hope that our keeping sailors, marines, or troops in the island will be but for a short time, until a permanent government has been formed.

Please consider whether it would not be well at first to limit, as far as possible, the places where we have to establish garrisons. I want to make it evident, beyond the possibility of a doubt, that we take no steps that we are not absolutely forced to by the situation, and, therefore, I should like to avoid taking possession in appearance of the entire island, if that is possible. Of course, I understand that it may not be possible to avoid this.

Of course, if it becomes necessary to answer any statement of Palma's and the Moderates point out the fact that you and Bacon only went down there when they had requested us to intervene by force of arms, and after Palma had notified us that he would resign, and that neither the vice-president nor the other members of the Cabinet would go on with the government, so that we were brought face to face with the island being left in absolute chaos, with no government at all, and all of this by the act of Palma and his government, before a single step had been taken by us.

I sympathize most heartily with your abhorrence of the insurrectionary spirit, and appreciate keenly the evil necessarily done by the recognition of the insurrectionary party into which we are forced, but this evil is not in the slightest degree due to any act of ours.

... concentration of power, and also a law making judges of the first instance immovable, as required by the constitution. New electoral law will be required to square with new municipal law, and a further condition should be an election within a reasonable time to fill the vacancies occasioned by the resignations. We do not know that we can enforce this compromise with the Moderates; think we can. Everything, however, must be dependent upon the condition that immediately upon entering into agreement, and the resignations in accordance with it, the insurgents in arms shall disband, and that a failure within five days to fulfill this condition will lead to forcible intervention by the United States. It seems to us in this way we put the insurgents in a position utterly indefensible if they remain in arms, and that we shall then probably be able to secure much more moral support from the people in the island if we have to intervene. At any rate, we shall have made every effort to avoid intervention, and coming as it then does after such an effort, it then remains for the United States to do its duty.

A conference is to be held this morning with Zayas, the leader of the Liberals, and tomorrow morning with military generals in charge of insurgents, and we should like your authority to say to them that a further movement toward or attack on Habana—for they are now within 2½ miles of the suburbs of the city and within that distance from the city waterworks—will be regarded as justification for forcible intervention, and secondly, that if they can not comply with the conditions along the lines above stated, which we deem reasonable, that then we shall move our forces into Habana. It may be under authority vested in me by Bonaparte's order I may find it necessary to land forces before hearing from you. I hope and think not. I need not say an early reply to this will be of assistance.

TAFT.

The Palma government lacks moral support of large majority of the people, and is without adequate preparation. Palma himself told us (and this is confirmed by information got directly from the chief of the secret police) that ramifications of this movement as a conspiracy were brought clearly to the knowledge of him and the government six months ago, and that no action was taken to avoid its necessary effect.

We cannot maintain the *Palma government except by forcible intervention against the whole weight of public opinion in the island.*

The Palma government, through its then minister of government, Andrade, openly need and abused its power to carry elections, and in doing so removed many municipal officers in many parts of the island. Undoubtedly it is usual for the government in such countries to attempt to control the election in its interests, but the open way in which it was here done seems to have made a deep impression on the minds of the people, especially because it was accompanied by wholesale removals from office. There are two elections under the law. The first or preliminary election is for the selection of the tribunal to determine the main elections. It was in the preliminary elections that such fraud and violence were practiced as to lead the Liberals to withdraw their candidate from main election. It is quite probable that the Liberals would have done the same thing as the Moderates had the power been theirs, but I can not think they would have done it in such an open way, entirely unnecessary to accomplish the purpose. If the present government could maintain itself, or if it had a moral support or following which would be useful in case of intervention, Bacon and I would be strongly in favor of supporting it as the regular and constitutional government, because the election was held under forms of law and has been acted upon and recognized as valid, but the actual state of affairs is such that we would be fighting the whole Cuban people in effect by intervening to maintain this government.

The insurgents, without our intervention, could drive the government out of Habana, and should they enter there would probably be an uprising in their favor. Is it not wiser, therefore, to continue the form of the present government by the resignation of the President and other officials and the succession of a temporary executive under the provisions of law?

We can possibly secure for this temporary executive, by agreement, a person indifferent between the parties and not closely affiliated with either party, who will have conservative tendencies. We shall try to procure the continuance of Palma in office with a new cabinet if possible, but there are two difficulties connected with this—first, that the insurgents are not likely to agree to it, and second, it is doubtful whether Palma would be an instrument in our hands for this purpose under the conditions which must accompany the arrangement, the chief of which are the resignation of one-half of the senate and one-half of the house elected at the last election and the restoration of the municipal officials who were removed from office by Andrade.

On the contrary, it is evident that only your going to Habana prevented that city and all of Cuba from falling immediately into the possession of the revolutionists. We have not caused the evil, we have simply dealt with it in the wisest possible manner under conditions as they have actually been.

THEODORE ROOSEVELT

CONCLUSION

On the whole, and to sum up the purpose of our going and what was done, we repeat that we went to Cuba for the purpose of securing peace; that when we went we knew the island was divided between two hostile and armed forces, and we desired to avoid a conflict between them for the reason that it would cause loss of life to the Cubans and a great destruction of property, a large part of which belonged to American citizens, and it would necessarily require the intervention of American troops and the expenditure of American lives and treasure. If *the insurrectionary habit persists, if again the Cubans divide into armed forces,* the strong hand of our Government will have to be imposed at whatever cost to life and property, and permanent peace should then certainly ensue because it should be of our own keeping.

We hope, however, that no such drastic remedy will be needed and that the lesson taught in this recent experience of the evil of unjust methods in elections will not be without its warning to future governments in Cuba. With the passage of proper laws for municipal governments, for elections, and for the independence of the judiciary, and with the holding of a fair election under the auspices of the United States for the vacancies effected in accordance with the compromise recommended, we are very hopeful that the Cuban Republic may be restored on even a more permanent basis than that which she enjoyed *during four years of prosperity under President Palma.*

WM. H. TAFT.
ROBERT BACON.

HABANA, *September 21, 1906.*

THE PRESIDENT, *Oyster Bay, N.Y.:*

With the assistance of Cairns and Ladd, and interviews we have had in last two days, our information as to the situation has increased greatly in accuracy and detail. It becomes clearer and clearer that present government under Palma can not maintain itself. It has about 5,500 rurales, 600 artillerymen, some militia, and the municipal police of Habana, but these are spread all over the island, about 3,000 being in the city of Habana. Artillery mostly is in the city.

The Government has had much difficulty in recruiting, notwithstanding that it pays $2.50 a day to recruits. It is quite probable, and the Government authorities expect that, should an attack be made on Habana, one-half of the Habana police force will join the insurgents. Within 5 miles of the city there is a force of 1,500 men, and within 20 miles, marching towards the city, there are 4,000 or 5,000. The truce is not being kept squarely on either side. The Government is perfecting blockhouses and attempting to mobilize. The insurgents are concentrating their troops near Habana. In addition to this there is a large force of insurgents in Santa Clara and other provinces, making force of insurgents in arms possibly 12,000, some with good arms, others with poor arms and with ammunition insufficient. We shall have definite statements with reference to sources of supplies for insurgents at noon. Know in advance that there were practically no American contributions, except some small sums from the Isle of Pines, but substantially all the money was by local contribution. Of course the fund is being added to by blackmail of property owners in fear of injury to their property. It is quite evident that no American interests in New York or elsewhere have initiated movement or contributed to its success. But for landing of troops of the *Denver* and publication of your letter, it is extremely probable that the insurgents would now be in control of Habana, with all the destruction and disaster that would have been certain to follow, not so much from the insurgents themselves as from mob which would have taken control.

HABANA CUBA, *September 28, 1906.*

THE PRESIDENT, *Oyster Bay:*
The following form of proclamation, in case we must establish provisional government, is suggested:

"To the people of Cuba:
"The failure of Congress to act on the irrevocable resignation of the President of the Republic of Cuba, or to elect a successor at this time when great disorder prevails in the country, requires that, pursuant to a request of President Palma referred to the President of the United States, the necessary step be taken by this proclamation in the name and by the authority of the President of the United States to restore order, protect life and property in the Island of Cuba and islands and keys adjacent thereto, and for this purpose to establish therein a provisional government.

"The provisional government hereby established will be maintained only long enough to restore order and peace and public confidence and then to hold such elections as may be necessary to determine those persons to whom the permanent government of the Republic should be turned back.

"In so far as is consistent with the nature of a provisional government, the constitution of Cuba will be observed. It will be a Cuban Government as far as possible and a mere continuance of the one for which it is temporarily substituted. All the executive departments will be as under President Palma. The courts will continue to administer justice and all laws not in their nature inapplicable by the reason of the temporary and emergent character of the government.

"President Roosevelt has been most anxious to bring about peace under the constitutional government of Cuba and has made every endeavor to avoid the present step. Longer delay, however, would be dangerous.

"In view of the resignation of the Cabinet, until further notice the heads of all departments of the central government will report to me for instructions, including General Alejandro Rodríguez, in command of the rural guard and other regular Government forces, and General Carlos Roloff, treasurer of Cuba.

"Until further notice, the civil governors and alcaldes will also report to me for instructions.

"I ask all citizens and residents of Cuba to assist in the work of restoring order, tranquility, and public confidence.

"WILLIAM H. TAFT,
"*Secretary of War of the United States,*
"*Provisional Governor of Cuba.*

"HABANA, *September 28, 1906.*"

TAFT.

PROPOSED COMPROMISE.

We had become convinced by our investigation that the compromise proposed by General Menocal, before we reached the island, with some modifications, was a fair basis for settlement. We were of opinion, from all we could learn, that President Palma would have been elected without any resort to the unfair methods which we believe to have been used under the Moderate secretary of government. We deemed it important, in order to maintain the good name of Cuba, and in order to show that a conservative man was retained in power, to have Mr. Palma remain as President. We thought it would preserve the continuity of the Government under the constitution, and perhaps prevent the injury to the credit of the island which a violent or abrupt change in chief executive would be likely to effect. Señor Palma seemed to us the most disinterested patriot in the island, and while we differed from him in some of his views and found defects in him as a successful administrator, we saw nothing to detract from his fame as a Cuban patriot and hero. We were certain that if the preliminary election had been fair, and the Liberals had gone to the polls at the final election, they would have been able to return some of their senatorial candidates, some of their candidates for the House of Representatives and some of their gubernatorial candidates, but it was impossible to say how many or which ones. There was no method, therefore, of reaching a satisfactory result, except to have a new election. This compromise would have continued the same chief executive, and in a Spanish country by tradition the power of the executive overshadows every other, whatever the legal relations of one branch to the other. Even if the Liberals should be generally successful in electing representatives and senators at the new election, there would be at least two provinces where the Moderates would be likely to return their candidates, and as they had a majority of the hold-over members of the house the parties would be fairly well balanced in the new Congress, especially if the new electoral law made provision as the constitution contemplated for minority representation. We thought that an election, if the compromise was fully concurred in and carried out in good faith, might be had in three months, and therefore that the remedy of any injustice which had been done with respect to the ayuntamientos, of which the Liberals complained so strenuously, might well await the result of the elections to be held under a new electoral law and new municipal law, in compliance with the requirements of the constitution. We thought that it would be wise to have a commission, consisting of an equal number of Moderates and Liberals, with at least one American on it, to prepare needed laws on the subject of municipalities, elections, independence of the judiciary, and the classified civil service, according to the merit system, so that these laws might be enforced and adopted by Congress, as a matter of course and of previous agreement after they had been settled by the commission. Immediately upon the tender of the resignations recommended, the rebels in arms were to lay down their arms and to disperse to their homes under a general amnesty. It should be said that although we thereafter ventured to intimate to President Palma the wisdom of accepting the tendered resignations of his then cabinet and appointing a nonpolitical one, it was not part of the compromise recommended either to the Liberal or the Moderate party.

On September 24 we explained the compromise to the representatives of the Liberal party, and although there was much objection to the failure to provide for an immediate restoration of the municipal governments and to an absence of a restriction upon President Palma's power to appoint such a cabinet as he saw fit, they indicated the probability of their acquiescence. The same day the proposition was submitted informally to Señor Capote, the head of the Moderate party, who said that he did not think the compromise proposed was a practical suggestion; that the government thus organized would not stand for three months, and that it was a mere patched up affair which simply postponed the evil day. He said, however, when we asked him for the resignations of the members of the Moderate party, which from previous informal assurances of himself and General Andrade we had reason to believe would be forthcoming at our request, that if we would give him the form of paper tendering their resignations such as we desired in the matter, he would bring it back to us in half an hour, signed. Instead of doing so, however, he sent a letter inclosing a resolution of the Moderate party passed some days before, which agreed to our arbitration of the difficulties if the insurgent Liberals would lay down their arms in advance. Having been advised by Doctor Capote's attitude of the probable unwillingness of the Moderate party to acquiesce in our proposed compromise, we deemed it wise to appeal to President Palma. We sought and had an appointment with him on the night of the 24th, in which we explained as fully as we could the reasons as to our conclusion as to the proper compromise, and asked him to aid us in carrying it out. There was an extended discussion. He maintained that the elections were fair and that we were prejudiced. Finally the President said that it was inconsistent with his dignity and honor to acquiesce in the resignation of members of his party who had been elected on the same ticket with him; that he did not think the compromise, if entered into, would last three months; that it was useless, and that he would not lend himself to it. We then withdrew, with expressions of regret that we could not come nearer reaching an agreement, and the same night we wrote him a letter embodying at length what we had stated to him in the conversation.

Meantime President Palma, having announced his intention to resign, summoned the Congress to receive his resignation on the 28th of September. Before Congress met efforts were made to secure an agreement between Liberals and a part of the Moderate party, which failed. We encouraged this effort as far as we could, but without success.

The strong desire of the Moderates was to secure our intervention, but they were most anxious to do it without incurring the criticism, as a party, which they knew would be directed against them if they were plainly and directly responsible for bringing intervention about. They therefore adopted the method of receiving the resignation of the President and of asking him to withdraw it, and on his failure to withdraw it, of failing to attend the adjourned meeting of Congress and leaving no quorum.

REPUBLIC OF CUBA,
EXECUTIVE MANSION,
Habana, September 28, 1906.

Appendix G:
Letters Relating to the Cuban Missile Crisis
Between John F. Kennedy and Nikita Khrushchev

PRESIDENT KENNEDY'S MESSAGE OF OCTOBER 22, 1962

[WASHINGTON,] *October 22, 1962.*

DEAR MR. CHAIRMAN: A copy of the statement I am making tonight concerning developments in Cuba and the reaction of my Government thereto has been handed to your Ambassador in Washington. In view of the gravity of the developments to which I refer, I want you to know immediately and accurately the position of my Government in this matter.

In our discussions and exchanges on Berlin and other international questions, the one thing that has most concerned me has been the possibility that your Government would not correctly understand the will and determination of the United States in any given situation, since I have not assumed that you or any other sane man would, in this nuclear age, deliberately plunge the world into war which it is crystal clear no country could win and which could only result in catastrophic consequences to the whole world, including the aggressor.

At our meeting in Vienna and subsequently, I expressed our readiness and desire to find, through peaceful negotiation, a solution to any and all problems that divide us. At the same time, I made clear that in view of the objectives of the ideology to which you adhere, the United States could not tolerate any action on your part which in a major way disturbed the existing over-all balance of power in the world. I stated that an attempt to force abandonment of our responsibilities and commitments in Berlin would constitute such an action and that the United States would resist with all the power at its command.

It was in order to avoid any incorrect assessment on the part of your Government with respect to Cuba that I publicly stated that if certain developments in Cuba took place, the United States would do whatever must be done to protect its own security and that of its allies.

Source: U.S. Department of State *Bulletin.* Vol LXIX no. 1795, November 19, 1973, p. 634–655; John F. Kennedy Library, Cambridge, Massachusetts.

Moreover, the Congress adopted a resolution expressing its support of this declared policy. Despite this, the rapid development of long-range missile bases and other offensive weapons systems in Cuba has proceeded. I must tell you that the United States is determined that this threat to the security of this hemisphere be removed. At the same time, I wish to point out that the action we are taking is the minimum necessary to remove the threat to the security of the nations of this hemisphere. The fact of this minimum response should not be taken as a basis, however, for any misjudgment on your part.

I hope that your Government will refrain from any action which would widen or deepen this already grave crisis and that we can agree to resume the path of peaceful negotiation.

Sincerely,
JOHN F. KENNEDY.

CHAIRMAN KHRUSHCHEV'S MESSAGE OF OCTOBER 23, 1962

Official Translation

MOSCOW, *October 23, 1962.*

MR. PRESIDENT: I have just received your letter, and have also acquainted myself with the text of your speech of October 22 regarding Cuba.

I must say frankly that the measures indicated in your statement constitute a serious threat to peace and to the security of nations. The United States has openly taken the path of grossly violating the United Nations Charter, the path of violating international norms of freedom of navigation on the high seas, the path of aggressive actions both against Cuba and against the Soviet Union.

The statement by the Government of the United States of America can only be regarded as undisguised interference in the internal affairs of the Republic of Cuba, the Soviet Union and other states. The United Nations Charter and international norms give no right to any state to institute in international waters the inspection of vessels bound for the shores of the Republic of Cuba.

And naturally, neither can we recognize the right of the United States to establish control over armaments which are necessary for the Republic of Cuba to strengthen its defense capability.

We reaffirm that the armaments which are in Cuba, regardless of the classification to which they may belong, are intended solely for defensive purposes in order to secure the Republic of Cuba against the attack of an aggressor.

I hope that the United States Government will display wisdom and renounce the actions pursued by you, which may lead to catastrophic consequences for world peace.

The viewpoint of the Soviet Government with regard to your statement of October 22 is set forth in a Statement of the Soviet Government, which is being transmitted to you through your Ambassador at Moscow.

N. KHRUSHCHEV.

PRESIDENT KENNEDY'S MESSAGE OF OCTOBER 23, 1962

[WASHINGTON,] *October 23, 1962.*

DEAR MR. CHAIRMAN: I have received your letter of October twenty-third. I think you will recognize that the steps which started the current chain of events was the action of your Government in secretly furnishing offensive weapons to Cuba. We will be discussing this matter in the Security Council. In the meantime, I am concerned that we both show prudence and do nothing to allow events to make the situation more difficult to control than it already is.

I hope that you will issue immediately the necessary instructions to your ships to observe the terms of the quarantine, the basis of which was established by the vote of the Organization of American States this afternoon, and which will go into effect at 1400 hours Greenwich time October twenty-four.

Sincerely,
JOHN F. KENNEDY.

CHAIRMAN KHRUSHCHEV'S MESSAGE OF OCTOBER 24, 1962

Official Translations

DEAR MR. PRESIDENT: I have received your letter of October 23, have studied it, and am answering you.

Just imagine, Mr. President, that we had presented you with the conditions of an ultimatum which you have presented us by your action. How would you have reacted to this? I think that you would have been indignant at such a step on our part. And this would have been understandable to us.

In presenting us with these conditions, you, Mr. President, have flung a challenge at us. Who asked you to do this? By what right did you do this? Our ties with the Republic of Cuba, like our relations with other states, regardless of what kind of states they may be, concern only the two countries between which these relations exist. And if we now speak of the quarantine to which your letter refers, a quarantine may be established, according to accepted international practice, only by agreement of states between themselves, and not by some third party. Quarantines exist, for example, on agricultural goods and products. But in this case the question is in no way one of quarantine, but rather of far more serious things, and you yourself understand this.

You, Mr. President, are not declaring a quarantine, but rather are setting forth an ultimatum and threatening that if we do not give in to your demands you will use force. Consider what you are saying! And you want to persuade me to agree to this! What would it mean to agree to these demands? It would mean guiding oneself in one's relations with other countries not by reason, but by submitting to arbitrariness. You are no longer appealing to reason, but wish to intimidate us.

No, Mr. President, I cannot agree to this, and I think that in your own heart you recognize that I am correct. I am convinced that in my place you would act the same way.

Reference to the decision of the Organization of American States cannot in any way substantiate the demands now advanced by the United States. This Organization has absolutely no authority or basis for adopting decisions such as the one you speak of in your letter. Therefore, we do not recognize these decisions. International law exists and universally recognized norms of conduct exist. We firmly adhere to the principles of international law and observe strictly the norms which regulate navigation on the high seas, in international waters. We observe these norms and enjoy the rights recognized by all states.

You wish to compel us to renounce the rights that every sovereign state enjoys, you are trying to legislate in questions of international law, and you are violating the universally accepted norms of that law. And you are doing all this not only out of hatred for the Cuban people and its government, but also because of considerations of the election campaign in the United States. What morality, what law can justify such an approach by the American Government to international affairs? No such morality or law can be found, because the actions of the United States with regard to Cuba constitute outright banditry or, if you like, the folly of degenerate imperialism. Unfortunately, such folly can bring grave suffering to the peoples of all countries, and to no lesser degree to the American people themselves, since the United States has completely lost its former isolation with the advent of modern types of armament.

Therefore, Mr. President, if you coolly weigh the situation which has developed, not giving way to passions, you will understand that the Soviet Union cannot fail to reject the arbitrary demands of the United States. When you confront us with such conditions, try to put yourself in our place and consider how the United States would react to these conditions. I do not doubt that if someone attempted to dictate similar conditions to you—the United States—you would reject such an attempt. And we also say—no.

The Soviet government considers that the violation of the freedom to use international waters and international air space is an act of aggression which pushes mankind toward the abyss of a world nuclear-missile war. Therefore, the Soviet Government cannot instruct the captains of Soviet vessels bound for Cuba to observe the orders of American naval forces blockading that Island. Our instructions to Soviet mariners are to observe strictly the universally accepted norms of navigation in international waters and not to retreat one step from them. And if the American side violates these rules, it must realize what responsibility will rest upon it in that case. Naturally we will not simply be bystanders with regard to piratical acts by American ships on the high seas. We will then be forced on our part to take the measures we consider necessary and adequate in order to protect our rights. We have everything necessary to do so.

Respectfully,
N. KHRUSHCHEV.

MOSCOW, *October 24, 1962.*

PRESIDENT KENNEDY'S MESSAGE OF OCTOBER 25, 1962

[WASHINGTON,] *October 25, 1962.*

DEAR MR. CHAIRMAN: I have received your letter of October 24, and I regret very much that you still do not appear to understand what it is that has moved us in this matter.

The sequence of events is clear. In August there were reports of important shipments of military equipment and technicians from the Soviet Union to Cuba. In early September I indicated very plainly that the United States would regard any shipment of offensive weapons as presenting the gravest issues. After that time, this Government received the most explicit assurances from your Government and its representatives, both publicly and privately, that no offensive weapons were being sent to Cuba. If you will review the statement issued by Tass in September, you will see how clearly this assurance was given.

In reliance on these solemn assurances I urged restraint upon those in this country who were urging action in this matter at that time. And then I learned beyond doubt what you have not denied—namely, that all these public assurances were false and that your military people had set out recently to establish a set of missile bases in Cuba. I ask you to recognize clearly, Mr. Chairman, that it was not I who issued the first challenge in this case, and that in the light of this record these activities in Cuba required the responses I have announced.

I repeat my regret that these events should cause a deterioration in our relations. I hope that your Government will take the necessary action to permit a restoration of the earlier situation.

Sincerely,
JOHN F. KENNEDY.

CHAIRMAN KHRUSCHEV'S MESSAGE OF OCTOBER 26, 1962

DEAR MR. PRESIDENT: I have received your letter of October 25. From your letter I got the feeling that you have some understanding of the situation which has developed and a sense of responsibility. I appreciate this.

By now we have already publicly exchanged our assessments of the events around Cuba and each of us has set forth his explanation and his interpretation of these events. Therefore, I would think that, evidently, continuing to exchange opinions at such a distance, even in the form of secret letters, would probably not add anything to what one side has already said to the other.

I think you will understand me correctly if you are really concerned for the welfare of the world. Everyone needs peace: both capitalists, if they have not lost their reason, and all the more, communists—people who know how to value not only their own lives but, above all else, the life of nations. We communists are against any wars between states at all, and have been defending the cause of peace ever since we came into the world. We have always regarded war as a calamity, not as a game or a means for achieving particular purposes, much less as a goal in itself. Our goals are clear, and the means of achieving them is worked. War is our enemy and a calamity for all nations.

This is how we Soviet people, and together with us, other peoples as well, interpret questions of war and peace. I can say this with assurance at least for the peoples of the Socialist countries, as well as for all progressive people who want peace, happiness, and friendship among nations.

I can see, Mr. President, that you also are not without a sense of anxiety for the fate of the world, not without an understanding and correct assessment of the nature of modern warfare and what war entails. What good would a war do you? You threaten us with war. But you well know that the very least you would get in response would be what you had given us; you would suffer the same consequences. And that must be clear to us—people invested with authority, trust and responsibility. We must not succumb to light-headedness and petty passions, regardless of whether elections are forthcoming in one country or another. These are all transitory things, but should war indeed break out, it would not be in our power to contain or stop it, for such is the logic of war. I have taken part in two wars, and I know that war ends only when it has rolled through cities and villages, sowing death and destruction everywhere.

I assure you on behalf of the Soviet Government and the Soviet people that your arguments regarding offensive weapons in Cuba are utterly unfounded. From what you have written me it is obvious that our interpretations on this point are different, or rather that we have different definitions for one type of military means or another. And indeed, the same types of armaments may in actuality have different interpretations.

You are a military man, and I hope you will understand me. Let us take a simple cannon for instance. What kind of a weapon is it—offensive or defensive? A cannon is a defensive weapon if it is set up to defend boundaries or a fortified area. But when artillery is concentrated and supplemented by an appropriate number of troops, then the same cannon will have become an offensive weapon, since they prepare and clear the way for infantry to advance. The same is true for nuclear missile weapons, for any type of these weapons.

You are mistaken if you think that any of our armaments in Cuba are offensive. However, let us not argue at this point. Evidently, I shall not be able to convince you. But I tell you: You, Mr. President, are a military man and you must understand: How can you possibly launch an offensive even if you have an enormous number of missiles of various ranges and power on your territory, using these weapons alone? These missiles are a means of annihilation and destruction. But it is impossible to launch an offensive by means of these missiles, even nuclear missiles of 100 megaton yield, because it is only people—troops—who can advance. Without people any weapons, whatever their power, cannot be offensive.

How can you, therefore, give this completely wrong interpretation, which you are now giving, that some weapons in Cuba are offensive, as you say? All weapons there—and I assure you of this—are of a defensive nature; they are in

Cuba solely for purposes of defense, and we have sent them to Cuba at the request of the Cuban Government. And you say that they are offensive weapons.

But, Mr. President, do you really seriously think that Cuba could launch an offensive upon the United States and that even we, together with Cuba, could advance against you from Cuban territory? Do you really think so? How can that be? We do not understand. Surely, there has not been any such new development in military strategy that would lead one to believe that it is possible to advance that way. And I mean advance, not destroy; for those who destroy are barbarians, people who have lost their sanity.

I hold that you have no grounds to think so. You may regard us with distrust, but you can at any rate rest assured that we are of sound mind and understand perfectly well that if we launch an offensive against you, you will respond in kind. But you too will get in response whatever you throw at us. And I think you understand that too. It is our discussion in Vienna that gives me the right to speak this way.

This indicates that we are sane people, that we understand and assess the situation correctly. How could we, then, allow [ourselves] the wrong actions which you ascribe to us? Only lunatics or suicides, who themselves want to perish and before they die destroy the world, could do this. But we want to live and by no means do we want to destroy your country. We want something quite different: to compete with your country in a peaceful endeavor. We argue with you; we have differences on ideological questions. But our concept of the world is that questions of ideology, as well as economic problems, should be settled by other than military means; they must be solved in peaceful contest, or as this is interpreted in capitalist society—by competition. Our premise has been and remains that peaceful coexistence of two different sociopolitical systems—a reality of our world—is essential, and that it is essential to ensure lasting peace. These are the principles to which we adhere.

You have now declared piratical measures, the kind that were practiced in the Middle Ages when ships passing through international waters were attacked, and you have called this a "quarantine" around Cuba. Our vessels will probably soon enter the zone patrolled by your Navy. I assure you that the vessels which are now headed for Cuba are carrying the most innocuous peaceful cargoes. Do you really think that all we spend our time on is transporting so-called offensive weapons, atomic and hydrogen bombs? Even though your military people may possibly imagine that these are some special kind of weapons, I assure you that they are the most ordinary kind of peaceful goods.

Therefore, Mr. President, let us show good sense. I assure you that the ships bound for Cuba are carrying no armaments at all. The armaments needed for the defense of Cuba are already there. I do not mean to say that there have been no shipments of armaments at all. No, there were such shipments. But now Cuba has already obtained the necessary weapons for defense.

I do not know whether you can understand me and believe me. But I wish you would believe yourself and agree that one should not give way to one's passions; that one should be master of them. And what direction are events taking now? If you begin stopping vessels it would be piracy, as you yourself know. If we should start doing this to your ships you would be just as indignant as we and the whole world are now indignant. Such actions cannot be interpreted otherwise, because lawlessness cannot be legalized. Were this allowed to happen then there would be no peace; nor would there be peaceful coexistence. Then we would be forced to take the necessary measures of a defensive nature which would protect our interests in accordance with international law. Why do this? What would it all lead to?

Let us normalize relations. We have received an appeal from U Thant, Acting Secretary General of the U.N., containing his proposals. I have already answered him. His proposals are to the effect that our side not ship any armaments to Cuba for a certain period of time while negotiations are being conducted—and we are prepared to enter into such negotiations—and the other side not undertake any piratical action against vessels navigating on the high seas. I consider these proposals reasonable. This would be a way out of the situation which has evolved that would give nations a chance to breathe easily.

You asked what happened, what prompted weapons to be supplied to Cuba? You spoke of this to our Minister of Foreign Affairs. I will tell you frankly, Mr. President, what prompted it.

We were very grieved by the fact—I spoke of this in Vienna—that a landing was effected and an attack made on Cuba, as a result of which many Cubans were killed. You yourself told me then that this had been a mistake. I regarded that explanation with respect. You repeated it to me several times, hinting that not everyone occupying a high position would acknowledge his mistakes as you did. I appreciate such frankness. For my part I told you that we too possess no less courage; we have also acknowledged the mistakes which have been made in the history of our state, and have not only acknowledged them but have sharply condemned them.

While you really are concerned for peace and for the welfare of your people—and this is your duty as President—I, as Chairman of the Council of Ministers, am concerned for my people. Furthermore, the preservation of universal peace should be our joint concern, since if war broke out under modern conditions, it would not be just a war between the Soviet Union and the United States, which actually have no contentions between them, but a world-wide war, cruel and destructive.

Why have we undertaken to render such military and economic aid to Cuba? The answer is: we have done so only out of humanitarian considerations. At one time our people accomplished its own revolution, when Russia was still a backward country. Then we were attacked. We were the target of attack by many countries. The United States took part in that affair. This has been documented by the participants in aggression against our country. An entire book has been written on this by General Graves, who commanded the American Expeditionary Force at that time. Graves entitled it *American Adventure in Siberia*.

We know how difficult it is to accomplish a revolution and how difficult it is to rebuild a country on new principles. We sincerely sympathize with Cuba and the Cuban people. But we do not interfere in questions of internal organization; we are not interfering in their affairs. The Soviet Union wants to help the Cubans build their life, as they themselves desire, so that others would leave them alone.

You said once that the United States is not preparing an invasion. But you have also declared that you sympathize with the Cuban counterrevolutionary emigrants, support them, and will help them in carrying out their plans against the present government of Cuba. Nor is it any secret to anyone that the constant threat of armed attack and aggression has hung and continues to hang over Cuba. It is only this that has prompted us to respond to the request of the Cuban Government to extend it our aid in strengthening the defense capability of that country.

If the President and Government of the United States would give their assurances that the United States would itself not take part in an attack upon Cuba and would restrain others from such action; if you recall your Navy—this would immediately change everything. I do not speak for Fidel Castro, but I think that he and the Government of Cuba would, probably, announce a demobilization and would call upon the people to commence peaceful work. Then the question of armaments would also be obviated, because when there is no threat, armaments are only a burden for any people. This would also change the approach to the question of destroying not only the armaments which you call offensive, but of every other kind of armament.

I have spoken on behalf of the Soviet Government at the United Nations and introduced a proposal to disband all armies and to destroy all weapons. how then can I stake my claims on these weapons now?

Armaments bring only disasters. Accumulating them damages the economy, and putting them to use would destroy people on both sides. Therefore, only a madman can believe that armaments are the principal means in the life of society. No, they are a forced waste of human energy, spent, moreover, on the destruction of man himself. If people do not display wisdom, they will eventually reach the point where they will clash, like blind moles, and then mutual annihilation will commence.

Let us therefore display statesmanlike wisdom. I propose: we, for our part, will declare that our ships bound for Cuba are not carrying any armaments. You will declare that the United States will not invade Cuba with its troops and will not support any other forces which might intend to invade Cuba. Then the necessity for the presence of our military specialists in Cuba will be obviated.

Mr. President, I appeal to you to weigh carefully what the aggressive, piratical actions which you have announced the United States intends to carry out in international waters would lead to. You yourself know that a sensible person simply cannot agree to this, cannot recognize your right to such action.

If you have done this as the first step towards unleashing war—well then—evidently nothing remains for us to do but to accept this challenge of yours. If you have not lost command of yourself and realize clearly what this could lead to, then, Mr. President, you and I should not now pull on the ends of the rope in which you have tied a knot of war, because the harder you and I pull, the tighter this knot will become. And a time may come when this knot is tied so tight that the person who tied it is no longer capable of untying it, and then the knot will have to be cut. What that would mean I need not explain to you, because you yourself understand perfectly what dread forces our two countries possess.

Therefore, if there is no intention of tightening this knot, thereby dooming the world to the catastrophe of thermonuclear war, let us not only relax the forces straining on the ends of the rope, let us take measures for untying this knot. We are agreeable to this.

We welcome all forces which take the position of peace. Therefore, I both expressed gratitude to Mr. Bertrand Russell, who shows alarm and concern for the fate of the world, and readily responded to the appeal of the Acting Secretary General of the U.N., U Thant.

These, Mr. President, are my thoughts, which, if you should agree with them, could put an end to the tense situation which is disturbing all peoples.

These thoughts are governed by a sincere desire to alleviate the situation and remove the threat of war.

Respectfully,
N. KHRUSHCHEV.

[MOSCOW,] *October 26, 1962.*

CHAIRMAN KHRUSHCHEV'S MESSAGE OF OCTOBER 27, 1962

DEAR MR. PRESIDENT, I have studied with great satisfaction your reply to Mr. Thant concerning measures that should be taken to avoid contact between our vessels and thereby avoid irreparable and fatal consequences. This reasonable step on your part strengthens my belief that you are showing concern for the preservation of peace, which I note with satisfaction.

I have already said that our people, our Government, and I personally, as Chairman of the Council of Ministers, are concerned solely with having our country develop and occupy a worthy place among all peoples of the world in economic competition, in the development of culture and the arts, and in raising the living standard of the people. This is the most noble and necessary field for competition, and both the victor and the vanquished will derive only benefit from it, because it means peace and an increase in the means by which man lives and finds enjoyment.

In your statement you expressed the opinion that the main aim was not simply to come to an agreement and take measures to prevent contact between our vessels and consequently a deepening of the crisis which could, as a result of such contacts, spark a military conflict, after which all negotiations would be superfluous because other forces and other laws would then come into play—the laws of war. I agree with you that this is only the first step. The main thing that must be done is to normalize and stabilize the state of peace among states and among peoples.

I understand your concern for the security of the United States, Mr. President, because this is the primary duty of a President. But we too are disturbed about these same questions; I bear these same obligations as Chairman of the Council of Ministers of the U.S.S.R. You have been alarmed by the fact that we have aided Cuba with weapons, in order to strengthen its defense capability—precisely defense capability—because whatever weapons it may possess, Cuba cannot be equated with you since the difference in magnitude is so great, particularly in view of modern means of destruction. Our aim has been and is to help Cuba, and no one can dispute the humanity of our motives, which are oriented toward enabling Cuba to live peacefully and develop in the way its people desire.

You wish to ensure the security of your country, and this is understandable. But Cuba, too, wants the same thing; all countries want to maintain their security. But how are we, the Soviet Union, our Government, to assess your actions which are expressed in the fact that you have surrounded the Soviet Union with military bases; surrounded our allies with military bases; placed military bases literally around our country; and stationed your missile armaments there? This is no secret. Responsible American personages openly declare that it is so. Your missiles are located in Britain, are located in Italy, and are aimed against us. Your missiles are located in Turkey.

You are disturbed over Cuba. You say that this disturbs you because it is 90 miles by sea from the coast of the United States of America. But Turkey adjoins us; our sentries patrol back and forth and see each other. Do you consider, then, that you have the right to demand security for your own country and the removal of the weapons you call offensive, but do not accord the same right to us? You have placed desctuctive missile weapons, which you call offensive, in Turkey, literally next to us. How then can recognition of our equal military capacities be reconciled with such unequal relations between our great states? This is irreconcilable.

It is good, Mr. President, that you have agreed to have our representatives meet and begin talks, apparently through the mediation of U Thant, Acting Secretary General of the United Nations. Consequently, he to some degree has assumed the role of a mediator and we consider that he will be able to cope with this responsible mission, provided, or course, that each party drawn into this controversy displays good will.

I think it would be possible to end the controversy quickly and normalize the situation, and then the people could breathe more easily, considering that statesmen charged with responsibility are of sober mind and have an awareness of their responsibility combined with the ability to solve complex questions and not bring things to a military catastrophe.

I therefore make this proposal: We are willing to remove from Cuba the means which you regard as offensive. We are willing to carry this out and to make this pledge in the United Nations. Your representatives will make a declaration to the effect that the United States, for its part, considering the uneasiness and anxiety of the Soviet State, will remove its analogous means from Turkey. Let us reach agreement as to the period of time needed by you and by us to bring this about. And, after that, persons entrusted by the United Nations Security Council could inspect on the spot the fulfillment of the pledges made. Of course, the permission of the Governments of Cuba and of Turkey is necessary for the entry into those countries of these representatives and for the inspection of the fulfillment of the pledge made by each side. Of course it would be best if these representatives enjoyed the confidence of the Security Council, as well as yours and mine—both the United States and the Soviet Union—and also that of Turkey and Cuba. I do not think it would be difficult to select people who would enjoy the trust and respect of all parties concerned.

We, in making this pledge, in order to give satisfaction and hope of [to] the peoples of Cuba and Turkey and to strengthen their confidence in their security, will make a statement within the framework of the Security Council to the effect that the Soviet Government gives a solemn promise to respect the inviolability of the borders and sovereignty of Turkey, not to interfere in its internal affairs, not to invade Turkey, not to make available our territory as a bridgehead for such an invasion, and that it would also restrain those who contemplate committing aggression against Turkey, either from the territory of the Soviet Union or from the territory of Turkey's other neighboring states.

The United States Government will make a similar statement within the framework of the Security Council regarding Cuba. It will declare that the United States will respect the inviolability of Cuba's borders and its sovereignty, will pledge not to interfere in its internal affairs, not to invade Cuba itself or make its territory available as a bridgehead for such an invasion, and will also restrain those who might contemplate committing aggression against Cuba, either from the territory of the United States or from the territory of Cuba's other neighboring states.

Of course, for this we would have to come to an agreement with you and specify a certain time limit. Let us agree to some period of time, but without unnecessary delay—say within two or three weeks, not longer than a month.

The means situated in Cuba, of which you speak and which disturb you, as you have stated, are in the hands of Soviet officers. Therefore, any accidental use of them to the detriment of the United States is excluded. These means are situated in Cuba at the request of the Cuban Government and are only for defense purposes. Therefore, if there is no invasion of Cuba, or attack on the Soviet Union or any of our other allies, then of course these means are not and will not be a threat to anyone. For they are not for purposes of attack.

If you are agreeable to my proposal, Mr. President, then we would send our representatives to New York, to the United Nations, and would give them comprehensive instructions in order that an agreement may be reached more quickly. If you also select your people and give them the corresponding instructions, then this question can be quickly resolved.

Why would I like to do this? Because the whole world is now apprehensive and expects sensible actions of us. The greatest joy for all peoples would be the announcement of our agreement and of the eradication of the controversy that has arisen. I attatch great importance to this agreement in so far as it could serve as a good beginning and could in particular make it easier to reach agreement on banning nuclear weapons tests. The question of the tests could be solved in parallel fashion, without connecting one with the other, because these are different issues. However, it is important that agreement be reached on both these issues so as to present humanity with a fine gift, and also to gladden it with the news that agreement has been reached on the cessation of nuclear tests and that consequently the atmosphere will no longer be poisoned. Our position and yours on this issue are very close together.

All of this could possibly serve as a good impetus toward the finding of mutually acceptable agreements on other controversial issues on which you and I have been exchanging views. These issues have so far not been resolved, but they are awaiting urgent solution, which would clear up the international atmosphere. We are prepared for this.

These are my proposals, Mr. President.

Respectfully yours,
N. KHRUSHCHEV.

[MOSCOW,] *October 27, 1962.*

PRESIDENT KENNEDY'S MESSAGE OF OCTOBER 27, 1962

[WASHINGTON,] *October 27, 1962.*

DEAR MR. CHAIRMAN: I have read your letter of October 26th with great care and welcomed the statement of your desire to seek a prompt solution to the problem. The first thing that needs to be done, however, is for work to cease on offensive missile bases in Cuba and for all weapons systems in Cuba capable of offensive use to be rendered inoperable, under effective United Nations arrangements.

Assuming this is done promptly, I have given my representatives in New York instructions that will permit them to work out this weekend—in cooperation with the Acting Secretary General and your representative—an arrangement for a permanent solution to the Cuban problem along the lines suggested in your letter of October 26th. As I read your letter, the key elements of your proposals—which seem generally acceptable as I understand them—are as follows:

1) You would agree to remove these weapons systems from Cuba under appropriate United Nations observation and supervision; and undertake, with suitable safeguards, to halt the further introduction of such weapons systems into Cuba.

2) We, on our part, would agree—upon the establishment of adequate arrangements through the United Nations to ensure the carrying out and continuation of these commitments—(a) to remove promptly the quarantine measures now in effect and (b) to give assurances against an invasion of Cuba. I am confident that other nations of the Western Hemisphere would be prepared to do likewise.

If you will give your representative similar instructions, there is no reason why we should not be able to complete these arrangements and announce them to the world within a couple of days. The effect of such a settlement on easing world tensions would enable us to work toward a more general arrangement regarding "other armaments", as proposed in your second letter which you made public. I would like to say again that the United States is very much interested in reducing tensions and halting the arms race; and if your letter signifies that you are prepared to discuss a detente affecting NATO and the Warsaw Pact, we are quite prepared to consider with our allies any useful proposals.

But the first ingredient, let me emphasize, is the cessation of work on missile sites in Cuba and measures to render such weapons inoperable, under effective international guarantees. The continuation of this threat, or a prolonging of this discussion concerning Cuba by linking these problems to the broader questions of European and world security, would surely lead to an intensification of the Cuban crisis and a grave risk to the peace of the world. For this reason I hope we can quickly agree along the lines outlined in this letter and in your letter of October 26th.

JOHN F. KENNEDY.

CHAIRMAN KHRUSHCHEV'S MESSAGE OF OCTOBER 28, 1962

DEAR MR. PRESIDENT: I have received your message of October 27, 1962. I express my satisfaction and appreciation for the sense of proportion you have displayed, and for your understanding of the responsibility you now bear for the preservation of peace throughout the world.

I regard with great understanding your apprehension and the apprehension of the people of the United States of America over the fact that the weapons which you describe as offensive are indeed terrible weapons.

Both you and we understand what kind of weapons they are.

In order to eliminate as rapidly as possible a conflict which endangers the cause of peace, to give confidence to all peoples longing for peace, and to reassure the people of America, who, I am sure, want peace as much as the peoples of the

Soviet Union, the Soviet Government, in addition to previously issued instructions for the cessation of further work at the weapons construction sites, has issued a new order to dismantle the weapons, which you describe as offensive, and to crate and return them to the Soviet Union.

Mr. President, I would like to repeat, as I have already stated in my previous letters, that the Soviet Government has extended economic aid as well as arms to the government of Cuba, since Cuba and the Cuban people have constantly been under the continual threat of an invasion of Cuba.

A piratical vessel has shelled Havana. It is said that irresponsible Cuban émigrés did the shooting. This is possibly the case. But the question arises: from where did they shoot? After all, these Cubans have no territory; they are fugitives from their homeland; they have no funds for conducting military actions.

This means that someone put into their hands the weapons for shelling Havana and for piratical acts in the Caribbean, in Cuban territorial waters. It is unthinkable in our time that a pirate ship could pass unnoticed, particularly considering the saturation of the Caribbean with American ships from which literally all of this is seen and observed. And in such circumstances pirate ships freely roam about Cuba, shell Cuba, and carry out piratical attacks upon peaceful cargo ships. It is, after all, known that they even shelled a British freighter.

In short, Cuba has been under a continual threat from aggressive forces that have not concealed their intention to invade Cuba's territory.

The Cuban people wish to build their life in their own interests without external interference. This is their right, and they cannot be blamed for wanting to be masters of their own country and to enjoy the fruits of their labor. The threat of a Cuban invasion and all the other designs aimed at surrounding Cuba with tension are designed to engender uncertainty in the Cuban people, to intimidate them, and to hinder them in freely building their new life.

Mr. President, I want to say clearly once again that we could not be indifferent to this, and so the Soviet Government decided to help Cuba with means of defense against aggression—means only for purposes of defense. We placed means of defense there, means which you call offensive. We placed them there in order that no attack might be made against Cuba and that no rash acts might be permitted.

I regard with respect and trust the statement you made in your message of October 27, 1962, that no attack would be made on Cuba and that no invasion would take place—not only on the part of the United States, but also on the part of other countries of the Western Hemisphere, as your same message pointed out. In view of this, the motives which prompted us to give aid of this nature to Cuba no longer prevail. Hence, we have instructed our officers (these means, as I have already reported to you, are in the hands of Soviet officers) to take the necessary measures to stop the construction of the facilities indicated, and to dismantle and return them to the Soviet Union. As I have already informed you in my letter of October 27, we are prepared to come to an agreement with you to enable representatives of the U.N. to verify the dismantling of these means.

In this way, on the basis of the assurances you have made and of our orders to dismantle, there appear to exist all the necessary conditions for the elimination of the conflict which has arisen.

I note with satisfaction that you have echoed my desire that this dangerous situation be eliminated and also that conditions be created for a more thorough appraisal of the international situation, which is fraught with great dangers in our age of thermonuclear weapons, rocket technology, space ships, global rockets, and other lethal weapons. All mankind is interested in ensuring peace.

Therefore, we who bear great trust and responsibility must not permit the situation to become aggravated but must eliminate breeding grounds where dangerous situations are created, fraught with serious consequences for the cause of peace. And if we, together with you and other people of good will, succeed in eliminating this tense situation, we must also concern ourselves with seeing that other dangerous conflicts do not arise which might lead to a world thermonuclear catastrophe.

In conclusion, I should like to say something about the improvement of relations between NATO and the states of the Warsaw Pact, which you mention. We spoke of this a long time ago, and are ready to continue exchanging opinions with you on this question and to find a reasonable solution. We also wish to continue to exchange opinions on the prohibition of atomic and thermonuclear weapons, on general disarmament, and on other questions relating to relaxation of international tensions.

Mr. President, I place belief in your statement. On the other hand there are irresponsible people who would like to carry out an invasion of Cuba at this time and thereby unleash a war. If we take practical steps and announce the dismantling and evacuation of the above-mentioned means from Cuba, in doing so we at the same time want the Cuban people to be sure that we are with them and are not relieving ourselves of the responsibility of granting aid to the Cuban people.

We are convinced that the peoples of all countries will, like yourself, Mr. President, understand me correctly. We do not threaten. We desire only peace. Our country is now on the upswing. Our people are enjoying the fruits of their peaceful labor. They have achieved tremendous successes since the October Revolution, and have created the greatest material, spiritual, and cultural values. Our people are making use of these values and want to develop their achievements further and by their steadfast labor to ensure even greater growth along the path of peace and social progress.

I should like, Mr. President, to remind you that military aircraft of a reconnaissance nature have violated the frontiers of the Soviet Union—over which matter we had a controversy with you, and an exchange of notes took place. In 1960 we shot down your U-2 aircraft, whose reconnaissance flight over the U.S.S.R. led to the disruption of the summit meeting in Paris. You took a correct position at the time in condemning that criminal action on the part of the previous Administration of the United States.

But during your term of office as President, a second case of violation of our frontier by an American U-2 aircraft has taken place in the Sakhalin area. We informed you of this violation on August 30. You then replied that this violation had occurred as a result of bad weather and gave assurances that it would not be repeated. We accepted your assurances because there was, indeed, bad weather in that area at the time.

However, if your aircraft had not been given a mission to fly near our territory, then even bad weather could not have led an American aircraft into our air space. The conclusion follows that this is done with the knowledge of the Pentagon, which tramples on international norms and violates the frontiers of other states.

An even more dangerous case occurred on October 28, when your reconnaissance aircraft invaded the northern area of the Soviet Union, in the area of the Chukotski Peninsula, and flew over our territory. One asks, Mr. President, how we should regard this. What is this—a provocation? Your aircraft violates our frontier, and this happens at a time as troubled as the one through which we are now passing, when everything has been put in battle readiness. For an intruding U.S. aircraft can easily be taken for a bomber with nuclear weapons, and that can push us toward a fatal step. All the more so, because the U.S. Government and the Pentagon have long been saying that you continually maintain bombers with atomic bombs in the air. Therefore, you can imagine what kind of responsibility you assume, especially during such an anxious time as the present.

I should like to ask you to assess this correctly and to take steps accordingly, to prevent it from serving as a provocation to touch off a war.

I should also like to express to you the following wish. Of course, this is the Cuban people's affair—you do not at present maintain diplomatic relations, but through my officers in Cuba I have reports that American planes are conducting flights over Cuba.

We are interested in not having any war at all in the world and in the Cuban people's being able to live in peace. But, in addition to this, Mr. President, it is no secret that we have our people in Cuba. By agreement with the Cuban Government, we have there officers and instructors who are training the Cubans; they are mainly ordinary people, including specialists, agronomists, animal husbandry technicians, irrigation and reclamation experts, common laborers, tractor drivers, and others. We have concern for them.

I should like to ask you, Mr. President, to bear in mind that a violation of Cuban air space by American aircraft may also have dangerous consequences. And if you do not want that, no cause should be given for the creation of a dangerous situation.

We must now be very cautious and refrain from any acts that would not help in the defense of the states involved in the controversy, but which could arouse only irritation, and even prove to be a provocation for a fatal step. We must therefore display sense and wisdom, and refrain from acts of that kind.

We value peace, perhaps even more than other peoples, because we experienced a terrible war against Hitler. But our people will not flinch in the face of any ordeal; our people trust their own government, and we assure our own people and world public opinion that the Soviet Government will not allow itself to be provoked. But if the provocateurs unleash a war, they will not escape the responsibility and the grave consequences that war will bring to them. We are confident, however, that reason will prevail, that war will not be unleashed, and that the peace and security of peoples will be ensured.

In regard to the current negotiations of Acting Secretary General U Thant, with representatives of the Soviet Union, the United States of America and the Republic of Cuba, the Soviet Government has sent to New York V.V. Kuznetsov, First Deputy Minister of Foreign Affairs of the U.S.S.R., with a view to assisting Mr. Thant in his noble efforts aimed at eliminating the present dangerous situation.

Respectfully yours,
N. KHRUSHCHEV.

[MOSCOW,] *October 28, 1962.*

PRESIDENT KENNEDY'S MESSAGE OF OCTOBER 28, 1962

[WASHINGTON,] *October 28, 1962.*

DEAR MR. CHAIRMAN: I am replying at once to your broadcast message of October twenty-eight, even though the official text has not yet reached me, because of the great importance I attach to moving forward promptly to the settlement of the Cuban crisis. I think that you and I, with our heavy responsibilities for the maintenance of peace, were aware that developments were approaching a point where events could have become unmanageable. So I welcome this message and consider it an important contribution to peace.

The distinguished efforts of Acting Secretary General U Thant have greatly facilitated both our tasks. I consider my letter to you of October twenty-seventh and your reply of today as firm undertakings on the part of both our governments which should be promptly carried out. I hope that the necessary measures can at once be taken through the United Nations, as your message says, so that the United States in turn will be able to remove the quarantine measures now in effect. I have already made arrangements to report all these matters to the Organization of American States, whose members share a deep interest in a genuine peace in the Caribbean area.

You referred in your letter to a violation of your frontier by an American aircraft in the area of the Chukotsk Peninsula. I have learned that this plane, without arms or photographic equipment, was engaged in an air sampling mission in connection with your nuclear tests. Its course was direct from Eielson Air Force Base in Alaska to the North Pole and return. In turning south, the pilot made a serious navigational error which carried him over Soviet territory. He immediately made an emergency call on open radio for navigational assistance and was guided back to his home base by the most direct route. I regret this incident and will see to it that every precaution is taken to prevent recurrence.

Mr. Chairman, both of our countries have great unfinished tasks and I know that your people as well as those of the United States can ask for nothing better than to pursue them free from the fear of war. Modern science and technology have given us the possibility of making labor fruitful beyond anything that could have been dreamed of a few decades ago.

I agree with you that we must devote urgent attention to the problem of disarmament, as it relates to the whole world and also to critical areas. Perhaps now, as we step back from danger, we can together make real progress in this vital field. I think we should give priority to questions relating to the proliferation of nuclear weapons, on earth and in outer space, and to the great effort for a nuclear test ban. But we should also work hard to see if wider measures of disarmament can be agreed and put into operation at an early date. The United States government will be prepared to discuss these questions urgently, and in a constructive spirit, at Geneva or elsewhere.

JOHN F. KENNEDY.

Appendix H:
Excerpts from the Speech Given by Fidel Castro Analyzing the Events in Czechoslovakia, 23 August 1968

We are appearing here tonight to analyze the situation in Czechoslovakia. We are going to make this analysis in the light of the revolutionary positions and international policy maintained by our Revolution and our Party....

Our people have a good deal of information about these events, and, although no, as we may say, official exposition of the position of our Party regarding those events has ever been presented—among other reasons because the events were still in progress, and we are not obliged to analyze each thing going on in the world every day—we were observing developments in the political process in that country....

A process of what was termed democratization began. The imperialist press invented another word, the word "liberalization," and began to differentiate between progressives and conservatives—calling progressives those who supported a whole series of political reforms, and conservatives the supporters of the former leadership. It was evident—and we must give our opinion about both: the conservatives and the liberals.... It rather reminds us of the past history of Cuba, that division between conservatives and liberals, a situation which, of course, was not to be expected in the political processes of socialist revolutions.

This had a series of repercussions throughout the world. Some began to sympathize with the so-called liberals or proponents of democratization. And we watched events unfold....

Here you see a whole series of things—the beginning of a "honeymoon" in the relations between the liberals and imperialism. I have simply referred to certain incidents of an economic nature occurring on different dates because throughout that entire process a whole series of events of a political nature took place. A real liberal fury was unleashed; a whole series of political slogans in favor of the formation of opposition parties began to develop, in favor of openly anti-Marxist and

Source: *Granma*, Havana, August 25, 1968, Year 3, No. 34

anti-Leninist theses, such as the thesis that the Party should cease to play the role which the Party plays within socialist society and begin to play the role there of a guide, supervising some things but, above all, exerting a sort of spiritual leadership—in short, that the reins of power should cease to be in the hands of the Communist Party; the revision of certain fundamental postulates to the effect that a socialist regime is a regime of transition from socialism to communism, a governmental form known as the dictatorship of the proletariat. This means a government where power is wielded in behalf of one class and against the former exploiting classes, by virtue of which in a revolutionary process political rights, the right to carry on political activities, cannot be granted to the former exploiters, whose objective would be precisely to struggle against the essence and the raison d'etre of socialism. A series of slogans began to be put forward, and in fact certain measures were taken such as the establishment of a bourgeois form of "freedom" of the press. . . .

Thus these tendencies were developing simultaneously, some of which justified the change and others of which turned that change toward an openly reactionary policy. And this divided opinion.

We, on the other hand, were convinced—and this is very important—that the Czechosolvak regime was dangerously inclined toward a substantial change in the system. In short, we were convinced that the Czechoslovak regime was heading toward capitalism and was inexorably heading toward imperialism. Of that we did not have the slightest doubt.

We must begin by saying this because we also want to say certain things about other matters related to the situation there. As to this matter, there are some people in the world who do not share these opinions. Many considered that this danger did not exist. Many tendencies favored certain freedom of artistic expression and some of those things. Because, naturally, there are many people in the world who are sensitive to these problems. . . .

Provisionally, we reached this conclusion: we had no doubt that the political situation in Czechoslovakia was deteriorating and going downhill on its way back to capitalism and that it was inexorably going to fall into the arms of imperialism. . . .

Nevertheless, it is not enough to simply accept the fact—and nothing more—that Czechoslovakia was headed toward a counterrevolutionary situation and that it was necessary to prevent it. It is not enough to simply come to the conclusion that there was no alternative there but to prevent this, and nothing more.

We must analyze the causes and ask what factors made this possible and created the necessity for such a dramatic, drastic and painful measure. What are the factors that created the necessity for a step which unquestionably entailed a violation of legal principles and international norms that, having often served as a shield for the peoples against injustice, are highly esteemed by the world? Because what cannot be denied here is that the sovereignty of the Czechoslovak State was violated. This would be a fiction, an untruth. And the violation was, in fact, of a flagrant nature.

And right here I wish to make the first important affirmation: we considered that Czechoslovakia was moving toward a counterrevolutionary situation, toward capitalism and into the arms of imperialism.

So this defines our first position in relation to the specific fact of the action taken by a group of socialist countries. That is, we consider that it was absolutely necessary, at all costs, in one way or another, to prevent this eventuality from taking place.

WE BELIEVE THAT IT IS A FUNDAMENTAL DUTY AND RESPONSIBILITY OF THE LEADERS OF A REVOLUTION TO AVERT THE DEVELOPMENT OF DEFORMATIONS CAPABLE OF PRODUCING SUCH CIRCUMSTANCES. . . .

In future stages it will be necessary for our revolutionary people to go deeply into the concepts of what they understand by a communist society. The ideal of the communist society cannot be the ideal of the industrialized bourgeois society; it cannot, under any circumstances, be the ideal of a bourgeois-capitalist consumers' society.

THOSE WHO STRUGGLE FOR COMMUNISM IN ANY COUNTRY IN THE WORLD CAN NEVER FORGET THE REST OF THE WORLD

The communist ideal cannot, for a single moment, exist without internationalism. Those who struggle for communism in any country in the world can never forget the rest of the world. They can never forget the suffering, underdevelopment, poverty, ignorance and exploitation that exist in a part of the world or how much poverty and destitution have accumulated there. They can never forget, for a single moment, the needs of that part of the world, and we believe that it is impossible to instill in the masses a truly internationalist outlook, a truly communist outlook, if they are allowed to forget the realities of the world, the dangers of confrontation with imperialism that those realities entail and the dangers of growing soft when the people are made to forget those real problems and when the attempt is made to move the masses through material incentives and the promises of more consumer goods alone.

And, together with this, the preaching of peace. There has been incessant, widespread preaching of peace within the socialist countries. And we ask ourselves, why all these campaigns? Do we say this because we are in favor of war? Do we say this because we are the enemies of peace? We are not the enemies of peace; we are not in favor of wars; we do not advocate universal holocaust....

The real promoters of war, the real adventurers, are the imperialists. Now then, these dangers are real; they are a reality! And those realities cannot be changed by simply preaching, in one's own house, an excessive desire for peace. In any case, the preaching should be done in the enemy's camp and not in one's own camp, because this would only contribute to stifling the combat spirit, to weakening the people's readiness to face the risks, sacrifices and all the consequences imposed by the international situation. That international situation demands all kinds of sacrifices, not only the possible ultimate sacrifice of one's life but also material sacrifices.

WHEN WE GIVE SOME TECHNICAL AID, WE DO NOT THINK OF SENDING A BILL TO ANYONE....

Technical aid. Gentlemen, our country is a country—as you know—which is in great need of technicians, great need of technicians! However, when we give some technical aid, we do not think of sending a bill to anyone, because we think that the least a developed country, a socialist country, a revolutionary country, can do to help the underdeveloped world is to send technicians.

We cannot imagine sending a bill to anyone for arms which we give him or sending a bill to anyone for technical aid, or even reminding him of it. Because if we are going to give aid and then bring up the fact every day, what we will be doing is constantly humiliating those whom we are aiding. I don't think there is any need to go around preaching about it too much....

There is more than one question that disturbs us. It disturbs us that, so far, there has been no direct imputation against Yankee imperialism in any of the statements made by the countries that sent their divisions to Czechoslovakia, or in the explanation of the events. We have been informed exhaustively concerning all the preceding events, all the facts, all the deviations, all about that rightist group, all about that liberal group; we have been informed of their activities.

The activities of the imperialists and the intrigues of the imperialists are known, and we are disturbed to see that neither the Communist Party nor the Government of the Soviet Union, nor the governments of the other countries that sent their troops to Czechoslovakia, have made any direct accusation against Yankee imperialism for its responsibility in the events in Czechoslovakia.

Certain vague references to world imperialism, to world imperialist circles, and some more concrete statements concerning the imperialist circles of West Germany have been made. But who doesn't know that West Germany is simply a pawn of Yankee imperialism in Europe, the most aggressive, the most obvious pawn—that it is a pawn of the CIA, a pawn of the Pentagon and a pawn of the imperialist Government of the United States? And, certainly, we wish to express our concern over the fact that in none of the statements is a direct imputation made against Yankee imperialism, which is the principal culprit in the world plot and conspiracy against the socialist camp. And it is necessary that we express this preoccupation.

At this very moment, in relation to the events in Czechoslovakia, the principal promoter of all of that policy of bourgeois liberalism, its principal defender, was the organization of the so-called Yugoslav Communists. They enthusiastically applauded all the liberal reforms, the concept of the Party ceasing to be the instrument of revolutionary power—that the exercise of power cease to be a function of the Party—because this is very closely allied to the concept of the League of Yugoslav Communists. All of those ideas of a political nature that completely depart from Marxism, all of those economic concepts, are closely tied to the ideology of the League of Yugoslav Communists. . . .

Nevertheless, as you know, in recent times, many Communist Parties, and among them the Communist Parties of the Warsaw Pact, began to forget the role and the nature of the League of Yugoslav Communists.

Yugoslavia began to be called a communist country; the League of Yugoslav Communists began to be called a communist party and be invited to meetings of socialist countries, to meetings of mass organizations and of the Communist Parties. And this is what gave rise to our constant opposition, our constant disagreement, our constant discrepancies—expressed on a number of occasions. And these are facts. This organization—as the agent of imperialism—was one of the principal promoters of the deformations of Czechoslovakia's political process. Some will say I am exaggerating, but I am going to prove this with facts.

Tito was received as a hero in Prague just a few weeks ago. And why was this? Because of ideological softening, of a political weakening in the awareness of the masses.

It is understandable that the countries of the Warsaw Pact sent their armies to destroy the imperialist conspiracy and the progress of counterrevolution in Czechoslovakia. However, we have disagreed with, been displeased at, and protested against the fact that these same countries have been drawing closer economically, culturally and politically to the oligarchic governments of Latin

America, which are not merely reactionary governments and exploiters of their peoples, but also shameless accomplices in the imperialist aggressions against Cuba and shameless accomplices in the economic blockade of Cuba. And these countries have been encouraged and emboldened by the fact that our friends, our natural allies, have ignored the vile and treacherous role enacted by those governments against a socialist country, the policy of blockade practiced by those countries against a socialist country.

And at the same time that we understand the need for the spirit of internationalism, and the need to go to the aid—even with troops—of a fraternal country to confront the schemes of the imperialists, we ask ourselves if that policy of economic, political and cultural rapprochement toward those oligarchic governments that are accomplices in the imperialist blockade against Cuba will come to an end....

These puppet governments have already begun to prepare the theory that Cuba must be invaded, because it is within their security area. And it is these countries—with the single exception of Mexico, whose government is the only one which has not participated in the blockade, aggressions and imperialist actions against Cuba—it is all these oligarchic governments, toward which they have shown great consideration and tact, which are the ringleaders in the United Nations of the clamor and the attacks on the socialist camp over the events in Czechoslovakia. Things have even gone so far as for these same countries of the Latin American bloc to propose a meeting of the General Assembly; they are the most rabid critics of the Soviet Union and the other countries of the socialist camp as a result of these events. And these are the countries which have been accomplices in the aggressions against Cuba; countries which have no moral right to talk about sovereignty or the like; countries which have no moral right to talk about interventions, because they have been accomplices in all the crimes committed by imperialism against the peoples, such as the brutal counterrevolutionary action perpetrated in the Dominican Republic, the aggressions against Cuba and many other countries and the aggressions against other peoples in Latin America. The oligarchic governments themselves, such as those of Brazil, Paraguay and other countries, sent troops to the Dominican Republic and are now leading the attack on and the condemnation of the socialist camp for the events in Czechoslovakia....

Men have to die, one way or another. The one sad way to die is to die in shame, with one's back to the enemy. We are not in favor of war, but revolutionaries would rather die in battle than as the result of natural causes. Naturally, we are not going to provoke wars just to avoid death by natural causes. Revolutionaries cannot always do what they want to do or whatever pleases them the most, for their duty will always come first and foremost....

The imperialists will begin by threatening us. The future will be much more entertaining than the past. We will never halt our work or our development plans. The enemy will not succeed even in this. Our present level of organization will help us carry out our plans. We will carry these plans ahead, strengthen our defenses and step up our combat training....

Appendix I:
The Constitution of the Republic of Cuba, 1976 Resolution on Approval

Approved February 15, 1976

The Council of Ministers was informed that all legal requisites were met and that 5,602,973 citizens voted; of those, 5,473,534 voted in favor and 54,070 against; 31,148 ballots were annulled and 44,221 were left blank.

The Draft Constitution and the Draft Law of Constitutional Transition, published in Special Issue No. 1 of the *Extraordinary Official Gazette* dated December 27, 1975, were approved by the citizens by means of a free, secret and direct vote.

THEREFORE the Council of Ministers, in accordance with Article 23 of Law No. 1299 of December 29, 1975, unanimously resolves:

FIRST: To declare that the Constitution of the Republic of Cuba and the Law Constitutional Transition have been approved by the free, direct and secret vote of the citizens.

SECOND: To delegate Comrade Blas Roca Calderio, chairman of the commission responsible for the drawing up of the Draft Constitution, to read the solemn proclamation at a mass rally to this effect scheduled for February 24.

THIRD: That the solemn proclamation be published in the *Official Gazette* of the Republic of Cuba on February 24 of this year.

FOURTH: That the Constitution of the Republic of Cuba and the Law of Constitutional Transition, approved by the citizens by means of a free, direct and secret vote, be published in the *Official Gazette*.

Issued in the Palace of the Revolution, in Havana, February 17, 1976.

Granma (Havana), 18 February 1976. Italics reflect words in the final ratified Constitution which were changed after the draft Constitution was circulated.

To be published in the *Official Gazette* of the Republic on February 24, 1976.

The Secretariat of the Presidency and of the Council of Ministers of the Republic of Cuba certifies that in the special session held by the Council of Ministers on February 17, 1976 the following resolution was adopted unanimously:

The Council of Ministers examined the report of the National Referendum Commission concerning the total number of ballots, the procedures and the results of the referendum.

Excerpts from the Constitution

PREAMBLE

WE, CUBAN CITIZENS,

by the workers, peasants, students, and intellectuals who struggled for over fifty years against imperialist domination, political corruption, the absence of people's rights and liberties, unemployment and exploitation by capitalists and landowners;

by those who promoted, joined and developed the first organizations of workers and peasants, spread socialist ideas and founded the first Marxist and Marxist-Leninist movements;

GUIDED

by the victorious doctrine of Marxism-Leninism;

AWARE

that all the regimes of the exploitation of man by man cause the humiliation of the exploited and the degradation of the human nature of the exploiters;

that only under socialism and communism, when man has been freed from all forms of exploitation—slavery, servitude and capitalism—can full dignity of the human being be attained; and

ADOPT

by means of our free vote in a referendum, the following:

CHAPTER I
POLITICAL, SOCIAL AND ECONOMIC
PRINCIPLES OF THE STATE

ARTICLE 1. The Republic of Cuba is a socialist state of workers and peasants and all other manual and intellectual workers.

ARTICLE 5. The Communist Party of Cuba, the organized Marxist-Leninist vanguard of the working class, is the highest leading force of the society and of the state, which organizes and guides the common effort toward the goals of the construction of socialism and the progress toward a communist *society.*

ARTICLE 8. The socialist state:

a) carries out the will of the working people and

—channels the efforts of the nation in the construction of socialism;

—maintains and defends the integrity and the sovereignty of the country;

—guarantees the liberty and the full dignity of man, the enjoyment of his rights, the exercise and fulfillment of his duties and the integral development of his personality;

—*consolidates* the ideology and the rules of living together and of conduct proper to a society free from the exploitation of man by man;

—protects the constructive work of the people and the property and riches of the socialist nation;

—directs in a planned way the national economy;

—assures the educational, scientific, technical and cultural progress of the country;

b) as the power of the people and for the people, guarantees

—*that every man or woman who is able to work have the opportunity to have a job with which* to contribute to the good of society and to the satisfaction of individual needs;

—that no disabled person be left without adequate means of subsistence;

—that no sick person be left without medical care;

—that no child be left without schooling, food and clothing;

—that no young person be left without the opportunity to study;

—that no one be left without access to studies, culture and sports;

c) works so that no family be left without a comfortable place to live.

ARTICLE 10. The Cuban socialist state exercises its sovereignty:

a) over the entire national territory, which consists of the island of Cuba, the Isle of Pines and all other adjacent islands, keys and *internal waters;* over the territorial waters in the extension prescribed by law; and over the air space corresponding to the above;

The Republic of Cuba rejects and considers illegal and null all treaties, pacts and concessions which were signed in conditions of inequality, or which disregard or diminish its sovereignty over any part of the national territory.

ARTICLE 12. The Republic of Cuba espouses the principles of proletarian internationalism and of the combative solidarity of the peoples and

a) condemns imperialism, the promoter and supporter of all fascist, colonialist, neo-colonialist and racist manifestations, as the main force of aggression and of war and the worst enemy of the peoples;

b) condemns imperialist intervention, whether direct or indirect, in the internal and external affairs of any state and, therefore, armed aggression and economic blockade, as well as any other form of economic coercion and of interference with or threat to the integrity of the states and to the political, economic and cultural elements of the nations;

c) considers wars of aggression and of conquest international crimes; recognizes the legitimacy of the wars of national liberation, as well as armed resistance to aggression and conquest; and considers that its help to those under attack and to the peoples that struggle for their liberation constitutes its internationalist right and duty;

ch) recognizes the right of the peoples to repel imperialist and reactionary violence with revolutionary violence and to struggle by all means within their reach for the right to determine freely their own destiny and the economic and social system in which they choose to live;

e) establishes its international relations on the principles of equality of rights, sovereignty and independence . . .

f) bases its relations with the Union of Soviet Socialist Republics and with other socialist countries on socialist internationalism and on the common objectives of the construction of the new society, fraternal friendship, cooperation and mutual assistance;

g) aspires to establish along with the other countries of Latin America and of the Caribbean—freed from foreign domination and internal oppression—one large community of nations joined by the fraternal ties of historical tradition and the common struggle against colonialism, *neo-colonialism* and imperialism, in the same desire to foster national and social progress;

h) develops fraternal relations and relations of collaboration with the *other* countries that uphold anti-imperialist and progressive positions;

i) maintains friendly relations with those countries which—although having different political, social and economic systems—respect its sovereignty, observe the rules of coexistence among states and the principles of mutual conveniences and adopt an attitude of reciprocity with our country;

ARTICLE 16. The state organizes, directs *and controls* the economic life of the nation in accordance with the central plan of socioeconomic development in whose elaboration and execution the workers of all the branches of the economy and of the other spheres of social life have an active and conscious participation.

The structure, powers and functions of the state enterprises and economic entities of production and of services and the system of their relations are prescribed by law.

ARTICLE 18. Foreign trade is the exclusive function of the state. The law determines the state institutions and officials authorized *to establish foreign trade enterprises and to standardize and regulate* export and import transactions and those invested with legal power to sign commercial agreements.

ARTICLE 20. The state recognizes the right of small farmers to own their lands and other means *and implements* of production, according to what the law stipulates.

ARTICLE 21. Small farmers have the right to sell their land with the previous authorization of the state agencies, as prescribed by law. In all cases, the state has preferential right to the purchase of the land while paying a fair price.

Land leases, *sharecropping*, mortgages and all other forms which entail a lien on the land or partial cession *to private individuals* of the rights and title to the land which is the property of the small farmers are all prohibited.

ARTICLE 22. The state guarantees the right to *personal ownership* of earnings and savings derived from one's own work, of *the dwelling to which one has legal title* and of the other possessions and objects which serve to satisfy one's material and cultural needs.

ARTICLE 24. The law regulates the right of citizens to inherit legal title to a place of residence and to other personal goods and chattels.

The land owned by a small farmer may only be inherited by the heirs who are personally involved in its cultivation, save for the exceptions prescribed by the law.

With regard to goods which are part of cooperatives, the law prescribes the conditions under which said goods may be inherited.

ARTICLE 25. The expropriation of property for reasons of public benefit or social interest and with due compensation is authorized.

CHAPTER VI
FUNDAMENTAL RIGHTS, DUTIES
AND GUARANTEES

ARTICLE 44. Work in a socialist society is a right and duty and a source of pride for every citizen.

Work is remunerated according to its quality and quantity; when it is provided, the needs of the economy and of society, the decision of the worker and his skill and ability are taken into account; this *is guaranteed* by the socialist economic system, that *facilitates* social and economic development, without crises, and has thus eliminated unemployment and the dead season.

Nonpaid, voluntary work carried out for the benefit of all society in industrial, agricultural, technical, artistic and service activities is recognized as playing an important role in the formation of our people's communist awareness.

Every *worker* has the duty to faithfully carry out tasks corresponding to him at his job.

ARTICLE 45. All those who work have the right to rest, which is guaranteed by the eight-hour workday, a weekly rest period and annual paid vacations.

The state contributes to the development of vacation plans and *facilities*.

ARTICLE 46. By means of the Social Security System the state assures adequate protection to every worker who is unable to work because of age, illness or *disability*.

If the worker dies, this protection will be extended to his family.

ARTICLE 47. The state protects by means of social aid *senior citizens lacking* financial resources or anyone to take them in or care for them and anyone who is unable to work and has no relatives who can help him.

ARTICLE 48. The state guarantees the right to protection, *safety* and hygiene on the job by means of the adoption of adequate measures for the prevention of accidents at work and occupational diseases.

ARTICLE 49. Everybody has the right to health protection and care.

ARTICLE 52. Citizens have freedom of speech and of the press in keeping with the objectives of socialist society. Material conditions for the exercise of that right are provided by the fact that the press, radio, television, movies and other organs of the mass media are state or social property and can never be private property. This assures their use at the exclusive service of the working people and in the interest of society.

The law regulates the exercise of these freedoms.

ARTICLE 53. The rights to assembly, demonstration and association are exercised by workers, both manual and intellectual; *peasants; women; students; and other sectors of the working people*, and they have the necessary means for this. The social and mass organizations have all the facilities they need to carry out those activities in which the members have full freedom of speech and opinion based on the unlimited right of initiative and criticism.

ARTICLE 54. The socialist state, which bases its activity and educates the people in the scientific materialist concept of the universe, recognizes and guarantees freedom of conscience and the right of everyone to profess any religious belief and to practice, within the framework of respect for the law, the belief of his preference.

The law regulates the activities of religious institutions.

It is illegal and punishable by law to oppose one's faith or religious belief to the revolution; to education; or to the fulfillment of one's duty to work, defend the homeland with arms, show reverence for its symbols and fulfill other duties established by the Constitution.

ARTICLE 57. Freedom and inviolability of persons is assured to all those who live in the country.

ARTICLE 58. Nobody can be tried or sentenced except by the competent tribunal by virtue of laws which existed prior to the crime and with the formalities and guarantees that the laws establish.

ARTICLE 59. Confiscation of property is only applied as a punishment by the authorities in the cases and by the methods determined by law.

ARTICLE 64. Defense of the socialist homeland is the greatest honor and the supreme duty of every Cuban citizen.

The law regulates the military service which Cubans must do . . .

CHAPTER VII
PRINCIPLES OF ORGANIZATION AND FUNCTIONING OF THE STATE ORGANS

ARTICLE 66. State organs are set up, function and carry out their activity based on the principles of socialist democracy, unity of power and democratic centralism. . . .

CHAPTER VIII
SUPREME ORGANS OF PEOPLE'S POWER

ARTICLE 67. The National Assembly of People's Power is the supreme organ of state power and represents and expresses the sovereign will of all the working people.

ARTICLE 68. The National Assembly of People's Power is the only organ in the Republic invested with constituent and legislative authority.

ARTICLE 69. The National Assembly of People's Power is composed of deputies *elected by the Municipal Assemblies of People's Power* according to the procedure and in the proportion established by law.

ARTICLE 70. The National Assembly of People's Power is elected for a period of five years.

ARTICLE 72. The National Assembly of People's Power elects, from among its deputies, the Council of State, which consists of one President, one First Vice-President, five Vice-Presidents, one Secretary and 23 *[24]* other members.

The President of the Council of State is, at the same time, the *Head of State* and Head of Government.

The Council of State is accountable for its action to the National Assembly of People's Power, to which it must render accounts of all its activities.

ARTICLE 73. The National Assembly of People's Power is invested with the following powers:

a) deciding on reforms to the Constitutions

b) approving, modifying and annulling laws and, *when it is considered necessary in view of the nature of the law in question, submitting it to the people for consultation*;

c) deciding on the constitutionality of laws, decree-laws, decrees and all other general provisions;

ch) revoking in total or in part the decree-laws issued by the Council of State;

d) discussing and approving the national plans for economic and social development;

e) discussing and approving the state budget;

f) approving the principles of the system for planning and the management of the national economy;

g) approving the monetary and credit system;

h) approving the general outlines of foreign and domestic policy;

[ratifying and denouncing international treaties.]

i) declaring a state of war in the event of military aggression and approving peace treaties;

k) electing the President, Vice-President and Secretary of the National Assembly;

l) electing the President, the First Vice-Presidents, the *Secretary* and the other members of the Council of State;

ll) appointing, at the initiative of the President of the Council of State, *the First Vice-President, the Vice-President and* the other members of the Council of Ministers;

m) electing the President, Vice-President and other judges of the People's Supreme Court;

n) electing the Attorney General and the deputy attorneys general of the Republic;

o) revoking the election or appointment of those persons elected or appointed by it.

ARTICLE 87. The Council of State is the organ of the National Assembly of People's Power that represents it in the period between sessions, puts its resolutions into effect and complies with all the other duties assigned by the Constitution.

It is collegiate, and for national and international purposes it is the highest representative of the Cuban state.

ARTICLE 88. The Council of State is invested with the power to:

c) issue decree-laws in the period between the sessions of the National Assembly of People's Power;

f) decree general mobilizations whenever the defense of the country makes it necessary and assume the authority to declare war in the event of aggression or to approve peace treaties—duties which the Constitution assigned to the National Assembly of People's Power—when the Assembly is in recess and cannot be called to session with the necessary security and urgency;

g) replace, at the initiative of its President, the members of the Council of Ministers in the period between the sessions of the National Assembly of People's Power;

m) *ratify* or denounce international treaties;

n) grant or refuse recognition to diplomatic representatives of other states;

q) *exercise all other powers conferred by the Constitution and laws or granted by the National Assembly of People's Power.*

ARTICLE 93. The Council of Ministers is the highest-ranking executive and administrative organ and constitutes the Government of the Republic.

ARTICLE 94. The Council of Ministers is composed of the Head of State and Government, as its President; the First Vice-President; the Vice-Presidents; the President of the Central Planning Board; the Ministers; the Secretary; and the other members that the law determines.

ARTICLE 96. The Council of Ministers is invested with the power to:

a) organize and conduct the political, economic, cultural, scientific, social and defense activities outlined by the National Assembly of People's Power;

b) propose the projects for the general plans for the socio-economic development of the state and, after these are approved by the National Assembly of People's Power, organize, conduct and supervise their implementation;

c) conduct the foreign policy of the Republic and relations with other governments;

ch) *approve* international treaties and submit them to ratification by the *Council of State; [National Assembly of People's power]*

d) direct and control foreign trade;

e) draw up the draft for the state budget and, once it is approved *by the National Assembly of People's Power*, see to its implementation;

h) see to national defense, the maintenance of order and security at home, the protection of citizens' rights and the protection of lives and property in the event of natural disasters;

ll) determine the general organization of the Revolutionary Armed Forces;

CHAPTER IX
LOCAL ORGANS OF PEOPLE'S POWER

ARTICLE 100. For politico-administrative purposes, the country is divided into provinces and municipalities; their number, boundaries and names are determined by law.

ARTICLE 105. In the limits of their jurisdiction, the Provincial and Municipal Assemblies of People's Power:

a) obey and help to enforce the general laws and regulations which come from the superior organs of the state;

k) *work to* strengthen socialist legality, uphold internal order and strengthen the country's defensive capacity.

ARTICLE 115. The election of the members of the Executive Committees of the Municipal *and Provincial* Assemblies takes place from among the ranks of Assembly delegates.

CHAPTER X
THE COURTS AND THE ATTORNEY GENERAL

ARTICLE 122. The courts constitute a system of state organs which are set up with functional independence from all other systems; they are only subordinate to the National Assembly of People's Power *and the Council of State.*

ARTICLE 124. The People's Supreme Court is the foremost judicial authority, and its decisions in this field are final.

Through its *Governing Council,* it can propose laws and issue regulations, make decisions and enact norms whose fulfillment is compulsory for all the people's courts. Based on their experience, it issues instructions which are also compulsory in order to establish uniform judicial practice in the interpretation and application of the law.

CHAPTER XI
ELECTORAL SYSTEM

ARTICLE 134. In all elections and in referenda, voting is free, equal and secret. *Every voter has only one vote.*

ARTICLE 137. Members of the Revolutionary Armed Forces and other military institutions of the nation have the right to elect and be elected, just like any other citizen.

ARTICLE 139. The Municipal Assemblies elect, *[from among their own ranks]* by means of secret balloting, the delegates to the *Provincial Assemblies of People's Power.*

CHAPTER XII
CONSTITUTIONAL REFORM

ARTICLE 141. This Constitution can only be totally or partially modified by the National Assembly of People's Power, by means of resolutions adopted by roll-call vote by a majority of no less than two thirds of the total number of members.

If the modification is total or has to do with the integration and authority of the National Assembly or People's Power or its Council of State or the rights and duties contained in the Constitution, the approval of the majority of citizens with the right to vote is required via a referendum organized for this purpose by the Assembly.

Source: Pamela S. Falk, "Cuba, 1974-78," in *Constitutions of the Countries of the World*, Albert P. Blaustein and Gisbert H. Flanz, ed. Dobbs Ferry, New York: Oceana, 1978.

Government Institutions under the Constitution

The Constitution contains twelve articles which articulate the structure and goals of the republic. Basically, the goals defined in the Constitution are to decentralize the state apparatus, to democratize the electoral process, and to reduce bureaucracy. The Constitution established three branches of government: executive, legislative, and judicial. The division of power among the branches, however, was not equal, and each branch is not independent as in the U.S. and British constitutional systems. The legislative and executive branches are responsible for foreign policy decision making.

The legislative branch consists of the National Assembly of People's Power. Significantly, delegates are chosen by the municipal assemblies of people's power for a term of five years, rather than by direct popular election. The deputies of the National Assembly choose a president, vice-president, and secretary (Chapter VIII, Articles 67–71). The National Assembly is the Cuban law-making body. It has the authority to: (1) approve, modify, and annul laws; (2) to reform the Constitution; and (3) to determine the constitutionality of laws and decrees (Article 73). In addition, the Assembly has economic policymaking powers, including approval of national plans for economic and social development, approval of the state budget, and approval of the system for planning and management of the national economy.[1] Finally, the Assembly has the power to approve the general outlines of foreign and domestic policy and it has the utmost authority to declare a state of war (Article 73). In practice, it should be noted, the Assembly convenes for only brief periods, twice a year. When not in session, its powers are delegated to the Council of State.

The Council of State is chosen by the National Assembly from among its deputies (Article 72).[2] The president, first vice-president, and secretary of the Council of State represent the National Assembly. The Council of State represents the National Assembly in the period between sessions and in that capacity exercises the powers of the Assembly, including the power of legislative initiative (Article 88) and the power to declare war "in the event of aggression . . . when the Assembly is in recess and cannot be called to session with the necessary security and urgency."

The president of the Council of State (Fidel Castro), according to the Constitution, is by definition the head of government (Article 72). The broad powers invested in this head of state and government include the authority to: (1) represent the state and the government and set general policy, (2) assume the leadership of any ministry or central agency of the administration, and (3) assume the leadership of the Revolutionary Armed Forces (Article 91).

The Council of Ministers is the "highest-ranking executive and administrative organ and constitutes the Government of the Republic" (Article 93).[3] As such, the Council of Ministers is charged with the overall direction of government. It organizes and conducts all activities mandated by the National Assembly including defense, political, economic, cultural, scientific, and social programs. The Council of Ministers conducts the foreign policy of the republic, directs and controls foreign trade, drafts the state budget, administers national defense and the maintenance of domestic order and security, and determines the organization of the Revolutionary Armed Forces (Article 96).

The Executive Committee of the Council of Ministers consists of the president, first vice-president, and the vice-presidents of the Council of Ministers. The Executive Committee controls and administers the ministries, and in emergency cases it may assume the powers of the Council of Ministers (Article 95).

Notes

1. The National Assembly of People's Power is the supreme organ of state power and is invested with legislative power (in addition to constituent power). However, Article 86

describes the proposal of laws as the responsibility of (1) the deputies to the National Assembly of People's Power, (2) the Council of State, and (3) the Council of Ministers—as well as other officials and groups, including the Office of the Attorney General and citizens.

2. The Council of State consists of: a president, a first vice-president, five vice-presidents, a secretary, and twenty-three other members (Article 72).

3. The Council of Ministers is composed of the head of state and government (president), a first vice-president, the vice-presidents, the president of the Central Planning Board, the ministers, a secretary, and other members as the law determines (Article 94).

Appendix J: Cuban Leadership and Government Structure before January 1980 Reorganization

Head of State: Dr. Fidel Castro Ruz

Council of State

President
 Dr. Fidel Castro Ruz

First Vice-President
 Gen. Raúl Castro Ruz

Vice-Presidents
 Juan Almeida Bosque
 Ramiro Valdés Menéndez
 Guillermo García Frías
 Blas Roca Calderío
 Dr. Carlos Rafael Rodríguez
  Rodríguez

Secretary
 Celia Manduley

Members
 Pedro Miret Prieto
 Dr. Osvaldo Dorticós Torrado
 Dr. Armando Hart Dávalos
 Vilma Espín Guilloys
 Dioclés Torralba González
 Bellarmino Castilla Mas
 Flavio Bravo Pardo
 Joel Domenech Benítez
 Luis Orlando Domínguez Muñiz
 Roberto Veiga Menéndez
 José Ramirez Cruz
 Haydée Santamaría Cuadrado
 Osmany Cienfuegos Gorriarán
 Dr. Raúl Roa García
 Severo Aguirre del Cristo
 Reinaldo Castro Yedra
 Marta Deprés Arozarena
 Gen. Senén Casas Regueiro
 Gen. Abelardo Colomé
  Ibarra
 Gen. Sergio del Valle
  Jiménez
 Dr. José Ramón Machado
  Ventura
 Arnaldo Milián Castro
 Jorge Lezcano Pérez

Council of Ministers

President
 Dr. Fidel Castro Ruz*

First Vice-President
 Gen. Raúl Castro Ruz*

---

*Member of the Executive Committee.

Vice-Presidents
Dr. Osvaldo Dorticós Torrado*
Dr. Carlos Rafael Rodríguez
  Rodríguez*
Ramiro Valdés Menéndez
Guillermo García Frías*
Joel Domenech Benítez*
Flávio Bravo Pardo*
Dioclés Torralba González*
Bellarmino Calsilla Mas*

Secretary
Osmany Cienfuegos Gorriarán*

Minister of Agriculture
Rafael Francia Mestre

Minister of Foreign Trade
Marcelo Fernández

Minister of Internal Trade
Serafin Fernández Rodríguez

Minister of Communications
Pedro Guelmes González

Minister of Construction
José López Moreno

Minister of Culture
Dr. Armando Hart Dávalos

Minister of Education
José Ramón Fernández Alvarez

Minister of Higher Education
Gen. Fernando Vecino Alegret

Minister of the Revolutionary Armed Forces
Gen. Raúl Castro Ruz

Minister of the Food Industry
Dr. José A. Naranjo Morales

Minister of the Sugar Industry
Ingeniero Marcos Lage Coello

Minister of Electricity Industry
Ingeniero José L. Beltrán
  Hernández

Minister, State Committee for Standardization
Ramón Darias Rodés

Minister, State Committee for Prices
Santiago Riera Hernández

Minister of Light Industry
Nora Frómeta Silva

Minister of the Construction Materials Industry
José Valle Roque

Minister of the Fishing Industry
Aníbal Velaz Suárez

Minister of the Iron and Steel and Metallurgical Industries
Léster Rodríguez Pérez

Minister of the Chemical Industry
Antonio Esquivel Yedra

Minister of the Interior
Gen. Sergio del Valle Jiménez

Minister of Justice
Dr. Armando Torres Santrayll

Minister of Mines and Geology
Manuel Céspedes Fernández

Minister of Foreign Affairs
Isidoro Malmierca Peoli

Minister of Public Health
Dr. José A. Gutiérrez Muñiz

Minister of Transport
Antonio E. Lussón Battle

Minister, President, Central Planning Board
José López Moreno
(replaced Humberto Pérez, 1985)

Minister, State Committee for Technical and Material Supplies
Irma Sánchez Valdés

Minister, State Committee for Science and Technology
Dr. Zoilo Marinello Vidaurreta

Minister, State Committee for Economic Cooperation
Héctor Rodríguez Llompart

Minister, State Committee for Construction
Levi Farah Balmaseda

Minister, State Committee for Statistics
Fidel Vasco González

Minister, State Committee for Finance
Francisco García Valls

Minister, State Committee for Labor and Social Security
Oscar Fernández Padilla

Minister, President of the Banco Nacional de Cuba
Raúl León Torras

Legislature

National Assembly of People's Power: 481 Deputies

President: Blas Roca Calderío
Vice-President: Dr. Raúl Roa García
Secretary: José Aranaburo García

Provincial Assemblies: 14

Municipal Assemblies: 169

Judiciary

Supreme Court President
Enrique Hart Ramírez*

Criminal Court President
José García Alvarez*

Court for State Security President
José Raúl Amaro Salup*

Civil and Administrative Court President
Fernando Alvarez Tabío*

Military Court President
Héctor Canciano Laborí*

Attorney-General
Dr. Santiago Cuba Fernández

---

*Members of the Governing Council.

Communist Party of Cuba (PCC)

Political Bureau Members
Fidel Castro Ruz
Raúl Castro Ruz
Osvaldo Dorticós Torrado
Juan Almeida Bosque
Ramiro Valdés Menéndez
Armando Hart Dávalos
Guillermo García Frías
Sergio del Valle Jiménez
Blas Roca Calderío
José Ramón Machado Ventura
Carlos Rafael Rodríguez Rodríguez
Pedro Miret Prieto
Arnaldo Milián Castro

Secretariat
Fidel Castro Ruz (First Sec.)
Raúl Castro Ruz
Blas Roca Calderío
Carlos Rafael Rodríguez Rodríguez
Antonio Pérez Herrera
Isidoro Malmierca Peoli
Jorge Risquet Valdés
Pedro Miret Prieto
Raúl García Peláez
José Ramón Machado Ventura
Amaldo Milián Castro

Central Committee: 112 members

Commissions: 5

Central State Agencies as of January 1980

Ministry of Agriculture
Ministry of Domestic Trade
Ministry of Construction
Ministry of Education
Ministry of the Revolutionary
  Armed Forces
Ministry of the Sugar Industry
Ministry of the Fishing Industry
Ministry of Justice
Ministry of Foreign Affairs
Ministry of Communications
Ministry of Culture
Ministry of Higher Education
Ministry of the Food Industry
Ministry of Basic Industry
Ministry of Light Industry

Central Planning Board
National Bank of Cuba
State Committee for Technical and
  Material Supply
State Committee for
  Economic Cooperation
State Committee for Statistics
State Committee for Finance
State Committee for Standardization
State Committee for Prices
State Committee for Labor and
  Social Security
Academy of Sciences of Cuba
Cuban Institute of Hydrography
Cuban Institute of Radio
  and Television

Source: Decree-Law 31 of the Council of State, *Granma Weekly Review*, 20 January 1980, p. 5.

Ministry of the Iron and Steel and
  Machine Industry
Ministry of the Interior
Ministry of Public Health
Ministry of Transportation

National Institute of Sports, Physical
  Education and Recreation
National Institute of Automated
  Systems and Computer Technology
National Institute of Tourism

Executive Committee of the Council of Ministers

President
Fidel Castro Ruz

First Vice-President
Raúl Castro Ruz

Vice-Presidents
Guillermo García
Carlos Rafael Rodríguez Rodríguez
Osvaldo Dorticós
Arnaldo Milián
Joel Domenech
Flávio Bravo
José R. Fernández Alvarez
José López Moreno
Osmany Cienfuegos
Ramiro Valdés
Dioclés Torralba
José A. López Moreno

Source: *Granma Weekly Review*, 20 January 1980, p. 5.

Role of Council of Ministers after Reorganization of January 1980

Council Member	Supervise	Minister
Fidel Castro	Ministry of Armed Forces Ministry of Interior Ministry of Public Health Ministry of Culture	
Raúl Castro	Assist President	
Guillermo García	Ministry of Communications	Minister of Transport
Carlos Rafael Rodríguez	State Committee for Economic Cooperation Ministry of Trade National Bank of Cuba Ministry of Foreign Relations	
Osvaldo Dorticós	State Committee for Normalization System of Arbitraje	Minister of Justice
Arnaldo Milián	Ministry of Food Industry	Minister of Agriculture
Joel Domenech	Ministry for Steel and Engineering Industry	Minister of Heavy Industry
Flávio Bravo	Ministry of Light Industry Ministry of Domestic Trade Ministry of Fisheries	
José R. Fernández Alvarez	Academy of Sciences Ministry for Higher Education National Institute for Sports, Physical Education and Recreation National Television and Radio Authority	Minister of Education

Appendix J • 257

Council of Ministers *Executive Committee Member*	*Supervise*	*Minister*
Humberto Pérez	State Committee on Prices and Statistics National Institute for Automation and Computer Techniques	President, Central Planning Board
Osmany Cienfuegos	State Committee for Industrial Supplies State Committee for Finance and Labor State Committee for Social Security Institute for National Tourism	Council Secretary
Ramiro Valdés		Minister of Interior
Dioclés Torralba		Minister of Sugar Industry
José A. López Moreno		Minister of Construction Industry

Source: Decree of Fidel Castro by Virtue of Article 18 of Law 1323, *Granma Weekly Review*, 11 January 1980.

Appendix K: Government and Communist Party of Cuba

Government

National Assembly of the People's Government

(499 Deputies elected)

Council of State

(29 Members)

Fidel Castro Ruz,
 President
Raúl Castro Ruz,
 First Vice President
Juan Almeida Bosque,
 Vice President
Ramiro Valdés Menéndez,
 Vice President
Guillermo García Frías,
 Vice President
Carlos Rafael Rodríguez Rodríguez,
 Vice President
Blas Roca Calderío
 Vice President
José M. Mlyar Barruecos,
 Minister-Secretary
Armando Acosta Cordero
Severo Aguirre del Cristo
Flavio Bravo Pardo
Senén Casas Regueiro
Reinaldo Castro Yedra
Osmani Cienfuegos Gorriarán
Abelardo Colomé Ibarra
Marta Deprés Arozarena
Joel Domenech Benítez
Luis Orlando Domínguez Muñiz
Vilma Espín Guillois
José Ramón Fernández Alvarez
Armando Enrique Hart Dávalos
José Ramón Machado Ventura
Braulio Maza Oliva
Pedro Miret Prieto
José Ramirez Cruz
Jorge Lezcano Pérez
Dioclés Torralba González
Sergio del Valle Jiménez
Roberto Veiga Menéndez

Council of Ministers

(38 Members)

Fidel Castro Ruz,
 President

Source: U.S. Department of State.
Note: Persons listed in rank order, as provided in official Cuban Communist Party publications.

Raúl Castro Ruz,
  First Vice President
Ramiro Valdés Menéndez,
  Vice President
Guillermo García Frías,
  Vice President
Carlos Rafael Rodríguez Rodríguez,
  Vice President
Adolfo Díaz Suárez,
  Vice President
Osmani Cienfuegos Gorriarán,
  Vice President, Executive Secretary
Humberto Pérez González,
  Vice President
José Ramón Fernández Alvarez,
  Vice President
Joel Domenech Benítez,
  Vice President
Pedro Miret Prieto,
  Vice President
Dioclés Torralba González,
  Vice President
Antonio Esquivel Yedra,
  Vice President
Juan Escalona Reguera
José López Moreno
Irma Sánchez Valdés
Hector Rodríguez Llompart
Fidel Vascos González
Francisco García Valls
Ramón Darias Rodés
Joaquin Benavides Rodríguez
Raúl León Torras
Wilfredo Torres Iribar
Ricardo Cabrisas Ruíz
Manuel Vila Sosa
Pedro Guelmes González
Armando Hart Dávalos
Fernando Vecino Alegret
Alejandro Roca Iglesias
José Manuel Millares Rodríguez
Jorge A. Fernández Cuervo-Vinent
Marcos Lage Coello

Isidoro Malmierca Peoli
Sergio del Valle Jiménez
Levi Farah Balmaseda
José A. Naranjo Morales
Marcos I. Portal Leon
Faustino Pérez Hernández,
  Deputy Secretary

Communist Party of Cuba

Central Committee

(146 Members)
(77 Alternate Members)

Political Bureau

(14 Members)

Fidel Castro Ruz,
  First Secretary
Raúl Castro Ruz,
  Second Secretary
Juan Almeida Bosque
Ramiro Valdés Menéndez
Guillermo García Frías
José Ramón Machado Ventura
Blas Roca Calderío
Carlos Rafael Rodríguez Rodríguez
Pedro Miret Prieto
Sergio del Valle Jiménez
Armando Hart Dávalos
Jorge Risquet Valdes
Julio Camacho Aguilera
Osmani Cienfuegos Gorriarán

(11 Alternate Members)

Abelardo Colome Ibarra
Senén Casas Regueiro
Sixto Batista Santana
Antonio Pérez Herrero

Humberto Pérez González
Jesus Montane Oropesa
Miguel José Cano Blanco
Vilma Espin Guillois
Roberto Veiga Menéndez
José Ramirez Cruz
Armando Acosta Cordero

Secretariat

(10 Members)

Fidel Castro Ruz,
  First Secretary
Raúl Castro Ruz,
  Second Secretary
Jaime Crombet Hernández
Pedro Miret Prieto
Jorge Risquet Valdes
Antonio Pérez Herrera
Lionel Soto Prieto
José Ramón Machado Ventura
Jesus Montane Oropesa
Julian Rizo Alvarez

Appendix L:
Note on Statistics

The most difficult aspect of conducting research on postrevolutionary Cuba is the status of statistical information. The principal problem is the disparity which exists between information provided by the Cuban government (or lack of it during certain periods) and the information published by outside sources such as the United Nations, U.S. government agencies, and secondary analyses.

Equally problematic, however, are the indices of economic growth. Statistical handbooks on the Cuban economy confuse gross national product (GNP), gross domestic product (GDP), gross material product (GMP), and the global social product (GSP). According to the Cuban government, because of Cuba's centrally planned socialist economy, the statistical offices make use of the standard GSP since it includes production and not personal and professional services which the government provides. The GSP is the value of gross production of all productive sectors; it is the sum of all goods and services produced in the country in one year. It does not include the value of other services such as education, defense, public administration, public health, housing, and professional services; these are classified as consumption and are calculated on a separate basis. The GMP is calculated by subtracting the value of the transportation, communications, and trade-sector services.

The most comprehensive article on the history of statistical development in Cuba is by Carmelo Mesa Lago, "Availability and Reliability of Statistics in Socialist Cuba" (*Latin American Research Review* 4, no. 2 [spring 1969]). An update was published by the author in 1979, "Cuban Statistics Revisited" (*Cuban Studies/Estudios Cubanos* 9, no. 2 [July 1979]). This article was published after Mesa Lago visited Cuba in December 1978. It clarifies some of the ambiguities in the statistics published by the Cuban government in earlier years, such as the failure to distinguish between constant and current prices. The article also describes the authority of the statistical offices of the Cuban government today, including a history of the Cuban Planning Board's Statistical Directorate (JUCEPLAN) and the new State Committee on Statistics (CEE) established in December 1976.

Methodological Notes

Mercantile Production

It is the sum of the values of all goods and services of the productive sectors (excluding trade) destined for sale. In general, it is an appropriate estimate of the level of economic activity and is used in national statistical practice as the basis for measuring economic behavior in periods of time of less than one year.

The process of improvement of the organizational structure of the productive sphere, which has been taking place during 1983 and through the early months of 1984, has modified the figures appearing in the chronological series of the mercantile production. The organization of the so-called agro-industrial complexes in the sugar economy sector encompasses the merging of the sugar cane enterprises with the sugar mills, this resulting in that the previously denominated finished and marketed products of the former now turn out to be intermediate products of the agro-industrial complexes. Given the above mentioned situation and with a view to maintain the data of the present report comparable to the previous ones, an adjustment has been made of the figures corresponding to the period taken as a comparative basis, this adjustment being suited to the new conditions of the period so analyzed. Such an adjustment permits to make an efficient analysis of the national economy rate of growth.

Gross Social Product

The Gross Social Product, one of the basic indicators of the system of balances of the national economy, is used to characterize annual results with comparable figures.

The Gross Social Product is the value of all goods and services generated in the country during one year. It is equal to the sum of value of gross production of all production sectors.

In Cuba, the Gross Social Product is determined by the material product system adopted by the UN Statistics Office (see, in this regard, the Study of Methods, Series F, No. 17, 1971). This indicator doesn't include the value of financial, housing, personal and professional, public health, education, public administration, defense and other related services defined as nonproductive.

Sales to the State

These are defined as the volume of agricultural finished products sold by state production enterprises and by nonstate producers to state procurement enterprises and other buyers in accord with planned delivery contracts. It should be borne in mind that all commercial activity in the country is carried out by state enterprises.

Balance of Payments and Foreign Trade Statistics

The apparent differences between foreign trade statistics and the corresponding items in the balance of payments are due to the following reasons.

Entry dates. In foreign trade statistics, exports are registered on the basis of bill of lading dates, and in imports, according to vessel cargo report dates. For the balance of payments purposes, the entry date corresponds to the date when the Banco Nacional de Cuba receives the documents.

Classification and Valuation of Trade by Countries and Groupings. Foreign trade statistics comprise all trade transactions with every country or grouping, both in convertible currency and in transferable rubles or in the corresponding bilateral payments agreements unit of account, as the case may be.

Exports to other socialist countries include supplies paid in convertible currency, and imports from those countries include supplies purchased in the market-economy countries that the importing country pays for in transferable rubles. In foreign trade statistics, exports are valued on FOB terms and imports on CIF terms, while, in the case of the balance of payments, both elements are recorded on FOB terms.

Exchange Rates

For purposes of control of the annual foreign trade plan and the balance of payments, fixed annual exchange rates are used for each convertible currency with respect to the Cuban peso.

Source: Banco Nacional de Cuba *Economic Report*, op. cit., annex 10. These methodological notes are reprinted exactly as they appear in the *Report*.

Appendix M:
Cuban Central Budget

Covers 1 January–31 December 1982

Revenue	Millions of Dollars
Contributions from the state sector of the economy	11,890.560
Taxes and other contributions from the nonstate sector of the economy	17.664
Taxes and duties from the population	140.288
Total revenue	12,048.512

Expenditures

Production	4,070.656
Housing and community services	618.752
Education and public health	2,611.584
Other sociocultural and scientific activities	1,978.240
Administration of the organs of People's Power, the courts, the Attorney General's Office, and other organs and agencies of the state	794.112
Defense and internal order	1,182.464
Other activities	696.704
Reserve	634.496
Total Expenditures	12,587.008
Deficit	538.496

The Central Budget for 1982 totals:

Revenues	8,699.008
Expenditures	3,477.504
Deficit	538.496

Source: *Granma Weekly Review*, 10 January 1982.

Covers 1 January–31 December 1983

Revenue	Millions of Dollars
Contributions from the state sector of the economy	13,214.208
Taxes and other contributions from the nonstate sector of the economy	20.736
Taxes and duties from the population	200.448
Total revenue	13,435.392

Expenditures

Production	4,554.112
Housing and community services	650.752
Education and public health	2,762.624
Other sociocultural and scientific activities	1,951.232
Administration of the organs of People's Power, the courts, the Attorney General's Office, and other organs and agencies of the state	813.312
Defense and internal order	1,427.840
Other activities	576.000
Reserve	448.000
Total Expenditures	13,183.872
Surplus	251.520

The Central Budget for 1983 totals:	
Revenues	9,723.44
Expenditures	9,521.92
Surplus	251.52

Source: *Granma Weekly Review*, 10 January 1983.

Appendix N: Cuban Military Capability

1984–85 Military Capacity

Army: 125,000 (incl. proportion of Ready Reserve) (some 75,000 conscripts).
3 Regional Commands, 2 Army, 4 Corps HQ.
3 armd divs (2 cadre).
3 mech divs.
13 inf divs (8 cadre, others at about 60%).
1 AB assault bde; Special Force (1,000) 2 bns.
8 indep inf. regts.
1 arty div (3 fd arty bdes).
AFV: 350 T-34, 350 T-54/-55, some 150 T-62 MBT; 40 PT-76 lt tks; some 150 BRDM-1/-2 armd cars; some 100 BMP MICV; 400 BTR-40/-60/-152 APC.
Arty: 1,200 guns/how incl: M-1942 76mm, 85mm, 100 SU-100 SP, 122mm, M-46 130mm, D-1, D-2, ML-20 152mm; BM-21 122mm, BM-14 140mm. BM-24 240mm MRL; 65 *FROG*-4/-7 SSM; M-43 120mm mor; additionally, some 60 JS-2 hy, T-34/85 tks, SU-100 SP guns may be static defence arty.
ATK: M-1943 57mm guns; 57mm RCL; *Sagger, Snapper* ATGW.
AD: At least 26 regts: 1,500 AA guns incl: ZU-23, 37mm, 57mm, 85mm. towed, ZSU-23-4 23mm, 30mm M-53 (twin) BTR-60P,ZSU-57 57mm SP,SA-7/-9 SAM.

RESERVES: Ready Reserves 190,000 (serve 45 days per year); to fill out Regular and 18 Reserve inf divs.

Navy: 12,000 (8,500 conscripts).
4 Sov subs: 3 *F*-class: 1 *W*-class (non-operational; trg).
2 Sov *Koni* frigates.
11 Sov large patrol craft: 9 SO-1, 2 *Kronshradt*.
26 Sov FAC(G) with *Styx* SSM: 5 *Osa*-1, 13 *Osa*-II, 8 *Komar*‹.
26 Sov FAC(T): 8 *Turya*, 6 P-6‹, 12 P-4‹.
22 Sov *Zhuk* FAC(P)‹; 12 coastal patrol craft‹.
12 Sov minesweepers: 2 *Sonya*, 10 *Yevgenya*‹.
2 *Polnocny* LSM, 7 T-4 LCM.

NAVAL INFANTRY: (some 350); 1 amph assault bn.

COASTAL DEFENCE:
M-1931/37 122mm, M-1937 152mm, SM-4-1 130mm guns; 50 *Samlet* SSM.

Bases: Cienfuegos, Cabañas, Havana, Mariel, Punta Ballenatos, Banes.

Air Force: 16,000, incl air defence forces (11,000 conscripts); 250 combat ac, some 38 armed hel.
4 FGA sqns: 1 with 15 MiG-17; 3 with 36 MiG-23BN *Flogger* F.
16 interceptor sqns: 2 with 30 Mig-21F; 3 with 34-21PFM; 2 with 20 -21PFMA;8 with 100 -21bis; 1 with 15 MiG-23 *Flogger* E.
4 tpt sqns: 16 Il-14, 35 An-2, 3 An-24, 22 An-26, 4 Yak-40.
8 hel sqns: 60 Mi-4, 40 Mi-8 (perhaps 20 armd), 18 Mi-24 *Hind* D.
Trainers incl 2 MiG-23U, 10 MiG-21U, some An-2, 30 Zlin 326, some L-39.
AAM: AA-1 *Alkali,* AA-2 *Atoll,* AA-8 *Aphid.*
30 SAM bns: 28 with 60 SA-2, 140 SA-3; 2 with 12 SA-6.
The Civil Airline has 9 Il-62, some 4 Tu-154, which are used as tp tpts.

Forces Abroad: Angola 19,000; Congo 750; Ethiopia 3,000; Mozambique 750; Other Africa 500; Iraq 2,000; Libya 3,000; S. Yemen 300; Nicaragua 3,000; Afghanistan ?500.

Para-Military Forces: Ministry of Interior: State Security 15,000; Frontier Guards 3,500; some 22 craft. Ministry of Defence: Youth Labour Army 100,000; Civil Defence Force: 100,000; Territorial Militia 530,000.

Source: International Institute for Strategic Studies (IISS), *The Military Balance,* 1984–85 (London: ISS, 1984 pp. 119–120.

Troop Strength of Cuba's Military, 1984

Division	Ministry	Member Number
Territorial Troop Militia	MINFAR	1,000,000
Civil Defense Force	MINFAR	100,000
Youth Labor Army	MINFAR	100,000
Armed Forces	MINFAR	250,000
Air Force	MINFAR	11,000
	MINFAR	16,000
Reservists	MINFAR	190,000
Border Guard	MININT	3,000
National Revolutionary Police	MININT	10,000
civilian auxiliaries		52,000
Department of State Security	MININT	10,000-15,000
Committee for the Defense of the Revolution		5,300,000

Key
MINFAR: Ministry of the Revolutionary Armed Forces
MININT: Ministry of the Interior

Sources
1. U.S., Department of State, "Cuban Armed Forces and the Soviet Military Presence," Special Report No. 103 (Washington, D.C.: Government Printing Office, August 1982).
2. *White House Digest,* "Soviet Cuban Threat and Buildup in the Caribbean" (Washington, D.C.: 6 July 1983).
3. U.S., Department of Defense, *Soviet Military Power,* 2d ed. (Washington, D.C.: Government Printing Office, March 1983).
4. Joseph B. Treaster, "Cuba Says Its Militia Forces Now Exceed a Million," *New York Times,* 2 May 1984.
5. Edward Gonzalez, *A Strategy for Dealing with Cuba* (Santa Monica, Ca.: Rand Corp., September 1982).
6. Fidel Castro, *Report to the 2nd Congress of the Communist Party* (Havana, Political Publishers, 1981).
7. U.S., Department of Defense. *Soviet Military Power, 1984, 3rd ed.* Washington, D.C.: Government Printing Office, April 1984.

Relative Military Strength

Country	Population (thousands)	People Military (thousands)	% of Population in Military
Cuba	9,800	227.0	2.32
Argentina	28,000	185.5	.66
Bolivia	5,500	26.6	.48
Brazil	124,780	272.6	.22
Chile	11,180	92.0	.82
Colombia	27,310	70.0	.26
Ecuador	8.250	38.8	.47
Paraguay	3,270	16.0	.49
Peru	18,075	130.0	.72
Uruguay	2,945	29.7	1.01
Venezuela	16,459	40.8	.25
Dominican Republic	5,835	22.5	.39
Guatemala	7,200	15.1	.21
Honduras	3,900	11.2	.29
Mexico	69,000	119.5	.17

Source: *Current Policy,* Special Report #103, "Cuban Armed Forces and the Soviet Military Presence," p. 2, Washington, D.C.: Dept. of State: Bureau of Public Affairs, August, 1982.

Appendix O:
Economic and Trade Data

Table O-1
Cuba's Military Expenditures
($ millions, current)

Year	Military Expenditures	GNP	Spending as % of GNP
1968	214	3994	5.3
1969	187	4288	4.4
1970	229	4707	4.9
1971	239	4675	5.1
1972	249	4705	5.3
1973	290	6235	4.7
1974	339	6082	5.6
1975	389	6318	6.2

Source: U.S., Arms Control and Disarmament Agency, *World Military Expenditures* (Washington, D.C.: Government Printing Office, July 1978).

Table O-2
Cuban Armed Forces

Year	People (Million)	Armed Forces (Thousand)	Armed Forces per 1000 People	GNP per Capita (Constant Dollars)	Military Expenditures per Capita (Constant Dollars)
1968	8.2	110	13.4	739	40
1969	8.3	140	16.8	743	32
1970	8.5	140	16.5	764	37
1971	8.6	140	16.3	712	36
1972	8.8	140	15.96	676	36
1973	8.9	140	15.7	833	39
1974	9.1	140	15.4	725	40
1975	9.3	120	12.97	683	42
1976	9.4	125	13.27	840	

Source: U.S., Arms Control and Disarmament Agency, *World Military Expenditures*, (Washington, D.C.: Government Printing Office, July 1978); and U.S., Central Intelligency Agency, *National Basic Intelligence Handbook*, USCIA:DC, January 1979.

Table 0-3
Soviet Assistance to the Cuban Economy, 1961–1976
($ millions)

	1961–1967	1968	1969	1970	1971	1972	1973	1974	1975[a]	1976[b]
Balance-of-payments aid	1,393	432	494	231	509	632	437	294	65	110
Trade deficit	1,180	382	436	162	427	535	404	259	30	75
Interest charges[c]	59	28	34	45	57	69	0	0	0	0
Other invisibles	154	22	24	24	25	28	33	35	35	35
Cumulative aid[d]	1,393	1,825	2,319	2,550	3,059	3,691	4,128	4,422	4,487	4,597
Sugar subsidy[e]	632	150	86	150	56	22	154	4	365	876
Petroleum subsidy[f]	0	0	0	0	0	0	0	370	300	375
Nickel subsidy[e]	0	0	0	0	0	0	48	40	27	22
Total cumulative aid	2,025	2,607	3,187	3,568	4,133	4,743	5,382	6,090	6,847	8,230

Source: U.S., Central Intelligence Agency, *The Cuban Economy: A Statistical Review, 1968–76*, December 1976, cited in *Business International*.
[a]Provisional.
[b]Estimated.
[c]Cuban-Soviet agreement of December 1972 exempted Cuba from further interest charges on debt.
[d]Includes balance-of-payments assistance and an estimated $550 million in development loans, the first payments of which will not fall due until 1986.
[e]Estimated as the difference between the sales values if sold on the world market.
[f]Reflects the difference between the value of petroleum purchased from the USSR and the value at world prices.
[g]Excludes Soviet hard-currency purchases of sugar.

Appendix O • 275

Table O-4
Loans and Credits to Cuba by Western Markets, 1973-1979

Source	Value	Date Authorized	Terms
Argentina	1,200	August 1973	Long-term credits for the purchase of Argentine industrial and transportation equipment, to be repaid in eight years from time of delivery.
Eurocurrency market	30	1973	Medium-term credits.
Spain	900	December 1974	Trade credits for the purchase of Spanish ships and plants.
Eurocurrency market	119	1974	Medium-term credits.
France	350	January 1975	Long-term credits for the purchase of French machinery, plants, and transportation equipment, to be repaid in ten years.
Canada	155	March 1975	$100 million credit to be repaid in ten years at competitive interest rates; $10 million development loan to be repaid over thirty years at 3 percent interest and a $3 million technical-assistance grant extended in February 1975. Credits of $24 million extended in December 1974 and $18 million in April 1974 for purchases of oil tankers and rail equipment.
United Kingdom	580	May 1975	Medium-term credits at less than 7.5 percent interest for the purchase of British capital goods.

Table O-4 continued

Source	Value	Date Authorized	Terms
Eurocurrency market	234	1975	Medium-term credit to be repaid in 5 years at 1.75 percent over LIBOR (London International Rate).
Eurocurrency market	134	1976	Medium-term credits to be repaid in 5 years at 1.75 percent over LIBOR.
Eurocurrency market	20	May 1977	Five-year credit at 1.75 percent over LIBOR, with minimum interest rate of 6.25 percent.

Source: Rosemary Warrett, *Cuba at the Turning Point* (New York: Business International Corporation, 1977); U.S., Central Intelligence Agency, *The Cuban Economy: A Statistical Review, 1968-76*, (Washington, D.C.: Government Printing Office, March 1981).

Table O-5
Eurocurrency Loans to Cuba, 1973-1976

Date	Amount (Million $U.S. equivalent)	Maturity	Interest Rate[a]	Lead Banks
May 1973	15.4	3 years	n.a.	Royal Bank of Canada
May 1973	14.8	4 years	+1½	Toronto Dominion Bank
January 1974	5.3	n.a.	+1-1-1/8	Credit Lyonnais, Eurobank
May 1974	59.3	5 years	+1-1-1/8	Toronto Dominion Bank
June 1975	93.0	5 years	+1-3/4	Deutsche Bank, Morgan Grenfel
October 1975	137.0	5 years	+1-3/4	Credit Lyonnais and 1 Southern
June 1976	77.6	5 years	+1-3/4	Union de Banque, Arabic et Francais, and 8 others
December 1976	62.9	5 years	+1-3/4	Credit Lyonnais
Total	519.3			

Source: Theriot.

[a]Indicate spread over the floating interbank lending rate in London.

Table O-6
Cuban-Soviet Sugar Trade

Year	Total Cuban Sugar Production (Metric Tons)	Export to the USSR (Metric Tons)	Soviet Share of Total Production %	Soviet Price Paid (U.S. per Pound)	Average World Price (U.S. per Pound)	Soviet to World %
1968	5.164	1.832	32.9	6.11	1.98	308
1969	4.459	1.332	30.0	6.11	3.37	181
1970	8.538	3.105	35.2	6.11	3.75	162
1971	5.925	1.581	25.1	6.11	4.52	135
1972	4.4	1.101	25.8	6.55	7.43	88
1973	5.5	1.603	29.1	12.83	9.61	133
1974	5.8	1.856	32.8	19.80	29.96	66
1975	6.4	3.187	49.8	30.4	20.50	148
1976	6.2	3.036	48.9	30.8	11.57	266

Source: Lawrence Theriot.

Appendix O • 279

Table O-7
Direction of Cuban Trade, 1971–1976
($ millions U.S.)

	1971		1974		1975		1976	
	Imports	Exports	Imports	Exports	Imports	Exports	Imports	Exports
Socialist Bloc								
USSR	731	304	1,240	981	1,531	2,011	1,800	1,925
Other Communist	238	253	389	555	426	404	450	400
Total	969	557	1,629	1,536	1,957	2,415	2,250	2,325
Western Countries								
Japan	60	100	212	458	468	268	195	75
West Germany	17	3	130	7	182	5	125	15
Canada	27	11	113	98	119	77	95	95
France	63	6	68	14	116	22	100	25
Spain	33	36	75	213	193	266	220	100
United Kingdom	61	17	102	54	166	15	110	35
Belgium-Luxembourg	5	3	36	4	24	7	15	10
Italy	55	9	55	34	134	19	85	25
Netherlands	16	5	48	12	68	7	50	6
Mexico	—	4	12	n.a.	30	n.a.	40	n.a.
Sweden	16	8	75	46	49	30	50	35
Argentina	0	—	69	n.a.	170	n.a.	100	n.a.
Other	81	106	112	213	74	409	65	179
Total	418	304	1,064	1,153	1,793	1,125	1,250	600
Total Trade	1,387	861	2,693	2,689	3,750	3,540	3,500	2,925
Western countries (%)	26	24	31	26	35	24	29	18
Japan (%)	4	12	8	17	13	8	5	3
Other Communist (%)	17	29	61	21	11	11	13	13
USSR (%)	53	35	46	36	41	57	51	66

Source: U.S., Central Intelligence Agency, *op. cit.*

Table O-8
Average Annual World Market Price for Sugar, 1968-1976
(cents per pound, U.S., FOB)

Year	Cents per Pound		Cents per Pound
1968	1.9	*1974*	
1969	3.2	First quarter	19.45
1970	3.7	Second quarter	22.91
1971	4.5	Third quarter	29.93
1972	7.3	Fourth quarter	46.84
1973	9.5		
		(November 20)	65.50
		1975	
		First quarter	32.89
		Second quarter	18.32
		Third quarter	17.57
		Fourth quarter	13.57
		1976	
		First quarter	14.10
		Second quarter	13.86
		Third quarter	10.75
		(October 24, 1976)	7.21

Source: Compiled from International Sugar Organization cited in National Bank of Cuba, Lawrence Theriot.

Table O-9
Cuba's GNP and Relation to Trade Composition
(U.S.$ billion)

Year	GNP	Exports as % of GNP	Imports as % of GNP
1974	9.9	27.2	27.2
1975	10.3	34.4	36.4
1976	10.6	30.2	33.3

Source: Computed from Lawrence Theriot, Foreign Trade, and U.S., Central Intelligence Agency, *National Basic Intelligence Handbook*, USCIA:DC, July 1979.

Table O-10
Exports to Non-Communist Countries, 1970-1974
(percentages)

Non-Communist Countries	1970	1971	1972	1973	1974
Japan	10.6	14.9	17.4	13.2	16.1
Spain	3.4	3.2	5.8	4.0	6.3
Canada	0.9	1.2	1.6	1.2	2.8
United Kingdom	1.3	1.6	1.5	2.4	1.7
Finland	0.0	0.0	0.4	0.4	1.5
Italy	1.1	1.3	1.7	1.4	1.0
Sweden	0.4	1.0	1.4	0.8	0.6
Netherlands	1.1	1.4	1.2	1.2	0.5
France	1.5	1.6	1.4	0.9	0.4
West Germany (FRG)	0.3	0.6	0.5	0.3	0.2
Switzerland	0.2	0.3	0.4	0.3	0.2
Other	7.6	6.5	12.8	9.0	14.2
Total	28.4	33.6	46.1	35.1	45.5

Source: *Area Handbook for Cuba.*

Table O-11
Balance of Payments (Hard Currency), 1974-1976
(U.S. million $)

	1974	1975	1976
Exports	1,153	1,125	600
Imports	1,064	1,793	1,250
Balance	89	-668	-650

Source: Compiled from U.S., Central Intelligence Agency, "The Cuban Economy: A Statistical Review, 1968-78," December 1976; and U.S., Central Intelligence Agency, *National Basic Intelligence Handbook*, USCIA:DC, July 1979.

Table O-12
Cuban Foreign Trade: Council of Mutual Economic Assistance (CMEA)

	Exchange		Exports		Imports	
	1958	1974	1958	1974	1958	1974
Total	100	100	100	100	100	100
CMEA	1	52	2	51		54
Socialist Nations of Asia		7	1	6		7
Latin America and Canada	9	6	5	4	13	8
Other European nations	15	20	15	18	14	23
Asia and Africa	6	15	10	21	3	8
United States	69		67		70	

Source: Cuban Ministry of Foreign Trade, *Fifteen Years of Cuban Trade*, Havana 1975.

Table O-13
Cuba: Structure of Imports, By Main Countries of Origin

	1977	1978	1979	1980(a)
USSR	100.0	100.0	100.0	—
Machinery in general (b)	27.4	30.8	30.1	—
Energy-related products (c)	23.2	25.4	27.6	—
Raw-materials (d)	15.6	15.1	13.7	—
Foodstuffs	16.4	11.3	12.9	—
Durable consumer goods (e)	4.3	4.4	3.9	—
Others non-specified goods	13.1	13.0	11.8	—
OECD	100.0	100.0	100.0	100.0
Federal Republic of Germany	6.6	8.4	10.8	7.4
Canada	15.4	22.0	22.8	22.5
Spain	13.5	11.5	20.7	13.1
France	5.0	5.1	4.6	17.3
Japan	32.1	24.1	14.1	17.8
Others (f)	27.4	28.6	27.0	21.9

Source: CEPAL on the basis of data from the *USSR Foreign Trade Yearbook* (several issues) and *Statistics of Foreign Trade*, OECD.

(a) January–September 1980.
(b) Includes machinery, equipment and means of transport.
(c) Includes coal, petroleum and related products.
(d) Includes metals, chemical products, textile fibers, paper and wood.
(e) Includes clothing, electro-domestic appliances and cultural articles.
(f) Includes the other OECD countries, except Yugoslavia.

Table O-14
Cuba: Main Indicators of Foreign Trade[a]
(Index 1970 = 100)

	1976	1977	1978	1979	1980
Exports of goods					
Value					
Soviet Union	309.6	390.5	471.8	448.0	425.9
Market economy countries	220.5	174.0	191.9	225.6	432.6
Volume					
Soviet Union	85.3	105.1	103.8	100.2	75.5
Market economy countries	65.2	84.8	98.0	99.5	106.2
Unit values					
Soviet Union	362.9	371.7	454.6	446.9	563.9
Market economy countries	258.7	285.2	195.9	226.7	407.2
Imports of goods					
Value					
Soviet Union	215.6	268.9	336.9	355.3	406.6
Market economy countries	334.0	284.8	184.0	159.6	253.6
Volume					
Soviet Union	119.8	145.9	172.0	179.7	—
Market economy countries	250.2	188.9	110.2	79.7	112.0
Unit values					
Soviet Union	180.0	184.3	195.9	203.3	—
Market economy countries	133.5	150.8	166.9	200.2	226.4
Terms of trade for goods					
Soviet Union	201.5	201.7	232.1	219.8	—
Market economy countries	193.8	136.1	117.4	113.2	179.9

Source: CEPAL estimates on the basis of data from the *Anuarios estadísticos de Cuba*, the State Statistical Committee of Cuba, the United Nations, *Monthly Bulletin of Statistics*.

[a]Not including trade with the socialist countries, apart from the Union of Soviet Socialist Republics.

Source: Economic Commission on Latin America, *ECLA Economic Survey, 1980*, New York, United Nations, 1980, p. 195 and other international statistics.

Table O-15
Cuba: Material Product by Economic Sectors[a]

	Millions of Constant-Value Pesos[b]					Percentage Breakdown			Growth Rates		
	1970	1977	1978	1979	1980[c]	1970	1975	1980[c]	1978	1979	1980[c]
Total material product	5 666	8 690	9 402	9 580	9 714	100.0	100.0	100.0	8.2	1.9	1.4
Agriculture	1 183	1 735	1 842	1 892	1 969	20.9	19.7	20.3	6.2	2.7	4.1
Sugar cane agriculture	559	629	684	707	689	9.9	6.8	7.1	8.7	3.4	-2.5
Non-sugar cane agriculture	261	382	378	390	414	4.6	4.5	4.3	4.4	3.2	6.2
Stock raising	345	658	687	707	773	6.1	7.4	8.0	4.4	2.9	9.3
Agricultural services	—	16	16	17	22	—	0.2	0.2	—	6.3	29.4
Forestry	18	70	77	71	71	0.3	0.8	0.7	10.0	-7.8	0.6
Industry	4 047	5 505	6 003	6 118	6 210	71.4	64.9	63.9	9.0	1.9	1.9
Electrical energy	122	184	206	240	268	2.2	1.8	2.7	12.0	16.5	11.0
Mining	70	72	73	74	86	1.2	0.7	0.9	1.4	1.4	15.6
Manufacturing[d]	3 855	5 249	5 724	5 804	5 856	68.0	62.4	60.3	9.0	1.4	0.9
Construction	436	1 450	1 557	1 570	1 535	7.7	15.4	15.8	7.4	0.8	-2.2

Source: CEPAL, on the basis of data from the State Statistical Committee of Cuba.

[a]The material product consists of the value of the gross production of the agricultural, mining, manufacturing, construction and electrical energy sectors.

[b]The *Anuarios estadísticos de Cuba* describe all this information as valued at current prices, whereas in *Desarrollo y perspectivas de la economía cubana*, (National Bank of Cuba) it is stated on page 23 that, with the exception of commerce and transport, the "other sectors"—those entering into the material product plus communications—are given at constant 1965 prices. In addition, sources in the State Statistical Committee explained that as of 1965 prices were frozen for inputs and final goods in the agricultural, industrial and construction sectors and only new products were valued at different prices from those fixed then, but also at prices frozen from the year in which they were incorporated in the Cuban economic system. Thus, according to the above mentioned official source, the terms "current prices" and "constant prices" are equivalent in the case of the material product (at producer prices), and bearing in mind that the group of new products is very small, it is considered that this does not affect the interpretation of the resulting real growth rates.

[c]Preliminary figures.

[d]Including the fishing industry.

Source: Economic Commission on Latin America, *ECLA Economic Survey, 1980*, New York United Nations, 1980, p. 184.

Table O-16
Latin America: Evolution of Global Gross Domestic Product
(Annual growth rates)

Country	1970–1974	1975–1978	1979–1980	1981	1982	1983[a]	1981–1983[a,b]
Argentina	4.0	0.5	4.0	-5.9	-5.4	2.8	-8.8
Bolivia	5.6	5.1	1.2	-1.1	-9.1	-7.6	-17.0
Brazil	11.1	6.4	7.3	-1.9	-1.1	-3.3	-4.1
Colombia	6.6	4.9	4.7	2.1	1.2	1.0	4.4
Costa Rica	7.1	5.7	2.8	-4.6	-9.0	—	-12.5
Cuba[c]	8.7[d]	6.0[e]	1.5	15.6	2.7	5.0	24.6
Chile	0.9	1.7	8.0	5.7	-14.3	-0.8	-10.2
Ecuador	11.5	7.0	5.1	4.5	1.4	-3.3	2.5
El Salvador	4.9	5.5	-5.4	-9.3	-6.4	—	-15.1
Guatemala	6.4	5.5	4.2	0.9	-3.7	-2.0	-4.8
Haiti	4.7	3.3	5.4	0.3	-3.6	0.5	-2.8
Honduras	3.9	5.8	4.8	0.4	-0.6	-0.3	-0.5
Mexico	6.8	5.3	8.8	7.9	-0.5	-4.5	2.5
Nicaragua	5.4	1.5	-9.5	8.7	-1.2	5.3	13.1
Panama	5.8	3.5	8.7	4.2	5.0	0.9	10.4
Paraguay	6.4	9.2	11.0	8.5	-2.0	-3.7	2.3
Peru	4.8	1.5	4.0	3.9	0.4	-11.8	-8.0
Dominican Republic	10.1	4.7	5.3	4.1	1.6	3.9	9.8
Uruguay	1.3	4.1	6.0	-0.1	-8.7	-4.7	-13.1
Venezuela	5.4	6.0	-0.4	0.4	0.6	-3.0	-2.1
Total[f]	**7.1**	**4.8**	**6.2**	**1.5**	**-1.0**	**-2.8**	**-2.3**

Source: ECLA, on the basis of official figures.
[a]Preliminary estimates subject to revision.
[b]Cumulative variation for the period.
[c]Refers to the concept of global social product.
[d]Relates to the period 1971–1974. These figures are not comparable with those of the following period 1976–1983 because of methodological reasons.
[e]Relates to the period 1976–1978.
[f]Average excluding Cuba.

Source: *Economic Survey of Latin America, 1983: Advance Summary* New York: Economic Commission for Latin America, United Nations, 1983, p. 8.

Table O-17
Latin America: Evolution of the Main Sectors of Economic Activity
(Growth rates)

	Agriculture			Manufacturing Industry				Construction			
	1981	1982	1983[a]	1981–1983[a,b]	1981	1982	1983[a]	1981–1983[a,b]	1981	1982	1983	1981–1983[a,b]
Argentina	2.4	7.1	0.8	10.5	−16.0	−4.8	9.9	−12.1	−7.9	−19.4	−6.5	−30.5
Bolivia	7.0	−2.2	−22.0	−18.4	−3.8	−15.3	−7.5	−24.6	−34.9	−40.0	—	−60.9
Brazil	6.9	−2.5	2.2	6.4	−6.4	0.1	−6.3	−12.3	−4.3	0.4	−19.0	−22.8
Colombia	3.0	−0.2	2.1	4.9	3.2	−2.0	−0.2	0.9	9.4	5.0	3.1	18.5
Costa Rica	1.2	−4.9	4.4	0.5	−3.7[c]	−14.9[c]	1.8[c]	−19.5[c]	−11.6	−32.6	−6.0	−44.0
Cuba[d]	13.1	−4.1	0.7	9.2	17.4	3.0	4.7	26.6	19.3	0.4	10.7	32.6
Chile	5.3	−2.3	−1.0	1.9	2.6	−21.6	3.0	−17.2	21.1	−29.0	0.2	−13.9
Ecuador	5.7	2.8	−14.9	−7.6	6.1	4.0	−5.6	4.1	1.4	−0.7	−15.4	−14.8
El Salvador	−9.2	−7.7	3.2	−13.5	−16.2	−8.4	−4.3	−26.6	−1.3	−2.0	7.3	−3.7
Guatemala	1.4	−2.2	−1.9	−2.7	−2.5	−5.8	−2.1	−10.0	16.0	−9.5	−10.6	−6.1
Haiti	−1.8	−4.2	3.3	−2.8	3.9	−3.3	—	0.4	4.1	−5.6	0.7	−1.4
Honduras	0.9	1.1	0.9	2.9	1.7	−1.3	0.6	1.0	−7.8	−4.2	−3.0	−14.2
Mexico	6.1	−0.6	3.2	8.8	7.0	−2.9	−8.5	−4.9	11.8	−5.0	−14.4	−9.1
Nicaragua	9.7	2.9	9.6	24.5	2.8	−1.7	4.6	5.7	34.9	−25.5	7.7	8.4
Panama	2.9	4.4	2.0	9.6	−2.7	5.6	−2.5	1.0	11.6	18.0	−20.0	5.4
Paraguay	6.7	−3.0	−4.8	−1.5	8.0	−4.5	−4.2	−1.2	16.7	−6.0	−5.4	.8
Peru	10.7	2.1	−11.4	0.1	−0.2	−2.5	−17.2	−19.4	11.1	2.3	−21.4	−10.7
Dominican Republic	5.5	3.6	3.8	13.4	2.7	5.2	1.7	9.9	0.6	−4.9	14.5	−18.2
Uruguay	1.0	−6.8	2.1	−3.9	−4.6	−17.1	−7.0	−26.2	0.3	−12.8	−26.5	−35.7
Venezuela	−1.9	3.6	0.7	2.3	−1.8	2.1	−2.7	−2.4	−2.8	−4.8	−10.8	−17.5
Latin America[e]	**4.6**	**0.1**	**0.8**	**5.5**	**−2.0**	**−2.5**	**−4.9**	**−9.2**	**2.0**	**−5.5**	**−13.8**	**−16.9**

Source: ECLA, on the basis of official statistics.
[a] Preliminary figures.
[b] Accumulated variations during the period.
[c] Includes mining.
[d] It refers to the concept of social product.
[e] Average excludes Cuba.
Source: ECLA, *Economic Survey of Latin America, 1983: Advance Summary*. New York: Economic Commission for Latin America, United Nations, 1983, p. 12.

Table O-18
Cuban Foreign Debt in Convertible Currency—Projections
(in millions U.S. dollars in 1985 prices)

	Total	1985	1986	1987	1988	1989	1990
Total debt disbursed[a]	3,430	1,671	423	315	225	210	224
Bilateral official debt	1,727	417	312	235	163	137	163
Intergovernmental loans	187	45	44	34	17	17	17
Development assistance credits	31	2	1	1	1	1	2
Government-insured export credits	1,508	371	267	200	145	139	145
Multilateral official debt	23	4	4	5	5	1	1
Suppliers	250	246	1	1	1	1	1
Financial institutions	1,430	1,005	105	75	57	51	58
Bank deposits and loans	1,333	908	105	75	57	51	58
Medium-term consortial and bilateral loans	543	117	105	75	57	51	58
Short-term deposits	790	790	—	—	—	—	—
Credits for current imports	97	97	—	—	—	—	—
Other credits	.1	.1	—	—	—	—	—

Source: National Bank of Cuba, "Economic Report, 1985." Havana, Cuba: National Bank of Cuba, February 1985.

[a]Including the obligtions assumed with maturities of up to and including one year.

Appendix P:
Joint Ventures in Cuba
(February 1982; Excerpts)

REPUBLIC OF CUBA
Council of State

WHEREAS: The nation's economic development in the last few years has made it possible to engage in commercial activities in association with foreign interests in various countries—activities which have been formalized by the constitution of Cuban-and foreign-capital joint enterprises and through other forms of bilateral and multilateral economic association.

WHEREAS: Certain forms of economic association with foreign interests have also been initiated within Cuban national territory in recent years, without having been specifically regulated by law.

WHEREAS: The country's economic development requires this type of association in those activities that call for more financial resources, raw materials, technologies and markets than we have available in order to employ our natural and human resources.

WHEREAS: These associations, freely promoted or accepted by the socialist state, help to consolidate our socioeconomic system.

WHEREAS: It is advisable to establish legal regulations under which the economic associations of Cuban state enterprises and other national entities with foreign entities may continue to be developed in Cuban national territory, within the guidelines of the policy in effect regarding this aspect of international economic relations, whose basic purposes include the expansion of exports and foreign tourism.

Source: Republic of Cuba, Permanent Mission of Cuba to the United Nations, 1984. (mimeo)

LEGISLATIVE DECREE NUMBER 50 ON ECONOMIC ASSOCIATION BETWEEN CUBAN AND FOREIGN ENTITIES

CHAPTER 1

Legal status

Article I. The Executive Committee of the Council of Ministers will appoint a commission empowered to authorize state enterprises and other national organizations to join in economic association with foreign interests within Cuban national territory in order to engage in profitable activities that promote the country's development.

The economic association to which the preceding paragraph refers may take the form of Cuban- and foreign-capital joint enterprises with their own legal status and patrimony, or other diverse forms that do not imply the creation of a body corporate.

The commission referred to in the first paragraph of this article will be referred to henceforth as "the Commission."

Article 2. The Executive Committee of the Council of Ministers may empower the Commission to authorize state enterprises or other national organizations to lease to the joint enterprises mentioned in the preceding article, or to furnish them, as capital contributions, for their temporary usufruct, with land and industrial, touristic or other types of installations that already exist or that may be built in Cuban national territory.

Article 3. In granting each authorization, the Commission will establish the conditions which the economic associations should abide by and those of the leases and contributions in temporary usufruct to joint enterprises.

The legislation in force on the regulation of leases does not apply to those mentioned in the preceding paragraph.

Article 4. The duration of the economic associations should enable both parties to recover their capital investments and obtain returns that make the undertaking attractive.

Article 5. The parties to the economic associations that are established in the country will be as follows:

Cuban: state enterprises and consortia and other national organizations.

foreign: state or private enterprises and/or other economic entities established abroad that are dedicated to business activities, no matter what their juridical form—including natural persons.

Article 6. Joint enterprises established under the provisions of this legislative decree will adopt the form of corporations, with nominal shares, and will be subject to the provisions of the Commercial Code in force.

Article 7. The joint enterprises will have Cuban nationality and legal addresses in Cuban territory. They may establish offices, representations, subsidiaries and branches in any other country and have interests in entities abroad.

Article 8. The functioning of the joint enterprises and the relations between the partners thereto will be governed by the memorandum of association and the articles of association that are subscribed to.

The memorandum of association will contain the basic agreements between the partners for carrying out and developing the operations of the joint enterprise and for attaining its objectives, including those which guarantee that the Cuban party will manage or comanage the enterprise and those concerning the market which each of the parties should guarantee for the products or services of the joint enterprise.

The articles of association of joint enterprises will include provisions on the organization and operation of the entity, including provisions concerning stockholders meetings and their powers and organization; required quorums; the requisites for exercising the right to vote at stockholders meetings; the structure and powers of the board of directors; the method these entities will use in making decisions at both stockholders meetings and those of the board of directors, which may entail anything from a simple majority vote to a unanimous vote; the appointment, powers, remuneration and responsibilities of the managing officers of the joint enterprise; the bases of the accounting system; the computation and distribution of profits; the method for liquidating capital assets; reasons for dissolution and the procedure to be followed in liquidating the joint enterprises; and other matters that derive from this legislative decree and are agreed to by both parties.

Article 9. The remaining forms of economic association will be formalized by means of partnership contracts.

The content of the partnership contracts will be agreed to by the parties, in line with the purpose of the association.

Article 10. Joint enterprises will acquire legal status and the contracts referred to in Article 9 will enter into force when they are recorded in the Registry that the Chamber of Commerce of the Republic of Cuba opens and controls for these activities, with no other procedures required for this purpose.

Article 11. Once a joint enterprise is established or an economic partnership contract is granted, those party to them cannot be changed except by unanimous agreement.

Article 12. Joint enterprises may be modified, dissolved and liquidated in conformity with the provisions of their articles of association, and the other forms of economic asociation, in accordance with their partnership contracts. In both cases, the Commercial Code will apply on a supplementary basis.

Modifications and dissolutions will be recorded in the Chamber of Commerce Registry referred to in Article 10.

Article 13. Any disputes that arise in the relations between the parties of a joint enterprise will be settled in accordance with the procedures set forth in the memorandum of association and in the articles of association of the enterprise.

Any disputes between the partners of other forms of economic association will be aired in accordance with the provisions of the partnership contracts.

CHAPTER II

Financial regulations

Article 14. The joint enterprises' capital and the contributions of the parties to other forms of economic association may consist of cash and other assets, including the temporary usufruct of land and other real estate, raw materials, other materials, tools and any other asset.

Capital contributions to a joint enterprise, and the contributions of the parties to the other forms of economic association in applicable cases, will be measured in the freely convertible currency and on the appraisal basis agreed on by the partners.

Article 15. Foreign participation in the capital of a joint enterprise will be limited to 49 percent, save in those exceptional cases for which the Executive Committee of the Council of Ministers authorizes greater participation.

Article 16. Before authorizing the establishment of a joint enterprise or of another form of economic association, the Commission may require the eventual foreign partner to furnish an adequate guarantee that he will provide his contribution.

If the guarantee is provided for in cash, it will draw the going rate of interest.

Article 17. After a guarantee is furnished in accordance with the previous article, it will be released:

a) if the Commission authorizes the establishment of the joint enterprise or of another form of economic association. In this case, if the guarantee consists of cash, the said guarantee and the interest it has accrued will be transferred to the association as part of the contribution of the foreign partner. If the guarantee consists of securities, they will be returned to the depositor; or

b) if the Commission turns down the application or renders no decision on it within 60 days. In this case, the guarantee and interests accrued, if applicable, will be placed at the disposal of the one who furnished it.

Article 18. Joint enterprises that are lessees or users of industrial, touristic or any other kinds of installations contributed thereto will insure those installations in favor of the Cuban lessor or the one who makes the contribution.

Cuban insurance enterprises will have first option on the sale of the policies, on the basis of internationally competitive premiums and other contract stipulations.

Article 19. The joint enterprises, and the parties to the other forms of economic association in applicable cases, will open freely convertible currency accounts in banks pertaining to the national banking system, through which they will make collections and payments related to their operations.

Article 20. The National Bank of Cuba's official rates of exchange will be used for

a) the appraisal, in freely convertible currency, of wages, services and other obligations when charged on the basis of rates expressed in national currency;

b) the conversion of taxes and other fiscal liabilities that are expressed in national currency; and

c) any other currency exchanges.

Article 21. The joint enterprises and the parties to the other forms of economic association may arrange loans in foreign currency

a) from banks pertaining to the national banking system or

b) from foreign banks, in accordance with the National Bank of Cuba's regulations in this regard.

Article 22. The joint enterprises, and the parties to the other forms of economic association in applicable cases, will draw on their profits to set up reserves to cover all contingencies that may arise in the course of their operations, within the limits of and in accordance with the regulations established by the State Committee for Finances.

Article 23. The Cuban state guarantees the foreign partner that, through the National Bank of Cuba, he may freely transfer, in freely convertible currency, his dividends or net profits, the payment he receives from the Cuban party if he agrees to transfer to the Cuban party all or part of his contribution and the share that corresponds to him from the liquidation of the economic association.

Article 24. The National Bank of Cuba may guarantee the foreign partner that, if the activities of the economic association are suspended as a result of a unilateral act by the Cuban state, he may repatriate the share that corresponds to him on the liquidation of that association.

CHAPTER III

Taxation

Article 25. The joint enterprises, along with their partners, managers and other officers, and the parties to the other forms of economic association, along with their managers and other offices, will be exempt from payment of the following taxes set forth in Law 998, of January 10, 1962:

a) on gross income of private enterprises.

b) on personal income and

c) on transfers of real estate and commercial establishments.

Article 26. The joint enterprises, and the parties to other forms of economic association in applicable cases, are subject to the following:

a) profits tax. The tax rate is 30 percent on net annual profits. That part of the profits which is plowed back into the joint enterprise as capital stock or into other kinds of economic association as contributions, plus that part which is earmarked for the workers' economic incentive fund and that part which is held in reserve for covering contingencies or for other purposes to which the parties agree, will be deductible from the net profits. This tax is determined yearly and is payable within the first two months of the following year:

b) workers' payroll tax. The tax rate is 25 percent on all wages and other income that the Cuban workers receive for any reason, except for that which they receive from the workers' economic incentive fund. This tax includes contributions to Social Security. It will be paid together with the wages and other remuneration paid the Cuban personnel;

c) tariffs and other customs duties;

d) assessments on the ownership or possession of motor vehicles for land transportation; and

e) document fees (for requesting, obtaining and/or renewing documents).

Article 27. The payment of taxes, tariffs, duties, assessment and fees will be made in convertible currency, even when their amount is expressed in national currency.

Article 28. In view of the benefits that these associations may bring the national economy, the State Committee for Finances is empowered to temporarily exempt—either in full or in part—the joint enterprises or the parties to the other forms of economic association from the profits tax and the tariffs and other customs duties.

Article 29. The joint enterprises and the parties to the other forms of economic association, in applicable cases, will provide the State Committee for Finances with the financial statements it requests, within the time limit and under the conditions that it sets, in addition to the official audits that the State Committee orders.

Article 30. The partners may freely determine the system of accounting that best suits the purposes of the economic association, as long as the system that is adopted conforms to the principles universally accepted in this field and meets fiscal requirements.

CHAPTER IV

Commercial regulations

Article 31. The joint enterprises and the parties to the other forms of economic association will have the right to export their products directly and to import, also directly, what they need.

Article 32. Without prejudice to the provisions of the preceding article and on the basis that they offer the joint enterprise, or the parties to the other forms of economic association in applicable cases, internationally competitive prices and other conditions, Cuban state enterprises will have first option on the following:

a) supplying fuel, raw materials, other materials, tools, equipment, spare parts, accessories and consumer goods;

b) purchasing the finished products or services provided by the economic association; and

c) shipping and providing marine insurance for the products.

Article 33. The joint enterprises, and the parties to the other forms of economic association in applicable cases, have first option on the Cuban state enterprises' purchases of the items that the economic associations can produce in Cuba to replace imports that those state enterprises plan to receive from countries with which Cuba does not have signed payment agreements, on the basis of internationally competitive prices and other conditions.

Article 34. Through contracts, the Cuban state enterprises will guarantee the joint enterprises, and the parties to the other forms of economic association in applicable cases.

a) the supplies and services agreed upon in accordance with the provisions of Article 32; and

b) supplies of electric power, gas and water; local and international telephone and teletype services; transportation services within Cuban national territory; and other services that cannot be obtained through foreign trade.

Article 35. The joint enterprises and the parties to the other forms of economic association are party to economic contracts as defined in Legislative Decree 15, of July 3, 1978, the signing and fulfillment of which are governed by the economic legislation in effect.

Any disputes between the joint enterprises or the parties to the other forms of economic association, on the one hand, and Cuban state enterprises or other national organizations, on the other, with regard to the signing or fulfillment of economic contracts will be submitted to the State Arbitration System.

CHAPTER V

Labor regulations

Article 36. The personnel of the joint enterprises will be Cuban, except for those filling certain managerial posts or some posts that require a high degree of technical specialization, as agreed to by the parties.

Article 37. Either the Cuban entity that participates in the joint enterprise or another Cuban entity or enterprise contracts with the joint enterprise regarding the use of the Cuban work force agreed upon by the two parties, through the payment of a monthly sum equivalent to the total wages and other remuneration due the Cuban personnel.

Article 38. No matter what their occupational category, the Cuban workers employed in the joint enterprise will maintain their labor contractual relations with the Cuban entity that contracts the work force for the enterprise.

The Cuban entity will pay these workers their wages and other remuneration.

Article 39. The joint enterprises must comply with the legislation in effect on work safety and hygiene.

Article 40. The Cuban entity that contracts the work force for the joint enterprise assumes payments of the wages and other rights and benefits due Cuban workers who, for any reason, do not continue to work for the joint enterprise, including indemnification when awarded by the appropriate authorities.

Article 41. The wages paid the Cuban personnel will conform to the rates set by the legislation in effect, except in the case of Cuban managerial personnel, whose salaries will be set by agreement between the parties to the economic association, in accord with the salaries of foreign managerial personnel.

Article 42. The joint enterprises must establish an economic incentive fund for the Cuban workers. The amount of the annual contributions to this fund, its purpose and its operation will be determined in accordance with the conditions that the Commission sets when it authorizes the establishment of the joint enterprise.

Article 43. The joint enterprises and the parties to the other forms of economic association may freely contract foreign administrative and technical personnel as required; this personnel will be subject to Cuban laws regarding immigration and aliens. The rights and duties of foreign workers will be determined by agreement of the parties.

Article 44. Foreign workers may remit abroad in convertible foreign exchange that percentage of their salaries determined by the National Bank of Cuba.

SPECIAL PROVISIONS

FIRST: With regard to areas of great importance for international tourism, as authorized by the Law on Protection of the Environment and the Rational Use of National Resources (Law 33, of January 10, 1981).

a) the State Committee for Finances is authorized to declare all or part of the area exempt from taxes, customs duties, tariffs and assessments;

b) the State Committee for Labor and Social Security is authorized to set up special work regulations; and

c) the Ministry of the Interior is authorized to set up special regulations for maintaining public order and to facilitate immigration procedures through the National Institute of Tourism.

SECOND: The Executive Committee of the Council of Ministers is empowered to authorize state enterprises or other national organizations to lease the installations referred to in Article 2 of this legislative decree to foreign entities.

In this case, the lessee will insure the installations leased in favor of the lessor.

Work regulations in the installations leased to foreign entities will be those set forth in Chapter V of this legislative decree, with the qualification that, in this case, the Cuban work force is contracted either by the lessor entity or by another Cuban entity or enterprise, as the Executive Committee of the Council of Ministers may determine.

The Executive Committee of the Council of Ministers will determine the other conditions of leasing when each authorization is granted.

The legislation in force on leases does not apply to these leases.

THIRD: The joint enterprises, the foreign parties to other forms of economic association and the foreign lessees will not be bound by the provisions of laws on classified information.

FOURTH: The provisions of this legislative decree do not apply to the international compensation agreements in which Cuban enterprises participate; rather, these agreements will be regulated

a) by the State Committee for Economic Cooperation, when they involve the purchase-sale or turn-key plants, production lines or other industrial installations involving long- or medium-term financing, and

b) by the Ministry of Foreign Trade in all other cases.

FIFTH: The stipulations of this legislative decree do not apply to the establishment of economic associations in Cuba by agreement of the Council for Mutual Economic Assistance or of the Latin-American Economic System or by bilateral agreements with CMEA member countries.

FINAL PROVISION

Any provisions of laws or regulations that run counter to the provisions of this legislative decree, which will go into effect on its publication in the Official Gazette of the Republic of Cuba, are herewith revoked.

Palace of the Revolution, Havana, February 15, 1982.

(Unofficial translation)

The wage scale that is applicable for Cuban personnel—excluding the executives, whose salaries will be comparable to those of foreign executives—sets the following monthly wages:

	(in Cuban pesos; 1 peso = US$2.25 ±)	
	From	To
Workers and other day laborers	93.39	249.69
Brigade foremen	106.74	265.00
Heads of shifts	111.00	280.00
Shop foremen	128.00	295.00
Administrative and service personnel	85.00	231.00
Basic-level technicians	128.00	198.00
Intermediate-level technicians	171.00	250.00
University-graduate technicians	211.00	325.00

Appendix Q:
Interviews by the Author

Informal as well as formal interviews were conducted during the research of this book. Several hours of background interviews were conducted in Washington, New York and Havana with the following government officials:

U.S. Government

Kenneth W. Skoug, Jr., Director of Cuban Affairs, U.S. Department of State
Myles Frechette, former Desk Officer, U.S. Department of State
Wayne Smith, former Head, U.S. Interests Section, U.S. Department of State, Havana

Cuban Government

Ramón Sánchez-Parodi, head, Cuban Interests Section, Ministry of Foreign Relations, Washington
Raúl Roa Kourí, former Ambassador of Cuba to the United Nations, New York
Oscar Oramas Oliva, Ambassador of Cuba to the United Nations, New York
Joaquin Más, Chief, Ministry of Foreign Relations, Havana
Fernando García, First Secretary, Cuban Mission to the United Nations, New York
Carlos Ciaño, former First Secretary, Cuban Mission to the United Nations, New York
Ramón Prado, Counsellor, Cuban Mission to the United Nations, New York
Manuel Davis, Counsellor, Cuban Mission to the United Nations, New York
Mary Gentile, Counsellor, Ministry of Foreign Relations, Havana
José Viera, Deputy Foreign Minister, Ministry of Foreign Relations, Havana

The following formal interviews were conducted by the author:

Enrique Alvarez,* president of the El Salvador Revolutionary Democratic Front (FDR). 28 July 1980. New York City.

Eugenio Rodríguez Balari, Cuban Institute for Consumer Research and Planning (IDI). 14 November 1980. New York City.

José Benítez, *Granma*, Cuba. 13 April 1981. New York City.

Rubén Berríos Martínez, Senator, Puerto Rican Legislature; head, Puerto Rican Independence Party (PIP). 3 April 1982. New York City.

Ernesto Betancourt, director, Radio Martí, and former advisor to Fidel Castro, 1959 as Representative of the Twenty-six of July Movement in New York. 6 May 1984. Washington, D.C.

H.E. Maurice Bishop,* Prime Minister of Grenada. 24 October 1979. New York City.

José Manuel Casanova, executive director, Inter-American Development Bank. 19 September 1983. Washington, D.C.

Ramón Castro, *Picadura Central,* 26 January 1980. Havana, Cuba.

Emilio Collado, former head, American Republics, 1940, Special Assistant to Ambassador Sumner Welles, U.S. Department of State; former vice chairman, Exxon Corporation; CEO, Adela Corporation. 14 July 1982. New York City.

Cuban Construction Workers. International Airport in Port Salene, Grenada. February 1981. Republic of Grenada.

Miguel de la Guardia, Radio Havana. 13 April 1982. New York City.

Régis Debray, minister of administration of François Mitterand, Republic of France, at International Conference on Corporation and Development. 22–23 October 1981. Cancún, Mexico.

Father Miguel D'Escoto, minister of foreign affairs, National Government of Reconstruction, Nicaragua. 2 October 1981. New York City.

Olga Fernández, Cuban Foreign Ministry; director of Radio Havana. 23 January 1980, Havana, Cuba, and 13 April 1984, New York City.

H.E. José Figueres, former President, Costa Rica. 10 October 1984. Panama City, Panama.

Carlos Franqui, former director of radio and press services during Sierra Maestra Campaign against Batista during the Cuban Revolution; former editor, *Revolución* magazine (Havana) and advisor to Fidel Castro; author, *Family Portrait with Fidel.* 10 April 1984. New York City.

Myles Frechette, U.S. Department of State, Office of Cuban Affairs, Head of Cuban Affairs. 20 November 1980.

Cheddi Jagan, former prime minister of Guyana. 26 June 1980. New York City.

Manuel Lee, U.S. Department of the Cuban Institute for Friendship with the People (ICAP). 14 November 1980. New York City.

Felix Loaces Romas, director of the Department of Commerce with Socialist Countries, Ministry of Foreign Commerce (MINCEX). 25 January 1980. Havana, Cuba.
Carlos Mora, sub-director general, *Prensa Latina*, Cuba. 13 April 1982. New York City.
Ambler Moss, U.S. ambassador to Panama. 2 October 1980. New York City.
Antonio Navarro, vice president, W.R. Grace and Company. 14 February 1984. New York City.
Oscar Oramas Oliva, ambassador of Cuba to the United Nations; former Director of Subsaharan African Ministry of Foreign Relations (MINREX). 24 January 1980. Havana, Cuba.
Edén Pastora Gómez, "Comandante Cero." Radio patch interview by the author to Nicaragua. 5 October 1983. San Jose, Costa Rica. 10 November 1983. New York City.
José Francisco Peña Gómez, Dominican Revolutionary Party. 10 November 1979. Santo Domingo, Dominican Republic.
Oscar Pino Santos, director of the Center of Investigations of the World Economy. 24 January 1980. Havana, Cuba.
Catherine Ribas, Director of International Relations, Federation of Cuban Women. 23 January 1980. Havana, Cuba.
Raúl Roa Kourí, Ambassador of Cuba to the United Nations. 6 June 1984. New York City.
Carlos Rafael Rodríguez, vice president of the Council of State and the Council of Ministers, Republic of Cuba. 17 June 1982. New York City.
Alejandro Romero, MINCEX. 25 January 1980. Havana, Cuba.
Ramón Sánchez-Parodi, head, Cuban Interests Section in the United States. 6 May 1984 and 16 April 1982. Washington, D.C.
Kenneth W. Skoug, Jr., Director of Cuban Affairs, U.S. Department of State. 25 July 1984. New York City.
Wayne Smith, former head, Interests Section, U.S. Department of State, Havana, Cuba. 21 January 1980. Havana, Cuba.
Felipe Suárez, director of foreign relations, Committee for the Defense of the National Revolution (CDR). 25 January 1980. Havana, Cuba.
Caldwell Taylor, foreign minister, Grenada. 5 March 1982. New York City.
Lawrence H. Theriot, acting deputy director, Office of East-West Policy and Planning, U.S. Department of Commerce. 25 January 1982. New York City.
Guillermo Manuel Ungo, vice president, El Salvador, Revolutionary Democratic Front. 9 October 1980. New York City.
Constantino Urcuyo Fournier, director, Department of Political Science, University of Costa Rica at San José. 4 June 1982. New York City.
H.E. Manuel Urrutia-Lleó,* first president of Cuba after the Revolution,

took power January 1959. Former President of Tribunal under Batista. 17 April 1975. New York City.

Telegram from Cuban vice foreign minister **José R. Viera** to Pamela Falk. 2 October 1981. Havana, Cuba, to New York City. Announcement of cancellation due to U.S. State Department denial of visa enter the United States. Grounds that were given were the Immigration and Naturalization Act which permits the Executive Branch to deny visas on policy grounds: Section 212A27.

Miguel Viñas, Prensa Latina, Cuba. 13 April 1982. New York City.

Hugo Yedra, Department of the United States, Ministry of Foreign Relations (MINREX). 24 January 1980. Havana, Cuba.

Carlos Zamora, sub-director, Direction America II, Ministry of Foreign Relations (MINREX). 26 January 1980. Havana, Cuba.

---

*Deceased.

Bibliography

Books

Aguilar, Luis E. *Cuba 1933: Prologue to Revolution.* Ithaca, N.Y.: Cornell University Press, 1972.
Allison, Graham T. *Essence of Decision: Explaining the Cuban Missile Crisis.* Boston, Mass.: Little, Brown & Co., 1971.
Alvarez Tabío, Pedro, ed. *Development and Prospects of the Cuban Economy.* Joint publication of the National Bank of Cuba and the Central Bureau of Statistics of the Central Planning Board. Havana: Cuban Book Institute, 1975.
Aranda, Sergio. *La revolución agraria en Cuba.* 6th ed. Mexico: Siglo XXI, 1975.
Azicri, Max. *The Governing Strategies of Mass Mobilization: The Foundations of Cuban Revolutionary Politics.* Latin American Monograph Series, no. 2. Erie, Pa.: Mercyhurst College, 1977.
Barkin, David P., and Manitzas, Nita R., eds. *Cuba: The Logic of the Revolution.* Andover, Mass.: Warner Modular Publications, 1973.
Barnet, Richard J. *Real Security: American Power in a Dangerous Decade.* New York: Simon and Schuster, 1981.
Batista, Fulgencio. *Cuba Betrayed.* New York: Vantage Press, 1962.
———. *The Growth and Decline of the Cuban Republic.* Translated by Blas M. Rocafort. New York: Devin-Adair Company, 1964.
Beals, Carleton. *The Crime of Cuba.* New York: Arno Press and *New York Times*, 1970.
Bekarevich, Anatolii; Bondarchuk, Vladimir N.; and Kukharev, N.M. *Cuba in Figures.* Translated by U.S. Department of Commerce. Moscow: Academy of Sciences of the USSR, Institute of Latin America, 1972.
Bekarevich, Anatolii, and Kukharev, N.M. *The Soviet Union and Cuba.* Moscow: Nauka, 1973.
Belyayev, Yuri. *CMEA and Competition between Two Systems.* Moscow: Novosti Press Agency, 1964.
Bender, Gerald J. *Angola under the Portuguese.* Berkeley, Calif.: University of California Press, 1978.
Benjamin, Jules Robert. *The United States and Cuba: Hegemony and Dependent Development, 1880–1934.* Pittsburgh, Pa.: University of Pittsburgh Press, 1977.
Bernardo, Robert M. *The Theory of Moral Incentives in Cuba.* Birmingham, Alabama: University of Alabama Press, 1971.

Blachman, Morris J., and Ronald G. Hellman, eds. *Terms of Conflict: Ideology in Latin American Politics.* Philadelphia, Pa.: Institute for the Study of Human Issues, 1977.
Black, Jan Knippers; Blutstein, Howard I.; Edwards, J. David; Johnston, Katheryn Therese; and McMorris, David S. *Area Handbook for Cuba.* Washington, D.C.: U.S. Government Printing Office, 1976.
Blasier, Cole. *Soviet Relations with Latin America in the 1970s.* Cambridge, Mass.: National Council for Soviet and East European Research, 1979.
———. *The Giants' Rival: The USSR and Latin America.* Pittsburgh, Pa.: University of Pittsburgh Press, 1983.
Blasier, Cole, and Mesa-Lago, Carmelo, eds. *Cuba in the World.* Pittsburgh, Pa.: University of Pittsburgh Press, 1979.
Bonachea, Ramón L., and San Martín, Marta. *The Cuban Insurrection.* New Brunswick, N.J.: Transaction Books, 1976.
Bonachea, Rolando, L., and Valdes, Nelson P., eds. *Che: Selected Works of Ernesto Guevara.* Cambridge, Mass.: MIT Press, 1969.
———. *The Selected Works of Fidel Castro: Revolutionary Struggle.* Cambridge, Mass.: MIT Press, 1971.
———. *Cuba in Revolution.* Garden City, N.Y.: Anchor Books, 1972.
Bonsal, Philip W. *Cuba, Castro and the United States.* Pittsburgh, Pa.: University of Pittsburgh Press, 1971.
Boorstein, Edward. *The Economic Transformation of Cuba: A First-Hand Account.* New York: Monthly Review Press, 1969.
Brunner, Heinrich. *Cuban Sugar Policy from 1963 to 1970.* Translated by Marguerite Borchardt and H.F. Broch De Rothermann. Pittsburgh, Pa.: University of Pittsburgh Press, 1977.
Butterworth, Douglas. *The People of Buena Ventura.* Chicago: University of Illinois Press, 1980.
Callahan, James Morton. *Cuba and International Relations: A Historical Study in American Diplomacy.* Baltimore: Johns Hopkins University Press, 1899.
Cannon, Terence. *Revolutionary Cuba.* New York: Thomas Y. Crowell, 1981.
Cardenal, Ernesto. *In Cuba.* Translated by Donald D. Walsh. New York: New Directions, 1974.
Cardoso, Fernando Henrique. *Cuba: Lesson or Symbol?* Module 267. Andover, Mass.: Warner Modular Publications, 1973.
Castro, Fidel. *Discursos para la história.* Havana: Impresa Emilio Gall, 1959.
———. *Palabras a los intelectuales.* Havana: Ediciones del Consejo Nacional de Cultura, 1961.
———. *History Will Absolve Me.* London: Grossman Publishers, 1967.
———. *The Cuban Revolution, National Liberation, and the Soviet Union.* New York: New Outlook, 1974.
———. *Discursos.* Vol. 3. Havana: Editorial de Ciencias Sociales, 1979.
———. *The World Economic and Social Crisis: Report to the Seventh Summit Conference of Non-Aligned Countries.* Havana, Cuba: Publishing Office of the Council of State, 1983.
Chapman, Charles E. *A History of the Cuban Republic.* New York: MacMillan, 1927.
Chester, Edmund A. *A Sergeant Named Batista.* New York: Henry Holt & Company, 1954.
Comisión Ecónomica para América Latina, CEPAL, *Balance Prelimar de la Economía Latinoamericana Durante 1983.* New York: United Nations, 16 Diciembre 1983.
Commission on United States–Latin American Relations. *The Americas in a Changing World.* Center for Inter-American Relations. New York: Quadrangle Books, 1975.

Crassweller, Robert D. *Cuba and the U.S.: The Tangled Relationship.* New York: Foreign Policy Association, 1971.
Cuba, Government of, Ministerio de Justicia. *Family Code.* Law no. 1289,*Official Gazette*, 15 February 1975. Havana, 1975.
——. *Ley de Procedimiento Penal Militar.* Law no. 6, *Official Gazette*, 18 August 1977. Havana, 1977.
——. *Ley de los Tribunales Militares.* Law no. 3, *Official Gazette*, 9 August 1977. Havana, 1979.
Cuban Economic Research Project. *Labor Conditions in Communist Cuba.* Coral Gables, Fla.: University of Miami Press, 1963.
——. *The Colonial and Republican Periods, the Socialist Experiment.* Coral Gables, Fla.: University of Miami Press, 1965.
——. *Cuba: Agriculture and Planning 1963-64.* Coral Gables, Fla.: University of Miami Press, 1965.
——. *Industrialization under Communism, 1959 to Date.* Coral Gables, Fla.: University of Miami Press, 1965.
——. *Stages and Problems of Economic Development.* Coral Gables, Fla.: University of Miami Press, 1965.
Cuban Women's Federation. 2d Congress. *Memories.* Havana: Editorial Orbe, 1975.
Debray, Régis. *Revolution in the Revolution? Armed Struggle and Political Struggle in Latin America.* New York: Monthly Review Press, 1967.
——. *Strategy for Revolution.* Edited by Robin Blackburn. New York: Monthly Review Press, 1969.
——. *Che's Guerrilla War.* Translated by Rosemary Sheed Hammondsworth. London: Penguin Books, 1975.
De la Cuesta, Leonel-Antonio. *Constituciones Cubanas desde 1812 hasta nuestros días.* Appendix: annotated bibliography by Rolando Alum Linera. New York: Ediciones Exilio, 1972.
Del Aquila, Juan M. *Cuba: Dilemmas of a Revolution.* Profiles/Nations of Contemporary Latin America. Boulder, Co.: Westview Press, 1984.
Dillon, Dorothy. *International Communism and Latin America: Perspectives and Prospects.* Latin American Monograph Series. Gainesvilla, Fla.: University of Florida Press for the Pan-American Foundation, 1962.
Dinerstein, Herbert S. *Soviet Policy in Latin America.* Rand Memorandum RM-4967-PR. Santa Monica, Calif.: Rand Corporation, May 1966.
Dirección Central de Estadística. *Anuario Estadístico de Cuba, 1972.* Havana: Junta de Planificación, 1974.
——. *Anuario Estadístico de Cuba, 1974.* Havana: Junta de Planificación, 1974.
——. *Anuario Estadístico de Cuba, 1973.* Havana: Junta de Planificación, 1973.
——. *Boletín Estadístico de Cuba, 1971.* Havana: Junta Central de Planificación, 1973.
——. *Boletín Estadístico de Cuba, 1970.* Havana: Junta Central de Planificación, 1972.
——. *Boletín Estadístico de Cuba, 1968.* Havana: Junta Central de Planificación, 1970.
——. *Censo de población y viviendas.* Havana: Junta Central de Planificación, 1971.
——. *Compendio Estadístico de Cuba, 1974.* Havana: Junta Central de Planificación, 1974.
——. *Compendio Estadístico de Cuba, 1968.* Havana: Junta Central de Planificación, 1968.
Dirección de Divulación y Relaciones Internacionales de Poder Popular. *Sobre la Constitutión del Poder Popular.* Havana: 1978.

Dolgoff, Sam. *The Cuban Revolution*. Montreal: Black Rose Books, 1976.
Domínguez, Jorge I. *Cuba: Order and Revolution*. Cambridge, Mass.: Belknap Press of Harvard University Press, 1978.
——. *Cuba: Internal and International Affairs*. Beverly Hills: Sage Publications, 1982.
Domínguez, Jorge I., ed. *Human Rights and International Relations*. New York: McGraw-Hill, 1978.
Domínguez, Jorge I., and Marc Lindenberg (forthcoming). *Headline Series* on Cuba and Central America. New York: Foreign Policy Associations, 1985.
Domínguez, Jorge I., and Watts, William. *The United States and Cuba: Old Issues and New Direction*. Washington, D.C.: Potomac Associates, 1977.
Dorschener, John, and Fabricio, Roberto. *The Winds of December*. New York: Coward, McCann, and Geoghegan, 1979.
Draper, Theodore. *Castro's Revolution: Myths and Realities*. New York: Praeger, 1962.
——. *Castroism: Theory and Practice*. New York: Praeger, 1965.
Dubois, Jules. *Fidel Castro*. Indianapolis, Ind.: Bobbs-Merrill, 1959.
Dumont, René. *Is Cuba Socialist?* New York: Viking Press, 1974.
Durch, William J. *The Cuban Military in Africa and the Middle East*. Professional Paper no. 201. Arlington, Va.: Center for Naval Studies, 1977.
Economic Commission on Latin America, ECLA. *Economic Survey of Latin America, 1983: Advanced Summary*. New York: United Nations, 22 March 1984.
Edwards, Jorge. *Persona Non Grata*. New York: Pomerica Press, 1973.
Einaudi, Luigi R., ed. *Latin America in the 1970s*. Santa Monica, Calif.: Rand Corporation, 1972.
——. *Beyond Cuba: Latin America Takes Charge of Its Future*. New York: Crane, Russak, 1974.
Einaudi, Luigi R.; Heymann, H.; Ronfeldt, D.; and Sereseres, C. *Arms Transfers to Latin America: Toward a Policy of Mutual Respect*. Santa Monica, Calif.: Rand Corporation, 1973.
Entralgo, Armando. *Africa Económica*. Segunda parte. Havana: Editorial de Ciencias Sociales, 1979.
——. *Africa Política*. Segunda parte. Havana: Editorial de Ciencias Sociales, 1979.
Erlich, Haggai. *The Struggle over Eritrea, 1962-1978: War and Revolution in the Horn of Africa*. Stanford, California: Stanford University/Hoover Institution Press, 1983.
Fagen, Richard R. *The Transformation of Political Culture in Cuba*. Stanford, Calif.: Stanford University Press, 1969.
Fagen, Richard R.; Brody, Richard A.; and O'Leary, Thomas J. *Cubans in Exile: Disaffection and the Revolution*. Stanford, Calif.: Stanford University Press, 1968.
Farber, Samuel. *Revolution and Reaction: A Political Sociology from Machado to Castro in Cuba, 1933-1960*: Middletown, Conn.: Wesleyan University Press, 1976.
Farer, Tom J. *War Clouds on the Horn of Africa: The Widening Storm*. 2d rev. ed. New York: Carnegie Endowment for International Peace, 1979.
Fermoselle, Rafael. *Política y color en Cuba: la guerrita de 1912*. Montevideo: Ediciones Geminis, 1974.
Fitzgibbon, Russell H. *Cuba and the United States, 1900-1935*. Menasha, Wis.: George Banter Publications, 1935.
Foner, Philip S. *A History of Cuba and Its Relations with the United States*. Vol. 1, 1492-1845. New York: International Publishers, 1962. Vol. 2, 1845-1895. New York: International Publishers, 1963.

——. *The Spanish-Cuban-American War and the Birth of American Imperialism.* 2 vols. New York: Monthly Review Press, 1972.
Fox, Geoffrey E. *Working-Class Emigrés from Cuba.* Palo Alto, Calif.: R & E Research Associates, 1979.
Franqui, Carlos. *Diary of the Cuban Revolution.* Translated by Georgette Felix. New York: Viking Press, 1980.
——. *Family Portrait with Fidel.* Translated by Alfred MacAdan. New York: Random House, 1984.
Gellman, Irwin F. *Roosevelt and Batista: Good Neighbor Diplomacy in Cuba, 1933–1945.* Albuquerque: University of New Mexico, 1973.
Gerassi, John. *Fidel Castro: A Biography.* Garden City, N.Y.: Doubleday & Co., 1973.
Gilly, Adolfo. *Inside the Cuban Revolution.* Translated by Felix Gutierrez. New York: Monthly Review Press, 1964.
Goldenberg, Boris. *The Cuban Revolution and Latin America.* New York: Praeger, 1965.
González, Edward. *Cuba under Castro: The Limits of Charisma.* Boston: Houghton Mifflin, 1974.
González, Edward, and Ronfeldt, David. *Post-Revolutionary Cuba in a Changing World.* Rand Memorandum R–1844–ISA. Santa Monica, Calif.: Rand Corporation, December 1975.
Goodsell, James Nelson, ed. *Fidel Castro's Personal Revolution in Cuba, 1959–1973.* New York: Knopf Publishing Co., 1975.
Gordon, Michael W. *The Cuban Nationalizations: The Demise of Foreign Private Property.* Buffalo, N.Y.: W.S. Hein, 1976.
Gott, Richard. *Rural Guerrillas in Latin America.* Middlesex, England: Penguin Books, 1973.
Goure, Leon, and Rothenberg, Morris. *Soviet Penetration of Latin America.* Miami: Center for Advanced International Studies, University of Miami, 1975.
Greanville, Patrick. *Cuba: Dictatorship or Democracy?* Westport, Conn.: Lawrence Hill & Company, 1980.
Green, Gilbert. *Revolution, Cuban Style.* New York: International Publishers, 1970.
Greig, Ian. *The Communist Challenge to Africa: An Analysis of Contemporary Soviet, Chinese, and Cuban Policies.* Richmond, Surrey: Foreign Affairs Pub., 1977.
Guevara, Ernesto Che. *Venceremos.* Edited by John Gerassi. New York: Macmillan Publishing Co., 1968.
——. *Obras, 1957–1967.* 2 vols. Havana: Casa de las Americas, 1977.
Haig, Alexander M., Jr. *Caveat: Realism, Reagan, and Foreign Policy.* New York: Macmillan Publishing Co., 1984.
Halper, Thomas. *Foreign Policy Crisis: Appearance and Reality in Decision-Making.* Columbus, Ohio: Charles E. Merrill Publishing Co., 1971.
Halperin, Ernst. *Castro and Latin American Communism.* Translated by William F. Griffith. Cambridge, Mass.: Center for International Studies, MIT Press, 1963.
Halperin, Maurice. *The Rise and Decline of Fidel Castro.* Berkeley, Calif.: University of California Press, 1973.
——. *The Taming of Fidel Castro.* Berkeley, Calif.: University of California Press, 1981.
Harnecker, Marta. *Cuba: Los Protagonistas de un Nuevo Poder.* Havana: Editorial de Ciencias Sociales, 1979.
——. *Cuba: Dictatorship or Democracy?* Translated by Patrick Greanville. Westport, Conn.: Lawrence Hill & Co., 1980.

Harsch, Ernest, and Thomas, Tony. *Angola: The Hidden History of Washington's War* New York: Pathfinder Press, 1976.
Heras, Leon. *Balance de la Economía Latinoamericana, 1959–1974*. Vol. 5, *El Sector Externo*. Havana: Editorial de Ciencias Sociales, 1978.
Herring, Hubert. *A History of Latin America: From the Beginning to the Present*. 3rd ed. New York: Alfred Knopf, 1968.
Hersh, Seymour M. *The Price of Power: Kissinger in the Nixon White House*. New York: Summit, 1983.
Holt-Seeland, Inger. *Women in Cuba*. Westport, Conn.: Lawrence Hill, 1982
Horowitz, Irving L., ed. *Masses in Latin America*. New York: Oxford University Press, 1970.
——. *Cuban Communism*. 5th ed. New Brunswick, N.J.: Transaction Books, January 1984.
Huberman, Leo, and Sweezy, Paul M. *Cuba: Anatomy of a Revolution*. 2d ed. New York: Monthly Review Press, 1969.
——. *Socialism in Cuba*. New York: Monthly Review Press, 1969.
——, eds. *Régis Debray and the Latin American Revolution*. New York: Monthly Review Press, 1968.
Hunt, E. Howard. *Give Us This Day*. New Rochelle, N.Y.: Arlington House, 1973.
Ignatyev, Oleg. *Secret Weapon in Africa*. Translated by David Fidlon. Moscow: Progress Publishers, 1977.
Instituto de la Demanda Interna. *Seminario Internacional de la Demanda en el Mundo*. Havana: Editorial Orbe, 1976.
——. *Investigaciones Científicas de la Demanda en Cuba*. Havana: Editorial Orbe, 1979.
International Commission of Jurists (ICJ). *Cuba and the Rule of Law*. Geneva, Switzerland: ICJ, 1962.
Jackson, D. Bruce. *Castro, the Kremlin, and Communism in Latin America*. Baltimore: Johns Hopkins University Press, 1969.
Jenks, Leland H. *Our Cuban Colony*. New York: Vanguard Press, 1928.
Johnson, Haynes. *The Bay of Pigs: The Leaders' Story of Brigade 2506*. New York: Norton & Company, 1964.
Johnson, Willis Fletcher. *The History of Cuba*. 5 vols. New York: B.F. Buck & Co., 1920.
Jorge, Antonio. *An Evaluation of Cuba's Post-Revolutionary Socio-Economic Models*. Coral Gables, Fla.: University of Miami, 1984.
Karol, K.S. *Guerrillas in Power: The Course of the Cuban Revolution*. Translated by Arnold Pomerans. New York: Hill and Wang, 1970.
Kaser, Michael. *Comecon: Integration Problems of the Planned Economies*. New York: Oxford University Press, 1967.
Khrushchev, Nikita. *Khrushchev Remembers*. Boston, Mass.: Little, Brown & Company, 1970.
Kozolchyk, Boris. *The Political Biographies of Three Castro Officials*. Rand Memorandum RM-4994-RC. Santa Monica, Calif.: Rand Corporation, 1966.
Krich, John. *A Totally Free Man: An Unauthorized Autobiography of Fidel Castro*. Berkeley, Calif.: Creative Arts Books Company, 1981.
Kwitney, Jonathan. *Endless Enemies: The Making of an Unfriendly World*. New York: Congdon and Weed, Inc., 1984.
LaFeber, Walter. *Inevitable Revolutions: The United States and Central America*. New York: W.W. Norton & Co., 1983.

Langley, Lester D. *The Cuban Policy of the United States: A Brief History.* New York: John Wiley and Sons, Inc., 1968.
——. *The United States, Cuba, and the Cold War: American Failure or Communist Conspiracy.* Lexington, Mass.: Lexington Books, D.C. Heath, 1970.
Lavan, George, ed. *Che Guevara Speaks.* New York: Merit Publishers, 1967.
Lavigne, Marie. *The Socialist Economies of the Soviet Union and Europe.* Translated by T.G. Waywell. White Plains, N.Y.: International Arts and Sciences, 1974.
Lazo, Mario. *Dagger in the Heart: American Policy Failures in Cuba.* New York: Funk and Wagnalls, 1968.
Leiner, Marvin, and Ubell, Robert. *Children Are the Revolution: Day Care in Cuba.* New York: Viking Press, 1974.
LaRiverend, Julio. *La República: Dependéncia y Evolución.* Havana: Editorial Universidad, 1966.
——. *Economic History of Cuba.* Havana: Instituto de Libro, 1967.
Levesque, Jacques. *The USSR and the Cuban Revolution: Soviet Ideological and Strategic Perspectives, 1959-1977.* Translated by Deanna Drendel Leboenf. New York: Praeger, 1978.
Lewis, Oscar; Lewis, Ruth M.; and Rigdon, Susan M. *Neighbors: Living The Revolution; An Oral History of Contemporary Cuba.* Urbana, Ill.: University of Illinois Press, 1978.
Llerena, Mario. *The Unsuspected Revolution: The Birth and Rise of Castroism.* Ithaca, N.Y.: Cornell University Press, 1978.
Llerena, Rafael, and Philipson, Lorrin. *Freedom Flights.* New York: Random House, 1981.
Lockwook, Lee. *Castro's Cuba, Cuba's Fidel.* New York: Vintage Books, 1969.
Lowy, Michael. *The Marxism of Che Guevara: Philosophy, Economics, and Revolutionary Warfare.* New York: Monthly Review Press, 1973.
McClintock, Cynthia. *Cuban Revolutionary Ideology and the Cuban Intellectual.* U.S., Department of State, Office of External Research, Foreign Affairs Research Paper, no. FAR 22538-P. Cambridge, Mass., July 1975.
MacEwan, Arthur. *Revolution and Economic Development in Cuba.* New York: St. Martin's Press, 1981.
Mankiewicz, Frank, and Jones, Kirby. *With Fidel: A Portrait of Castro and Cuba.* New York: Ballantine Books, 1975.
Marcum, John A. *The Angolan Revolution: Exile Politics and Guerrilla Warfare, 1962-1976.* Cambridge, Mass.: MIT Press, 1978.
Martell, Raúl. *La Empresa Socialista.* Havana: Editorial de Ciencias Sociales, 1978.
Martí, José. *Inside the Monster.* Edited by Philip S. Foner. Translated by Elinor Randall. New York: Monthly Review Press, 1975.
——. *On Education.* Edited by Philip S. Foner. Translated by Elinor Randall. New York: Monthly Review Press, 1979.
Martínez Alier, Juan, and Martínez Alier, Verena. *Cuba: economía y sociedad.* Paris: Ruedo Ibérico, 1972.
Matthews, Herbert L. *Return to Cuba: An Analysis of Developments.* Stanford, Calif.: California Institute of International Studies, 1964.
——. *Fidel Castro.* New York: Simon and Schuster, 1969.
——. *Revolution in Cuba: An Essay in Understanding.* New York: Charles Scribner's Sons, 1975.
Mesa-Lago, Carmelo. *The Labor Sector and the Socialist Distribution in Cuba.* New York: Praeger, 1968.

———, ed. *Revolutionary Change in Cuba*. Pittsburgh, Pa.: University of Pittsburgh Press, 1971.

———. *Cuba in the 1970s: Pragmatism and Institutionalization*. 2d ed. Albuquerque: University of New Mexico Press, 1978.

———. *The Economy of Socialist Cuba: A Two Decade Appraisal*. Albuquerque, N.M.: University of New Mexico Press, 1981.

Meyer, Karl E., and Szulc, Tad. *The Cuban Invasion: The Chronicle of Disaster*. New York: Praeger, 1962.

Millette, James. *Cuba since 1959: A Commonsense View of Economic Development*. Port of Spain, Trinidad: United Independence Party, 1973.

Mills, C. Wright. *Listen Yankee: The Revolution in Cuba*. New York: McGraw-Hill, 1960.

Montaner, Carlos A., ed. *Diez años de revolución Cubana*. San Juan, Puerto Rico: Editorial San Juan, 1970.

Montaner, Carlos A. *Secret Report on the Cuban Revolution*. Translated by Eduardo Zayas-Bazan. New Brunswick, N.J.: Transaction Books, 1981.

———. *Cuba, Castro and the Caribbean: The Cuban Revolution and the Crisis in Western Conscience*. New Brunswick, N.J.: Transaction Books, 1985.

Moreno Fraginals, Manuel. *The Sugarmill: The Socio-Economic Complex of Sugar in Cuba, 1760–1860*. Translated by Cedric Belfrage. New York: Monthly Review Press, 1976.

Moss, Ambler H. *Reflections on U.S. Policy toward Central America: The Transition from Carter to Reagan*. Coral Gables, Fla.: University of Miami, 1983.

Navarro, Antonio. *Tocayo: A Cuban Resistance Leader's True Story*. Westport, Conn.: Sandown Books, Shamrock Publishing Co., 1981.

Nelson, Lowry. *Cuba: The Measure of a Revolution*. Minneapolis: University of Minnesota Press, 1972.

Newman, Phillip C. *Cuba before Castro: An Economic Appraisal*. Ridgewood, N.J.: Foreign Studies Institute, 1965.

Nicolson, Joe, Jr. *Inside Cuba*. New York: Sheed and Ward, 1974.

O'Connor, James. *The Origins of Socialism in Cuba*. Ithaca: Cornell University Press, 1970.

Oramas, Oscar. *Angola: Ha nacido una nueva generación*. Havana: Editorial de Ciencias Sociales, 1978.

Ortíz y Fernández, Fernando. *Cuban Counterpoint: Tobacco and Sugar*. New York: Random House, 1970.

Pando, Magdalen M. *Cuba's Freedom Fighter, Antonio Maceo: 1845–1896*. Gainesville, Fla.: Felicity Press, 1980.

Pardeiro, Francisco A. *História de la Economía de Cuba*. Havana: Editorial Universidad de la Havana, 1966.

Parkinson, F. *Latin America, the Cold War, and the World Powers, 1945–1973*. Beverly Hills, Calif.: Sage Publications, 1974.

Paz, Octavio. *Democracy and Dictatorship in Latin America*. New York: Foundation for the Study of Independent Social Ideas, 1982.

Pérez, Louis A., Jr. *Army Politics in Cuba 1898–1958*. Pittsburgh, Pa.: University of Pittsburgh Press, 1976.

———. *Cuba between Empires, 1878–1902*. Pittsburgh, Pa.: University of Pittsburgh Press, 1982.

Phillips, Ruby Hart. *Cuba: Island of Paradox*. New York: McDowell, Obolensky, 1959.

Phillipson, Lorrin, and Llerena, Rafael. *Freedom Flights*. New York: Random House, 1980.

Pino Santos, Oscar. *El asalto a Cuba por la oligarquía financiera Yanqui*. Havana: Casa de las Americas, 1973.
Plank, John, ed. *Cuba and the United States: Long-Range Perspectives*. Washington, D.C.: The Brookings Institution, 1967.
Poklad, B., and Shchevchenko, E. *Council for Mutual Economic Assistance: Its Present and Future*. Moscow: Novosti Press Agency, 1973.
Radosh, Ronald, ed. *The New Cuba: Paradoxes and Potentials*. New York: Morrow Publishers, 1976.
Randall, Margaret. *Women in Cuba: Twenty Years Later*. New York: Smyrna Press, 1981.
——— . *Breaking the Silences: 20th Century Poetry by Cuban Women*. Vancouver, Canada: Pulp Press, 1982.
Ratliff, William E. *Castroism and Communism in Latin America, 1959-1976*. Washington, D.C.: American Enterprise Institute for Public Policy Research, 1976.
Reckford, Barry. *Does Fidel Eat More Than Your Father?* New York: Praeger, 1971.
Riding, Alan. *Distant Neighbors: A Portrait of the Mexicans*. New York: Alfred A. Knopf, 1985.
Ripoll, Carlos. "The Cuban Scene: Censors and Dissentors," reprinted from *Partisan Review* 47, no. 4. Washington, D.C.: The Cuban-American Foundation, 1982.
——— . *Martí: Democracy and Anti-Imperialism*, Coral Gables, Fla.: University of Miami, 1984.
——— . *Martí, the United States, and the Marxist Interpretation of Cuban History*. New Brunswick, N.J. Transaction Books, 1984.
Ritter, Archibald R.M. *The Economic Development of Revolutionary Cuba: Strategy and Performance*. New York: Praeger, 1974.
Rivero, Nicolas. *Castro's Cuba: An American Dilemma*. Washington, D.C.: Luce Publishers, 1962.
Roberts, C. Paul, and Hamour, Mukhtar, eds. *Cuba, 1968: Supplement to the Statistical Abstracts of Latin America*. Los Angeles: University of California Press, Latin American Center, 1970.
Roca Calderío, Blas. *The Cuban Revolution*. New York: New Century Publishers, 1961.
Roca Calderío, Blas; Rodríguez, Carlos Rafael; and Luzardo, Manuel. *En defensa del pueblo*. Havana: Arrow Press, 1945.
Rodríguez, Carlos Rafael. *José Martí and Cuban Liberation*. New York: International Publishers, 1953.
——— . *Letra Con Fila* (Writings with an Edge). 3 volumes. Havana, 1983.
Roig de Leuchsenring, Emilio. *Los Estados Unidos Contra Cuba Libre*. 2 volumes. Santiago de Cuba: Government of Cuba, 1982.
Ronfeldt, David F. *Superclients and Superpowers: Cuba: Soviet Union/Iran: U.S*. Rand Memorandum P-5945. Santa Monica, Calif.: Rand Corporation, April 1978.
Roosevelt, Theodore. *The Rough Riders*. New York: Charles Scribner's Sons, 1899.
——— . *The Letters of Theodore Roosevelt*. Selected and edited by E. Morison. 8 volumes. Cambridge, Mass.: Harvard University Press, 1951-54.
Rubinstein, Alvin Z. *Soviet and Chinese Influence in the Third World*. New York: Praeger, 1975.
Ruíz, Ramón Eduardo. *Cuba: The Making of a Revolution*. New York: W.W. Norton, 1970.
Russell, Philip. *Cuba in Transition*. Amarillo, Texas: Armadillo Press, 1971.
Saíz Cidoncha, Carlos. *Guerrillas en Cuba y otros paises de Ibero-América*. Madrid: Nacional, 1974.

Salkey, Andrew. *Writing in Cuba since the Revolution.* London: Ouverture Publications, 1977.
Samuels, Michael, et al. *Implications of Soviet and Cuban Activities in Africa for U.S. Policy.* Washington, D.C.: Georgetown University Center for Strategic and International Studies, 1979.
Santamaría, Haydée. *Moncada: Memories of the Attack That Launched the Cuban Revolution.* Secaucus, N.J.: Lyle Stuart, 1980.
Santos, Francisco Fernández, and Martínez, José. *Cuba, una revolución en marcha.* Colombes, France: Ediciones Ruedo Ibérico, 1967.
Sartre, Jean Paul. *Sartre on Cuba.* New York: Ballantine Books, 1961.
Schaefer, Henry Wilcox. *Comecon and the Politics of Integration.* New York: Praeger, 1972.
Schlesinger, Arthur M., Jr. *A Thousand Days: John F. Kennedy in the White House.* Boston, Mass.: Houghton Mifflin, 1965.
Schroeder, Susan. *Cuba: A Handbook of Historical Statistics.* Boston, Mass.: G.K. Hall & Co., 1982.
Seers, Dudley, ed. *Cuba: The Economic and Social Revolution.* Chapel Hill: University of North Carolina Press, 1964.
Serra, Carmen, et al. *La educacíon empieza con la vida.* Havana: Instituto de la Infancia, 1979.
Sheer, Robert, ed. *The Diary of Che Guevara.* New York: Bantam Books, 1968.
Silva Leon, Arnold. *Cuba y el Mercado Internacional Azucarero.* Havana: Editorial de Ciencias Sociales, 1975.
Silverman, Bertram, ed. *Man and Socialism in Cuba: The Great Debate.* New York: Athenaeum, 1971.
Sinclair, Andrew. *Che Guevara.* New York: Viking Press, 1970.
Smith, Earl E.T. *The Fourth Floor: An Account of the Castro Communist Revolution.* New York: Random House, 1962.
Smith, Robert Freeman. *The United States and Cuba: Business and Diplomacy, 1917–1960.* New York: Bookman Associates, 1960.
——, ed. *Background to Revolution: The Development of Modern Cuba.* 1966. 2d ed. New York: Huntington Press, 1979.
Sorenson, Theodore C. *Kennedy.* New York: Harper & Row, 1965.
Stockwell, John. *In Search of Enemies: A CIA Story.* New York: W.W. Norton & Company, 1978.
Suarez, Andres. *Cuba: Castroism and Communism, 1959–60.* Cambridge, Mass.: MIT Press, 1967.
Suchlicki, Jaime. *University Students and Revolution in Cuba, 1920–1968.* Coral Gables, Fla.: University of Miami Press, 1969.
——, ed. *Cuba, Castro and Revolution.* Coral Gables, Fla.: University of Miami Press, 1972.
——. *Cuba: From Columbus to Castro.* New York: Charles Scribner's Sons, 1974.
——. *Cuba: Continuity and Change.* Coral Gables, Fla.: University of Miami, 1984.
Sutherland, Elizabeth. *The Youngest Revolution: A Personal Report on Cuba.* New York: Dial Press, 1969.
Szulc, Tad. *Twilight of the Tyrants.* New York: Holt, Rinehart, and Winston, 1959.
Taber, Michael, ed. *Fidel Castro Speeches.* New York: Pathfinder Press, 1981.
Taber, Robert. *M-26: The Biography of a Revolution.* Secaucus, N.J.: Lyle Stuart, 1961.
Theberge, James D. *Soviet Seapower in the Caribbean: Political and Strategic Implications.* New York: Praeger, 1972.

———. *The Soviet Presence in Latin America.* New York: Crane, Russak and Company for the National Strategy Information Center, 1974.
Theberge, James D., and Fontaine, Roger W. *Latin America: Struggle for Progress.* Lexinton, Mass.: Lexington Books, D.C. Heath, 1977.
Thomas, Hugh. *Cuba: The Pursuit of Freedom.* New York: Harper and Row, 1975.
———. *The Cuban Revolution.* Harper Torchbooks, 1977.
Thurber, Clarence E., and Graham, Laurence S., eds. *Development Administration in Latin America.* Durham, N.C.: Duke University Press, 1973.
Tomasi, Lydio, ed. *In Defense of the Alien: Immigration and Refugee Policy.* Vol. VI. New York: Center for Migration Studies, 1984.
Torres Ramírez, Blanco. *Las relaciones Cubano-Soviéticas, 1959-1968.* México: El Colegio de México, 1971.
Tretiak, Daniel. *Cuba and the Soviet Union: The Growing Accommodation.* Rand Memorandum RM-4935-PR. Santa Monica, Calif.: Rand Corporation, July 1966.
Ulibarri Eduardo, *U.S. Options in Central America.* Washington, D.C.: The Cuban-American National Foundation, 1982.
Urrutia-Lleó, Manuel. *Democracía falsa y falso socialismo: pre-castrismo y castrismo.* Englewood Cliffs, N.J.: Vega Publishing Co., 1975.
U.S. Congress, House, Committee on Foreign Affairs. *Castro's Communist Subversion in the Western Hemisphere.* HR 195, 88th Cong., 1st sess. 4 April 1963.
———, Subcommittee on Inter-American Relations, Committee on Foreign Affairs. *Communist Activities in Latin America.* 90th Cong., 1st sess. July 1967.
———, Committee on International Relations. *Cuba, Study Mission: A Fact-Finding Survey, June 26-July 2, 1975.* 94th Cong., 1st sess. Washington, D.C.: Government Printing Office, 15 July 1975.
———, Permanent Select Committee on Intelligence, Subcommittee on Oversight and Evaluation. *U.S. Intelligence Performance in Central America.* 97th Cong., 2d sess. Washington, D.C.: Government Printing Office, 1982.
U.S. Congress, Joint Committee Print: House, Committee on Foreign Affairs; Senate, Committee on Foreign Relations. *Country Reports on Human Rights Practices for 1979.* 96th Cong., 2d sess. Washington, D.C.: Government Printing Office, 1980.
U.S. Congress, Senate, Judiciary Committee, Internal Security Subcommittee. Published as *Communist Threat to the United States through the Caribbean: Hearings*, part 9. 30 August 1960. Washington, D.C.: Government Printing Office, 1960.
———. *Chronology of Important Events in United States-Cuban Relations, 1957-62.* Hearings before the International Security Subcommittee of the Senate Judiciary Committee. Appendix 2. 87 Cong., 1st sess., March-July 1961. Washington, D.C.: Government Printing Office, 1962.
———, Committee on Foreign Relations. Subcommittee on Western Hemisphere Affairs. *U.S. Policy Toward Cuba: Hearings.* 93rd Cong., 1st sess., 26 March and 18 April 1973. Washington, D.C.: Government Printing Office, 1974.
———. Committee on Foreign Relations. *Cuba: A Staff Report.* 93rd Cong., 2d sess. Washington, D.C.: Government Printing Office, 1974.
———. Committee on Foreign Relations. *The United States and Cuba: A Propitious Moment.* Report by Senator Jacob K. Javits and Senator Claiborne Pell to the Committee on their trip to Cuba. 27-30 September 1974. Washington, D.C.: Government Printing Office, 1974.
———. Committee on Foreign Relations. *Détente: Hearings.* 93rd Cong., 2d sess., 15, 20,

21 August; 10, 12, 18, 19, 24, 25 September; and 1, 8 October 1974. Washington, D.C.: Government Printing Office, 1975.

U.S. Congress, Senate, Committee on Foreign Relations. *Cuban Realities: May 1975.* Report by Senator George S. McGovern. 94th Cong., 1st sess. Washington, D.C.: Government Printing Office, 1975.

———. United States Congressional Record, vol. 126, no. 92. Comments by Senator Edward M. Kennedy, Friday, June 6, 1980. 96th Cong., 2d sess. Washington, D.C.: Government Printing Office, 1980.

———. Joint Economic Committee, Congress of the United States. *The Political Economy of the Western Hemisphere: Selected Issues for U.S. Policy.* Selected Essays Prepared for Use of The Subcommittee on International Trade, Finance, and Security Economics. 97th Cong., 1st sess. Washington, D.C.: Government Printing Office, 1981.

U.S. Congress. American Papers: Documents, Legislature and Executive, of the Congress of the United States. Second Series, Volume V, Foreign Relations. Washington, D.C.: Gales & Seaton, 1858.

U.S., Department of State. *Responsibility of Cuban Government for Increased International Tensions in the Hemisphere.* Washington, D.C.: Government Printing Office, August 1960.

———. *Cuba.* Publication 7171 (White Paper on Cuba) Inter-American Series, no. 66. Washington, D.C.: Government Printing Office, April 1961.

———. *The Castro Regime in Cuba.* August 1961.

———. *Horn of Africa.* Current Policy, no. 141, 25 February 1980.

———. *Regional Strategy for Southern Africa.* Current Policy, no. 308, 29 August 1981.

———. *Cuban Support for Terrorism and Insurgency in the Western Hemisphere.* Current Policy, no. 376, 12 March 1982.

———. *Radio Martí and Cuban Interference.* Current Policy, no. 392, 10 May 1982.

———. *Cuban Armed Forces and the Soviet Military Presence.* Special Report no. 103, August 1982.

———. *A New Partnership with Africa.* Current Policy, no. 438, 19 November 1982.

———. *Dealing with the Reality of Cuba.* Current Policy, no. 443, 14 December 1982.

———. Bulletin. *Khruschev-Kennedy Letters,* May 8, 1961, pp. 659–87.

———. Report of the Secretary of War, Appendix E, "Cuban Pacification: Report of William H. Taft, Secretary of War, and Robert Bacon, Assistant Secretary of State, of "What Was Done under the Instructions of the President in Restoring Peace in Cuba." Washington, D.C.: Government Printing Office, 1906.

U.S. Government. *Papers Relating to the Foreign Relations of the United States.* Washington, D.C.: Government Printing Office, 1904.

———. "Papers of President Kennedy, Presidential Recordings." Off-the-Record Meeting on Cuba, October 16, 1962, 11:50 a.m.–12:57 p.m. Transcript released by J.F.K. Library October 1983.

U.S. Government. General Advisory Committee on Arms Control and Disarmament. "A Quarter Century of Soviet Compliance Practices under Arms Control Commitments: 1958–83." Washington, D.C.: Arms Control and Disarmament Agency, October 1984.

Valdés, Nelson P. *Cuba socialismo democrático o burocratismo colectivista?* Bogotá: Editores Tercer Mundo, 1973.

Valdés Vivo, Raul. *Angola: Fin del mito de los mercenarios.* Havana: Editorial de Ciencias Sociales, 1978.

Valdés Vivo, Raul. *Ethiopia's Revolution.* New York: International Publishers, 1978.
Warrett, Rosemary. *Cuba at the Turning Point.* New York: Business International Corporation, 1977.
Weinstein, Martin, ed. *Revolutionary Cuba in the World Arena.* Philadelphia: Institute for the Study of Human Issues, 1979.
Welles, Sumner. *The Time for Decision.* New York and London: Harper & Brothers, 1944.
Weyl, Nathaniel. *Red Star over Cuba.* New York: Devin-Adair, 1960.
Wilczynski, Josef. *Technology in Comecon: Acceleration of Technological Progress through Economic Planning and the Market.* New York: Praeger, 1974.
Wilkerson, Loree. *Fidel Castro's Political Programs from Reformism to Marxist-Leninism.* Gainesville: University of Florida Press, 1965.
Willetts, Peter. *The Non-Aligned Movement: The Origins of the Third World Alliance.* New York: Nichols Publishing Company, 1978.
Wise, David, and Ross, Thomas B. *The U-2 Affair.* New York: Random House, 1962.
Wood, Bryce. *The Making of the Good Neighbor Policy.* New York: Colombia University Press, 1961.
Wyden, Peter. *Bay of Pigs: The Untold Story.* New York: Simon and Schuster, 1979.
Yglesias, José. *In the Fist of the Revolution: Life in a Cuban Country Town.* New York: Pantheon Books, 1968.
Zeitlin, Maurice. *Revolutionary Politics and the Cuban Working Class.* Princeton, N.J.: Princeton University Press, 1967.
Zeitlin, Maurice, and Sheer, Robert. *Cuba: Tragedy in Our Hemisphere.* New York: Grove Press, 1963.

Articles and Periodicals

Al-Khawas, Mohamed A., and Cohen, Barry. U.S. National Security Council Interdepartmental Group of Africa. *Study in Response to National Security Study Memorandum 39: Southern Africa.* Published in *The Kissinger Study of Southern Africa.* Westport, Conn.: Lawrence Hill and Co., 1976.
Americas Watch. "The Treatment of Political Prisoners in Cuba and the American Response." An Americas Watch Report written by Gregory Wallace. New York: Americas Watch, September 1983.
Aufricht, Hans, ed. League of Nations, *Guide to League of Nations Publications.* League Documents. Annex to the Covenant, p. 418. Geneva: League of Nations. Reprint of 1951 edition.
Balari, Eugenio R. "Trabajo y desarrollo del Instituto de la Demanda Interna." *Economía 7 desarrollo,* no. 21 (January–February 1974).
Bank of London. "Cuba: A Sustained Economic Recovery." *Bank of London and South American Review* 9, no. 101 (May 1975).
Barkin, David P. "Agricultura: El sector clave del desarrollo de Cuba." *Comercio Exterior* (Mexico City) 20, no. 3 (March 1970).
―――. "La estratégia Cubana de desarrollo." *Foro Internacional* (Mexico City), 2, no. 2 (October–December 1971).

Barkin, David P. "The Redistribution of Consumption in Socialist Cuba." *Review of Radical Political Economics* 14, no. 5 (February 1972).
——. "Cuban Agriculture: A Strategy of Economic Development." *Studies in Comparative International Development* 17, no. 1 (spring 1972).
Barquin, Ramón. "Cuba: The Cybernetic Era." *Cuban Studies* no. 5, issue 2 (July 1976).
Bender, Gerald J. "Angola: Left, Right, and Wrong." *Foreign Policy*, no. 43 (summer 1981):53–70.
——. "Angola, the Cubans and American Anxieties." *Foreign Policy*, no. 31 (summer 1978):3–30.
Bender, Lynn Darrell. "U.S.-Cuban Policy: Subtle Modifications and the Implication of the American-Soviet 'Understandings.'" *Potomac Review* 5, no. 2 (1972).
——. "Guantánamo: Its Political, Military, and Legal Status." *Caribbean Quarterly* (Kingston, Jamaica) 19, no. 1 (March 1973):80–86.
Benglesdorf, Carol, and Locker, Michael. "Perfect Identification of Government and Community." *Cuban Review Newsletter* 4, no. 4 (December 1974).
Berman, Jesse. "The Cuban Popular Tribunals." *Columbia Law Review* 60, no. 8 (December 1969).
Betancourt, Ernesto F., and Dizard, Wilson P. "Castro and the Bankers: The Mortgaging of a Revolution—1983 Update." Washington, D.C.: The Cuban-American National Foundation, 1983.
Bialer, Seweryn, and Stepan, Alfred C. "Cuba, the U.S., and the Central American Mess." *The New York Review of Books*, 27 May 1982, pp. 17–21.
Blechman, Barry M., and Levinson, Stephanie E. "Soviet Submarine Visits to Cuba." *United States Naval Institute Proceedings*, no. 101, Issue 9/871 (September 1975).
Boudin, Leonard B. "The Cuban Travel Case," *Cuba Update* 4, no. 4 (4 August 1983). Center for Cuban Studies, New York.
Casal, Lordes. "On Popular Power: The Organization of the Cuban State during the Period of Transition." *Latin American Perspectives*, 7, supplement (1975).
——. "Cuban Communist Party: The Best among the Good." *Cuba Review*, 6 (September 1976).
Casal, Lordes, and Pérez-Stable, Marifeli. "Sobre Angola y los negros de Cuba." *Areito* (summer 1976).
Castro, Fidel. "The USSR-Cuba Economic Agreements: A Model of Fraternal Relations." *New World Review*, 41, no. 2 (1973).
——. Speech by Fidel Castro as a response to the Soviet Invasion of Czechoslovakia. *Granma*, year 3, no. 34, Havana, Cuba, 25 August 1968.
Castro, Raúl. Sabemos que el imperialismo se debilita." *Verde Olivo* 17, no. 29 (20 July 1975).
Center for Cuban Studies Newsletter. "The First Party Congress: Institutionalization of the Cuban Revolution" 3, nos. 2 and 3 (March–June 1976).
Current Intelligence Weekly Summary. Washington, D.C.: Office of the Current Intelligence Weekly, 9 February 1961, 16 March 1961.
Central Committee of the Communist Party of Cuba. "Report of the Central Committee of the PCC to the First Congress." Havana, 1977.
——. Speech by Humberto Pérez, president of the Central Planning Board at the 2d period of sessions of the National Assembly of People's Power. Department of Revolutionary Orientation. Havana, 1978.

Comisión Internacional de Juristas. *El Imperio de la ley en Cuba*, Ginebra, 1962.
——. "Variaciones constitucionales en Cuba." *Boletín de la Comisión Internacional de Juristas*, no. 13 (May 1962).
Comisión Nacional de Implantación del sistema de dirección y planificación de la economía. "Plenaria nacional de chequeo sobre el sistema de dirección y planificación de la economía." Havana, 16 February 1979.
Comité Estatal de Ciencia y Técnica. *Resúmen nacional sobre política científica y tecnológica*. Havana, 1978.
Comité Estatal de Estadísticas. *Compendio Estadístico de Cuba, 1975*. Havana, 1975.
——. *La Economía Cubana, 1975*. Havana, 1975.
——. *Compendio Estadístico de Cuba, 1976*. Havana, 1976.
——. *La Economía Cubana, 1976*. Havana, 1976.
——. *La Economía Cubana, 1977*. Havana, 1977.
——. *La Economía Cubana, 1978*. Havana, 1978.
"Concursos literarios e históricos de los CDR." Havana: Editorial Orbe, 1977.
Crain, David A. "Guatemalan Revolutionaries and Havana's Ideological Offensive of 1966-68." *Journal of Inter-American Studies and World Affairs* 17, no. 2 (1975).
Crozier, Brian. "Soviet Pressures in the Caribbean: The Satellization of Cuba." *Conflict Studies* 35 (May 1973).
Cuban-American National Foundation. "Castro's Narcotics Trade." Washington, D.C.: Cuban-American National Foundation Publications, 1983.
Da Gama Pinto, Clarence. "Who Sells What to Whom." *South* (London), August 1983, pp. 15-16. Citation of The World Armaments and Disarmament, *Yearbook, 1983*. Stockholm International Peace Research Institute.
De la Cuesta, Leonel-Antonio. "The Cuban Socialist Constitution: Its Originality and Role in Institutionalization." *Cuban Studies* 6, no. 2 (July 1976).
——. "Los nuevos municipios de Cuba." *Reunion* (Madrid), September-October 1976.
De la Torriente, Cosme. "Cuba, the United States of America and the League of Nations." Address delivered at the closing banquet of the Cuban Society of International Law, Havana, 5 March 1922, pp. 361-377.
Dinerstein, Herbert S. "Castro's Latin American Comintern." Rand Memorandum P-3678, September 1967.
Domínguez, Jorge I. "Cuban National Security in the 1970s: Critique and Evaluation." Paper delivered at the Conference on the International Relations of the Cuban Revolution. New York: Ibero-American Language and Area Center, New York University, 1 November 1975.
——. "Institutionalization and Civil-Military Relations." *Cuban Studies* 6, no. 1 (1976).
——. "Revolutionary Values and Development Performance: China, Cuba, and the Soviet Union." In *Values and Development*, edited by Harold Lasswell, Daniel Lerner, and John Montgomery. Cambridge, Mass.: MIT Press, 1976.
——. "The Cuban Operation in Angola: Costs and Benefits for the Armed Forces." Cuban Studies 8, no. 1 (January 1978).
——. "Cuban Foreign Policy." *Foreign Affairs*, 57, no. 1 (fall 1978).
——. "The Success of Cuban Foreign Policy." Occasional Papers, no. 27. New York: New York University Center for Latin American and Caribbean Studies, January 1980.
——. "On U.S.-Cuban Ties." *New York Times*, 26 February 1981.

Domínguez, Jorge I., and Mitchell, Christopher. "The Roads Not Taken: Institutionalization and Political Parties in Cuba and Bolivia." *Comparative Politics* 9 (January 1977).
Dórticos, Osvaldo. "Análisis y Perspectivas del Desarrollo de la Economía Cubano." *Revista Interamericana de Planificación* (Bogotá) 7, nos. 28–29 (December 1973–March 1974).
Dumont, Rene. "The Militarization of Fidelismo." Translated by Adrienne Foulke. *Dissent*, September–October 1970.
Duncan, W. Raymond. "Soviet Policy in Latin America since Khrushchev." *Orbis* 15, no. 2 (1971).
Durch, William J. "The Cuban Military in Africa and the Middle East: From Algeria to Angola." Professional Paper no. 201. Alexandria, Va.: Center for Naval Analysis, September 1977.
———. "Revolution from a F.A.R.: The Cuban Armed Forces in Africa and the Middle East." Alexandria, Va. Center for Naval Analysis, September 1977, Professional Paper 199.
Eckstein, Susan. "Capitalist Constraints on Cuban Socialist Development." *Working Papers*, no. 6. Washington, D.C.: Latin American Program of the Wilson Center, 1978.
Edwards, J. David. "The Consolidation of the Cuban Political System." *World Affairs* 139, issue 1 (summer 1976).
"El Futuro es el Internacionalismo: Recorrido del Comandante Fidel Castro por Paises de Africa y Europa Socialista." Havana: Instituto Cubano del Libro, 1972.
Estefania Seoane, M. "Cuba-USSR: Fraternal Cooperation." *Foreign Trade* (Moscow) 8 (1976).
Fagen, Richard R. "Charismatic Authority and the Leadership of Fidel Castro." *Western Political Quarterly* 18, no. 2, pt. 1 (June 1965).
———. "Continuities in Cuban Revolutionary Politics." *Monthly Review* 23, no. 11 (April 1972).
Falcoff, Mark. "Thinking about Cuba." *Washington Quarterly* 7, no. 2 (spring 1983). Washington, D.C.: Georgetown University, Center for Strategic and International Studies.
———. "Thinking about Cuba: Unscrambling Cuban Messages." Washington, D.C.: The Cuban-American National Foundation, 1983.
Falk, Pamela S. "Cuba, 1974–78." In *Constitutions of the Countries of the World*, edited by Albert P. Blaustein and Gisbert H. Flanz. Dobbs Ferry, N.Y.: Oceana, 1978.
Fontaine, Roger W. "On Negotiating with Cuba." Washington, D.C.: American Enterprise Institute for Public Policy Research, 1975.
Frechette, Myles R.R. "Letter to the Editor." *Foreign Policy*, no. 48, Carnegie Endowment for International Peace, fall 1982.
Friscia, A. Blake. "Cuba's Potential for U.S. Business." *International Finance*. New York: The Economics Group of the Chase Manhattan Bank, 23 January 1978.
Gall, Norman, and Teodoro Petkoff. "The Crisis of the Professional Revolutionary. Part I: Years of Insurrection." *American Universities Field Staff*, 16. Hanover, N.H.: American Universities Field Staff, 1972.
García Márquez, Gabriel. "Colombian Author Writes on Cuba's Angola Intervention." *Washington Post*, 10 January 1977.
———. "Castro in the War Room: Tactical Advice to Angola." *Washington Post*, 11 January 1977.

———. "Cuba en Angola: Operación Carlota." *Proceso*, January 1977.
Gardiner, C. Harvey. "The Japanese and Cuba." *Caribbean Studies* 12, no. 2 (July 1972).
Goldenberg, Boris. "Radicalization of a Latin-American State: The Establishment of Communism in Cuba." *Studies on the Soviet Union* (West Germany) 11, no. 4 (1971).
González, Edward. "Castro's Revolution, Cuban Communist Appeals and the Soviet Response." *World Politics* 21, no. 1 (October 1968).
———. "A Comparison of Soviet and Cuban Approaches to Latin America." *Studies in Comparative Communism* 5 (spring 1972).
———. "New Perspectives on Cuba." *Journal of Inter-American Studies and World Affairs* 15 (November 1973).
———. "Castro and Cuba's New Orthodoxy." *Problems of Communism* 25 (January 1976).
———. "Political Succession in Cuba." *Studies in Comparative Communism* 9, no. 1 (spring 1976).
———. "Complexities of Cuban Foreign Policy." *Problems of Communism* 26, no. 6 (1977).
———. "Letter to the Editor," *Foreign Policy*, no. 48, Carnegie Endowment for International Peace, fall 1982.
———. "A Strategy for Dealing with Cuba in the 1980s." Prepared for the U.S. Air Force and Department of State. Santa Monica: Rand Publications, 1982.
———. "U.S. Strategic Interests in the Caribbean Basin," San Juan, Puerto Rico: Universidad Interamericana de Puerto Rico, Centro de Investigaciones del Caribe y America Latina, no. 3 (April 1983).
Goure, Leon, and Weinkle, Julian. "Cuba's New Dependency." *Problems of Communism* 21, no. 2 (March–April 1972).
Grabendorff, Wolf. "Cuba's Involvement in Africa." *Journal of Interamerican Studies and World Affairs*, 22, no. 1 (February 1980):3–29.
Grayson, George W. "Cuba's Development Policies." *Current History* 72, no. 424 (February 1977).
Halloran, Richard. "Soviet Said to Add Troops in Cuba." *New York Times*, 10 June 1984.
Hennessy, C.A.M. "The Roots of Cuban Nationalism." In *Background to Revolution*, edited by Robert F. Smith. 2d ed. New York: Huntington Press, 1979.
Hollarbach, Paula, and Díaz-Briquets, Sergio. *Fertility Determinants in Cuba*. With appendix by Kenneth H. Hill. New York: Center for Policy Studies, no. 102, December 1983.
Horowitz, Irving L. "Military Origins of the Cuban Revolution." *Armed Forces and Society*, no.1, issue 4 (summer 1975).
———. "The Cuba Lobby." *Washington Review of Strategic and International Studies*, Washington, D.C.: July 1978.
Junta Central de Planificación. Republic of Cuba. Centro de Información Científica Técnica. *Clausura del Congreso Constituyente de la Asociación de Economistas de Cuba*. Discurso por Humberto Peréz, 14 June 1979. Havana, October 1979.
Kirkpatrick, Jeane J. "Cuba and the Cubans." Washington, D.C.: The Cuban-American National Foundation, 1983.
Klare, Michael. "The Global Reach of the Superpowers." *South* (London), August 1983, pp. 9–14.
Kokorev, Vladimir. "La Solaridad de Cuba con Angola." *América Latina* 1 (1979). Moscow: Editorial Progreso, Instituto de América Latina.
Kopilow, David J. "Castro, Israel and the PLO." Washington, D.C.: The Cuban-American National Foundation, 1983.

Kovalyov, Y. "Latin America: The Struggle for Agrarian Reform." *International Affairs* (Moscow) 2 (1974).

Lamberg, Robert F. "Che in Bolivia: The 'Revolution' That Failed." *Problems of Communism* 19 (1974).

Latin American Perspectives. "Cuba: La revolución en marcha." *LAP* 12, no. 4, issue 7 (supplement 1975).

LeoGrande, William. "Cuban Dependency: A Comparison of PreRevolutionary and Post-Revolutionary International Economic Relations." *Cuban Studies* 9, no. 2 (July 1979).

———. "The Revolution in Nicaragua: Another Cuba?" *Foreign Affairs* 58 (fall 1979): pp. 28-50.

LeoGrande, William. "Cuba's Policy in Africa, 1959-1980." Berkeley, Calif.: Institute of International Affairs, 1980.

———. "Evolution of the Non-Aligned Movement." *Problems of Communism*, January-February 1980.

———. "Cuba's Policy Recycled." *Foreign Policy*, no. 46 (spring 1982). Carnegie Endowment for International Peace.

LeRiverend, Julio. "Etapas del proceso revolucionario." *América Latina* 21, no. 1. Moscow: Editorial Progreso, 1979.

Lernoux, Penny. *Fear and Hope: Toward Political Democracy in Central America*. New York: The Field Foundation, 1984.

Lowenthal, Abraham F. "Cuba: Time for a Change." *Foreign Policy* 20 (fall 1975).

———. "Cuba's African Adventure." *International Security* 2 (summer 1977).

McColm, R. Bruce. "Negotiating with Castro." Washington, D.C.: The Cuban-American National Foundation, 1983.

McShane, John. "Cuban Foreign Policy: Global Orientations." *Latin Americanist* 14, no. 3 (31 May 1979).

MacEwan, Arthur. "Equality and Power in Revolutionary Cuba." *Socialist Revolution* 4, no. 2 (October 1974).

———. "Ideology, Socialist Development and Power in Cuba." *Politics and Society* 5, no. 1 (August 1975).

Mallin, Jay. "Phases of Subversion: The Castro Drive on Latin America." *Air University Review* 25, issue 1 (1973).

Marchant, Herbert. "Castro's Cuba and the Soviet Union." *World Survey* (Great Britain) 91-92 (1976).

Maso, Calixto. "Una isla singular." *Aportes* (Paris) 11 (January 1969).

Mesa-Lago, Carmelo. "Availability and Reliability of Statistics in Socialist Cuba." *Latin American Research Review* 4, no. 1 (spring 1969).

———. "Economic Significance and Unpaid Labor in Cuba." *Industrial and Labor Relations Review*, April 1969.

———. "The Revolutionary Offensive." *Transaction* 6, no. 6 (April 1969).

———. "Ideological, Political, and Economic Factors in the Cuban Controversy on Material versus Moral Incentives." *Journal of InterAmerican Studies and World Affairs* 16, no. 1 (February 1972).

———. "Tipología y valor económico del trabajo no renumerado en Cuba." *El Trimestre Económico* (México City) 40, no. 149 (July-September 1973).

———. "Castro's Domestic Course." *Problems of Communism* 22, no. 5 (September-October 1973).

Mesa-Lago, Carmelo, and Hernández, Robert E. "La organización del trabajo y el sistema salarial en Cuba." *Revista de Política Social* (Madrid) 95 (September 1972).
Meyer, Karl E. "Report on Rebel Cuba." 14–19 September 1958. "Six-Part Series; *Washington Post*. 14 September 1958, "Report on Rebel Cuba"; 15 September 1958, "Castro Says He Fights for Rights and Opportunities Found in U.S."; 16 September 1958, "Teen-Age Boys Tortured, Murdered for Sympathy with Castro's Cause"; 17 September 1958, "Rotarians, Doctors, Women Back Castro Revolt"; 18 September 1958, "Foes Attack Batista-Called Elections"; 19 September 1958, "Neutrality Difficult in Castro's Revolt."
Middleton, Drew. "U.S. Officers Report a Buildup by Cuba," *New York Times*, 28 March 1983.
Migdail, Carl J. "How African War is Hitting Home in Cuba." *U.S. News and World Report* 84, no. 24 (14 June 1978).
Moran, Theodore. "The International Political Economy of Cuban Nickel Development." *Cuban Studies* 7, no. 2 (July 1977).
Nordheimer, Jon. "Twenty Years with Fidel." *New York Times*, 31 December 1978, Sunday Magazine.
Of Human Rights 4, no. 1 (winter 1981). Washington, D.C.: Georgetown University.
Organization of American States, General Secretariat. Inter-American Commission on Human Rights. "Sixth Report on the Situation of Political Prisoners in Cuba." Washington, D.C.: OAS, 14 December 1979, pp. 1–79.
Oswald, J. Gregory. "Soviet Diplomatic Relations with Mexico, Uruguay, and Cuba." *Texas Quarterly* 15, no. 1 (1972).
Pellicer de Brody, Olga. "Cuba y América Latina: Coexistencia pacífica o solaridad revolucionaria?" *Foro Internacional* (México) 12, no. 47 (1972).
Pérez, Louis A., Jr. "Army Politics in Socialist Cuba." *Journal of Latin American Studies* 8 (November 1976).
Pérez-López, Jorge F., and Pérez-López, René. "A Calendar of Cuban Bilateral Agreements 1959–1975: Descriptions and Uses." *Cuban Studies* 7 (July 1977).
Pérez-Stable, Marifeli. "Whither the Cuban Working Class." *Latin American Perspectives* 2, nos. 4–7 (supplement 1975).
———. "Institutionalization and Worker's Response." *Cuban Studies* 6, no. 2 (July 1976).
———. "The Making of a Conference on Cuba's Foreign Policy." *Journal of Political Science and Modern History* 2 (winter 1977).
"Política Cultural de la Revolución Cubana." Havana: Editorial de Ciencias Sociales, 1977.
Pollis, Adamantia. "Human Rights, Third World Socialism and Cuba." *World Development* 9, no. 9/10 (1981).
Pope, Ronald R. "Soviet Foreign Policy toward Latin America." *World Affairs* 135, no. 2 (1972).
Purcell, Susan Kaufman. "Containing Cuba" An unpublished manuscript for the study group on "U.S.–Cuba Relations" of the Council on Foreign Relations. Fall 1984.
Ratcliff, William E. "Communist China and Latin America, 1949–71." *Asian Survey*, 12, no. 10 (1972).
Republic of Cuba, *Possibility of Joint Ventures in Cuba*, Havana, Cuba: Council of State, February 1982.
Revista Interamericana de Planificación (Bogotá). "Las Perspectives del Desarrollo de la Economía Cubana, 1971–75." vol. 7, nos. 28–29, December 1973–March 1974.

Riog de Leuchsenring, Emilio. "La colonia superviva." El Siglo (Havana) 20 (1925).
Ripoll, Carlos. "The Cuban Scene: Censors and Dissenters," reprinted from *Partisian Review* 47, no. 4. Washington, D.C.: The Cuban-American National Foundation, 1982.
Ritter, Archibald R.M. 'The Transferability of Socioeconomic Development Models of Revolutionary Cuba." *Cuban Studies* 7, no. 2 (July 1977).
Roca, Sergio. "Cuban Economic Policy and Ideology: The Ten Million Ton Sugar Harvest." *Sage Professional Papers in International Studies* 4, no. 02–044 (1976).
Rodríguez, Carlos Rafael. "The Advantages of Socialism Are the Basis of Our Achievements." *New Times*, no. 1 (January 1974).
Rogers, William D. "Department Discusses U.S. Policy toward Cuba." *Department of State Bulletin* 73, no. 1880 (7 July 1975): pp. 30–35.
Russell, George. "Cuba: From Spontaneity to Stagnation." *Time*, 16 January 1984, pp. 48–49.
Schecter, Danny. "The Havana-Luanda Connection." *Cuba Review* 6, no. 1 (March 1976).
Schlesinger, Arthur M., Jr. "Russians and Cubans in Africa." *Wall Street Journal* 191 (2 May 1978):22.
Schriffrin, André. "Cuba's Fourth World." *New Republic* 158 (29 July 1968).
Shaffer, Harry G., and Mitchell, Stephen G. "Cuba: Present and Future." *Queen's Quarterly* (Canada) 79, no. 2 (1972).
Sheinin, Eduard. "Vínculos internacionales de la economía Cubana." *América Latina* (Moscow) 21, no. 1 (1979).
Silverman, Bertram. "A New Direction in Cuban Socialism." *Current History* 68, no. 401 (January 1975).
Silvert, Kalman H. "A Hemispheric Perspective." In *Cuba and the United States*, edited by John N. Plank. Washington, D.C.: Brookings Institute, 1967.
Silvert, Kalman H., and Silvert, Freida M. "Fate, Chance, and Faith: Some Ideas Suggested by a Recent Trip to Cuba." American Fieldstaff Reports. North America Series 2 no. 2, Hanover, New Hampshire: AUFS, September 1974.
"Sistema de Arbitraje Estatal y Normas Básicas para los Contratos Ecónomicos." Havana: Editorial Orbe, 1978.
Sklar, Barry. "Cuba in the Mid-1970s." *Foreign Service Journal* 53 (November 1976).
Smallwood, Lawrence L., Jr. "African Dimensions in Cuba." *Journal of Black Studies* 6, no. 2 (1975).
Smith, Wayne. "Dateline Havana: Myopic Diplomacy." *Foreign Policy*, no. 48, Carnegie Endowment for International Peace (fall 1982).
——. "Cuba: Time for a Thaw." *New York Times Magazine*. 29 July 1984, pp. 22–25, 54–56.
Suarez, Andres. "La construcción del socialismo en Cuba: El papel de partido." San Juan, Puerto Rico, January 1975.
Szulc, Tad. "Relax Nicaragua Isn't Another Cuba." *New York Times*, 7 August 1979, p. 15.
——. "Friendship is Possible, But . . . " *New York Daily News Parade Magazine*, 1 April 1984.
Taubman, Philip. "U.S. Officials Cite Cuba-Backed Drive In Urging Latin Aid," *New York Times*, 24 April 1984, pp. 1, 4.
Theriot, Lawrence. "U.S.-Cuba Trade: Question Mark?" *Commerce America*, 24 April 1978.
Thomas, Hugh. "The Revolution on Balance." Washington, D.C.: The Cuban-American National Foundation, 1983.

Treaster, Joseph B. "Cuba Says Its Militia Forces Now Exceed a Million." *New York Times*, 2 May 1982, p. 12.
Treverton, Gregory F. "Cuba After Angola." *World Today* (London) 33 (January 1977).
U.S., Central Intelligence Agency. Information Report. Telegram, 17 November 1963. Subject: Plan by anti-Castro Cubans in New York.
——. *Directory of Personalities of the Cuban Government, Official Organizations, and Mass Organizations*. Washington, D.C.: Government Printing Office, March 1974.
——. *The Cuban Economy: A Statistical Review*. Washington, D.C.: Government Printing Office, 1981.
U.S., Department of Commerce. Office of East-West Policy and Planning. Soviet Economic Relations with Non-European CMEA: Cuba, Vietnam and Mongolia." Staff research report by Lawrence H. Theriot and JeNelle Matheson. From *Soviet Economy in a Time of Change*. Vol. 2. Joint Economic Committee, U.S., Congress, 10 October 1979.
U.S., Department of State. Memorandum for the President of the United States. Secretary of State Dean Rusk, 24 February 1961. Secret memorandum declassified 13 March 1975. Subject: Exports from Cuba.
——. *Bulletin. Khrushchev-Kennedy Letters*. 8 May 1961, pp. 659–687.
——. *The Castro Regime in Cuba*. Washington, D.C.: Government Printing Office, August 1961.
——. U.S. Department of State staff summary, 17 April 1961. Top secret, eyes only for designated recipient, declassified 5 February 1975. Subject: Latin American Resolution on Cuba Appraised.
——. Memorandum to Mr. McGeorge Bundy from L.D. Battle, executive secretary of the U.S. Department of State, 9 February 1962. Confidential Memorandum Declassified 2 December 1975. Subject: Service of Cuban Volunteers in the United States Armed Forces.
——. Memorandum comments by United States Department of State on Dudley Seers' account of Cuba in 1962, 4 April 1962. Secret classification, declassified 10 May 1975.
——, Extension. Telegram from the United States, Department of State from New York from Stevenson to Secretary of State, 29 October 1962. Confidential document declassified 10 August 1973. Priority limited distribution. Subject of the telegram is the meeting of Stevenson, McCloy, and Yost with Kuznetzov.
——. Telegram for Stevenson and David McCloy, 7 December 1962. Confidential document declassified, 10 August 1974.
——. Airgram memo from Embassy of El Salvador, first secretary of the embassy, Robert M. Philips, to Department of State. Information passed on to U.S. embassies in Guatemala, Madrid, Managua, Mexico, San Jose, Tegucigalpa, Panama. Date: 29 April 1964. Confidential airgram declassified 16 September 1975. Subject of the airgram is anti-Castro Cuban groups announcing government in exile.
——. *Bulletin*. Vol. 54, pp. 707–713, 2 May 1966. "Review of Movement of Cuban Refugees and Hemisphere Policy Toward Cuba." Statement by Robert M. Sayre.
——. *Bulletin*. Vol. 69, no. 1795. 19 November 1973. Messages exchanged by President Kennedy and Chairman Khrushchev during the Cuban Missile Crisis of October 1962.
——. *United States Treaties and Other International Agreements, vol. 28, part 6, 1976–1977*. Washington, D.C.: Government Printing Office, 1978.

U.S., Department of State. From Washington to New York, from E.S. Little. Telegram concerns interview with Che Guevara and Department of State response and interpretation. Reference no. 439F.

——. Airgram to the United States Department of State from American embassy in San Salvador. Subject: A statistical framework for understanding the violence in El Salvador. 15 January 1982.

——. George Shultz, Secretary of State. Address before the Washington Plenary Meeting of the Trilateral Commission. "Power and Diplomacy in the 1980's." Distributed 3 April 1984.

U.S., Department of State and Department of Defense. *Background Paper: Nicaragua's Military Buildup and Support for Central American Subversion.* Released 18 July 1984, Washington, D.C.

U.S., National Security Council. Notes and background paper on Tunisia, Morocco, Algeria, 3 October 1956. Classification: secret. Declassified 4 March 1981.

——, Department of Defense. *Soviet Military Power,* 2d ed. Washington, D.C.: U.S. Government Printing Office, March 1983.

——, White House. *White House Digest.* "Soviet/Cuban Threat and Buildup in the Caribbean." Washington, D.C.: White House Office of Media Relations and Planning, July 6, 1983.

University of Pittsburgh Center for Latin American Studies. *Cuban Studies/Estudios Cubanos.* Published twice yearly, January and July.

Valdés, Nelson P. "Cuba: Socialismo democrático o burocratismo colectivista?" *Aportes* (Paris) 23 (January 1972).

——. "Revolution and Institutionalization in Cuba." *Cuban Studies* 6, issue 1 (January 1976).

Valenta, Jiri. "The Soviet-Cuban Alliance in Africa and the Caribbean." *The World Today* (London), Royal Institute of International Affairs. Vol. 37, no. 2, February 1981, pp. 45–53.

Valenta, Jiri, and Valenta, Virginia. "Soviet Strategy and Policies in the Caribbean Basin." In Howard Wiarda, *Rift and Revolution: The Central American Imbroglio.* Washington: American Enterprise Institute, 1984, pp. 197–252.

Vellinza, M.E. "The Military and the Dynamics of the Cuban Revolutionary Process." *Comparative Politics* 8, issue 2 (January 1976).

Volsky, George. "Cuban Foreign Policy." *Current History* 70, no. 413 (1976).

Zafesov, G. "Cuba: Signs of Momentous Changes." *International Affairs* (Moscow) 9 (September 1974).

Zeitlin, Maurice. "Inside Cuba: Workers and Revolution." *Ramparts* 8 (March 1970).

Zorn, Jean G., and Mayerson, Harold A. "Cuba's Joint Venture Law: New Rules for Foreign Investment," *Columbia Journal of Transnational Law.* (New York) Vol. 21, no. 2, 1983.

Cuban Newspapers and Periodicals

Adelante (Camaguey)
ANAP (National Association of Small Peasants: Havana)
Bohemia (Havana)

Cuba Internacional (Havana)
Con la Guardia en Alto (Committees for the Defense of the Revolution: Havana)
Granma Weekly Review (Communist party: Havana)
Granma (Communist party: Havana)
Juventud Rebelde (Young Communist League: Havana)
Juventud Técnica (Havana)
Mujeres (Federation of Cuban Women: Havana)
Opina (Institute of Internal Demand: Havana)
Pionero (Cuban Pioneers' Union: Havana)
Sierra Maestra (Santiago de Cuba)
Vanguardia (Matanzas)
Venceremos (Guantánamo)
Verde Olivo (Revolutionary Armed Forces: Havana)

Index

AALAPSO (Afro-Asian and Latin American Peoples Solidarity Organization), 28
Abdelazziz, Mohamed, 116
Abreu, Ramiro, 65
Abshire, David M., 87
Acheson, Dean, 154
AD (Democratic Action) (Venezuela), 28, 29, 59, 65, 73, 156, 157, 158, 159
AEFU (All Ethiopia Farmers' Union), 102
Afghanistan, 47, 52, 67, 115, 116, 158, 160
African policy, costs of Cuba's, 102-106, 143
Agramonte, Ignacio, 3, 5
AIE *(A la Izquierda Estudiantil)*, 13
Alberto Consalvi, Simon, 73
Albizu Campos, Pedro, 6, 22
Alessandri, Arturo, 32
Alfonsín, Raúl, 159
Algeria, 83, 102
All-Ethiopia Trade Union, 97
Allende Gossens, Salvador, 32-33, 44, 45, 156, 157
Alliance for Progress, 29, 59
Alvarez Córdoba, Enrique, 61
Alves, Nito, 89
Aman Andom, 96
ANAPO (National Popular Alliance) (Colombia), 67
Anarchist party, 13
Anarchist-Syndicalist movement, 11
Andino, Mario Antonio, 60
ANEC (National Association of Economists of Cuba), 75
Angola, 46, 53, 83-91, 95, 101, 102, 103, 104-105, 106, 114, 118, 122-123, 143, 158, 161, 165, 168
Angolan People's Union, 84
APRA (Popular American Revolutionary Alliance) (Peru), 26, 28, 29
Araujo, Arturo, 58
Arce, José, 11

ARDE (Revolutionary Democratic Alliance) (Nicaragua), 52
ARENA party (El Salvador), 60
ARG (Acción Revolucionaria Guiteras), 17
Argentina, 10, 11, 24, 32, 33, 43, 44, 45, 71-73, 74, 75, 76, 151, 157-158, 159
Arias Stella, Javier, 73
Armed forces, Cuban, 8, 121-123, 143, 158, 161
Armed Forces Movement (Portugal), 84
Asencio, Diego, 68, 75
Atnafu Abate, 96
Austria, 6, 115, 144
Auténtico party, 17

Bacon, Robert, 8-9, 152
Bahamas, the, 48
Bahía Honda, 7, 8, 9
Bahr, Egon, 104
Balari, Eugenio, 162
Bangladesh, 116
Barbados, 45
Barnes, Michael D., 63
Barnet, José Antonio, 15
Bateman Cayón, Jaime, 67, 69-70
Batista y Zaldívar, Fulgencio, 4, 13, 14, 15, 16, 17-18, 41, 58, 106, 117, 121, 153, 154-155
Bay of Pigs invasion (1961), 33, 106, 156, 168
Beaulac, Willard L., 153-154, 155
Belgium, 84, 85, 115
Berríos Martínez, Rubén, 6, 23, 70
Betancourt, Ernesto, 43, 156
Betancourt, Rómulo, 25, 28, 30, 31, 157
Betancur Cuartas, Belisario, 69
Bishop, Maurice, 46, 47, 158
Blanco, Rogaldo, 100
Bogotá, Colombia, 23
Bogotazo, the (1948), 23, 66, 71

Bolívar, Simón, 6, 76
Bolivia, 3, 10, 13, 22, 24, 28, 29, 30, 32, 34, 35, 43, 153, 157, 158
Bonsal, Philip, 14
Boorstein, Edward, 128
Bosch Gaviño, Juan, 23, 31
Botha, P.W., 90
Bowdler, William D., 50
Boyatt, Thomas D., 69
Braden, Spruille, 43
Bras, Juan Mari, 70
Bravo, Douglas, 30, 31
Bravo, Flavio, 45, 87
Brazil, 24, 32, 33, 35, 43, 73, 76, 159
Bridge, John, 164
Britain. *See* Great Britain
Brizola, Lionel da Moria, 33
Bru, Federico Laredo, 15
Bryan, William Jennings, 7
Burma, 116

CACM (Central American Common Market), 59
Caetano, Marcello, 84, 85, 86
Caldera Rodríguez, Rafael, 44, 65
Calderío, Francisco. *See* Roca Calderío, Blas
Calvani, Aristides, 65
Cambodia. *See* Kampuchea
Cámpora, Héctor J., 72
Canada, 44, 46, 51, 104, 144
Carazo, Rodrigo, 48
Carbó, Sergio, 14
Cárdenas, Lázaro, 16, 113, 156
Caribbean Legion (La Legión del Caribe), 17
CARIBEX, 131
Carlucci, Frank C., 63
Carter, Jimmy, 49, 60, 97, 165
Casey, William, 63
Castro, Fidel: address to U.N. (1979), 143; aid to Africa and, 104, 106; Allende and, 32-33; Angola and, 87, 89; armed forces and, 121-122; arrest and imprisonment of (1953), 18; attacks on Communists, 29; attempts to assassinate, 164, 169; Batista and, 18; Betancourt (Ernesto) and, 43, 156; Betancourt (Rómulo) and, 25, 28, 30, 157; Bishop and, 47; the *bogotazo* (1948) and, 23, 66; CEPAL and, 43; CMEA and, 134; Communist party and, 24, 106, 113, 119, 155-156, 159; Constitution of 1975 and, 119, 120; Council on Foreign Relations and, 43; Cuban dependence on the Soviet Union and, 169; Debray and, 28-29, 76; Declaration of Havana (1960) and, 42; difference between Guevara and, 27; Dominican Republic guerrilla movement (1947) and, 23; Eisenhower and, 43, 156; El Salvador and, 62; ELN and, 66; Eritrea and, 99; Escalante and, 113; Ethiopian-Somali dispute and, 98-99; Figueres and, 25-26, 157; *foco* guerrilla movement and, 34-35; Fonseca and, 48; foreign policy goals of, 170-171; foreign policy tools of, 120-121; Gaitán and, 66; *Granma* landing (1956) and, 18; Haig and, 165; Haya de la Torre and, 28; Herter and, 42; Latin American communism and, 27-18, 31-32; Majano and, 65; Mao and, 113; Martí and, 5, 151- 152; Marxism and, 41; Masferrer and, 16; Mella and, 11; Monada army barracks and, 18; NAM and, 46, 73; 1960s revolutionary strategy of, 24, 26-27; Nixon and, 43; OLAS and, 29; Operation Falcon (Venezuela) and, 24, 30-31; Ortodoxo party and, 17; Paz and, 28; Pazos and, 156; Prebisch and, 75; release from prison (1955), 18; Royo and, 65-66; Sandinistas and, 48; Second Declaration of Havana and, 44, 156; Sierra Maestra guerrilla campaign (1956-58) and, 18; Social Democratic movements and, 28; South Atlantic crisis and, 71, 73; strained Cuban-Soviet relations and, 162-163; student experiences of, 22-23; Torrijos and, 65; trade and, 141; Tri-Continental Conference (1966) and, 29; trial (1953) of, 117; Trujillo and, 48; Twenty-sixth of July Movement and, 18; U.N. and, 42, 43; Urrutia-Lleó and, 155; visits to the U.S., 42-43, 156; Walters and, 165
Castro, Raúl, 121, 122
Catholic Church. *See* Roman Catholic Church
Cayo Confites, 16, 23
CDRs (Committees for the Defense of the Revolution), 47, 161
CELU (Confederation of Ethiopian Labor Unions), 97
Central American dictatorships, Cuban opposition to, 90
CEPAL (U.N. Economic Commission on Latin America), 43
Cerezo, Vinicio, 65
Céspedes, Carlos Manuel de, 3, 5, 14
Chaco War (Bolivia-Paraguay, 1932-35), 3; Cuba and the, 13, 153
Chamorro, Pedro Joaquin, 49
Ch'en Yi, 113
Cheysson, Claude, 115
Chibás, Eduardo, 15, 17
Chile, 10, 24, 28, 32, 43, 44, 45, 69, 73, 157
China, People's Republic of (PRC), 27, 41, 67, 85, 86, 113-114, 159, 164, 166, 167

330 • *Cuban Foreign Policy*

Christian Democratic party(ies): Chile, 32; Costa Rica, 48; El Salvador (PDC), 58, 59, 60, 65; Guatemala, 65; Venezuela, 59
CIA (Central Intelligence Agency), 52, 63, 70, 86
Cienfuegos, Cuba, 7, 162–163, 164
Cienfuegos, Osmani, 28
CIES (Inter-American Economic and Social Council), 44
Clark, William, 90
CMEA (Council for Mutual Economic Assistance), 127, 128, 132–135, 136, 137, 139, 140, 141, 157, 169, 170
CNOC (Cuban National Workers Confederation), 12
Colombia, 6, 10, 13, 21, 22, 23, 24, 27, 44, 66–70, 73, 157
Communist party(ies): anti-Communist feelings in Cuba, 17, 29–30, 66, 155; Bolivia, 28; Castro and the, 24, 106, 113, 119, 155–156, 159; Colombia (PCC), 66, 67; Cuba, 11, 12, 15, 16, 24, 30, 53, 74, 75, 106, 113, 118–119, 122, 155–156, 163; Cuban Revolution and the, 50; El Salvador (PCS), 57, 58, 61; Latin American communism, 27, 28, 29, 31, 32; opposition to guerrilla movements, 35; students and the, 13; Venezuela (PCV), 28, 31
Congo, People's Republic of the, 30, 86, 87, 90, 101, 143
Conservative party (Colombia), 69
Constitution of Guainaro (1869), 5
Constitutions, Cuban, 41; (1901), 7, 152, 154; (1940), 16, 117, 154, 155; (1975), 117, 118–120, 155; Fundamental Law of 1959, 42, 118, 155
Contadora initiative, 167
Coolidge, Calvin, 12
Corona, Eduardo, 23
Corruption, Cuban, 8–9, 10, 11, 14, 153, 154
Cortina, José Manuel, 16
COSEP (Supreme Council of Private Enterprise), 49
Costa Méndez, Nicanor, 72–73, 74
Costa Rica, 21, 25–26, 32, 42, 44, 46, 48, 49, 50, 57, 157
Council on Foreign Relations, 43
Crocker, Chester, 91
Crowder, Enoch, 10
Cruz, Arturo J., 52
CUBAEXPORT, 131
CUBANIQUEL, 131
Cuban Peoples (Ortodoxo) party, 17, 18
Cuban relations with: Afghanistan, 116, 158; Algeria, 83; Angola, 46, 83, 85, 86, 87–91, 95, 101, 102, 103, 105, 106, 114, 118, 122–123, 143, 158, 161, 163, 165, 168; Argentina, 33, 43, 44, 45, 71–73, 74, 75, 76, 151, 157–158, 159; Austria, 6, 115, 144; the Bahamas, 48; Bangladesh, 116; Barbados, 45; Belgium, 115; Bolivia, 2, 3, 13, 22, 24, 30, 32, 43, 157, 158; Brazil, 43, 76, 159; Burma, 116; Canada, 44, 46, 104, 144; Chile, 32–33, 44, 45, 69, 157; China, 41, 43, 113–114, 159; Colombia, 6, 21, 22, 44, 66–70, 157; Congo, the, 30, 90, 101, 143; Costa Rica, 21, 25–26, 44, 46, 48, 157; Cyprus, 115; Czechoslovakia, 170; Denmark, 115; Dominican Republic, 22, 24, 48, 75, 156, 157; Ecuador, 21, 43, 76, 159; El Salvador, 44, 45, 51, 52, 57, 62, 63, 64–65, 66, 68, 158, 159, 163, 166, 170; Ethiopia, 83, 90, 95, 97, 98, 99, 100–102, 103, 105, 106, 118, 143, 158, 165, 168, 169; Finland, 115; France, 6, 10, 115, 144; Germany, 6, 8, 10, 16, 17; Great Britain, 6, 71–72, 74, 115, 144; Greece, 115; Grenada, 44, 46–47, 158, 159, 163; Guatemala, 22, 44, 52, 157; Guinea-Bissau, 90; Haiti, 22, 24, 156, 157; Honduras, 44, 45, 65; Iceland, 115; India, 116; Iran, 116; Iraq, 116; Israel, 116; Italy, 6, 16, 115; Jamaica, 21, 44, 45, 70; Japan, 16, 114, 140, 144, 153; Jordan, 116; Kampuchea, 115, 159; Kuwait, 116; Laos, 115; Lebanon, 116; Luxembourg, 115; Malaysia, 115; Maldives, 115; Malta, 115; Mexico, 3, 5, 6, 16, 33, 43, 44, 45, 46, 140, 157; Mongolia, 114; Morocco, 116; Mozambique, 90, 101, 159; Namibia, 158, 168; Nepal, 116; Netherlands, 115; Nicaragua, 21, 22, 24, 44, 45, 48–53, 63, 64, 65, 68, 75, 157, 158, 159, 166, 170; North Korea, 114; Norway, 115; the OAS, 18, 21, 22, 42, 43, 44, 45, 72, 74, 128, 156, 157, 158, 165; the OAU, 46, 103; Oman, 116–117; Pakistan, 116; Panama, 22, 24, 26, 45, 46, 65, 66, 75, 156, 157; Paraguay, 3, 13; Peru, 21, 22, 26–27, 44, 45, 48, 157; Portugal, 115; Puerto Rico, 6, 22–23, 70; Rhodesia, 143; Sahara Arab Republic, 116; Somalia, 97, 98, 169; South Africa, 88, 103, 158, 168; South Yemen, 116–117; the Soviet Union, 5, 6, 12, 16–17, 22, 28, 29, 32, 47, 70, 75, 89, 102–103, 113, 114, 115, 127, 128, 134, 135, 136, 137, 138, 139, 141, 142, 151, 156, 157, 158, 159, 160, 161, 162–163, 164, 166, 170–171; Spain, 4–5, 15–16, 22, 115, 140, 144, 151, 152, 170, 171; Sri Lanka, 115, 116; Sweden, 115; Switzerland, 115, 144, 160; Syria, 116; Tanzania, 101; Thailand, 115; Trinidad and Tobago, 44, 45, 69; Turkey,

116; the U.N. 18, 42, 45, 46, 64, 67–68, 70, 114, 128, 143, 162, 168, 170; the U.S., 3–5, 6–7, 8–10, 11, 12–13, 14, 15, 16, 17–18, 22, 28, 29, 33, 41–43, 47–48, 62, 63, 64, 65, 69, 70, 72, 73, 74, 103, 115, 117, 128, 134, 151, 152, 153–156, 157, 158, 159–160, 162, 163–171; Uruguay, 44, 76, 159; the Vatican, 115; Venezuela, 5–6, 7, 21, 22, 24, 30–31, 32, 44, 45, 48, 156, 157, 158, 159; Vietnam, 115; West Germany, 115, 144; Yemen, 116, 159; Yugoslavia, 115; Zaire, 165; Zanzibar, 83
Cuban Revolutionary party, 5
CUBARTESANIA, 131
CUBATOBACO, 131
CUBAZUCAR, 131
Cyprus, 115
Czechoslovakia, 170

D'Aubisson, Roberto, 60, 65, 66
De la Torre, Carlos, 11
Debray, Régis, 25, 28–29, 30–32, 33, 34–35, 76, 114
Debt, Cuba's, 138–140, 142, 144, 160
Declaration of Havana (1960), 42; Second Declaration of Havana, 44, 156
Del Pino, Rafael, 23
Denmark, 115
Dergue (Armed Forces Coordinating Committee) (Ethiopia), 96, 97, 100
D'Escoto, Miguel, 49, 50, 51
Díaz Arguellas, Raul, 87
Dillon, C. Douglas, 29
Dobrynin, Anatoly, 164
Dominican Republic, 10, 22, 23, 25, 31, 48, 68, 73, 75, 156, 157
Dos Santos, José Eduardo, 88, 89, 105, 168
DRU (United Unified Revolutionary Directorate) (El Salvador), 62
Durate, José Napoleón, 59, 61, 64, 65, 66, 158
Duzán Maria Jimena, 70

East Germany, 50, 52. *See also* Germany; West Germany
ECLA (Economic Commission for Latin America), 75; Cuba and, 114
Economic aid from Cuba, 10, 44, 45, 50, 83, 100–104, 118, 143
Economy, Cuban, 41–42, 45, 46, 51, 104–105, 114, 127, 135, 141–142, 153–155, 157, 160–161, 169; U.S. investment in, 3, 8, 10, 12, 16, 42, 103, 153–154, 156. *See also* Trade, Cuban
Ecuador, 10, 21, 24, 43, 45, 76, 159

Egypt, 98
Eisenhower, Dwight D., 42, 43, 152, 156
El Salvador, 10, 44, 45, 51, 52, 53, 57–66, 68, 71, 158, 159, 163, 165, 166, 170
ELF, the (ELF-RC, Revolutionary Council) (Eritrea), 98–99
ELF-PLF (Eritrean Liberation Front–Popular Liberation Front), 99
ELN (Colombian Army of National Liberation), 66, 67, 68
Embargo (1962) against Cuba, 156, 164, 165, 167–168
England. *See* Great Briatin
EPL (Popular Army of Liberation) (Colombia), 67
EPLA (Eritrean People's Army), 99
EPLF (Eritrean People's Liberation Front) (Ethiopia), 95, 99
Eritrea region (Ethiopia), 95, 96, 97, 98–99, 100, 102, 103, 163
ERP (People's Revolutionary Army (El Salvador), 59, 61
Escalante, Aníbal, 13, 30, 113, 163
Estrada-Palma, Tomás, 7–9, 152
Ethiopia, 53, 64, 65, 83, 90, 95–102, 105, 106, 118, 143, 158, 168, 169

Falange (El Salvador), 60
Falkland Islands/Islas Malvinas, 23. *See also* South Atlantic crisis
FAR (Fuerzas Armadas Revolucionaria) (Revolutionary Armed Forces), 121
FARC (Colombian Revolutionary Armed Forces), 67, 69
FARN (Armed Forces of National Liberation) (El Salvador), 59
FDN (Revolutionary Democratic Force) (Nicaragua), 52
FDR (Democratic Revolutionary Front) (El Salvador), 57, 60–62, 65
Febres Cordero, Leon, 159
FECCAS (Christian Peasant's Federation) (El Salvador), 59
Fernández Font, Marcelo, 138
Figueres Ferrer, José, 25–26, 157
Finland, 115
FMLN (Farabundo Martí National Liberation Front) (El Salvador), 57, 61–62, 65
FNLA (National Front for the Liberation of Angola), 84, 86, 87, 88, 89
Foco guerrilla movement, 24, 30, 34–35
Fonesca Amador, Carlos, 48
Ford, Gerald, 165
Foreign Policy Association, 60

Foreign policy decision making, Cuban, 117–123; Castro and, 120–121, 170–171; ideological/political motivations of, 106
FPL (Popular Liberation Forces) (El Salvador), 59, 61
Franca, Porfirio, 14
France, 6, 10, 13, 52, 65, 115, 144
Franqui, Carlos, 23
Frei Montalva, Eduardo, 32
Frondizi, Arturo, 33
FSLN. *See* Sandinista National Liberation Front
Fundamental Law (1959), 42, 118

Gairy, Eric, 46
Gaitán, Jorge Eliécer, 66
García Frías, Guillermo, 116
García Marquéz, Gabriel, 88
GATT (General Agreement on Tariffs and Trade), 114, 128
Germany, 6, 8, 10, 13, 16, 17. *See also* East Germany; West Germany
Gómez, José Miguel, 9–10, 13
Gómez, Miguel Mariano, 15
Good Neighbor Policy, 13
Goodwin, Richard, 33
Goulart, João, 32, 33
Granma landing (1956), 18
Granma Weekly Review, 119, 120, 121, 162
Grau San Martín, Ramón, 14, 15, 17, 23
Great Britain, 6, 23, 71–72, 74, 76, 84, 96, 115, 144
Greece, 115
Grenada, 44, 46–47, 158, 159, 163
Grito de Yara rebellion, 5
Group of 77, the, 45
Guantánamo, 7, 8, 10, 15, 152, 168
Guatemala, 22, 27, 33, 44, 52, 157
Guerra, Ramiro, 153
Guerrilla movements, 18, 99, 157, 166; Cuban support for, 21, 22, 23, 24–26, 28, 29, 30–31, 34–35, 43, 44, 46, 48–53, 57, 62–70, 89, 97, 98, 103, 116, 156, 158, 163, 165, 167–168
Guevara, Ernesto (Che), 22, 27, 29, 30, 31–32, 33, 34, 41, 113, 157
Guggenheim, Harry F., 12–13
Guillén, Nicolás, 16
Guinea-Bissau, 90
Guiteras, Antonio, 15, 17
Gutiérrez, Jaime Abdul, 60

Haig, Alexander, 62, 165
Haile Selassie I, 95, 96, 97, 99
Hailu Kebede, 97, 101
Haiti, 22, 25, 27, 156, 157
Hassan Mahmud, Abdullahi, 98

Havana Radio, 71
Havana Youth Conference (1960), 41, 42
Haya de la Torre, Víctor Raúl, 26, 28, 29
Hearst, William Randolph, 6
Hernández Martínex, Maximiliano, 58
Herrera Campíns, Luís, 59, 65
Herter, Christian, 42
Hevia, Carlos, 15
Hinton, Deane, 60
Holland. *See* Netherlands
Honduras, 27, 44, 45, 52, 59, 65, 73
Hoover, Herbert, 13
Hull, Cordell, 14
Hungary, 50

IBEC (International Bank for Economic Co-operation), 133
Iceland, 115
IIB (International Investment Bank), 133
Independence from Spain, Cuban war of (1895–98), 4–7, 152
India, 115, 116
INRA (Institute of Agrarian Reform), 41
Institute of Internal Demand, 162
Iran, 116
Iraq, 64, 116
Irisarri, José María, 14
ISA (International Sugar Agreement), 128, 136–138, 142
Isle of Pines/Isle of Youth, 7, 90
Israel, 116
Italy, 6, 16, 96, 115

Jamaica, 21, 44, 45, 48, 70, 73
Japan, 16, 114, 115, 140, 144, 153
Johnson, Lyndon, 164
Jordan, 116
Jóven Cuba, 17
Juárez, Benito, 5
JUCEPLAN (Junta Central de Planificación), 131

Kampuchea (Cambodia), 115, 159
Kennedy, John F., 29, 31, 156
Kennedy administration, 59, 164
Kenya, 98
Kissinger, Henry, 164
Kuwait, 116

Laos, 115
Latin American League of Students, 11
Lebanon, 116
Legum, Colin, 103
Lemos Simmones, Carlos, 67
Liberal party, 11
Libya, 51, 98
López Migoya, Manuel, 14

López, Narcisco, 6
Lusinchi, Jaime, 159
Luxembourg, 115

Maceo, Antonio, 3
Machadato, the, 14
Machado, Gerardo, 11-12, 13, 14-15, 16, 17, 153
McKinley, William, 7, 152
Maderne, Feliciano, 23
Magaña, Alvaro, 66
Magoon, Charles E., 9
Maine, U.S.S., 4
Majano Ramos, Adolfo Arnoldo, 60, 64, 65
Malaysia, 115
Maldives, 116
Malmierca Peoli, Isidoro, 64, 74, 90-91, 116
Malta, 115
Malvinas, Islas/Falkland Islands, 23. *See also* South Atlantic crisis
Manifesto of Monte Cristi, 5
Manley, Michael, 70
Mao Zedong, 113
Márquez Sterling, Manuel, 15
Martí, Agustín Farabundo, 58
Martí, José, 3, 5, 21, 151-152
Martínez Sáenz, Joaquín, 17
Masferrer, Rolando, 16
Matanza (El Salvador massacre, 1932), 57
Mauroy, Pierre, 115
Mayorga Quiróz, Román, 60
Mella, Julio Antonio, 11, 12, 153
Mendieta, Carlos, 15
Menelik II, 95
Mengistu Haile Mariam, 83, 89, 95, 96, 97, 99, 100, 101, 102, 103, 106, 163, 165
Menocal, Mario García, 10, 13
Mexican Revolution (1910), 58
Mexico, 3, 5, 6, 10, 12, 13, 16, 33, 43, 45, 46, 51, 57, 59, 65, 67-68, 73, 113, 140, 157, 167
Military aid from Cuba, 21, 47, 49, 50, 53, 62, 63, 64-65, 83, 85, 86, 87-91, 95, 97, 98, 99, 102-103, 105, 116, 118, 121, 122-123, 143, 156, 158, 161, 163, 165, 166, 168, 169-170
Miller, Edward G., Jr., 155
MINCEX (Ministry of Foreign Trade), 131
MINFAR (Ministry of Revolutionary Armed Forces), 53
MINREX (Ministry of Foreign Relations), 21, 87
MINSAP (Ministry of Public Health), 101
Missile crisis (1962), 113, 156, 162
Mitterand, François, 115
M-19 (Nineteenth of April movement) (Colombia), 66-70

MNR (National Revolutionary Movement) (Bolivia), 28, 29
MNR (National Revolutionary Movement) (El Salvador), 58
MOEL (Worker, Student, and Peasant Movement) (Colombia), 67
Molina Barraza, Arturo Armando, 59
Moncada army barracks, 18
Monge, Luis Alberto, 48
Mongolia, 114
Monroe Doctrine, 8, 9; Roosevelt Corollary to the, 8
Monroe, James, 8, 9, 13
Montane Oropesa, Jesus, 74-75
Morales Bermúdez, Francisco, 27
Morgan, J.P., 12
Morgan, Stokely, 12
Morocco, 116
Moss, Ambler H., 57
Mozambique, 86, 90, 91, 101, 159
MPLA (Popular Movement for the Liberation of Angola), 84, 85, 86, 87, 88, 89, 102, 103, 105, 158
MSR (Movimiento Socialista Revolucionaria), 17, 23
Muñoz Ledo, Porfirio, 68

NAM (Non-Aligned Movement), 47, 67, 73, 74, 90, 103, 104, 114-115, 159; Cuba and the, 46, 71-72, 73, 74, 90, 103, 104, 114-115, 159
Namibia, 86, 87, 90, 91, 105, 158, 168
NAMUCAR (Caribbean Multinaitonal Shipping Enterprise), 45, 114
Nasser, Ahmad Muhammad, 98
National Front (Colombia), 66
National Liberation party (Costa Rica), 25
Nationalization of foreign property by Cuba, 41-42, 156
Nepal, 116
Netherlands, 51, 115
Neto, Antônio Agostinho, 83, 87, 88, 89, 106
New Jewel movement (Grenada), 46, 47, 158
Nicaragua, 21, 22, 25, 44, 45, 46, 48-53, 63, 64, 65, 68, 75, 157, 158, 159, 165, 166, 168, 170
Nineteenth of April movement (Colombia). *See* M-19
Nipé, 7
Nixon, Richard, 43, 85, 156
Nixon administration, 159-160, 164
North Korea, 114
Norway, 115
Noyola, Juan, 75
Nur, Ramadan Muhammad, 99

OAS (Organization of American States), 33, 49; Cuba and the, 18, 21, 22, 42, 43, 44, 45, 72, 74, 128, 156, 157, 158, 165
OAU (Organization of African Unity), 46, 88, 103, 116
Ochoa Sanchez, Arnaldo T., 52-53
Ogaden region (Ethiopia), 95, 97, 98, 99, 101
OLAS (Latin American Solidarity Organization), 29
Oman, 116-117
OPEC (Organization of Petroleum Exporting Countries), 27
Operation Carlota (Angola), 88
Operation Falcón (Venezuela), 21, 24, 30-31, 156
Operation Zulu (Angola), 87
Opina, 162
Oramas Oliva, Oscar, 87, 88
ORDEN (Order) (El Salvador), 60
Orfila, Alejandro, 74
Organization for Economic Cooperation and Development, 104
Ortega, Daniel, 53
Ortodoxo (Cuban Peoples) party, 17, 18
Osman Saleh Sabbe, 99
Osorio, Oscar, 58
Ospina, Ivan Marino, 69-70
Ovimbundu tribe (Angola), 84, 89

Padillo, Heberto, 30
PAHO (Pan-American Health Organization), 45, 114
Pakistan, 116
Pan-American Conference: 1928 (Havana), 12; 1948 (Bogotá, Colombia), 23
Panama, 13, 22, 24, 25, 26, 45, 46, 49, 50, 65, 73, 75, 156, 157
Panama Canal, 4
Papandreou, Andreas, 115
Paraguay, 10, 27; Chaco War (1935), 3, 13, 153
Partido Liberación (Costa Rica), 48
Pastora Gómez, Edén (Commandante Cero), 52
Paz Estenssoro, Víctor, 28
Pazos, Felipe, 156
PCC (Colombian Communist party), 67
PCN (Party of National Conciliation) (El Salvador), 58, 59
PCS (Communist party in El Salvador), 57, 58, 61
PCV (Communist Party of Venezuela), 31
PDC (Christian Democratic party) (El Salvador), 48, 59, 65
Pedraza, José, 14
Pentarquía, the, 14, 15
Peoples Militia, 161

Pérez Jiménez, Marcos, 25, 31
Perón, Juan Domingo, 23, 33, 72
Peru, 10, 21, 22, 24, 26-27, 28, 29, 32, 35, 44, 45, 48, 73, 157
Petkoff, Teodoro, 30-31
Pezzullo, Lawrence A., 24
Phillips, Ruby Hart, 15
Piñeiro, Manuel, 75
Pinilla, José Maria, 26
Pinochet Ugarte, Augusto, 69
PIP (Puerto Rican Independence party), 6, 70
Platt Amendment (1903), 3, 7, 13, 15, 152
Platt, Orville H., 7
Plaza, Galo, 45
PLO (Palestine Liberation Organization), 52; Cuba and the, 116
PMAC (Provisional Military Administrative Council) (Ethiopia), 96, 97, 98
PMG (Provisional Military Government) (Ethiopia), 96
Polisario Front (Sahara Arab Democratic Republic), 116
Portugal, 83-84, 85, 86, 88, 115
Prado y Ugarteche, Manuel, 26
Prebisch, Raúl, 75
Prío Socarrás, Carlos, 6, 17, 31, 117, 154
PRTC (Central American Revolutionary Workers' party), 61
PRUD (Revolutionary Party of Democratic Unification) (El Salvador), 58
PSP (Puerto Rican Socialist party), 70
Puerto Rican Solidarity Conference (Havana, 1975), 70
Puerto Rico, 4, 6, 22-23, 70, 75
Puerto Rico Pro-Independence Committee, 22
Pulitzer, Joseph, 6
Punta del Este (Uruguay) meetings, 29, 33, 43

Rabasa, Emilio, 45
Radio Havana, 162
"Radio Martí," 5, 152, 166
Reagan administration, 5, 52, 62, 91
Reagan, Ronald, 47-48, 62, 90, 117, 165, 166, 167
Revolución, 23
Revolution in the Revolution?, 30, 31, 34
Revolutionary Directorate, 23
Revolutionary Students' Congress, 11
Rhodesia, 143
Rio Treaty, 73
Rivera, Julio, 58
RN (National Resistance) (El Salvador), 59, 61
Rao García, Raúl, 13, 14
Roa Kourí, Raúl, 130
Roberto, Holden, 84, 86
Roca Calderío, Blas, 13, 16, 118

Rodríguez, Carlos Rafael, 13, 16, 23–24, 49, 50, 51, 64–65, 71, 75, 100, 114, 115, 121, 122, 162, 165
Rodríguez, Pablo, 14
Rodríguez Loeches, Enrique, 23
Roig de Leuchsenring, Emilio, 153
Rojas Pinilla, Gustavo, 67
Roman Catholic Church, 50, 59
Romero, Carlos Humberto, 59, 60, 62–63
Romero, Oscar Arnulfo, 59, 60
Roosevelt, Franklin D., 13, 14, 16
Roosevelt, Theodore, 7, 8, 9
Roosevelt Corollary (1904) to the Monroe Doctrine, 8
Root, Elihu, 9
Royo, Aristides, 65, 66, 73
Russia. *See* Soviet Union
Russian Revolution (1917), 12, 58

Sahara Arab Republic, 116
Saladrígas, Carlos, 17
Salazar, Antônio de Oliveira, 83–84, 86
SALF (Somali Abo Liberation Front), 98
Sánchez Hernández, Fidel, 59, 60
Sánchez Parodi, Ramón, 95, 100
Sandinista National Liberation Front (FSLN), 48, 49, 50, 51, 52, 53, 169
Sandino, Augusto César, 48–49
Sanguinetti, Julio María, 159
Sarney, José, 159
Saudi Arabia, 98
Savimbi, Jonas, 84, 88, 89, 102
Seaga, Edward, 48
SELA (Latin American Economic System), 45, 114, 138
Sepúlveda, Bernardo, 167
Shahi, Agha, 116
Sierra Maestra guerrilla campaign (1956–58), 18, 28
Smith, Wayne, 74
Social Democratic movements/parties: Cuba, 17; Latin American, 28, 29, 32; 48; El Salvador, 60
Socialist parties: Cuba, 11, 13; Puerto Rico (PSP), 70
Somalia, 95, 97, 98, 99, 169
Somoza Debayle, Anastasio, 46, 48, 49
Somoza García, Anastasio, 49
South Africa, 84, 85, 86, 88, 89, 90, 103, 158, 168
South Atlantic crisis, 69, 75, 114; Cuba and the, 71–73, 74, 76
South-West Africa. *See* Namibia
South Yemen. *See* Yemen, People's Democratic Republic of
Soviet Union, 27, 41, 44, 50–51, 52, 57, 61, 66, 67, 72, 73, 74, 85, 86, 88, 97, 99, 100, 105, 116, 117, 167, 168; Cuba and the, 5, 6, 12, 16–17, 22, 28, 29, 32, 47, 70, 75, 89, 102–103, 113, 114, 115, 127, 128, 134, 135, 136, 137, 138, 139, 141, 142, 151, 156, 157, 158, 159, 160, 161, 162–163, 164, 166, 170–171
Spain, 4–5, 15–16, 22, 31, 85, 115, 140, 144, 151, 152, 170, 171
Spanish-American War, 4
Spanish Civil War, 15–16
Sri Lanka, 115, 116
Stimson, Henry L., 12
Stockwell, John, 86
Students' Federation (FEU), 11
Sugar, 4, 10, 16, 17, 41, 42, 45, 100, 127, 128, 129, 130, 134, 135, 136–138, 139, 140, 141–142, 153, 156, 160–161, 169
SWAPO (South West Africa People's Organization), 90, 91, 168
Sweden, 51, 115
Switzerland, 115, 144, 160
Syria, 116
Szulc, Tad, 25

Taft, William H., 8–9, 152
Tafari Makonnen, Ras. *See* Haile Selassie I
Tanzania, 101
Teferi Banti, 96
Tahiland, 115
Thomas, Hugh, 13
Torres Restrepo, Camilo, 66
Torrijos Herrera, Omar, 46, 49, 65
Trade, Cuban, 127–131, 160–161, 164, 167–168, 169, 170; international agreements and, 138–144; with nonsocialist countries, 136–138; with socialist countries, 131–136, 157. *See also* Economy, Cuban
Treaty of Paris (1898), 4, 152
Tri-Continental Conference (1966), 28
Trinidad and Tobago, 44, 45, 69
Trudeau, Pierre, 46
Trujillo Molina, Rafael Leonidas, 23, 48
Truman, Harry S., 154
Turbay Ayala, Julio César, 68, 69
Turkey, 116
Twenty-sixth of July Movement, 18, 23, 43, 50, 53, 155

UDN (National Democratic Union) (El Salvador), 58, 59
UIR (Unión Insurrecional Revolucionaria), 17, 23
UNCTAD (United Nations Conference on Trade and Development), 114
UNDP (United Nations Development Program), 114

UNESCO (United Nations Educational, Scientific, and Cultural Organization), 114
Ungo Revelo, Guillermo Manuel, 60, 61
Unidad Popular (Chile), 28
UNIDO (United Nations Industrial Development Organization), 142
UNITA (National Union for the Total Independence of Angola), 84, 85, 86, 87, 88, 89
United Front of South Yemen, 102
United Kingdom. *See* Great Britain
United Nations, 43, 47, 73, 85, 90, 96, 100, 115, 142; Cuba and the, 18, 42, 45, 46, 64, 67–68, 70, 114, 128, 143, 162, 168, 170
United States: Africa and the, 84, 85, 86–87, 97–98, 105, 106; anti-American feeling in Cuba, 162; Bay of Pigs invasion (1961), 33, 156, 168; Castro's visits to the, 42–43, 156; Costa Rica and the, 48; Cuban-Soviet alliance and the, 163–165, 168, 169–170; Cuba's African involvement and the, 103; Cuba's aid to South Yemen and the, 117; Cuba's aid to Vietnam and the, 115; El Salvador and the, 59, 60, 61, 62–65, 158, 165; Grenada and, 47; interrelationship of U.S. and Cuban interests, 166–167; intervention in Cuban internal affairs, 3, 4–5, 8, 9, 11, 12–13, 14–15, 17–18, 22, 152, 153–155; investment in Cuban economy, 3, 8, 10, 12, 16, 42, 103, 153–154, 156; military aid to Cuba, 3; military bases in Cuba, 6–7, 8, 9–10; missile crisis, 113, 156, 162; Monroe Doctrine, 8, 9; nationalization of U.S. property by Cuba, 41–42, 156; Nicaragua and the, 49–50, 51, 52, 53, 165; OAS and the, 42; occupation (1906–1909) of Cuba, 9–10, 152; opposition to guerrilla movements, 24, 29, 31, 35, 44, 49–50, 51, 52, 53, 62–65, 66, 69, 97–98, 103, 117; Platt Amendment, 7, 15, 152; pro-American feeling in Cuba, 162; provisional government in Cuba, 9; Puerto Rico and the, 70; Roosevelt Corollary (1904) to the Monroe Doctrine, 8; South Atlantic crisis and the, 69, 72, 73, 74, 75; Soviet Union and the, 115; Spanish-American war and the, 4, 6; rising tensions with Cuba, 157; strategies for U.S. policymakers in dealing with Cuba, 167–171; trade embargo of Cuba (1962), 156, 164, 165, 167–168; trade with Cuba, 4, 10, 16, 41, 42, 134, 137, 156, 169; Venezuela and the, 27, 156; view of Cuban affairs, 159–160; White Paper on Cuba (1961), 43; White Paper on El Salvador (1981), 62–65, 165
UNO (National Opposition Union) (El Salvador), 59, 60
Urrutia-Lleó, Manuel, 31, 155
Urrútia Parilla, Bolívar, 26
Uruguay, 10, 13, 24, 32, 44, 76, 159

Vaky, Viron P., 63
Vance, Cyrus, 97
Vatican, the, 115
Veiga Menendez, Roberto, 161
Velasco Alvarado, Juan, 26, 27
Venezuela, 10, 27, 43, 49; AD, 28, 29, 59, 65, 73, 156, 157, 158, 159; Cuba and, 5–6, 7, 21, 22, 24, 30–31, 32, 44, 45, 48, 156, 157, 158, 159
Versailles Summit Conference (1982), 115
Vides Cassanova, Carlos Eugenio, 65
Vietnam, 64, 65, 115
Voice of America, 152

Walters, Vernon, 165
Welles, Sumner, 14, 15, 16
West Germany, 51, 104, 115, 144. *See also* East Germany; Germany
White, Robert, 62, 63
White Paper on Cuba (1961), 43
White Paper on El Salvador (1981), 62–65, 165
Williams, Eric, 44
Wilson, Woodrow, 10
Wood, Leonard, 6–7, 8, 152
World War I, 3, 10, 152–153
World War II, 16–17, 153
WSLF (Western Somalia Liberation Front), 97, 98

Yemen, People's Democratic Republic of (South Yemen), 98, 99, 102, 116–117
Yemen Arab Republic (Yemen), 117, 159
Yugoslavia, 115

Zaire, 84, 85, 86, 89, 165
Zambia, 84
Zanzibar, 83
Zayas, Alfedo, 10–11
Zia ul-Haq, Mohammad, 116

About the Author

Pamela S. Falk is associate professor at Hunter College of the City University of New York, where she has taught courses in Cuban government, Latin American foreign debt, and international relations in the Political Science Department since 1979. She was director of Latin American Affairs at the Americas Society Inc./Center for Inter-American Relations and Senior Advisor to the Western Hemisphere Commission on Public Policy Implications of Foreign Debt. She studied Spanish colonial history at the University of Madrid. She received her Ph.D. from New York University.

Dr. Falk's articles have been published in the *New York Times,* the *Wall Street Journal,* the *Los Angeles Times,* and in the *New York Times Book Review.* She is editor of anthologies on Brazil and Mexico and editor of *Puerto Rico's Political Status* (Lexington Books, forthcoming). She is author of "Cuba," in *Constitutions of the Countries of the World.* She is a member of the Cuba Study Group of the Council on Foreign Relations and the Cuba Task Force of the Latin American Studies Association.

Dr. Falk is a member of the Council on Foreign Relations and is on the Board of Directors of the Caribbean Cultural Center and the National Advisory Council of the Center for the Study of the Presidency.